DECnet Phase V

A _(signature)_ BOOK

DECnet Phase V

An OSI Implementation

James Martin

Joe Leben

digital

Digital Press

Printed in the United States of America.

9 8 7 6 5 4 3 2 1

Order number EY-H882E-DP.

The publisher offers discounts on bulk orders of this book. For information, please write:

Special Sales Department
Digital Press
12 Crosby Drive
Bedford, MA 01730

Design: Susan Marsh Design
Production: Nancy Benjamin
Composition: TSI Graphics, Inc.
Printing: Hamilton Printing Co.

Library of Congress Cataloging-in-Publication Data

Martin, James
    DECnet phase V: an OSI implementation/James Martin, Joe Leben.
        p.   cm.
    Includes index.
    ISBN 1–55558–076–9
    1. Computer network architectures.   2. DECnet (Computer network architecture)
I. Leben, Joe.   II. Title.
TK5105.5.M366 1992
004.6—dc20

To Corinthia—JM

To the Dweebs. I'll miss you.—JL

CONTENTS

PREFACE

Computer networks of increasing complexity and diversity are being built at a rapidly increasing rate. The exponential growth of computer networks that we are experiencing is being driven by two complementary technologies: very high speed local area and wide area communication links and incredibly powerful microprocessors. The computer industry is faced with the requirement to create networking technology that will permit the construction of massively large computer networks on the scale of the global telephone network. Such networks are required to create the distributed computer applications that will be built in the 1990s.

During the mid-1970s, several of the major computer manufacturers perceived that a large part of their future market was to come from distributed data processing. A wide range of machines would be hooked together into all manners of configurations. A user or an application program at one machine would want to employ the facilities, data, or processing power of another machine, easily and inexpensively. For widely varying devices to be linked together, the hardware and software of those devices would have to be compatible; if compatibility was not achieved, complex interfaces would have to be built for meaningful communication to take place. To facilitate this compatibility, hardware manufacturers have developed network architectures that allow complex networks to be built using diverse types of equipment.

One of the most widely used of these manufacturers' architectures is Digital Equipment Corporation's Digital Network Architecture (DNA). DNA, which has evolved through a series of phases, is implemented in the DECnet family of hardware and software networking products. This book presents a detailed explanation of the concepts, protocols, functions, and capabilities constituting Phase V of DNA and its DECnet implementations.

Acknowledgments   This project began in the spring of 1989, and the writing of this book was very much a collaborative effort between the authors and the people responsible for developing Phase V of DNA. Without the help and co-operation of the people at Digital, this book could never have been written. There are a great many people whom we wish to thank.

We will begin by thanking Mike Meehan, our editor at Digital Press, for all his help. We know Mike is glad this book finally has been completed because he just told us the correspondence associated with this project has completely filled his file cabinets and he had begun to fear for the trees of New England.

Mahendra Patel also has our heartfelt thanks. Without Mahendra's enthusiastic cooperation, we would not have been able to gain access to the key people and the important proprietary information we required.

Mahendra's able assistant, Israel Gat, played an extremely important role in this project. Without Israel's patience, diplomacy, and tireless efforts to keep the review process organized, this project would never have come to completion.

On every book project of this nature there is always one individual who bears the brunt of the review burden, reviewing portions of the manuscript that need to be looked over right now and for which no other volunteer can quickly be found. The "master reviewer" on this project was Paul Koning, and he has our thanks for the review job he did for us.

An important part of the research we conducted during the development of this book took the form of lengthy meetings with Mahendra and the senior architects responsible for Phase V of DNA. As a result of these meetings, we began to understand the philosophy behind Digital's networking strategy and came to realize how important Phase V of DNA was to Digital's future and to the computer industry as a whole. We would like to thank all of these people, including John Adams, Lois Frampton, John Harper, Bill Hawe, Tony Lauck, and Dave Oran, for the time they gave us.

Equally important was the process of refining our initially imperfect understanding of the technical details surrounding Phase V of DNA. We accomplished this mainly through many iterations of a long review and revision process involving the people already mentioned and the following Digital staff members: Ross Callon, Carl Cargill, Dah-Ming Chiu, Eric Davison, Frank Dolan, Nick Emery, Len Fehskens, Elliot Gerberg, Art Harvey, Jerry Hutchison, Charles Kaufman, Jeffrey

Lukowsky, Peter Mierswa, Radia Perlman, Judy Pomper, Dave Robinson, Mike Shand, Mark Sylor, Pat Stetson, Peg Tillery, Roy Varughese, Kathy Vogel, and Henry Yang.

Last, but not least, thanks are due to Jim Miller, Rodger Miles, Molly Garcia, and everyone else involved in operating and maintaining the worldwide internal Digital computer network. The Digital network allowed us almost instant access to anyone in Digital anywhere in the world. It would not have been possible to coordinate the many details associated with this project using more conventional forms of communication. That, in the end, is what this book is really all about.

James Martin
Joe Leben

HOW TO READ THIS BOOK

This book can be read from front to back, but it is likely that many readers will wish to skip around—at least at a first reading—and read those sections that appear to be of the most interest. This can be done, especially by those readers at least somewhat conversant with OSI concepts. We recommend, however, that a reader not familiar with the OSI model read at least the chapters in the Prolog and in Part I before dipping into the more technical chapters.

A good way to get an initial feel for DNA Phase V is to skim through the book and look at the diagrams. We tried to include enough information in the diagrams so they are understandable on their own without the reader having to consult the text.

The text of each chapter describes the technical details surrounding Phase V of DNA and DECnet. But this book also attempts to provide some insights behind the engineering tradeoffs the network architects made while the architecture was in development. The vehicles for these insights are the unnumbered boxes labeled "Network Architect." These boxes, rather than containing technical content, contain the opinions of those Digital staff members who were instrumental in the development of key parts of the architecture.

The numbered boxes contain background information that can be skipped on a first reading, unless the reader is specifically interested in the technical content of a particular box.

To take a good short path through the book, read Chapters 1, 2, 3, 4, 9, 11, 12, 15, 16, and 17.

LIST OF ACRONYMS

ABM	asynchronous balanced mode
ACSE	Association Control Service Element
ADM	asynchronous disconnected mode
AM	Amendment
ANSI	American National Standards Institute
APDU	application-protocol-data-unit
API	application programming interface; application-process-invocation
ARM	asynchronous response mode
ASC	Accredited Standards Committee
ASE	application-service-element
ASN	abstract syntax notation
ASN.1	Abstract Syntax Notation One
AUI	Attachment Unit Interface
BER	basic encoding rules
CA	certification authority
CCITT	International Telegraph and Telephone Consultative Committee
CD	Committee Draft
CDAM	Committee Draft Amendment
CLNS	Connectionless-mode Network service
CMIP	Common Management Information protocol
CONS	Connection-mode Network service
CRC	cyclic redundancy check
CSMA/CD	Carrier Sense Multiple Access with Collision Detection
DA	dynamic assignment
DAC	dual-attachment concentrator
DAD	Draft Addendum
DAM	Draft Amendment
DAS	dual-attachment station

MAN metropolitan area network
MDI medium dependent interface
MEN management event notification
MICE management information control and exchange
MOP Maintenance Operations Protocol
MTA message transfer agent
NCL Network Control Language
NCP Network Control Program
NDM normal disconnected mode
NET network entity title
NPDU network-protocol-data-unit
NSAP network-service-access-point
NSCTS namespace creation timestamp
NSDU network-service-data-unit
NSP Network Service Protocol
PCI protocol-control-information
PDAD Proposed Draft Addendum
PDU protocol-data-unit
PDV presentation-data-value
PPDU physical-protocol-data-unit; presentation-protocol-data-unit
PSAP physical-service-access-point; presentation-service-access-point
PSDU physical-service-data-unit; presentation-service-data-unit
RPC remote procedure call
RSA Rivest, Shamir, and Adleman
SABM Set Asynchronous Balanced Mode
SABME Set Asynchronous Balanced Mode Extended
SACF single-association-control-function
SAP service-access-point
SAS single-attachment station
SDLC Synchronous Data Link Control
SDU service-data-unit
SNA Systems Network Architecture
SNACP Subnetwork Access Protocol role (Subnetwork Access role)
SNAP Subnetwork Access Protocol
SNDCP Subnetwork Dependent Convergence Protocol role (Subnetwork Dependent Convergence role)
SNICP Subnetwork Independent Convergence Protocol role (Subnetwork Independent Convergence role)
SNRM Set Normal Response Mode
SPDU session-protocol-data-unit
SSAP session-service-access-point; source-service-access-point

SSDU session-service-data-unit
SVC switched virtual circuit
TCP/IP Transmission Control Protocol/Internet Protocol
TPDU transport-protocol-data-unit
TR Technical Report
TSAP transport-service-access-point
TSDU transport-service-data-unit
UA user agent
UI Unnumbered Information
UID Unique identifier
UT Universal Time
UTC Coordinated Universal Time
VC virtual call
WAN wide area network

Prolog

CHAPTER 1

The Future of Networking

The 1990s will be a decade of revolutionary change in computer networking.

Revolutions occur frequently in the computer industry. The first information systems revolution occurred in the 1950s, when business discovered the computer. What was at first viewed as a market that would require perhaps 10 large computers expanded overnight into a market for many thousands of these machines.

Another revolution occurred in the 1960s, when we discovered that one computer could "speak" to another over telecommunications lines. Computers have been speaking to one another ever since.

In the 1970s two parallel revolutions began. Microprocessors dramatically reduced the cost of computation, and computer manufacturers began developing comprehensive *architectures* for interconnecting their computers using communication facilities. One of these architectures is the *Digital Network Architecture* (DNA), which has evolved through five phases since the mid-1970s. Digital uses the term *DECnet* to refer to hardware and software implementations of this architecture.

The visible revolution of the 1980s was the discovery by business of the personal computer and the technical workstation. By the end of the 1980s, most knowledge workers had computers they could call their own. A less visible revolution of the 1980s was the development of optical fiber cables with bit rates of billions of bits per second.

The revolution occurring in the 1990s is that the network architectures we began developing in the 1970s are beginning to bear their fruit: we can now begin to hook together all the computers of the world. This will be the most wide-reaching revolution of them all.

Computer networking really began in the 1970s, so we have had about two decades of experience with this technology. Those who have contributed heavily to computer networking, and to the technology described in this book, feel that it will take about another decade to accomplish the task of interconnecting all the world's computers. The technology described in this book will help us achieve that end.

A Computer on Every Desk

It is clear now that there should be a computer on everyone's desk and that these machines should be able to access a vast diversity of information resources. Every desktop computer should be able to communicate with every other computer, just as the telephone handsets of the world can intercommunicate. Machines running the processes of commerce, often without operators, should be able to communicate automatically with the corresponding machines of their trading partners. The world will become a vast mesh of computers interacting automatically with one another over high-speed networks.

Worldwide Standards

To create worldwide computer networks that interlink everybody's desks, we need standards—like the telephone network. Telephony standards, established by the *International Telegraph and Telephone Consultative Committee* (CCITT) are essential to the connectivity the telephone industry achieves. Standards for computer networking, set by the *International Organization for Standardization* (ISO) working with the CCITT, are essential for connectivity in the computer industry.[*] Both CCITT and ISO are described in Chapter 2.

Computer networking standards are highly complex. A reference model that guides the development of these standards is the *Reference Model for Open Systems Connection*, or OSI model. This seven-layer reference model is introduced in Chapter 3 and described in detail throughout this book. The OSI model is now accepted by all computer vendors, although some vendors, notably IBM, also use network architectures that date back to an era before the recognition that worldwide networking standards are essential. In inventing the protocols and algorithms needed for networking millions of computers, Digital Equipment

---

[*] Both CCITT and ISO are acronyms whose letters do not match up with their spelled-out names. This is because the acronyms are based on the "official" names of these organizations, which are in the French language. We are using the English translations of the French names as they appear in the documents published in the English language by CCITT and ISO.

Corporation has made vital contributions to the standards for the OSI model. Phase V of DNA and its DECnet hardware and software products represent innovative implementations of those standards.

High-Speed Communications

Over the short history of data communication and computer networking, the speed with which computers communicate with one another has been steadily increasing. The first computers that exchanged streams of bits did so at a miserably low speed. When I wrote my first book on data communication, the standard transmission speed was 14.8 7-bit characters per second. As modems dropped in price, it became increasingly common to communicate at 1200 bits per second (bps), and then at 2400 bps. Today it is commonplace for computers to communicate over ordinary telecommunications facilities at 9600 and 19,200 bps, using inexpensive modems.

Along with the increase in the speed with which data can be transferred over conventional telecommunications facilities was the explosive growth of local area networking (LAN) technology. In 1980 Digital, Intel, and Xerox published the *Ethernet Specification*, which defined a low-cost method by which computers of all sizes could exchange data over relatively short distances (up to 2.8 kilometers) at a rate of 10 million bps. Today thousands of inexpensive Ethernet networks are in daily use, connecting mainframes, minicomputers, personal computers, and workstations. Ethernet has been the high-speed communications medium of choice throughout the 1980s. The *Fiber Distributed Data Interface* (FDDI) technology that is emerging in the 1990s will allow machines to exchange data at 100 million bps. Companies such as Digital and IBM have designed LAN protocols operating at a billion bits per second for use during the second half of the 1990s. Still higher speeds will be needed and will become economically achievable.

Today we are used to computers operating over Ethernet networks at 10 million bps within buildings, and we are beginning to operate FDDI LANs at 100 million bps. LAN usage is widespread. Most buildings have LANs; much software and hardware have been built for use on LANs. However, when we transmit beyond a building over wide area networks (WANs), we frequently throttle the transmission speed down, often to 9600 bps, which has resulted in islands of computing. Computers interact within a building differently from the way they interact over long distances. Within a building we can build distributed systems that give subsecond response times. When we interact with a faraway computer, the increase in response time is often cripplingly frustrating.

One of the great needs of the 1990s is to remove the extreme speed differences between local area networks and wide area networks. A great opportunity is to extend LAN services nationwide and eventually worldwide. WANs should be as fast as LANs. Optical fiber trunks make that possible and economically desirable.

Standards have been created for *metropolitan area networks* (MANs), with the assumption that high-capacity cabling can be built across a city, whereas it may not be economical over long distances. In practice, continent-wide optical fiber trunks have been built. LANs, MANs, and WANs need to be integrated, leading to an era of worldwide computer networking at today's LAN speeds and higher.

Telecommunications common carriers are beginning to make wideband communication facilities available at a reasonable cost. Today the T1 facility allows communication at 1.544 million bps (Mbps) and is used in business as commonly as 9600-bps facilities were just a few years ago. T3 facilities, which provide a data rate of 45 Mbps, are starting to become commonplace in North America. By the end of the decade, 200 Mbps will be as common as T1 is today, and 1 or 2 gigabits per second will be available as a premium service.

The optical fiber was invented just in time for the computer industry. The gigabit fibers of today will evolve into fibers that can transmit hundreds of billions and eventually trillions of bits per second. Major telecommunications highways will use mass-produced cables containing hundreds and eventually thousands of optical fibers. We are building prodigious transmission capacity. Most of today's optical-fiber trunks are grossly underutilized, especially in their transmission of computer data. In some telephone companies demand has been increasing at 6 percent per year, but the bit capacity of long-distance trunks has been increasing at 100 percent per year, resulting in much unused transmission capacity, often referred to as "dark fiber."

With the increases in speed in both local area networks and wide area networks, a question that comes to mind is how much bandwidth is enough.

NETWORK ARCHITECT

Gordon Bell sponsored a meeting a few years ago at which a number of computer networking pioneers talked about the future of computer networking. One of their conclusions was that by the year 2000 it would be technically feasible to send somewhere around 10^{15} bits per second down a single cable. I think *this was a cable containing 100 optical fibers. It is interesting, however, that the observation was made at the meeting that the maximum bandwidth a person at a workstation would need is about a gigabit per second. This is the bandwidth you need to send high-resolution motion pictures. A human being simply can't absorb data any faster than that.*

An obvious question we might ask is that if a person's bandwidth is limited to a gigabit per second, do we really need networking technology that lets us send data at 10^{15} bps, which is roughly a million times faster than the human bandwidth limit. This question leads to a discussion of *computing paradigms*.

Computing Paradigms

A computing paradigm refers to a mindset that governs how we view the way computers are used. Two completely different computing paradigms have developed in parallel, leading to two divergent views of the world of computing and networking. The companies that grew up in the world of large, centralized processors tend to have one view of computing and networking, and the companies that grew up in the world of small, decentralized processors tend to have another view.

The Large, Centralized Paradigm

The large, centralized paradigm tends to look at the world of computing and networking as having a hierarchical structure, with terminals and workstations at the bottom and large computers at the top. The computer network exists to provide human users with access to computing power. Computing applications run on a relatively small number of large, centralized processors, and computing system users use terminals and workstations to access the computing applications. In this paradigm, when a centralized processor runs out of computing power, it is replaced with a bigger and faster model. The large, centralized paradigm leads to a model of computing in which the user submits a request or a job, the centralized processor computes a result, and the result is sent back to the user.

With the large, centralized paradigm, it is difficult to envision a need for extremely high bandwidth communication, except to create high-capacity trunks that are multiplexed to funnel traffic from large numbers of individual users into mainframe computer centers.

The Small, Decentralized Paradigm

The small, decentralized paradigm tends to look at the world of computing and networking as being characterized by mesh-structured networks of computers, in which each computer is a peer of all the other computers. A computer network exists to allow computers to talk to each other. Computing applications run on a large number of decentralized processors, and sometimes multiple processors cooperate to produce a single result. A peer-to-peer networking environment is ideally suited to the creation of a distributed computing environment, where the computing power is spread over a large number of processors. In a distributed computing environment, when an application needs more computing power, the computing power often can be provided by plugging another processor into the network rather than by replacing the processor with a bigger one.

With such a paradigm, very high bandwidth communication is extremely important. There is essentially no limit to the communication bandwidth that can be used in such an environment. This is because the communication facilities are used not only by people talking to computers, they are also used by computers talking to computers. In such an environment, it might be necessary to send billions of bits from one machine to another very quickly, to satisfy the needs of a distributed computing application.

Digital's View of Networking	In the past, IBM believed in the paradigm of large, centralized computing, while Digital subscribed to the paradigm of small, distributed computing. Today both organizations know that an enterprise should have both centralized and decentralized computing.

IBM's pioneering work in networking led to a hierarchical networking model with mainframes at the top exercising much of the control. Digital's pioneering led to peer-to-peer networks with highly distributed control. Today computer manufacturers no longer are as divided into the two camps as they were in the 1970s. Everyone now agrees that peer-to-peer networking will be a requirement in the future, and all computer manufacturers, including IBM, are moving their networking technology in that direction.

Digital's vision of networking does not look on networks as primarily a medium for *communication* but rather as a medium for *computing*. The communication facilities that a network provides are simply by-products of a networked, distributed computing environment. Most of the communication that takes place in a distributed computing environment has nothing to do with a person sitting at a terminal or workstation. Rather, communication consists of computers talking to other computers.

| The Future Is Everything | The enterprise of the future will use both centralized computing and networks of small computers. Both have essential roles to play. A major trend today is the consolidation of mainframe centers. A mainframe center with its building, operating staff, and software is expensive. If networks are reliable and use high-capacity trunks, a large enterprise does not need 10 mainframe centers. It saves money to consolidate those centers into one (or possibly two, for disaster protection). A consolidated center can afford to have large computers that can solve large problems. Some computing centers will have supercomputers of immense power. |

The large enterprise of the late 1990s will also have a computer on everyone's desk, connected by LANs to a diversity of file servers, database servers, and the like, with wideband networks linking the individual LANs and connecting them to a small number of corporate computer centers with massive computing power. Notebook computers will link into this network, sometimes using cellular radio techniques, such as are used today to provide mobile telephone service. The computers within the corporation will interact directly with the computers of the corporation's trading partners, sending and receiving transactions and information. There will be direct links to many service organizations that provide information and all forms of specialized processing.

| Digital's Networking Strategy | Although Digital began as a minicomputer company, it is evolving into a computer networking company. This is a necessary by-product of the fact that in order to bring the power of many processors to bear on a large problem, those processors must be able to communicate effectively with one another. It is of strategic importance that Digital support the creation of a standardized, global computer networking infrastructure because this will substantially expand the market for Digital's products and services. Digital is essentially a high-volume company, and a high-volume company must adopt one of two strategies: |

- **Fragmentation.** One strategy is to *fragment* the market and attempt to compete in that market by dominating more fragments than anyone else. This strategy is essentially a strategy of financial control, in which a company attempts to make a market relatively static by fragmenting it.

- **Homogenization.** The other strategy is to *homogenize* the market in order to expand and enlarge it. A company that adopts this strategy has to be the best at that part of the market it wants to participate in and it must have leadership products.

Digital's approach has been to drive for the adoption of international standards in an attempt to enlarge the market through homogenization. This book describes how international standards have been incorporated into Digital's networking strategy at all levels.

The Distributed Computing Environment

The goal that Digital is trying to achieve with its networking technology is nothing less than to provide the technical capability to create a global distributed computing environment. Such an environment would allow all of the world's computers to participate in a single, integrated network in much the same way as today's telephones are interconnected. We can divide the technology that is required to create such a distributed computing environment into three categories:

- network infrastructure
- distributed computing services
- distributed computing applications

Network Infrastructure

The network infrastructure consists, first, of physical things, such as cabling, telecommunications facilities, modems, repeaters, and other components that physically connect computers. On top of the physical things are the necessary software subsystems—such as operating systems and networking software—that turn a set of equipment into a logically coherent network that can be reliably used to move a string of bits from one computer in the network to any other computer. The chapters in Part I, Part II, and Part V are concerned with building the network infrastructure.

A large problem in developing the network infrastructure that will support a global network is *scale*. The networking technologies that have been used in the past reach their limits when a few tens of thousands of computers are hooked together. What is needed is the technology to create a network infrastructure capable of supporting millions of computers so we can eventually have an infrastructure roughly on the scale of the global telephone network.

Distributed Computing Services

If we are using a network infrastructure to create a true distributed computing environment, then we must begin to view the entire network as a *distributed operating system.*

An operating system that runs on a single computing system provides application programs with essential services, such as providing a means for giving an object a name, requesting the date and time of day, and allowing one procedure to invoke another procedure through a subroutine call facility. In a distributed computing environment, a computing application should be able to call on the services of the network to provide a similar set of services on a network-wide basis. For example, a distributed computing application should be able to access resources by name without needing to know where in the network those resources reside. An application should be able to request the date and time of day and not need to be concerned with how the clocks on all the processors in the network are synchronized. And a procedure running on one computing system should be able to pass control to a procedure running on some other computing system in the same way it passes control to a local subroutine.

Distributed computing services, described in Chapters 15 and 16, use the underlying network infrastructure to provide high-level services to distributed computing applications without requiring those applications to have detailed knowledge of the underlying network infrastructure.

Distributed Computing Applications

Distributed computing applications are applications that use distributed computing services and the underlying network infrastructure to do useful work. These applications are introduced in Part III. If the network infrastructure exists and the distributed computing services provide the right kind of functions, it should be possible to create distributed computing applications much easier than the distributed applications of the past. Of course, creating a distributed computing application will never be as easy as creating an application that runs on a single computing system or one that uses simple data communication facilities.

Problems of Worldwide Networking

To achieve networking with a vast number of computers worldwide and in different enterprises, some difficult problems need to be solved. In creating Phase V of DNA, Digital has developed ingenious solutions to many of these problems, and many of these solutions have found their way into international standards.

Names and Addresses

A complex addressing problem exists when a computer network is worldwide and links machines of many organizations. Worldwide addressing schemes have now been standardized, and support for these standards are included in DNA Phase V. Mechanisms that allow symbolic names to be assigned to users and to network resources are also important. A comprehensive distributed naming service is an important component of DNA Phase V. Network addressing is described in Chapter 7, and the DNA Phase V naming service is described in Chapter 16.

Routing

A DECnet network uses devices called routers to select the optimum path over which to transmit packets of data. The optimum route varies, depending on the current network topology and whether any circuits or nodes are out of action. On a very large network, with perhaps hundreds of thousands or millions of nodes, the routing problem is much more difficult to solve than on a small network. DNA Phase V defines a powerful distributed routing algorithm that is effective on very large networks. This routing algorithm has been accepted by ISO as an international standard and is described in Chapter 9.

Congestion

Associated with the routing problem is congestion control. Traffic jams can occur on a network just as they do in a city at rush hour. Drivers in a city listen to helicopter reports and try to avoid the worst congestion. Congestion avoidance is important in a computer network as well. In a computer network there is no traffic helicopter, so ingenious techniques are needed to prevent congestion from occurring, especially when networks are very large. When queues build up, it is desirable to stop pumping more traffic over an overloaded link. DNA Phase V includes innovative congestion avoidance mechanisms, which are described in Chapter 10.

Management

As networks become larger, their control and management become complex. It is essential that network management functions that were performed by humans in earlier generations of networks be done automatically in the future. A user should be able to simply plug a machine into the network and start using it—"plug and play." The network should automatically update its routing databases and other tables to reflect the existence of the new machine. In DNA Phase V, many mechanisms previously controlled by human network managers have been integrated into the underlying communication protocols. Digital's view of network management is that the network manager's main concern should be with setting policy rather than with day-to-day operation of the network. Network management is described in Chapter 17.

Conclusion

By the mid 1980s, the personal computer and the technical workstation had become widespread in the world of business and government. Nothing has been the same since. The ability to have one's own computer has freed millions of knowledge workers to use the computer in ways we could not have foreseen just a short time ago.

The world will seem small from the viewpoint of a computer connected to a worldwide computer network. You have probably seen Wall Street's or Chicago's trading rooms on television. These rooms where stock, bond, and futures traders work appear to be filled with human chaos, the traders frantically gesturing and shouting at one another. Such communication could be done better with the aid of a computer network. Some trading rooms are being automated, and once they are, the traders need not be in one room in Chicago; they could be in Tokyo, Paris, Auckland, and Gaborone all linked together. Computer networks take a localized activity and make it worldwide. This globalization is happening at a furious rate in many different spheres of activity.

Already money flashes around the world at the speed of light on optical fibers. Hundreds of billions of dollars are moved daily over electronic funds transfer networks. Market crashes are worldwide and happen with computerized speed. Computerized stock markets will need to operate 24 hours a day.

What American Airlines did with its Sabre airline reservation system, Nippon Life can do in the insurance business—worldwide. New chains of commerce, like the Benneton clothing chain, can spread worldwide at high speed. Many corporations will seek strategic partners worldwide, their operations linked with computer-to-computer transmissions. When all the millions of computers used by these organizations are connected to each other and can easily communicate, the world of information systems will never be the same. More important, the world of commerce will never be the same again.

PART I

The Digital Network Architecture

CHAPTER 2

Network Architecture

In the early days of computer networking, individual computer manufacturers produced communication products that worked only in conjunction with their own computing equipment, and data communication links between equipment of different manufacturers were difficult to implement. Today networks have increased in capability and complexity. In modern computer networks, the functions relating to data transmission are performed by complex hardware, firmware, and software operating in the various devices making up a network. To make it easier to manage this complexity, the functions performed in network devices are divided into independent *functional layers*, much like the skins of an onion. Each functional layer hides the complexities and the evolution of the lower layers from the layers above. It would be of great benefit to users of computing equipment for the computing industry to standardize the interfaces between the layers and to define the rules governing the way in which complementary layers in different network machines exchange messages with one another. This standardization is one of the roles of modern computer network architectures.

A network architecture is a comprehensive plan that governs the design of the hardware and software components making up a computer network. Before we discuss the nature of network architectures, we will introduce the functions of a computer network by using an analogy to describe the benefits of independent functional layers in complex systems.

Human Communication Analogy

An analogy can be made between the communication functions performed in a computer network and the functions performed in ordinary human communication. Figure 2.1 shows how we might divide the func-

FIGURE 2.1   Layers of human communication.

tions performed during human communication into three independent layers.

The Physical Layer

In the *Physical* layer, the two parties must select and use a common communication medium. A typical communication medium used in human communication might be sound waves in air. For example, Figure 2.2 shows the physical medium used when two parties are involved in a face-

FIGURE 2.2   Physical layer: human speech.

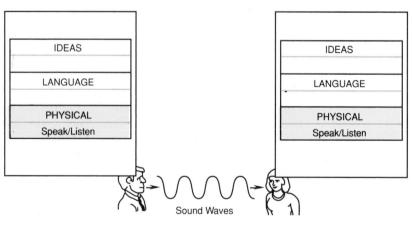

Sound Waves

to-face conversation. In human communication, it is important that both parties agree upon and use the same communication medium. For example, if one party is speaking, but the other party is deaf and can only read written words, no communication takes place.

The Language Layer

Once a common physical medium has been chosen, each party involved in a conversation must use a language understood by the other. If one party speaks only French and the other only English, little communication will take place. Figure 2.3 shows the *Language* layer when two parties are conducting a conversation using the English language. With no common language, there is no successful dialog, even though both parties may have agreed to use the same communication medium. If I call a Tokyo hotel and get a clerk who does not speak English, I will not be able to book a room, even though I might have an excellent telephone connection.

The Ideas Layer

We might think of the highest layer in human communication as the *Ideas* layer. In this layer, each person involved in a conversation must have some idea of what the conversation is about and must understand the concepts being discussed. Figure 2.4 shows the Ideas layer when two parties are discussing horticulture. If an English-speaking gardener es-

---

FIGURE 2.3   **Language layer: English.**

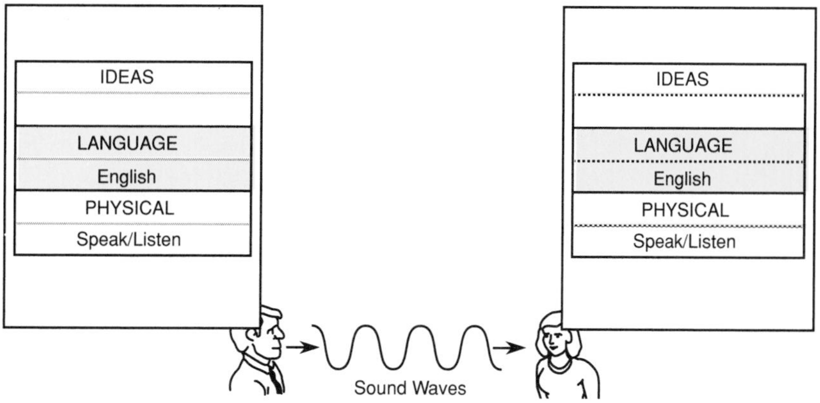

FIGURE 2.4   **Ideas layer: Horticulture.**

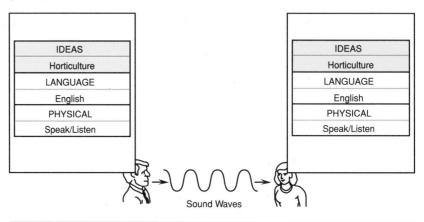

tablishes a good telephone connection with another English-speaking person and begins a technical discussion on horticulture, little real communication is likely to take place if the second party is a two-year-old child.

Protocols

In each layer in any communication system, a set of precisely defined *rules* must be agreed to and followed by both parties for communication to be successful. The rules governing communication at a given layer are called *protocols*. Each set of protocols can be thought of as a *rule book* that specifies a set of procedures governing communication. Each layer on one side communicates with a complementary layer on the other side using a protocol. Both parties must adhere exactly to the protocol; otherwise, communication is not possible.

Human Communication Protocols

The protocols involved in the Physical layer of human communication are simple and involve mechanical procedures. When two parties agree to use a common communication medium, they must both observe the same rules in using that medium. For example, on some long-distance telephone circuits, both people are not able to talk at the same time. If both people speak at once, no communication takes place. For the Language layer, the protocols involve procedures described by the rules of grammar and syntax for the common language. When two parties agree to use English, they agree to abide by the rules of grammar and syntax that govern the English language. For the Ideas layer, the protocols involve procedures described by the body of knowledge concerning the subject being discussed. If two parties are discussing horticulture, the protocols might involve technical details concerning botany and agriculture.

Changing Protocols

When people communicate, they can change the protocol for a given layer as long as both parties agree and change to the same new protocol. In effect, they agree to change the rule book for one of the layers. The protocols can be changed for one layer without requiring the protocols to be changed for the other layers. This makes the protocols used in each layer independent of the protocols used in the other layers. For example, in business people often begin a transaction by exchanging letters and then mutually decide a telephone conversation is needed. They may then decide a face-to-face meeting is required to continue the discussion. The rules, or protocols, governing the Ideas and Language layers remain the same each time the discussion is resumed, even though the protocol governing the Physical layer may change. Multilingual people might shift a conversation to a second language. As long as both parties agree to do so, the change in protocol for the Language layer does not necessitate changes in the Physical or Ideas layer.

Message Transmission

In human communication, a dialog between two communicating parties can be viewed as taking place via *messages* transmitted back and forth between the two parties (see Figure 2.5). For each message, there must be a *sender* and a *receiver*. On the sending end, an idea generates a message, which is transmitted to the second party via the agreed-upon communications medium. At the receiving end, the message is received and converted back into the original idea.

Functional Layers

Messages sent from a sender to a receiver in a human dialog can be viewed as passing through a number of *functional layers*. Messages are processed by *hardware* and *software* residing in, or controlled by, the two communicating parties. For example, in a face-to-face conversation, the hardware consists of the nervous systems, the mouths, and the ears of the two people. The software consists of the thought processes, both

FIGURE 2.5 **Message transmission.**

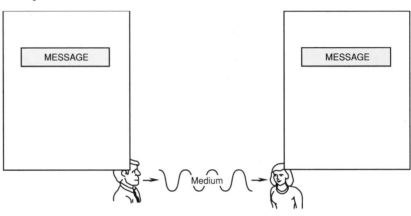

conscious and unconscious, used to conduct the conversation. There is an *interface* between each pair of layers, and each functional layer provides a set of *services* to the layer above it. A message passes down through the functional layers on the sending end, flows over a communications medium to the receiver, and moves up through corresponding functional layers on the receiving end.

Some interfaces in communication systems are concrete and define the characteristics of cables, connectors, and signals; others are abstract and define the semantics of the services one layer provides to another. Concrete interfaces must be adhered to exactly to achieve portability from one implementation to another; abstract interfaces need not be as rigidly standardized. It does not matter if the layer boundaries are a little fuzzy in the two communicating systems, as long as concrete interfaces and protocols are rigidly adhered to. As we will see in later chapters, the emphasis in determining conformance to communication standards is on concrete interfaces and protocols and not on abstract layer interfaces. However, standard layer interfaces are important because they define the services a protocol must supply, and they allow a protocol operating in one layer to be changed without affecting the protocols operating in the other layers.

Coming back to our human communication analogy, Figure 2.6 shows how the sender uses a high-level set of functions operating in the Ideas layer to formulate a message. Another set of functions, operating in the Language layer, is used to place that message into words. Still another function set, operating in the Physical layer, controls the mouth and the tongue in sending the message orally over the communications

FIGURE 2.6   **Layers of software.**

medium. The ear of the receiver is controlled by a low-level set of functions, operating in the Physical layer, that detects the sound waves carrying the message. A function set operating in the Language layer translates those sounds into words. A set of functions operating in the Ideas layer reconstructs the meaning of the original message from those words.

Computer Network Functional Layers

A computer network can be viewed on a number of different levels, just as can human communication. At each level, a functional layer—implemented using hardware, firmware, or software—provides a useful set of functions. As with the model of human communication discussed earlier, each functional layer should be as independent as possible of the others. Independence of the layers gives a computer network great flexibility.

Network Architectures

Network architectures define the way in which communication functions are divided into functional layers. They also define the layer protocols, the concrete interfaces, and the abstract interfaces between the functional layers. Protocols and interfaces make up the standards to which different machines and software modules must conform in order to effectively communicate. When new products are created that conform to the architecture, they will be compatible and can be linked with other products that also conform to the architecture. The goals and standards of a network architecture are important to both the users of computer networks and the organizations that provide computer networking equipment and services. A network architecture must provide users with a variety of choices in the configuration of computer networks, and it must allow users to change a configuration with relative ease as their systems evolve. For the providers of networking products and services, architectures permit the mass production of hardware and software building blocks that can be used in a variety of different systems. They also provide standards that allow development laboratories to create new machines and software that will be compatible with existing products. These new products can then be integrated into existing computer networks without the need for designing costly conversion mechanisms or making extensive software modifications.

The Nature of Architecture

Although network architectures provide rules for the development of new products, these rules can change. This is because the term architecture in the computer industry often implies an overall scheme or plan that may be evolving. The architecture defines an overall framework that allows the architecture to evolve and change to support new technologies. In Digital's view, an architecture also defines all the details needed to guide implementors in creating products that will fully conform to the architecture and, therefore, that will interoperate with all other implementations of the architecture. One of the DNA architects characterizes architecture in this way:

NETWORK ARCHITECT

An architecture must be always complete, *but it is never* finished. *It must provide a framework that permits change.*

A good architecture ought to relate primarily to the needs of the end users rather than to enthusiasms for particular techniques. A well-architected house, for example, is one that reflects the desired lifestyle of its owners rather than one designed to exploit a building technique that is currently in vogue. Fred Brooks, author of *The Mythical Man-Month* [1], defined architecture in a way that makes a clear distinction between architecture and engineering:

By the *architecture* of a system, I mean the complete and detailed specification of the user interface. For a computer this is the programming manual. For a compiler it is the language manual . . . . For the entire system it is the union of the manuals the user must consult to do his entire job . . . . The architect of a system, like the architect of a building, is the user's agent. It is his job to bring professional and technical knowledge to bear in the unalloyed interest of the user, as opposed to the interests of the salesman, the fabricator, etc.

The view of architecture that Digital engineers have is somewhat different from that of Fred Brooks. At Digital, architecture is not viewed as being associated only with the user.

NETWORK ARCHITECT

I think we would see architecture as being equally concerned with the needs of the user and *with the needs of the fabricator. There's no point in having a wonderful architecture that can't be implemented! In Digital, architecture is an integral part of the engineering process.*

Proprietary Network Architectures

Network architectures can be based on either accepted standards or proprietary standards developed by a particular organization, such as a computer manufacturer. Until recently, proprietary network architectures have played a more important role in the computer industry than architectures based on widely accepted standards. This is because computer manufacturers began providing advanced data communication capabilities long before today's standards were developed. Computer manufacturers were forced to develop proprietary network architectures to give an overall cohesiveness to their product lines. In today's information systems environment, architectures based on accepted standards are, in the long run, more desirable from the point of view of computer users, since they give the user the widest possible range of choices in configuring a network. Any vendor who implements the applicable standards can then be a candidate as a supplier. However, the standards underlying an architecture must be carefully chosen so they are likely to live a long time, provide for low-cost implementations, provide a broad range of functions, and are widely accepted.

The two most commonly used proprietary network architectures today are Digital's *Digital Network Architecture* (DNA) and IBM's *Systems Network Architecture* (SNA). The first products that conformed to each of these architectures were released at about the same time, in the mid 1970s. In the past, a computer manufacturer's architecture was designed for computer networks built with the products of only that manufacturer. The early manufacturer's architectures often made it difficult to interconnect machines offered by competing vendors. Most computer manufacturers, including Digital and IBM, however, provided facilities that allowed connections between otherwise incompatible equipment. As we saw in Chapter 1, in the future much more extensive forms of internetworking will be required to allow the machines of many different vendors to be interconnected to form an integrated, global computer network. It is a major goal of today's network architecture development to allow diverse equipment from many different vendors to be interconnected using standard interfaces and protocols. Because of this, widely accepted standards are playing an increasingly important role in network architecture development.

Standards Organizations

A number of organizations around the world are actively involved in developing standards and architectures for data communication and computer networking. Three important standards organizations for the information systems and communication industries are ISO, IEC, and CCITT, all of which we discuss next. Other important standards organizations are described briefly in Box 2.1. Some important terms making up the alphabet soup of information systems standardization are defined in Box 2.2. [2]

International Organization for Standardization

A prominent standards organization is the International Organization for Standardization (ISO), the largest standards organization in the world. ISO produces large numbers of standards on nearly every subject, from humane animal traps to screw threads. It is also the dominant information technology standardization organization in the world. The members of ISO are individual national standards organizations; only national positions—positions representing an entire country—are discussed in ISO. The ISO member organization from the United States is the American National Standards Institute (ANSI); all major industrialized countries have a similar standards organization that represents its national interests in ISO. ISO technical meetings take place at various locations around the world.

The secretariat of ISO, located in Geneva, Switzerland, is the organization charged with running the day-to-day affairs of ISO, including keeping track of its numerous Technical Committees (TCs) and publish-

BOX 2.1

**Other Standards
Organizations**

American National Standards Institute (ANSI)

Virtually every country in the world has a national standards organization responsible for publishing standards to guide that nation's industries. In the United States, this organization is ANSI. ANSI is a non-profit organization that writes the rules for standards bodies to follow and publishes standards produced under its rules of consensus. ANSI accredits standards committees to write standards in areas of their expertise. The major accredited standards committees (ASCs) in the information technology arena are:

- **JTC1 TAG.** This is the U.S. technical advisory group (TAG) for the ISO/IEC JTC1. This group provides U.S. positions on JTC1 standards and is the single interface to ISO/IEC JTC1 in the United States.

- **ASC X3.** This committee produces approximately 90 percent of the standards for U.S. information technology and provides the technical expertise for a majority of U.S. technical advisory groups to the subcommittees and working groups in ISO/IEC JTC1.

- **ASC T1.** This group is the voluntary standards-making body for the U.S. telecommunications industry and sets U.S. national telecommunications standards. T1 helps the State Department with CCITT positions.

- **ASC X12.** This group is responsible for standards relating to electronic data interchange (EDI) in the United States. It acts to set national positions for the United Nations EDIFACT group, which is establishing EDI standards worldwide.

ANSI has a small secretariat located in New York City whose function is organizational and administrative rather than technical. ANSI is not a government organization; it is funded by its members and through the sale of standards. ANSI standards can be obtained directly from ANSI or from OMNICOM or Global Engineering Documents.

National standards organizations from other countries include:

- **France.** Association Francaise de Normalisation (AFNOR)
- **United Kingdom.** British Standards Institute (BSI)
- **Canada.** Canadian Standards Association (CSA)
- **Germany.** Deutsches Institut fur Normung e.V. (DIN)
- **Japan.** Japanese Industrial Standards Committee (JISC)

These standards organizations have the same general role and organization as ANSI and provide a discussion forum for individuals. Some of those individuals then participate in international meetings and

BOX 2.1

continued

represent the agreed views of their countries. It is the national bodies that vote in the formal approval process for standards.

European Computer Manufacturers Association (ECMA)

ECMA was originally formed by a group of European companies. Since then, its membership has grown to become international and includes representatives from such organizations as IBM, Digital, AT&T, British Telecom, and Toshiba. ECMA is considered a regional standards organization and develops information technology standards for the European region. ECMA standards are often forwarded to ISO/IEC JTC1 for development as international standards. Such cooperation between organizations can result in a faster standards development process, since consensus has already been demonstrated. ECMA has a small secretariat in Geneva, and its members meet in various places throughout Europe.

Comite European de Normalization (CEN) and Comite European de Normalisation dans le domain Electrique (CENELEC)

CEN and its associated organization CENELEC have a relationship similar to that between ISO and IEC. They are concerned with the adoption of standards by the countries of the European Economic Community (EEC) and other European countries. Standards adopted by CEN/CENELEC are called European Norms (ENs) and are binding for procurement purposes on the CEN's member countries. CEN normally does not develop its own standards but instead relies heavily on standards developed by other organizations, especially ISO. Where there is no ISO or IEC standard, however, CEN will develop its own standard and forward it to ISO for development as an international standard.

National Institute for Science and Technology (NIST)

NIST (formerly known as the National Bureau of Standards) is a U.S. government organization. ISO standards often cover broad ranges of function and allow many choices to be made by individual implementors. The NIST has taken a leadership role in creating *profiles* that define preferred groups of choices from among the many options documented in ISO standards. Initially this was done in an informal workshop that developed *implementors' agreements*. As the importance of these profiles has increased and other organizations have started similar work internationally, the NIST workshop has become more for-

BOX 2.1

continued

mally organized. NIST is one of the three major international contributors to the development of Internationally Standardized Profiles (ISPs), which are the profiles formally ratified by ISO.

European Workshop on Open Systems (EWOS)

EWOS has the same role in Europe as the NIST workshop has in the United States. EWOS was started primarily by members of SPAG (see below) to ensure that Europe had a voice in the development of profiles. It also serves as the Technical Committee to support the technical activity of CEN. EWOS and NIST work closely together to achieve and maintain harmonization of their profiles. EWOS is located in Brussels.

Promotion of OSI/Asia and Oceania Workshop (POSI/AOW)

AOW is another organization that contributes to the international adoption of profiles. POSI is a Japanese organization concerned with promoting the adoption of ISO standards for the OSI model, while AOW is an open workshop that includes Australia and other Pacific countries as well as Japan.

Corporation for Open Systems (COS)

COS was initiated as a consortium of computer manufacturers and others to encourage the adoption of ISO information systems standards. It has initially directed its efforts toward the development of testing procedures to allow vendors to demonstrate conformance to ISO standards. COS operates as a non-profit organization funded by its members. It does not produce standards nor does it contribute to the development of standards. COS is located in McLean, VA.

Standards Promotion and Application Group (SPAG)

SPAG was initially a private consortium of European companies, set up with objectives similar to those of COS. Like COS, it has now directed its efforts primarily toward the development of testing procedures, and it cooperates closely with COS in that regard. Membership in SPAG is now open, and many U.S. companies are members.

Electrical Industries Association (EIA)

EIA is an association of companies involved in electrical and related industries. EIA undertakes some standardization projects and operates in that capacity as an accredited organization (AO) under the rules of consensus

BOX 2.1

continued

standards formulated by ANSI. The standards developed by the EIA are concerned primarily with physical communication interfaces and electrical signaling. A well-known EIA standard is EIA-232-D, which documents the way in which a terminal or computer is attached to a modem.

Institute of Electrical and Electronic Engineers (IEEE)

IEEE is a professional society whose members are individual engineers rather than companies. Most of its activities are only peripherally related to information technology, but it became the focus for development of local area network standards under its project 802 (see Chapters 21 and 22). The IEEE is also an AO, which operates under ANSI guidelines when it develops standards. Like the EIA, it rarely develops complex anticipatory systems standards, such as those falling under the OSI model umbrella, but ordinarily concentrates instead on product standards.

Conference of European PTTs (CEPT)

CEPT was established by the European PTTs primarily to develop technical standards that could be used in Europe prior to the development of corresponding CCITT standards. With the establishment of ETSI (see below), CEPT remains a closed forum that is concerned mainly with marketing and lobbying.

European Telecommunications Standards Institute (ETSI)

ETSI was established by the European Economic Commission to formalize many of the activities formerly undertaken by CEPT. Membership is open to suppliers of telecommunications equipment and services, PTTs, and other industrial organizations, with formal voting on a national basis. ETSI develops European telecommunications standards (ETSs). Some of these are intended as a basis for the provision of services and as a foundation for CCITT work, while others are oriented toward permission to connect testing for the attachment of equipment to public networks. ETSI is based in Sophie Antipolis, France. It has its own permanent technical staff and depends on the participation of its members.

Open Systems Foundation (OSF)

OSF is a non-profit organization established by a number of computer manufacturers to develop a common foundation for open computing. It is not directly concerned with standards but rather with the develop-

BOX 2.1

continued

ment of an agreed collection of software around a UNIX-like operating system kernel. OSF has its own permanent technical staff and depends on the participation of its members.

X/Open

X/Open was set up by European computer manufacturers to develop a consistent UNIX-like suite of application programming interfaces to permit application portability. Membership is open and worldwide.

ing the standards the Technical Committees produce. The Technical Committees, which not only create the standards but also determine what standards to produce, are composed of thousands of volunteers from computer manufacturers, suppliers of communication products, major computer users, governments, and consulting organizations. To participate, these delegates operate under the aegis of the national body. So a delegate from the United States not only brings technical expertise to the committee but also represents his or her sponsoring organization, ANSI, and the United States itself. A TC is ordinarily divided into Subcommittees (SCs) and Working Groups (WGs), which write the standards. The standards then receive the approval of the Technical Committee as a whole before they finally become accepted as international standards.

Closely associated with ISO is the International Electrotechnical Commission (IEC). IEC has a role similar to that of ISO but is restricted to electrical and electronic matters. There is an agreement between ISO and IEC to ensure that their work does not overlap. In the field of information technology standards, IEC's role is limited to Physical layer aspects, such as electrical safety. ISO and IEC have recently merged their Technical Committees working on information technology into a single organization, called ISO/IEC Joint Technical Committee 1 (JTC1), to ensure and improve continued close cooperation.

JTC1 is the ISO/IEC Technical Committee responsible for a particularly important framework for a computer network architecture called the Reference Model for Open Systems Interconnection, or the OSI model. The OSI model is introduced in Chapter 3 and forms the basis for the latest phase of Digital's own DNA. JTC1 is also publishing a comprehensive set of standards for the various functional layers defined by the OSI model. Many of those standards are described in this book.

BOX 2.2

Other Standards
Terminology

Manufacturing Automation Protocol (MAP)

MAP is a project started in the United States by General Motors to develop a single standard for communication between devices in a factory automation environment. Its work has been based on U.S. national and ISO standards and also defines additional standards specific to factory automation applications.

Technical and Office Protocol (TOP)

TOP is a complementary project to MAP started by Boeing to extend the applicability of MAP into other environments, such as office information systems and computer-aided design.

Government Open Systems Interconnection Profile (GOSIP)

GOSIP is a name for procurement-oriented standard profiles specifying how ISO standards will be used for U.S. government computing. The acronym GOSIP has been adopted by other countries to describe their own government procurement specifications.

European Procurement Handbook for Open Systems (EPHOS)

EPHOS is a project similar to GOSIP for government computing throughout Europe.

Open Distributed Processing (ODP)

ODP is a project started within ISO to develop standards for a heterogeneous distributed computing environment. It is defining an overall reference model for distributed computing that goes beyond the OSI model.

POSIX

POSIX is a standard developed by IEEE under its project 1003 that defines a UNIX-like interface to basic operating system functions to provide application portability.

There are four major steps in the standardization process. A standard begins its journey through the standardization process as a *working document*. After the working group or subcommittee agrees the working document should be developed into an international standard, it becomes a *committee draft*, at which time ISO/IEC assigns a unique number to it.

At this stage, the standard is referred to with the letters "CD," such as ISO CD 12345. (A committee draft was formerly called a *draft proposal* and was abbreviated DP.) After the subcommittee or working group agrees that the standard is close to being accepted as an international standard, it is given *draft international standard* status and is referred to using its number and the letters DIS, such as ISO DIS 12345. A standard may go through multiple revisions at both the committee draft and draft international standard phases. A standard that has made it all the way through the standardization process and has been accepted by ISO is called an *international standard* and is referred to only by its number, such as ISO 12345. ISO sometimes produces documents called *technical reports* when support cannot be obtained for the publication of a standard, when a subject is still under technical development, or when a Technical Committee has collected information of a different kind from that normally published as a standard. The identification number of a technical report is preceded by the letters TR, such as ISO TR 12345.

ISO also produces amendments to international standards as changes to them are required. Like the international standards themselves, amendments go through four phases. An amendment to an international standard begins as a *working draft* and then progresses to a *committee draft amendment* (CDAM), goes on to become a *draft amendment* (DAM), and finally becomes an *amendment* (AM) when it is approved. Generally, amendments are eventually incorporated into the text of their associated standards after the amendment is accepted. Amendments were formerly called *addenda* (ADs), draft amendments were called *draft addenda* (DADs), and committee draft amendments were *proposed draft addenda* (PDADs).

Most of the standards described in this book are accepted international standards, but some are currently in draft status and a few exist in the form of committee drafts. However, because standards often change their status quickly from CD to DIS and from DIS to accepted international standards, we will refer to standards using only their numbers, such as ISO 7498. Check with your country's national standards organization or with one of the many organizations that sell copies of international standards of the actual status of any particular ISO standard. ISO/IEC standards documents and technical reports can be obtained in the United States from ANSI, Inc., 1430 Broadway, New York, NY 10018. The following organizations also stock copies of ISO standards: OMNICOM, 501 Church Street, N.E., Vienna, VA 22180, (703) 281-1135; and Global Engineering Documents, 2805 McGaw Avenue, Ervine, CA 92714, (800) 854-7179.

International Telegraph and Telephone Consultative Committee

The International Telegraph and Telephone Consultative Committee (CCITT) has existed since around the turn of the century and is the leading organization involved in the development of standards relating to telephone and other telecommunications services. CCITT is a part of the International Telecommunications Union (ITU), which in turn is a body of the United Nations. The delegation to the ITU from the United States is the Department of State. In other countries, the ITU delegation is often the governmentally controlled Postal, Telephone, and Telegraph (PTT) organization.

CCITT deals with standards for interconnecting the world's telephone networks and for the signaling systems used by modems in sending computer data over telephone lines. CCITT calls the standards it produces *recommendations,* which have such names as *Recommendation X.25* and *Recommendation X.400.* It was a natural outgrowth of the data aspects of telephone service that CCITT should become involved in information system standards, particularly those directly related to public data networks. In the last decade, CCITT has also been involved in a major effort to define standards for a worldwide Integrated Services Digital Network (ISDN) for providing unified public voice and data communication services.

The principal contributors to CCITT are individuals representing the public and private telecommunications organizations, although nonvoting memberships are also open to industrial organizations. CCITT maintains a secretariat in Geneva, where most of the meetings take place. However, representation is international. As with ISO, all of the technical contribution comes from individual volunteers drawn primarily from telephone companies and other companies that supply telecommunications products and services. Again, membership is limited to national body representation — it is the State Department, not U.S common carriers, that represents the U.S. national position.

CCITT recommendations are published at four-year intervals, with the color of the covers changed with each new edition. Although the recommendations are newly published every four years, each new version represents evolutionary change from the previous version; many of the recommendations change little from one version of the recommendations to another. The color for the set of 1988 CCITT recommendations is blue, so that set of CCITT recommendations is called the *Blue Book.* The *Blue Book* contains new recommendations and all the revisions to existing ones approved from 1985 through 1988. The *Blue*

Book was published a piece at a time beginning in 1989. The *Blue Book* recommendations will be in common use through about 1993, after which all revisions approved since 1989 will be incorporated into a new set of recommendations. Each set of CCITT recommendations is published in the form of a series of volumes, each of which is divided into separately bound fascicles. Each fascicle can be ordered separately. CCITT recommendations can be obtained from the United States Department of Commerce, National Technical Information Service, 5285 Port Royal Road, Springfield, VA 22161. They can also be obtained from OMNICOM and Global Engineering Documents, whose addresses were given previously.

ISO, IEC, and CCITT cooperate quite closely. ISO and CCITT, in particular, have a strong interest in aligning their standards and thus try not to duplicate work between them. (Unfortunately, duplication of effort still sometimes occurs.) Standards of mutual interest typically are developed in one organization and then published by both. For example, the OSI model was developed principally by a subcommittee of ISO and is documented in ISO 7498; CCITT also publishes the OSI model as Recommendation X.200. Similarly, CCITT has developed Recommendation X.400, which standardizes electronic mail facilities. Recommendation X.400 has been adopted by ISO, which publishes it as ISO 10021. The technical people participating in committees of ISO are very often the same people as on CCITT committees, and the technical development activities associated with information systems standardization are often undertaken jointly by ISO and CCITT.

Conclusion

ISO's publication of the Reference Model for Open Systems Interconnection (the OSI model) was an extremely important development in the world of computer networking. The definition of international standards that fit into the OSI model framework is even more important. The OSI model and ISO's complete architecture for computer networking are introduced in Chapter 3.

References

1. Frederick P. Brooks, *The Mythical Man-Month: Essays on Software Engineering*, Addison-Wesley Publishing Company, Reading, MA, 1975.

2. Carl F. Cargill, *Information Technology Standardization: Theory, Process, and Organizations*, Digital Press, Bedford, MA, 1989.

CHAPTER 3

The OSI
Reference Model

Given the immense proliferation of intelligent computing devices now occurring, one of the activities most important to the future of information technology is the setting of standards to enable machines of different manufacturers to communicate. In 1984, as a start in the setting of such standards, ISO accepted as an international standard ISO 7498, *Open Systems Interconnection—Basic Reference Model*. ISO 7498 is a short document that describes the seven-layer Reference Model for Open Systems Interconnection that provides a common basis for the coordination of standards development for the purpose of interconnecting *open systems.* The term *open* in this context means systems open to one another by virtue of their mutual use of applicable standards. The OSI model describes how machines can communicate with one another in a standardized and highly flexible way by defining the functional layers that should be incorporated into each communicating machine. The OSI model does not define the networking software itself, nor does it define detailed standards for that software; it simply defines the broad categories of functions each layer should perform.

OSI Model Layers   The OSI model defines the seven independent functional layers shown in Figure 3.1. Each layer performs a different set of functions, and the intent is to make each layer as independent as possible from all the others. However, complete layer independence is difficult to achieve.

NETWORK ARCHITECT

Each layer provides a defined set of services by building on the layers below it. It is impossible for them to be completely independent. But the mechanisms of each layer are always independent of the mechanisms of the adjacent layers.

FIGURE 3.1   **OSI model functional layers.**

| Application Layer |
| Presentation Layer |
| Session Layer |
| Transport Layer |
| Network Layer |
| Data Link Layer |
| Physical Layer |

The ISO working group responsible for defining the OSI model began by establishing a number of principles that guided the development of the reference model. These principles are listed in Box 3.1. While it may be difficult to prove that the seven layers selected represent the best possible solution, the general principles listed in Box 3.1 guided the ISO working group in answering the questions of where a boundary should be placed and how many layers there should be. Organizations have now had much experience with developing network architectures based on the seven OSI model layers. For the most part, the layer divisions of the OSI model have proven to be well thought out. But there is still some controversy.

NETWORK ARCHITECT

There is still a general tension in standardization. If you have a group of people who are very focused on a certain area—whether it's a certain technology, like FDDI, or a certain layer, like the Session layer—there's a great tendency for them to say, "Well, everything we have to do to make this work—not just work but to be really useful—we should do in our layer, because you can't trust those people who are working on the other layers." This leads to something that has been called the "49-layer model" because all of the functions that are put in the seven layers start reappearing in each of the seven layers. We have to guard against this because you end up with the problems being solved in each layer becoming as complex as the entire original problem.

We next provide brief descriptions of each of the seven layers of the OSI model, beginning with the lowest layer. After we describe the seven OSI model layers, we will show how the OSI model relates to the complete OSI architecture and introduce concepts important in the OSI envi-

BOX 3.1

The Principles of
Layering

Principle 1. Collect similar functions in the same layer.

Principle 2. Create separate layers to handle functions that are manifestly different in the process performed or the involved technology.

Principle 3. Allow changes in functions or protocols to be made within a layer without affecting other layers.

Principle 4. Create a layer of easily localized functions so the layer could be totally redesigned and its protocols changed in a major way to take advantage of new advances in architectural, hardware, or software technology without changing the expected services from and provided to the adjacent layers.

Principle 5. Create a layer where there is a need for a different level of abstraction in the handling of data.

Principle 6. Create for each layer boundaries with adjacent layers only.

Principle 7. Select boundaries at a point that past experience has demonstrated to be successful.

Principle 8. Create a boundary at a point where the description of services can be small and the number of interactions across the boundary minimized.

Principle 9. Create a boundary where it may be useful at some time to have the corresponding interface standardized.

Principle 10. Do not create so many layers as to make the system engineering task of describing and integrating the layers more difficult than necessary.

ronment. Part II of this book examines each of the layers in detail, describes the ISO standards that apply to each, and shows how the DNA Phase V architecture incorporates the ISO standards.

The Physical Layer

The lowest layer of the OSI model is the *Physical layer*. It allows signals, such as electrical signals, optical signals, or radio signals, to be exchanged among communicating machines. The Physical layer, shown in Figure 3.2, typically consists of hardware permanently installed in the

FIGURE 3.2   **The Physical layer is concerned with sending and receiving signals.**

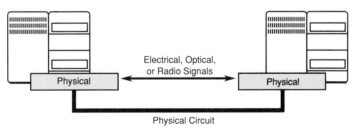

communicating devices. The Physical layer also addresses the cables, connectors, modems, and other devices used to connect machines. Mechanisms in each of the communicating machines control the generation and detection of signals that are interpreted as 0 bits and 1 bits. The Physical layer does not assign any significance to the bits. For example, it is not concerned with how many bits make up each unit of data, nor is it concerned with the meaning of the data being transmitted. In the Physical layer, the sender simply transmits a signal and the receiver detects it.

The Data Link Layer

Control mechanisms in the *Data Link* layer handle the transmission of data units over a physical circuit. Functions operating in the Data Link layer allow data to be transmitted, in a relatively error-free fashion, over a sometimes error-prone physical circuit (see Figure 3.3). This layer is concerned with how bits are grouped into collections and performs synchronization functions with respect to failures occurring in the Physical layer. The Data Link layer implements error-detection mechanisms that identify transmission errors. With some types of data links, the Data

FIGURE 3.3   **The Data Link layer is responsible for the transmission of data units over a physical circuit.**

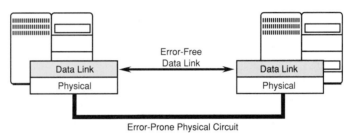

Link layer may also perform procedures for flow control, for data unit sequencing, and for recovering when transmission errors occur.

Some data links interconnect only two computers, such as with a point-to-point telecommunications facility. Other types of data links allow many computers to be interconnected, such as in a typical local area network. When more than two computers are attached to a single data link, any computer can be viewed as being connected by a single link with any other computer attached to the data link, even though there may be devices, such as repeaters or bridges, between any two stations.

The Network Layer

We will refer to a device containing an instance of the Network layer and the Data Link and Physical layers below it as a *node*.[*] Nodes that act as the source or the final destination of data are called *end nodes*. Between any two end nodes may be nodes acting as intermediaries that perform routing and relaying functions. These are called *intermediate nodes*. The facilities provided by the Network layer supply a service that higher layers employ for moving bits from one end node to another, where the bits may flow through any number of intermediate nodes. End nodes generally implement all seven layers of the OSI model, allowing application programs to exchange information with each other. It is possible for intermediate nodes performing *only* routing and relaying functions to implement only the bottom three layers of the OSI model, as shown in Figure 3.4.[†] Notice that the path between any two nodes may at one instant be via a number of data links. The application programs running in two end nodes that wish to communicate should not need to be concerned with the route data units take nor with how many data links they travel over. The Network layer functions operating in end nodes and in intermediate nodes together handle these routing and relaying functions. Whereas the Data Link layer provides for data transmission between *adjacent* nodes across

---

[*] OSI documentation uses the term *system* instead of *node*. However, we feel the term *system* is overused in information systems literature, and we prefer *node* to the more formal OSI term *system*.

[†] In actual practice, for an intermediate node to communicate with network management mechanisms, all seven layers are required, although some of the upper layers may implement a minimum set of functions. The term *skinny stack* is sometimes used to refer to such an implementation of only a minimum set of functions in one or more of the upper layers.

FIGURE 3.4   The Network layer allows communication across multiple data links.

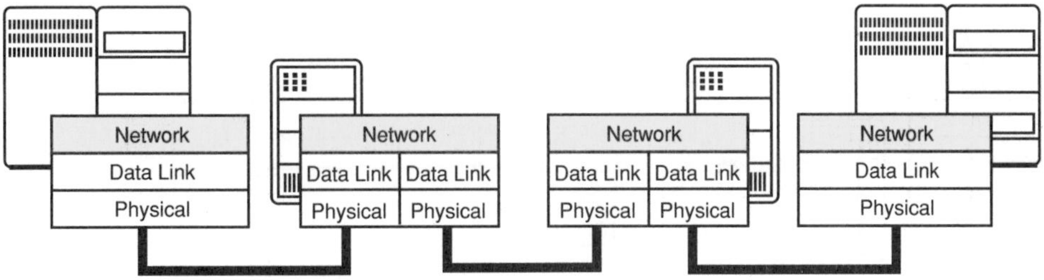

a single data link, the Network layer provides for the much more complex task of transmitting data between *any* two nodes in the network, regardless of how many data links may need to be traversed.

The Transport Layer

The Transport layer builds on the services of the Network layer and the layers below it to form the uppermost layer of a reliable end-to-end data transport service. The Transport layer hides from the higher layers all the details concerning the actual moving of data from one computer to another and shields network users from the complexities of network operation. The lowest three layers of the OSI model (see Figure 3.1) implement a common physical network many machines can share independently of one another, just as many independent users share the postal service. It is possible for the postal service to occasionally lose a letter. To detect the loss of a letter, two users of the postal service might apply their own end-to-end controls, such as sequentially numbering their letters. The functions performed in the Transport layer can include similar end-to-end integrity controls to recover from lost, out-of-sequence, or duplicate messages.

Transport layer functions handle addressing of the processes, such as application programs, that use the network for communication. The Transport layer can also control the rate at which messages flow through the network to prevent and control congestion. Whereas the Network layer is concerned with the interface between network nodes and operates in end nodes and intermediate nodes, the Transport layer provides an end-to-end service that programs can use for moving data back and forth between them. The Transport layer is the lowest layer required only in the computers running the programs that use the network for communication (see Figure 3.5).

FIGURE 3.5   **The Transport layer is the lowest layer required *only* in the computers that are communicating.**

End-to-End Transport Connection

| Transport |
| Network |
| Data Link |
| Physical |

| Network |
| Data Link | Data Link |
| Physical | Physical |

| Network |
| Data Link | Data Link |
| Physical | Physical |

| Transport |
| Network |
| Data Link |
| Physical |

The Session Layer

There is a fundamental difference in orientation between the bottom four layers and the top three. The bottom four layers are concerned more with the network itself and provide a data transport service; the top three layers are more concerned with the application programs that use the network for communication. (See Figure 3.6.)

The Session layer is the lowest of the layers associated with the application programs and is responsible for organizing the dialog between two application programs and for managing the data exchanges between them. To do this, the Session layer imposes a structure on the interaction between two communicating programs. (See Figure 3.7.) The Session layer defines three types of dialogs: two-way simultaneous interaction, where both programs can send and receive concurrently; two-way alternate interaction, where the programs take turns sending and receiving;

FIGURE 3.6   **The layers of the OSI model can be divided into those that provide a data transport service and those that supply application program services.**

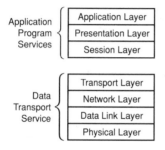

Application Program Services
- Application Layer
- Presentation Layer
- Session Layer

Data Transport Service
- Transport Layer
- Network Layer
- Data Link Layer
- Physical Layer

FIGURE 3.7   **The Session layer organizes the dialog between two application programs.**

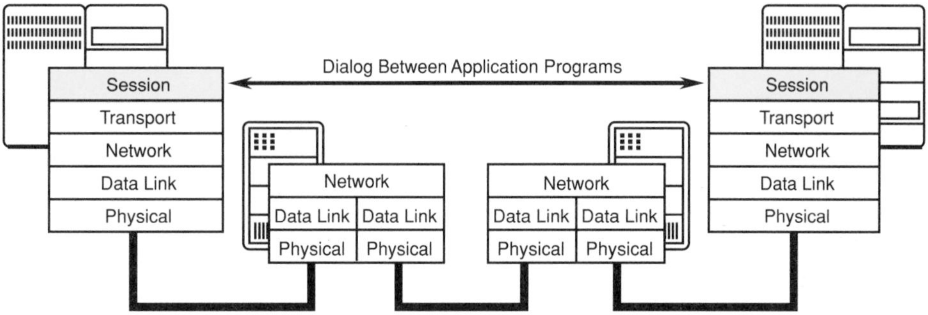

and one-way interaction, where one program sends and the other only receives.[*] In addition to organizing the dialog, Session layer services include establishing synchronization points within the dialog, allowing a dialog to be interrupted, and resuming a dialog from a synchronization point.

The Presentation Layer

The five layers below the Presentation layer are all concerned with the orderly movement of a string of bits from one program to another. The Presentation layer is the lowest layer interested in the *meaning* of those bits and deals with preserving the *information content* of data transmitted over the network. (See Figure 3.8.)

The Presentation layer is concerned with three types of *data syntaxes* that can be used for describing and representing data:

- **Abstract Syntax.** An *abstract syntax* consists of a formal definition of the information content of the data two programs exchange. An abstract syntax is concerned only with information content and not with how that information content is represented in a computer or how it is encoded for transmission. For example, an abstract syntax might define a data type called AccountNumber, values of which consist of integers. ISO 8824 *Abstract Syntax Notation One* (ASN.1) defines an international standard notation that is often used in practice to define abstract syntaxes in the OSI environment.

---

[*] Although one-way interaction is defined in ISO 7498, no ISO protocol uses this type of dialog.

FIGURE 3.8   The Presentation layer is responsible for preserving the information content of the data transmitted over the network.

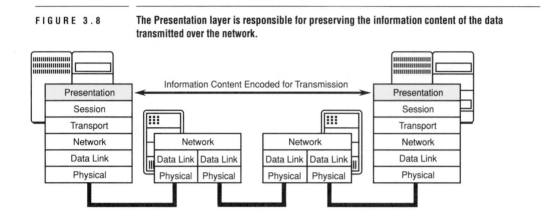

- **Local Concrete Syntax.** A *local concrete* syntax defines how the information content of data is actually represented in a computing system. Two communicating systems might use different local concrete syntaxes. For example, one system might represent an integer as a binary number using 2's complement notation; another system might use a string of decimal digits. ISO standards do not address the local concrete syntax, and programs are free to represent data in any desired way.

- **Transfer Syntax.** A *transfer syntax* defines how the information content of data is encoded for transmission over the network. A value of the AccountNumber type might be transferred over the network using some form of encoding scheme that identifies the value as being of the AccountNumber type, specifies that it consists of an integer, and encodes that integer's value using a minimum number of bits. ISO 8825, *Specification of Basic Encoding Rules for ASN.1*, specifies one way in which the information content of data units defined using ASN.1 notation can be encoded for transmission. The basic encoding rules are often used in the OSI environment to produce transfer syntaxes.

The OSI model defines two major functions for the Presentation layer. The first is for the two communicating Presentation entities to negotiate a common transfer syntax to be used to transfer the data units defined by a particular abstract syntax. The second is to ensure that one system does not need to care what local concrete syntax the other system is using. If the local concrete syntaxes in the two communicating systems are different, the Presentation layer is responsible for transforming from the local concrete syntax to the transfer syntax in the sending system and from the transfer syntax to the local concrete syntax in the receiving system.

The Application Layer

The topmost layer, the one user processes plug into, is the Application layer. (See Figure 3.9.) The Application layer is concerned with high-level functions that provide support to the application programs using the network for communication. The Application layer provides a means for application programs to access the system interconnection facilities to exchange information. It provides all functions related to communication between systems not provided by the lower layers. The Application layer is more open ended than the layers below. Due to the wide variety of applications that will ultimately use networks for communication, many standards for the Application layer are likely to be developed.

The OSI Network Architecture

Now that we have briefly described the functions of the seven layers of the OSI model, we will show how the OSI model relates to the complete OSI architecture ISO is defining and introduce the major concepts underlying the OSI architecture.

There is widespread confusion between the OSI *model* and ISO's ultimate plan for a complete *network architecture* based on the OSI model. After the OSI model became accepted as an international standard, a major part of ISO's work in the area of information system standardization has been to develop and publish comprehensive standards for each of the seven OSI model layers. These standards provide detailed descriptions of the services provided by each layer and the protocols each layer employs for communication. The standards ISO is devel-

FIGURE 3.9 The Application layer is the topmost layer into which user processes plug.

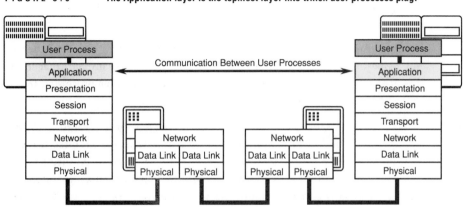

oping for the seven layers of the OSI model will ultimately define a fully standardized network architecture. At the time of this writing, many of the standards making up the OSI architecture are now accepted international standards. Others exist as draft international standards and as draft proposals, so all work has not yet been fully completed for all seven layers. Appendix A lists many of the standards that make up the OSI architecture. Since the statuses of international standards change rapidly, all standards are shown using the ISO designation, even though some of them may be in committee draft (CD) or draft international standard (DIS) status. Consult your country's national standards organization or an organization such as OMNICOM or Global Engineering Documents (see Chapter 2) for the current status of each international standard. Even though some standards may not currently have full international standard status, the standardization process is at a sufficiently advanced stage that full implementation of the OSI network architecture has been started by many organizations. The latest version of the Digital Network Architecture is based on many of the ISO standards that now exist for OSI architecture.

There is no requirement on the part of any hardware or software vendor to adhere to the principles set forth in the documentation of the OSI model or to adopt the ISO standards that are emerging for the seven layers of the OSI model. However, there is a worldwide trend in the information technology industry toward acceptance of and conformance to the ISO standards that make up the OSI architecture.

OSI Concepts

The OSI model is concerned with the interconnection of systems—the way in which they exchange information—and not the internal functions performed by a given system. In OSI terminology, a system is defined as:

> A set of one or more computers, the associated software, peripherals, terminals, human operators, physical processes, transfer means, etc., that forms an autonomous whole capable of performing information processing and/or information transfer.

The OSI model provides a generalized view of a layered architecture. With the broad definition given for a system, the architecture can apply to a very simple system, such as a point-to-point connection between two computers, or to a very complex system, such as the interconnection of two entire computer networks. As we stated earlier, we will often use the term *node* in place of the ISO term *system*.

Services and Protocols

The ISO standards making up the complete OSI architecture define for each layer a single *service definition* and one or more *protocol specifications*. A service definition defines the specific services a layer provides to the layer above it but says nothing about *how* those services are to be provided. A protocol specification describes the formats of the data units exchanged and specifies the procedures a layer must perform in exchanging those data units in providing the services of that layer. The relationship between the services layer N provides and the protocol governing its operation are shown in Figure 3.10. As shown there, the layer N protocol uses the services of layer $N–1$ to provide a defined set of services to layer $N+1$ above it.

FIGURE 3.10   The relationship between a layer's *service definition* and its *protocol specification*.

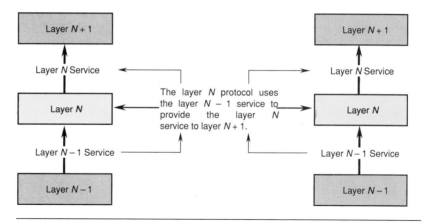

Many earlier network architectures and network implementations did not make a clear distinction between the services a layer provides and the protocols it uses in supplying those services. This meant that if a protocol needed to be changed, perhaps to enhance network efficiency, the changes often directly affected users of the network. By clearly separating services from protocols, such problems can be minimized. One of the underlying concepts in the standards making up the OSI architecture is that the service definition for a layer is always independent of protocol specifications.

Service Definition

Before we examine what is contained in the service definition for a layer, we must define the following two OSI terms:

- **Entity.** An entity is an active element within a layer. Two communicating entities within the same layer but in different network nodes are called *peer entities*. Entities in the Application layer are called *Application entities*, entities in the Presentation layer are called *Presentation entities*, and so on. A particular layer provides services to entities running in the layer above.

- **Service-Access-Point (SAP).** A service-access-point is the point at which the services of a layer are provided. Each layer provides service-access-points at which entities in the layer above request the services of that layer. Each service-access-point has an *SAP address*, by which the particular entity that is employing a layer service can be differentiated from all other entities that might also be able to use that layer service.

Abstract Interfaces

Layer *N* is the *service provider*, and layer *N*+1 operating above layer *N* is the *service requester* or *service user*. The service definition for layer *N* defines the services layer *N* provides to entities running in layer *N*+1 via a service-access-point into layer *N*. The set of services provided by layer *N* defines the *abstract interface* between layer *N* and layer *N*+1. (See Figure 3.11.) There is an abstract interface between any two adjacent layers of the architecture. The service definitions for the various OSI model layers describe these abstract interfaces. An abstract interface describes the semantics of the interactions between two architectural layers. An abstract interface does not specify implementation details, nor does it describe the syntax that must be used to implement the interface. The inter-

FIGURE 3.11   **A service provider provides a defined set of services to a service requester via a service-access-point. The set of services provided by layer *N* defines a abstract interface between layer *N* and layer *N* +1.**

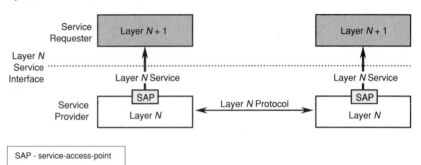

actions between two adjacent layers are described only in terms of an abstract set of services that layer N provides to layer $N+1$.

Concrete Interfaces

In addition to abstract interfaces, *concrete interfaces* are also important at some points in the architecture, especially in the Physical layer and at points where application programming interfaces (APIs) must be specified. A concrete interface might describe a point in the architecture at which a physical connector is used, for example, to connect a physical device to a transmission medium. A concrete interface might provide specific electrical and mechanical specifications for the cables and connectors that must be used for devices and cables to properly implement the architecture. A concrete interface might also define an application programming interface a programmer must adhere to in writing programs to request the services of a layer.

Service Primitives

The ISO service definition for a layer documents the services a layer provides to the layer above in terms of a set of *service primitives*, each of which has a defined set of *parameters*. The service primitives precisely define the abstract interface between a layer and the layer above it. The ISO standards define four general types of service primitive:

- **Request.** Issued by a service requester to request that a particular service be performed by a service provider and to pass parameters needed to fully specify the requested service.
- **Indication.** Issued by the service provider to notify a service requester that a significant event has occurred.
- **Response.** Issued by the service requester to acknowledge or complete some procedure previously invoked by the service provider through an indication primitive.
- **Confirm.** Issued by a service provider to notify the service requester of the results of one or more *request* primitives the service requester previously issued.

A particular service typically uses two or more service primitives. Figure 3.12 shows two *time-sequence diagrams* that show the sequence in which service primitives might be issued using the ISO model of ser-

FIGURE 3.12   Time-sequence diagrams for a nonconfirmed service and a confirmed service.

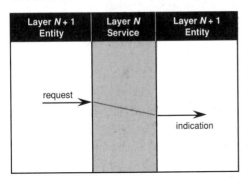
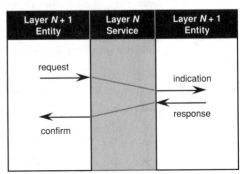

Nonconfirmed Service   Confirmed Service

vice primitives. In a time-sequence diagram, service primitives are represented by arrows, and time flows down. The first diagram shows an example of a *nonconfirmed service*, in which the service requester is not informed of the completion of the service request. In the normal case, a request invoked at one end results in an indication being invoked at the other. The second service shown in Figure 3.12 is a *confirmed service*, in which the service requester is informed by the distant peer entity of the success or failure of the service request.

Semantics versus Syntax

A set of service primitives and their parameters together define the abstract interface between two adjacent architectural layers. It is important to realize that an abstract interface defines only the *semantics*, or *meaning*, of service primitives. The standard does not specify any particular method for invoking a particular service, nor does it define how a service is to be implemented. Implementation details are the responsibility of the vendors that build networking products. In Part II, when we examine each of the layers in detail, we describe the ISO service primitives for each layer and also introduce the way in which Digital defines the abstract interfaces between layers in the DNA architecture.

Service-Data-Units

Some layer services are intended to be used to transmit units of data from a layer entity in one node to a peer layer entity in another node. A layer does this by issuing a data transfer request service primitive to the layer below and passing the data unit to be transferred as a parameter of the request primitive. Data units passed from a service requester to a service provider are called *service-data-units* (SDUs). The name of the SDU passed from a layer to the layer below begins with the name of the layer to which the SDU is passed. The SDUs passed to the Physical layer by the Data Link layer are called *physical-service-data-units* (PSDUs), the SDUs passed from the Network layer to the Data Link layer are called *data-link-service-data-units* (DLSDUs), and so on. The SDU for a particular layer is an abstract definition. In an actual implementation, the data making up an SDU can be passed from a layer to the layer below in any desired way (for example, as parameters in a procedure call) and need not all be passed at the same time.

Protocol Specifications

Another principle of the OSI model is that when two network nodes are communicating with one another, an entity in each layer in the first node communicates with its peer entity in the second node using a *protocol*. Figure 3.13 illustrates protocols operating in each of the seven layers of the OSI model. The ISO standards for each of the OSI model layers document one or more protocol specifications for the protocol(s) that control the operation of that layer. In some layers, ISO standards define more than one protocol that can be used to provide the services of that layer. For example, a number of separate protocol specifications describe the operation of the Network layer. Each Network layer protocol specification describes a different element of the Network layer's functions.

A protocol specification describing the procedures layer N performs in supplying its services to layer $N+1$ defines the following:

- the formats of the data units exchanged between peer layer N entities

FIGURE 3.13   **A separate protocol controls the operation of each of the layers in the OSI model.**

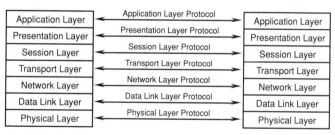

- the interactions that occur between peer layer N entities in exchanging data units
- the way in which layer N and layer $N+1$ interact in exchanging the service primitives defined in the service definition for layer N
- the way in which the layer N and layer $N-1$ interact in exchanging the service primitives defined in the service definition for layer $N-1$

Protocol-Data-Units

Data units sent from a layer entity in one node to a peer layer entity in another node are called *protocol-data-units* (PDUs). In many cases, a layer constructs a protocol-data-unit from the service-data-unit passed down from the layer above simply by adding *protocol-control-information* (PCI) to it. (See Figure 3.14.) Some of the information making up the protocol information may be passed down from layer $N+1$ to layer N

FIGURE 3.14   A layer accepts a service-data-unit from the layer above and adds protocol-control-information
to it to create a protocol-data-unit, which it sends to its peer entity.

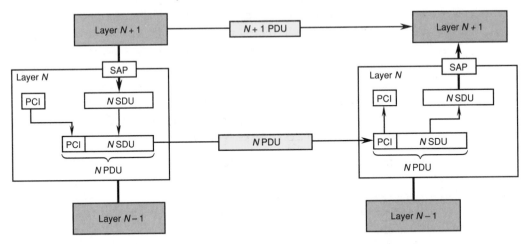

in the form of service primitive parameters. The PCI is used to control the peer-to-peer protocol operating in a particular layer. Protocol-control-information is carried in the form of a header (and, in the case of the Data Link layer, also a trailer) that are added to the SDU. The PDUs appear to flow from a layer N entity in the sending node to a layer N entity in the receiving node using the layer N protocol. From this perspective, functions performed in layer N-1 and below are hidden from layer N.

A layer N entity can also itself generate PDUs apart from the PDUs it creates from the SDUs it receives from layer N+1. Such generated PDUs are typically transmitted between peer layer N entities to control the operation of the layer N protocol. The layer N+1 service requester is not directly aware of the existence of these PDUs, although the service requester might be aware of effects caused by them.

Interface-Data-Units

The OSI model precisely defines the way in which the SDU is actually passed across the interface between layer N+1 and layer N in the form of *interface data* and *interface-control-information* (ICI). A set of interface data plus its associated ICI makes up an *interface-data-unit* (IDU). An interface-data-unit is defined as the data unit passed across the abstract interface at the service-access-point in a single interaction. Figure 3.15 shows how a single service-data-unit might be passed across the interface in three pieces, each of which makes up a single interface-data-unit. Layer N accepts the interface-data-units and extracts the interface-control-information and the interface data from them to create the protocol-control-information and the service-data-unit. Once all the interface-data-units have been passed across the interface, layer N uses the protocol-control-information and the service-data-unit to construct a protocol-data-unit for transmission to the peer entity. The service-data-unit can be passed across the interface in the form of multiple interface-data-units in the sending node, the receiving node, or both. The number of interface-data-units need not be the same in the sending and receiving nodes.

Although ISO standards define the way in which information is passed across the interface between layer N+1 and layer N, the reader must realize that ISO service definitions define *abstract* interfaces, and they are not meant to serve as implementation models. An abstract interface can be implemented in any desired way, and it may not be possible in an actual implementation to identify the data units described above.

FIGURE 3.15   Interface data together with interface-control-information (ICI) make up an interface-data-unit (IDU), which is defined as the data unit that is transferred across the abstract interface in a single interaction. In this example, the service-data-unit is passed across the interface using three interactions in the form of three separate IDUs.

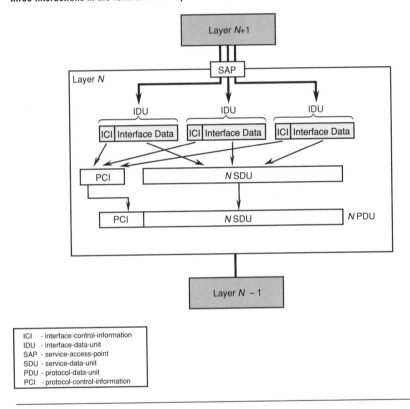

ICI	- interface-control-information
IDU	- interface-data-unit
SAP	- service-access-point
SDU	- service-data-unit
PDU	- protocol-data-unit
PCI	- protocol-control-information

Segmentation and Concatenation

A layer supporting a *segmentation* function may slice up an SDU into multiple segments. It then adds PCI to each segment to create multiple PDUs that it transmits separately. This is shown in Figure 3.16. A layer supporting a *concatenation* function may group multiple PDUs into a single block that it transmits as a single unit between peer layer entities. The layer N+1 service requester is not aware of the operation of the segmentation or concatenation functions when they are used. Note that the segmentation and blocking functions are completely separate from the notion of the SDU being possibly passed across the layer interface in multiple interface-data-units. The layer N+1 service requester is not aware that the segmentation or blocking functions are taking place and

FIGURE 3.16   A layer protocol may support a segmentation capability that allows it to break a service-data-unit into pieces, each of which it sends in the form of a separate protocol-data-unit.

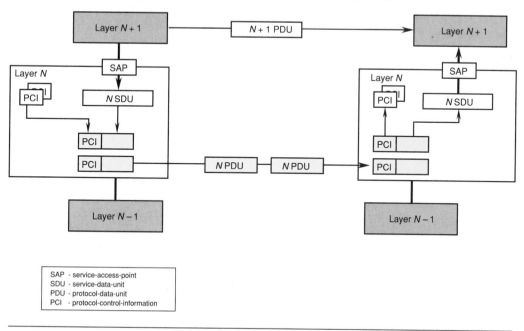

SAP - service-access-point
SDU - service-data-unit
PDU - protocol-data-unit
PCI - protocol-control-information

perceives only the service-data-unit itself, which might be passed across the interface in multiple interface-data-units.

Informal Protocol-Data-Unit Names

Certain protocol-data-units handled by the lower layers have come to have informal names that are often used in networking literature. The data-link-protocol-data-units (DLPDUs) passed between peer Data Link layer entities are often called *frames*. The network-protocol-data-units (NPDUs) passed between Network layer entities are typically called *packets*. These informal names predate the OSI model and are often not used consistently. To avoid confusion, the committees responsible for creating the OSI model have assigned the new formal names to the data units. However, some networking experts find exclusive use of the formal names for the data units a bit cumbersome:

> This language is often known as **internationalbureaucratspeak**. We will avoid it where possible in favor of more familiar nomenclature actually used by working scientists and engineers. [1]

The engineers who invented the terms feel less hostile toward them.

NETWORK ARCHITECT

OSI terminology is weird and wonderful. ISO doesn't use the same terms people in the United States grew up with in computer networking. This is partly because some of the informal terms don't translate well—some of them are not neutral in other languages. So in order to be international, we invented these new terms that have now taken on important meanings.

We will adopt a middle ground and use the *internationalbureaucrat-speak* where necessary, but we will avoid it where using the more informal terms will not confuse matters. For example, in the chapters discussing the Network layer, we will typically use the informal term *packet* instead of NPDU. But in a world that is becoming increasingly oriented to OSI, it is necessary that we all become familiar with its "weird and wonderful" terminology.

Conformance to Standards

Unlike service-data-units, which can be physically implemented in any desired way, protocol-data-units must be formatted exactly as they are defined in the ISO protocol specification. They are the basis for successful communication between network machines. As we have seen, the ISO service definition for a particular layer defines the services that a layer must provide to the layer above it. However, the service definition does not provide implementation details, and the interfaces between the layers within an actual device or software system are often fuzzy. They are fuzzy sometimes because of past history and sometimes to satisfy specific implementation objectives, such as achieving good performance, conforming to packaging constraints, and accommodating non-OSI protocols.

Conformance to ISO standards is not based on conformance to the abstract interfaces described in service definitions; it is based on conformance to the protocol specification and to any concrete interfaces the standards may define. The protocol specification defining the procedures for a given layer must be adhered to precisely if two nodes are to interoperate properly. And the data units flowing between machines at a given layer must conform exactly, bit by bit, to the protocol-data-unit formats defined in the standard. While service-data-units are abstract, protocol-data-units are real. By employing appropriate test equipment, we can actually see the PDUs flowing across the wires or other physical circuits that implement the network, and we can examine the various headers and see exactly how the bits are set. The protocol specification for a layer precisely defines each type of PDU peer entities in that layer can exchange and specifies the purpose of each bit in the headers. These bits must be set precisely as the protocol specification describes for two computers to communicate using an OSI protocol. Any concrete inter-faces defined in a standard, such as the specification of signal characteris-tics or for a plug or a connector, must also be adhered to exactly; other-wise, a device attempting to implement the standards will not be plug-compatible with other devices conforming to the standards.

Connection-Mode versus Connectionless-Mode Service

The service definitions and protocol specifications for all layers above the Physical layer of the OSI model define both a *connection-mode* and a *connectionless-mode* style of operation. A given layer may provide a connection-mode service, a connectionless-mode service, or both to the layer above it. A connection-mode service provides a service similar to that provided by the telephone system. It consists of three distinct phases:

1. connection establishment (we dial a call)

2. data transfer (we talk over the connection)

3. connection release (we hang up the phone)

A connectionless-mode service works more like the postal system. The service accepts each data unit for transmission and tries its best to deliver it, just as the postal system accepts addressed letters and attempts to deliver them to their intended recipients.

The OSI model, as described in ISO 7498, originally defined only a connection-mode style of operation. At any given layer, communication could originally take place only after a connection was established be-tween two peer entities in a given layer. Soon after ISO 7498 was first published, it was realized that this dependence on the establishment of a connection at each layer limited the power and scope of the reference model by specifically excluding entire classes of technology that are in-herently connectionless in nature. An ISO committee then developed an amendment to ISO 7498 specifying an alternative connectionless-mode style of operation for each layer above the Physical layer. The service definition for each layer now defines connection-mode services and con-nectionless-mode services. Protocol specifications are also provided that describe protocols to provide each type of service. Documentation of connectionless-mode services and protocols has often been added in the form of amendments to the original standards. Let us look at the characteristics of connection-mode and connectionless-mode operation.

Connection-Mode Operation

With a connection-mode style of operation, communication takes place in the three phases described earlier: connection establishment, data transfer, and connection release. There must be a three-party agreement between the two communicating partners and the provider of the service before data transfer can take place. With a connection-mode service, data transfer always involves a pair of peer layer entities. If a layer entity wishes to transmit a PDU to two or more other peer layer entities, it must establish a separate connection with each, and it must transmit the PDU to each peer entity in a separate operation. With a connection-mode service, the full address of the recipient need be specified only when the connection is established. Enough information must be provided with each data unit transferred only to identify the connection with which it is associated. A connection-mode service is often described as providing *reliable* and *sequential* data transfer. As long as the connection remains established, the sender can generally assume each data unit sent is successfully received and that the data units are received in the same order sent. If something goes wrong, the connection is either reset or released, and all parties are informed of the reset or release. The connection can be reset or released at any time by either of the communicating parties or by the service provider. This is an inherent property of a connection-mode service because any of the three parties can independently fail at any time.

The mechanisms used in various layers to supply a connection-mode service must perform two functions related to error correction: *sequence checking* and *message acknowledgement*. If layer N is supplying a connection-mode service to layer $N+1$, these two functions must be performed either by the layer N protocol itself or by at least one of the protocols operating below layer N. To perform the sequence checking function, PDUs being sent are assigned sequence numbers. As PDUs are received, the sequence number of each incoming PDU is checked to ensure that PDUs have arrived in the sequence in which they were sent and that none have been sent twice. Periodically, the receiving layer entity sends an acknowledgement so the sending entity knows the PDUs have arrived successfully. If problems occur and the receiving entity informs the sending entity that PDUs were not successfully received, the sending entity retransmits them.

Connectionless-Mode Operation

With a connectionless-mode style of operation, communication takes place in a single phase. The service requester hands an SDU to the service provider and gives the service provider the full address of the destination to which the SDU is to be sent. The service provider then packages the SDU in a PDU and attempts to deliver the PDU to its destination. Each PDU must contain the full address of its intended recipient and is handled independently from all other PDUs. A connectionless-mode service may incur less protocol overhead than a connection-mode service, especially when small amounts of data must be transferred. The delay involved in sending small amounts of data is also often less with a connectionless-mode service because no time is spent in setting up a connection before the data are sent. With a connectionless-mode service, there is no need to establish a logical connection between the sending and the receiving entities, and each PDU is sent and processed independently of any other PDU. No sequence checking is done to ensure that data units are received in the same sequence in which they were sent, and the receiver sends no acknowledgement that it has received a PDU. No flow control or error recovery is provided as part of a connectionless-mode service. With a connectionless-mode service, PDUs can be sent to one destination or to several destinations using the same service request. When a connectionless-mode service is used at a given layer, any flow control and error recovery services required must be provided either in a higher layer or by the communicating application programs.

A connectionless-mode service is typically described as providing a *best-efforts* delivery service. It is also sometimes called a *datagram* service. The sender does not know for sure a data unit being sent will actually be received by its intended recipient. A connectionless-mode service is not a reliable service. It is important to point out here that the term *reliable* used in this context is perhaps not the best term that could be used. *Reliable* has a "good" connotation that does not apply here. For example, a connection-mode service, although considered reliable, may provide a very poor service if frequent failures cause the connection to be constantly broken, thus requiring new connections to be established to continue data transfer. On the other hand, a connectionless service may deliver 999,999 data units out of every 1,000,000 sent. However, we cannot consider it reliable because we don't know for sure.

NETWORK ARCHITECT

Take this thing of reliability and guarantee of delivery. A connection-oriented person would say: "A connectionless service does not provide reliable delivery." But a connection-oriented service, even though it is described as reliable, doesn't provide reliable delivery either. When they refer to the service as reliable, what they really mean is: "If we don't give it to you, we will usually tell you we're not giving it to you." I say "usually" here because even the failure detection can never be 100 percent guaranteed. It is also interesting to note that with a "reliable" connection-mode service, the breaking of connections also voids the delivery and sequencing guarantees, thus still requiring recovery procedures in the higher layers. We need new terminology. Instead of using the term "reliable," perhaps we should start saying "positive notification of failure" or something like that.

Connectionless-Mode versus Connection-Mode Applications

The OSI model makes a distinction between connectionless-mode applications and connection-mode applications. A connectionless-mode application is one that simply sends data units into the network at the level of the Application layer and does not need the network to tell it whether the data unit was successfully received. Such an application may not care whether the data unit was received, or it might implement its own procedures for implementing end-to-end controls.

A connection-mode application is one that needs to establish a connection with another application and to have the network itself perform the required end-to-end controls. Most of today's applications that use the facilities of a computer network are connection-mode applications that want the network to accept the burden of providing a connection-mode, reliable data transfer service. However, there are some applications that require only a best-efforts datagram service, all the way up to the Application layer, and these may begin to increase in number over the years.

A network might implement a connectionless service at each layer to support connectionless-mode applications and a connection-mode service at each layer to support connection-mode applications. However, things often are not that straightforward. It is quite possible to provide a connection-mode service at one layer using a connectionless-mode service at the layer below. It is also possible to provide a connectionless-mode service at a particular layer by using a connection-mode service at the layer below. Consistent with the definitions of each of the layers, the combinations of connectionless-mode and connection-mode service shown in Figure 3.17 are possible within the context of the OSI model. The Physical layer provides a service that cannot be categorized as either a connectionless-mode or a connection-mode service. The Data Link layer can provide either a connection-mode or a connectionless-mode service. Likewise, the Network layer can provide either a connectionless-mode or a connection-mode service on top of either form of Data Link service. And the Transport layer can provide either a connectionless-mode or a connection-mode Transport service on top of either form of Network service. Above the Transport layer, conversions are not allowed. The Session, Presentation, and Application layers must together provide a connectionless-mode service for connectionless-mode applications or a connection-mode service for connection-mode applications.

At the level of the Data Link layer, there is generally little controversy concerning whether a connection-mode or a connectionless-mode style of operation should be supported. Analyzing such factors as transmission speed, average error rate, and cost determines whether a data link protocol should provide a connection-mode service or a connectionless-mode service. In a wide-area networking environment, speed and throughput typically are relatively low and the cost and the error rate are relatively high. So most wide-area networking data link protocols provide a reliable data transfer service. In a local area networking environ-

FIGURE 3.17   **A variety of combinations of connectionless-mode and connection-mode services are possible in the context of the OSI model.**

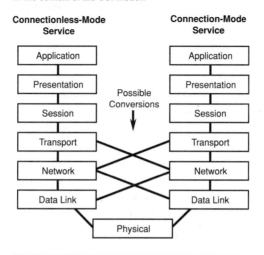

ment, transmission speed is very high, and the error rate and the cost are typically low. Therefore, a connectionless-mode style of operation is more appropriate. The broadcast nature of the local area network transmission medium also favors a connectionless approach.

The protocols operating in the Network layer generally are designed to operate using both connection-mode and connectionless-mode Data Link services, depending on the types of data link employed. At the level of the Transport layer, there is also little controversy. The majority of today's network applications require a reliable Transport service, and little use is made of a connectionless-mode Transport service. It is possible, however, that this may change in the future as connectionless-mode applications grow in number.

The Network Layer Controversy

Things are not as straightforward for the Network layer as they are for the other layers. There is great controversy in networking circles regarding whether the Network layer should provide a connection-mode service or whether a connectionless-mode Network service is sufficient. Digital is in the connectionless-mode camp and says only a datagram service is required in the Network layer, although the DNA Phase V architecture provides a connection-mode Network service for those requiring it. Many of the operators of public data networks, on the other hand, want to provide a connection-mode Network service. IBM also tends to be in the connection-mode camp with its SNA architecture. We will have more to say about the differences between connection-mode and connectionless-mode services in Part II, when we examine each of the OSI model layers in detail.

Conclusion	The DNA Phase V architecture is an implementation of the OSI architecture, and the ISO standards developed for the OSI architecture play important roles in the architecture. Chapter 4 introduces DNA Phase V and examines the way in which the DNA architecture has embraced ISO standards for the seven layers of the OSI model.
Reference	1. Andrew S. Tanenbaum, *Computer Networks—Second Edition*, Prentice Hall, Englewood Cliffs, NJ, 1988.

CHAPTER 4

The Digital Network Architecture

This chapter discusses Digital's approach to computer networking by introducing the *Digital Network Architecture* (DNA). We will see that a primary thrust of the latest version of DNA is to incorporate into the DNA architecture the ISO standards for the OSI model introduced in Chapter 3.

DNA and DECnet

Many users of Digital equipment and software are familiar with the term DECnet, which is used in the names of Digital's networking products. We will begin our examination of the Digital Network Architecture by discussing the relationship between DECnet and DNA.

The Digital Network Architecture consists of an architectural overview document, a set of specifications for each layer, and descriptions of each protocol that operates within each layer. These together constitute DNA. DNA, as a network architecture, is essentially a set of paper specifications, not a hardware or software product. All the components of DNA described in this book, while controlled by Digital and copyrighted, are available to the public. It is not necessary to have a license with Digital to purchase the detailed functional specifications of DNA. Be forewarned, however, that the detailed specifications of DNA make up a stack of manuals about three feet high, and are not for the faint of heart.

DECnet refers to a specific set of products that *implement* the Digital Network Architecture. The DECnet product line consists of hardware products, software products, and documentation for those products. Examples of DECnet hardware products are *routers* that relay messages from node to node through the network and *host computing systems*. An example of a DECnet software product might be the DECnet networking software that runs in a host computer. The DECnet products, unlike the architecture, are licensed products. They are paid for, and they have support policies associated with them, just like other Digital products.

DNA Architectural Specifications

The specifications that make up the Digital Network Architecture precisely define the architecture. A list of the most important DNA Phase V architectural specifications is included in Appendix B. The architectural specifications are designed to guide Digital engineers in developing DECnet hardware and software products so they all adhere to the same set of standards, thus allowing the products to be easily interconnected to form networks. They can also be used by other vendors in creating hardware and software products that can participate in a DECnet network on an equal basis with Digital products. The various types of information contained in the DNA architectural specifications are listed in Box 4.1.

Architectural Design Principles

Digital has been involved in the development of network architectures since the early 1970s. Since then, Digital network architects have developed a number of design principles that have been refined as architectures have evolved. Some of the important design principles that guided the development of DNA are listed below:

- **Self-Stabilization.** No matter what sort of failure occurs, algorithms and protocols should be constructed so the system always attains a correct, stable state when the failure is corrected or the failing component is removed from the network. The best example of this principle is found in the routing algorithm. The Phase V routing algorithm stabilizes in finite time to "good routes," provided no continuous topological changes occur.

- **No Single Point of Failure.** Algorithms and protocols should be designed, where feasible, so there will be no single component whose failure will cause the entire network to fail. It should be possible to add redundant equipment and software to the network and expect that higher reliability and availability will result. For example, in routing, algorithms will always find a path if a physical path exists, and in naming, replication of directories allows for continued operation even if one or more name servers fail.

- **Locality.** Individual parts of the system should self-stabilize even if continuous failures are occurring that affect the system on a global basis.

BOX 4.1

**DNA Architectural
Specifications**

Protocols

A *protocol* defines the way a layer entity in one node communicates
with a peer entity in another node. A protocol defines the formats of
the data units handled by a particular layer and the way in which information is exchanged among computers in the network in that layer.
Precise specification of protocols and accurate implementations of
those protocols allow diverse network machines to communicate successfully with one another across the network. The specifications for
each architectural layer describe the protocols that apply to that layer.

Abstract Service Interfaces

An *abstract service interface* defines the way a layer in a node communicates with the layer above it in the same node. Descriptions of
abstract service interface specifications constitute one of the fundamental characteristics of a layered architecture. Service interface specifications allow the complexities of a lower layer to be hidden from the layers above it. ISO standards define service interfaces in terms of abstract
service primitives and parameters; DNA architectural specifications
define abstract service interfaces in terms of a set of function and procedure declarations written in the Modula 2+ programming language.
The function and procedure declarations for an abstract service interface precisely define the services a layer can request of the layer below
it. Digital defines DNA service interfaces in terms of programming language functions and procedures rather than English language statements because a formal specification language allows a service interface
to be defined with precision and without ambiguity. The use of a particular programming language to define a service interface, however,
should not be taken to imply that implementations of the architecture
must use this language or must even be constrained to using procedure
calls. The architecture can be implemented in any desired way, for
example, using hardware or software interrupts or mechanisms operating in integrated circuits instead of procedure calls.

Concrete Interfaces

In addition to abstract service interfaces, which are defined for all
pairs of adjacent layers in the architecture, the architecture also defines
concrete interfaces at key points. A concrete interface is defined at any
point where it is necessary to describe the physical characteristics of a
plug or a connector and the characteristics of the signals flowing over
the interface. A concrete interface might also describe an application

BOX 4.1

continued

programming interface (API) that defines how an application program requests network services.

Configuration Mechanisms

Configuration mechanisms are the means by which the network automatically adapts to a changing environment. These include mechanisms that allow the network to modify its operation in response to changing network topologies and to control adaptive algorithms to improve the performance of the network. For example, when a new computing system is connected to the network, the architecture specifies the mechanisms used to allow that system to become, automatically, an active part of the network.

Network Management Mechanisms

Network management mechanisms describe the means by which a distributed network can be controlled and monitored. In Digital's view, network management constitutes all those elements of network operation that cannot be done automatically by the underlying network protocols. It also concerns the gathering of information for offline analysis and processing to measure the performance, reliability, and availability of the network.

Again, the best example of this principle can be found in routing. The network should stabilize locally to good routes even if there are continuous topology changes occurring elsewhere in the network.

- **Minimal Dependence on Network Management.** The algorithms and protocols should depend as little as possible on explicit human network management actions. The system should be self-managing as much as possible, and network management should concentrate on the setting of policy rather than on day-to-day operation. Algorithms and protocols should be designed so components can be plugged into the network and become part of it with little or no human intervention.

- **Invariants in System Operation.** The invariants of the system must be stated so the system is never permitted to enter an incorrect state.

- **Determinism.** The state of the system must be determined only by the characteristics of the system itself and must not depend on history. The best example of this is in routing. The routes calculated must be a function only of the network topology, not a function of past events that have occurred. This makes the operation of the network entirely predictable.

- **Scalability.** Algorithms and protocols should be designed so they scale well to support very large networks.

- **Interoperability.** Algorithms and protocols should be designed so they facilitate the interconnection of a variety of different types of network equipment.

- **No Cliffs.** Algorithms and protocols should be designed so when parameters exceed their design limits, no catastrophic failure occurs as soon as the limit is exceeded. The effect of adding one to anything should be to make things slightly worse than they were before, but there should be no point where adding one will cause the entire network to fail.

- **Configurable Redundancy.** It should be possible to configure a range of network topologies to make tradeoffs among cost, performance, and availability. For example, it should be possible to configure a network so a critical application can continue to operate despite the failure of a node or a data link.

The Evolution of DNA

Before we describe the actual architectural layers constituting the current version of the Digital Network Architecture, we will discuss how DNA has evolved over the years. We will then see how the latest version of DNA has incorporated ISO standards into the architecture. The development of DNA began in the early 1970s, when most of the major computer vendors were beginning to discover the value of computer communication across networks. Digital published its first DNA specification at about the same time IBM announced its Systems Network Architecture (SNA). Since then, DNA has evolved through a series of five phases.

DNA Phase I

Phase I of DNA was introduced in 1974. DECnet implementations of Phase I of DNA included support only for PDP-11 computing systems running the RSX-11 operating system. These implementations provided the ability to communicate in a standardized manner over point-to-point links between pairs of processors.

DNA Phase II

DNA Phase II was introduced in 1976. A major enhancement over Phase I was that the architects guaranteed they would not make incompatible changes from one version to the next. The Phase II architecture was also defined with sufficient precision that it was possible to have multiple, different implementations of the architecture that could interoperate with one another. DECnet implementations of Phase II of DNA were implemented for many of the Digital operating systems commonly used in that era, such as RSTS, TOPS-10, and TOPS-20. Phase II still provided only for point-to-point communication between pairs of processors; no intermediate node routing capabilities were included.

DNA Phase III

DNA Phase III was introduced in 1980 and provided the user with the ability to construct networks of up to 255 processors in any desired configuration. To handle such networks, this phase introduced an adaptive routing capability that allowed the computers themselves to determine the location of each node and to relay messages from one computer to any other computer, possibly through a number of intermediate nodes. An architecture for network management was also introduced in Phase III, and Digital developed gateways to other types of network, such those conforming to IBM's SNA standards and CCITT Recommendation X.25. Recommendation X.25 defines the means by which a computer is attached to a packet-switched data network. (The various roles that X.25 plays in the context of DNA are introduced in Chapters 7 and 8 and are discussed in detail in Chapter 18.)

DNA Phase IV

Phase IV of DNA was introduced in 1982. Phase IV defined a 16-bit network address that allowed users to construct networks theoretically containing up to about 64,000 nodes. However, network management constraints limited the practical size of networks to networks somewhat smaller than this because it is difficult to use the 16-bit address space that densely. DNA Phase IV added support for high-speed communication over short distances by integrating into the architecture support for the Ethernet form of local area network (developed jointly by Digital, Intel, and Xerox). The support for local area networks made it easy to connect large numbers of devices to the network. Phase IV also expanded the adaptive routing capability to include support for hierarchical routing. Hierarchical routing is a technique that allows adaptive routing to operate efficiently in large networks by dividing the network into subdivisions called *areas*. Hierarchical routing is discussed in detail in Chapters 7 and 9.

The layers of the Phase IV architecture have much similarity to the layers of the OSI model, especially at the lower levels of the architecture. However, at the time DNA Phase IV was introduced, ISO standards for many of the protocols had not yet emerged; therefore, many of the DNA Phase IV protocols remained Digital's own. Figure 4.1 illustrates the functional layers of the DNA Phase IV architecture, and Box 4.2 contains a brief description of each layer.

DNA Phase V

DNA Phase V, the subject of this book, was first introduced in 1987, and the first DECnet Phase V products to implement the architecture were brought to the market by Digital in 1991. The development of DNA Phase V took place over a number of years and was guided by the following five major objectives:

- support for very large networks (1,000,000+ nodes)
- integration of ISO standards into the architecture
- definition of a new network management model
- compatibility with DNA Phase IV
- equal or better performance than Phase IV implementations

The following sections discuss each of these five major objectives.

Support for Very Large Networks DNA Phase V was specifically designed to support very large networks. The theoretical maximum size of

---

FIGURE 4.1   **DNA Phase IV Functional layers.**

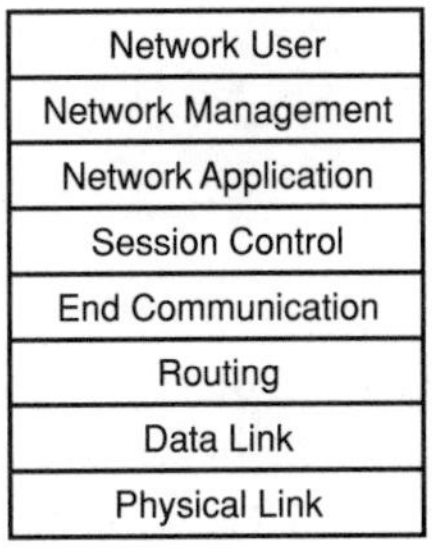

| Network User |
| Network Management |
| Network Application |
| Session Control |
| End Communication |
| Routing |
| Data Link |
| Physical Link |

BOX 4.2

DNA Phase IV
Functional Layers

The Physical Link Layer

The DNA Phase IV Physical Link layer corresponds exactly with the Physical layer of the OSI model. It is concerned with the transmission of bits across a physical medium, such as a telephone connection or a local area network cable. The Phase IV architecture uses international standards for describing the operation of this layer.

The Data Link Layer

The Phase IV Data Link layer corresponds exactly to the Data Link layer of the OSI model. The Data Link layer supports the proprietary Digital Data Communication Message Protocol (DDCMP) for wide area networking and the *Ethernet Specification* for local area networking.

The Routing Layer

The Routing layer is analogous to the Network layer in the OSI model. The Routing layer uses the building blocks of nodes and links implemented by the Physical and Data Link layers to implement a network of any desired configuration. The Routing layer allows a node to send data units to any other node in the network, independently of how many intermediate nodes the data units have to pass through to arrive at their destinations. The Phase IV Network layer provides a connectionless-mode datagram service. The addressing structure of DNA Phase IV allows for a theoretical maximum of about 64,000 nodes.

The End Communication Layer

There is a close correspondence between the functions performed by the End Communication layer and the functions performed by the OSI Transport layer. A major purpose of the End Communication layer is to provide for reliable communication between programs using the underlying datagram Routing layer service. The Data Link layer itself

a network conforming to the DNA Phase V architecture is essentially un-limited; implementation considerations rather than architectural con-straints limit the size of DECnet Phase V networks that can be built. The initial products supporting Phase V make it possible to build networks of

BOX 4.2

continued

may in some cases provide an essentially error-free data communication service between a pair of network nodes. However, since the Routing layer provides a connectionless-mode datagram service, the End Communication layer must ensure packets are placed into their proper sequence, duplicate packets are eliminated, and retransmission is requested when packets are lost.

The Session Control Layer

The Session Control layer performs some of the functions specified for the three uppermost layers of the OSI model: the Session, Presentation, and Application layers. It deals with such things as assigning names to objects in the computing environment, controlling access to those objects, and requesting communication services.

Higher Layers

Above the Session Control layer in the Phase IV architecture are three more layers that each directly access Session Control layer services. All of these layers operate above the operating system interface and are perceived by the operating system as network applications:

The Network Application Layer. The Network Application layer implements commonly used network facilities, such as transferring files from one computing system to another, providing facilities for logging onto a remote computing system, and electronic mail.

The Network Management Layer. The Network Management layer uses the facilities of the network to exchange messages concerning the status of network nodes, communication links, and other network components. This layer implements a variety of user interfaces network managers can use to monitor the status of the network and to gather statistics on network operation.

Network User Layer. The Network User layer represents the actual users of the network. These are the people and the application programs that use the network to perform useful work.

up to a million or so nodes. In addition, internetworking capabilities are defined that allow a DECnet Phase V network to be interconnected with other DECnet networks and with any other network implementing the ISO standards for the OSI model, leading ultimately to a single global data network. The very large OSI network addresses Phase V uses (up to 20 octets* compared to 16 bits in Phase IV) allow for addresses on all networks to be globally unique. When networks begin to be interconnected, the network addresses of the nodes will remain unique in a manner similar to global telephone numbers. To support such large networks, the routing algorithm that handles the relaying of messages from a source node to a destination node has been improved over that in Phase IV so it performs well in a very large network.

Integration of ISO Standards ISO standards for the OSI architecture have been integrated into DNA to allow computers from any vendor supporting the ISO standards to participate as a full partner in a DECnet Phase V network. The approach Digital has taken with respect to the integration of ISO standards and protocols is twofold:

1. Where an ISO protocol exists that duplicates functions previously performed by a Digital protocol, Digital has replaced its own protocol with the appropriate ISO protocol. Where a Digital protocol has been replaced, Digital has also retained support for its own protocol for the purposes of compatibility with Phase IV.

2. Where there is an ISO protocol that performs a similar function as a DNA protocol, but where the Digital protocol has some important advantage, such as higher performance, or a greater range of functions, DNA supports both the ISO and the DNA protocols, allowing the user to employ either one. Automatic network mechanisms select the required protocols as needed.

Digital's stated motivation for integrating the ISO standards directly into the DNA architecture is to provide support for multivendor networks. In Digital's view, the market for networking products has been constrained by the ability to interconnect equipment from various vendors. Digital believes that by supporting multi-vendor connectivity, it will greatly expand its own market for networking products.

---

* ISO standards and other documentation concerning the OSI model typically refer to a collection of 8 bits as an *octet*. Much of the DNA documentation also uses the term *octet* for a collection of 8 bits. Even though the term *byte* is today more common than *octet*, we will adopt the OSI terminology and use the term *octet* to refer to an arbitrary collection of 8 bits, such as when it is used to describe a networking protocol. But we will continue to use the term *byte* when referring to a collection of 8 bits in a storage system.

NETWORK ARCHITECT

The only company that can bet its business on Digital's proprietary network architecture is Digital. So if you buy into this vision of very large networks, then, by definition, these large networks must be based on standards. The standards must be extremely good technically to solve these kinds of problems because they are very difficult problems to solve. The essential problem facing the industry, and the real challenge, is that we must have extremely well thought out standards that everyone agrees to and implements consistently. Digital's approach says that ISO standards should be an integral part of the network. This means that wherever there is a place ISO standards should play a role, then that is the place they get slotted in. In Digital's view, ISO standards are not a means just for interoperability between DECnet networks and anyone else's network. Digital's goal is one of total interoperability with anyone who chooses to implement the ISO standards.

We believe the computer industry cannot afford to have artificial boundaries between networks conforming to entirely different architectures—such as connecting an OSI network to one conforming to IBM's SNA—because this forces you into a gateway model. With gateways, you get the Union of the liabilities and the Intersection of the capabilities of the two architectures being connected. If you are forced to use gateways to interconnect a group of incompatible networks, you will be too restricted. If you think of it strictly from a user-to-computer view, then there are all sorts of translation mechanisms you can get away with that really do not cost you very much. But in a computer-to-computer environment, with very large numbers of nodes, these translation mechanisms would very seriously limit the kinds of networks you could build.

New Network Management Model   DNA Phase V defines a new network management model that allows for either centralized or decentralized management of both small and large networks. The new network management model promotes the distribution of function among various processors in the network but allows users to employ a single central focus for network management if they choose to do so. The network management model allows for continuous network operation. It is never necessary to shut a DECnet network down to perform network management functions or to reconfigure portions of the network. The network management model was strongly influenced by early drafts of the ISO standards for network management, and Digital's work has also influenced the development of those standards. Digital feels it will be relatively simple to provide support of OSI network management when it becomes accepted as an international standard. The characteristics of the

DNA Phase V network management model are introduced later in this chapter and are examined in detail in Chapter 17.

Compatibility with Phase IV   A network that conforms to DNA Phase V is fully capable of supporting equipment and software conforming to Phase IV of the architecture in order to provide an orderly transition from a Phase IV environment to a Phase V environment. A major reason for providing compatibility with Phase IV is that networks behave in many ways like living organisms. It is not possible with a large computer network simply to shut it down to install a new release of the networking software on all the computers. The transition to new software must be made in an orderly manner on one portion of the network at a time. During the transition period it must be possible for the network to continue in operation with some nodes running Phase V software and others continuing to run in a Phase IV environment. Another reason for providing backward compatibility is that many hardware and software implementations of DNA Phase V are more sophisticated and more complex and require more resources than those for Phase IV. Certain older implementations of DNA, running on older hardware, will not be converted to Phase V. To allow Digital customers to continue using such hardware, it is necessary to support those Phase IV implementations on a continuing basis. The Phase V network management model discussed previously also provides for coexistence with nodes conforming to Phase IV of the architecture. From a network management perspective, it is not possible for a Phase IV node to manage Phase V nodes, but Phase V nodes do have the capability to manage Phase IV nodes.

Performance   A guiding principle in the design of the Phase V protocols and mechanisms is that their implementations must be capable of providing performance at least equal to the performance provided by the Phase IV facilities they replace. In many cases, Phase V implementations provide better performance than their Phase IV counterparts.

DNA Phase V Functional Layers   The layer structure of the Phase V architecture is shown in Figure 4.2. In Phase V of DNA, the lowest four layers of the architecture conform exactly to the OSI model and use the ISO standards defined for those layers. Above the Transport layer, the user can choose between Digital proprietary protocols and ISO standard protocols for the upper three layers of the OSI model. As stated earlier, the intent in DNA Phase V is to use ISO standard protocols wherever possible. However, both ISO standard protocols and DNA proprietary protocols are supported in the lower layers for compatibility with earlier versions of the architecture. This view of the

FIGURE 4.2   **DNA Phase V Functional layers.**

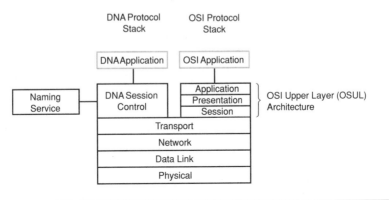

architecture as supporting multiple protocol stacks is a key to the flexibility of the DNA Phase V architecture. DNA Phase V has been designed so other important protocol stacks, such as the Transmission Control Protocol/Internet Protocol (TCP/IP) suite, can be supported as needed.

The Physical Layer

The Physical layer of the Phase V architecture is similar in function to the Phase IV Physical Link layer. It is analogous to the Physical layer of the OSI model and includes architectural specifications that define three major forms of physical link:

- **Modem Connect.** This specification defines support for international standards that govern the way a computer is connected to an analog or digital data transmission facility in a wide area networking environment.

- **CSMA/CD LAN.** This specification covers both the Physical and Data Link layers and documents specifications for how a computer is attached to a *carrier sense multiple access with collision detection* (CSMA/CD) form of local area network (LAN). The CSMA/CD LAN specification supports the CSMA/CD form of LAN defined by the IEEE 802.2/802.3 and ISO 8802-2/8802-3 standards. Support is also provided for the Ethernet form of LAN, described by the *Ethernet Specification* jointly published by Digital, Intel, and Xerox. CSMA/CD and Ethernet LANs are compatible and support a data transmission rate of 10 megabits per second over a multiaccess transmission facility using various types of transmission media. Digital's implementations of the CSMA/CD and Ethernet LAN standards are described in Chapter 22.

• **FDDI LAN.** This specification describes both the Physical and Data Link layers and defines how a computer is attached to a *Fiber Distributed Data Interface* (FDDI) form of local area network. FDDI is described by the ANSI X3T9.5 standards and by ISO 9314. An FDDI LAN supports a data transmission rate of 100 megabits per second over a ring-structured network, typically using a fiber-optic transmission medium. Digital's implementation of the FDDI form of LAN is described in Chapter 23.

The architecture is designed so other forms of local area network, such as the IEEE/ISO token ring and token bus forms of LAN, can be accommodated easily if needed. The main differences between Phase IV and Phase V in the Physical layer is that Phase V has added support for the IEEE/ISO CSMA/CD and ISO FDDI forms of LAN. The Phase V Modem Connect specification also provides a network management interface that is more explicit than the Phase IV equivalent of Modem Connect. Chapter 5 discusses the Physical layer in detail.

The Data Link Layer

The Data Link layer in the Phase V architecture is similar to the Data Link layer in the Phase IV architecture. It is analogous to the OSI model Data Link layer and includes architectural specifications for five forms of data links:

• **HDLC.** The HDLC specification includes support for ISO's High Level Data Link Control (HDLC) protocol, defined by ISO 3309, 4335, 7809, and 8885.

• **LAPB.** The LAPB specification defines a subset of the HDLC protocol used for compatibility with X.25 networks, defined by CCITT Recommendation X.25 and ISO 7776.

• **CSMA/CD LAN.** The Data Link layer portion of the CSMA/CD LAN specification includes support for the CSMA/CD and Ethernet forms of LAN, defined by IEEE 802.3, ISO 8802-3, and Version 2 of the *Ethernet Specification.*

• **FDDI LAN.** The Data Link layer portion of the FDDI LAN specification includes support for the ISO FDDI forms of LAN, defined by the ANSI X3T9.5 standards and ISO 9314.

• **DDCMP.** The DDCMP specification continues support for the *Digital Data Communication Message Protocol* (DDCMP) included in DNA Phase IV.

The main differences between Phase IV and Phase V in the Data Link layer is that Phase V has added support for HDLC and for the

CSMA/CD and FDDI forms of LAN. Chapter 6 discusses the Data Link layer in detail, and the chapters in Part V describe the various protocols supported by the DNA Data Link layer.

The Network Layer

The Network layer in the Phase V architecture is similar to the Routing layer in the Phase IV architecture. The Phase V Network layer is the same as the OSI model Network layer, and Network layer architectural specifications include support for the following ISO standards:

- The normal mode of operation of the DNA Phase V Network layer is to provide the ISO connectionless-mode Network service (CLNS) described in ISO 8348 Amendment 1 using the network addressing structure defined in ISO 8348 Amendment 2. The CLNS is provided using the protocols described in ISO 8473, ISO 9542, and ISO 10589.

- Optional support is also provided for the ISO connection-mode Network service (CONS), described in ISO 8348, using the network addressing structure defined in ISO 8348 Amendment 2. The CONS is provided to allow for communication between a DNA Phase V node and a node on an X.25 network that supports only the CONS using the protocols described in ISO 8878 and ISO 8208.

The main thrust of the changes Digital has made in the Network layer is to accommodate very large networks, to support the attachment of devices from multiple vendors to a DECnet network, and to interconnect the separate networks of different organizations. Key to this are the use of the ISO Network layer standards and the support of ISO network addressing standards that specify the use of globally unique addresses. DNA Phase V defines a unique distributed routing algorithm that supports very large networks. This routing algorithm has been accepted by ISO for standardization as a Network layer protocol described in ISO 10589. The Network layer also includes support for the connection-mode Network service to allow DNA Phase V nodes to communicate directly with other nodes on X.25 packet-switched data networks, but the strategic thrust of Phase V is to provide a datagram Network service. Chapters 7, 8, and 9 describe the Network layer in detail.

The Transport Layer

The Transport layer of the DNA Phase V architecture is similar to the End Communication layer of Phase IV. It provides support for the OSI

Transport protocol and also for Digital's own Transport protocol:

- The Phase V Transport layer provides the OSI Transport service defined in ISO 8072 and implements classes 0, 2, and 4 of the OSI Transport protocol defined by ISO 8073. Class 4 Transport is the preferred operating mode.

- A second protocol defined for the Transport layer is the DNA Network Services Protocol (NSP) implemented in the DNA Phase IV End Communication layer. Much of the experience Digital gained in building Digital's NSP Transport protocol was used by ISO in specifying the Class 4 ISO Transport protocol.

The main difference between the Phase IV and Phase V architectures in the Transport layer is that Digital has adopted the ISO standards for this layer. However, Digital's NSP protocol is still supported for compatibility with Phase IV systems. Chapter 10 describes the Transport layer in detail.

Higher Layers

Above the Transport layer are two separate protocol stacks that provide support for two separate classes of application. Other protocol stacks are likely to be added as well to meet the needs of Digital's customers. The higher layers are where the networking and communication pieces of the DNA architecture are integrated with the rest of the computing environment, such as the operating system, the applications that run on it, and system management facilities. DNA Phase V is designed to support both proprietary DNA applications and applications conforming to ISO standards.

- **DNA Session Control Layer.** DNA applications communicate with other DNA applications using the DNA Session Control layer. Even though the fifth layer of the OSI model is named the Session layer, it has little in common with the DNA Session Control layer. Chapter 11 examines the DNA Session Control layer.

- **OSI Higher Layers.** OSI applications communicate with other OSI applications using the OSI Session, Presentation, and Application layers. Support for the three OSI upper layers is defined by the architectural specification for the *OSI Upper Layer (OSUL) architecture.* Chapter 12 describes the OSUL architecture in detail.

To send a message from one user process to another using the network, a DNA application passes a user message to an implementation of the DNA Session Control layer using an application programming interface defined by the local operating system environment. An OSI application passes a user message to an implementation of the OSUL architecture. An application that needs to communicate with other DNA applications and with other OSI applications can use the facilities of both protocol stacks. It would then employ the interface appropriate for the partner with which it is communicating.

The DNA Session Control layer or the OSI upper layers add protocol-control-information (PCI) to each user message in the form of headers to create a transport-service-data-unit (TSDU), which it passes down to a Transport layer entity. The Transport layer is not concerned with whether the TSDU originated in the DNA protocol stack or in the OSI protocol stack. It simply knows the service-access-point address of the peer Transport entity to which the message is to be delivered. The Transport entity operates using the ISO protocol for the Transport layer whether a message originated from a DNA Session Control layer entity or from an OSI Session layer entity.

The support for both DNA applications and OSI applications using separate protocol stacks should not be viewed as a compromise that makes the DNA Phase V architecture somehow less than compliant with ISO standards. The support for both stacks reflects the real-world fact that there are currently more DNA applications running on DECnet networks than there are OSI applications. This is likely to be the case for some time to come. There would have been no advantage in attempting to merge the DNA Session Control layer with the three OSI upper layers. Digital's view is that as OSI applications continue to be developed and as they grow in capability, more use will begin to be made of the OSI upper layer stack by applications running on DECnet networks. Over time, the DNA proprietary upper-layer protocol stack will become less important.

The Naming Service

A growing problem in computer networking, especially with large networks, involves identifying, locating, and accessing network resources and the people that use them. Network resources include anything that can be accessed via the network, including devices, files, databases, and application programs. A computer network requires an easy-to-use directory service for locating resources by name. The DNA Phase V *naming service* provides such a directory facility. Conceptually, the function of the naming service is simple: a user provides the naming service with a name, and the naming service passes back the set of attributes associated with that name. The naming service can store attribute values for any type of named object the user finds useful. An important attribute associated with a named object is the address of the node on which the object resides. Storing the address of a resource as an attribute of its name allows the user to locate network resources by name alone without regard to where in the network they reside.

The naming service allows network users to create a single *namespace* containing the names of all the objects that can be referenced, anywhere in a possibly global network. For good performance and high availability, the naming service implements the namespace in the form of *directories* stored in a distributed database. The namespace directories can be both *partitioned* (different sets of directories are maintained by different nodes) and *replicated* (the same sets of directories can be maintained by multiple nodes). The naming service is central to the operation of a DECnet Phase V network, and each node in the network implements a naming service component called a *clerk*. Users employ a clerk to request naming service operations. Certain nodes in the network also implement naming service components called *name servers*, each of which is responsible for maintaining a portion of the namespace. Clerks communicate with name servers to satisfy name lookup operations. Chapter 16 describes the naming service in detail.

Network Management

The DNA Phase V approach to *network management* is based on an overall approach to the management of distributed systems, in which the communication network is viewed as only one aspect of the distributed system. Digital's overall approach to distributed system management is described by the *enterprise management architecture* (EMA). The enterprise management architecture defines a distributed system as a collection of individual computing systems tied together by a communication network for the purposes of sharing resources between the various computing systems. The EMA can be viewed as a *meta-architecture* that ensures consistency among a family of management architectures in the same way an individual architecture ensures consistency among a family of implementations. The DNA Phase V network management architecture is one of a series of management architectures that fall under the EMA umbrella. The DNA Phase V network management architecture describes how the components of a DNA Phase V communication network are managed. Other management architectures describe how various other components in the total distributed system are managed.

Each major component of the DNA Phase V architecture, including each architectural layer, has interfaces with a network management component. DNA Phase V network management allows network managers to monitor the operation of a network component and to change its operating characteristics. It allows parameter values to be specified that describe how various aspects of the network are to operate and also allows parameter values automatically set by DNA Phase V protocols to be fine-tuned as necessary. DNA network management also allows network managers to start and stop network components as needed, to monitor the operation of the network, and to extract information relating to network traffic and network performance characteristics. Chapter 17 describes the DNA network management architecture in detail.

| Conclusion | With DNA Phase V, Digital has solved a great many of the problems associated with building very large networks. These solutions include a sophisticated, distributed routing algorithm capable of scaling into the millions of nodes, a global naming service that allows users to access resources without having to know where they are located, and a network management scheme that allows automated monitoring and controlling of network resources in a global network.

Chapter 5 begins Part II of this book, which examines in detail each of the functional layers making up the DNA Phase V architecture. Chapter 5 discusses the lowest layer of the architecture, the Physical layer.

PART II

DNA Functional Layers

CHAPTER 5

The Physical Layer

The DNA Physical layer is responsible for the transmission of signals across a physical transmission medium connecting two or more devices. Some Physical layer implementations must also provide support for the establishment and release of calls, as over a switched telephone line. Typically the hardware associated with the Physical layer consists of electrical cables, appropriate connectors, and two or more communicating devices capable of both generating and detecting voltages or other types of signal, such as microwave transmissions or light flowing through an optical fiber. The hardware might also include modems, transceivers, repeaters, concentrators, or other signaling devices. Hardware or firmware permanently installed in the communicating machines typically controls the generation and detection of these signals. A physical link might involve the concatenation of a series of data circuits, such as in a typical long-distance telephone link. The Physical layer hides the complexity of such a concatenation of circuits from users of the Physical layer and makes the circuits appear to be a single physical circuit. A user of the Physical layer is typically an entity running in the Data Link layer, but the Network layer and network management entities also sometimes directly access the services of the Physical layer.

Physical Layer Functions

The documentation of the OSI model (ISO 7498) and the DNA architectural specifications list the following major functions of the Physical layer:

- **Circuit Establishment and Release.** Allows a physical circuit to be dynamically established when it is required and released when the circuit is no longer needed. This function is provided for a circuit implemented by a temporary facility, such as a dial-up line in the telephone network.

- **Bit synchronization.** Establishes synchronization in a receiving device with a stream of bits coming in and clocks data in from the communication circuit at the correct rate.
- **Physical-Service-Data-Units.** Defines the physical-service-data-unit (PSDU) passed down from a user of the Physical layer in the sending device and up from the Physical layer to its user in the receiving device. A PSDU typically consists of a single bit.
- **Data Transfer and Sequencing.** Allows electrical signals to be exchanged over the circuit connecting two communicating devices and allows bits to be accepted by the receiving device in the same order in which they are delivered by the sending device.
- **Fault Condition Notification.** Notifies the Physical layer user when fault conditions occur.
- **Network Management.** Controls and monitors the operation of functions operating in the Physical layer. Network management functions include setting the operating characteristics of the communication link, activating and deactivating physical circuits, monitoring the status of physical links, and performing diagnostic procedures, such as loopback tests.
- **Medium Specific Control Functions.** Provides control functions for specific forms of transmission medium, such as encoding/decoding, carrier sensing, collision detection, and collision announcement functions for CSMA/CD LAN data links, and detection of illegal cabling topologies for FDDI data links.

Transmission Alternatives

The circuit used to connect communicating devices that the Physical layer addresses has several characteristics, including:

- duplex or half-duplex transmission
- point-to-point, multipoint, or multiaccess circuits
- synchronous or asynchronous transmission

Duplex or Half-Duplex Transmission

Some types of physical circuits permit communication in both directions at the same time. These are called *duplex*, or *full-duplex*, circuits. *Half-duplex* circuits allow communication in both directions but in only one

FIGURE 5.1   **A point-to-point circuit using a direct cable connection.**

direction at a time. A third form of circuit, called a *simplex* circuit, allows communication in only one direction. Simplex circuits are not ordinarily used for data communication because even if information needs to be transmitted in one direction, control signals of some kind generally must flow in the opposite direction to control communication functions.

Point-to-Point, Multipoint, or Multiaccess Circuits

In the Physical layer three types of circuits can be used for interconnecting devices in the network: point-to-point, multipoint, and multi-access.

The simplest circuit consists of a *point-to-point* connection between a pair of devices. An example of a point-to-point circuit is shown in Figure 5.1, in which two devices are directly attached by a cable. A more complex type of point-to-point circuit might be implemented by a pair of modems and a telephone line, as shown in Figure 5.2. Collections of point-to-point circuits can be used to create any desired network configuration. In a typical DECnet Phase V network, routers are usually connected to one another using point-to-point circuits to form a mesh structure. Certain types of local area network, such as FDDI, also use collections of point-to-point links to create ring structures. Examples of the mesh and ring configurations are shown in Figure 5.3. In most cases, point-to-point circuits are implemented by a direct electrical or optical connection between each pair of devices. But another type of point-to-

FIGURE 5.2   **A point-to-point circuit using a telecommunications link.**

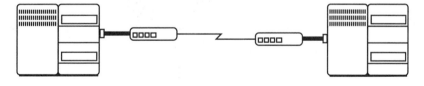

FIGURE 5.3   Mesh and ring configurations using point-to-point circuits.

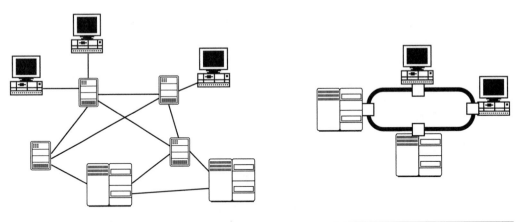

point connection can be implemented via a *virtual circuit* connecting a pair of computers that communicate using a packet-switched data network, typically implementing CCITT Recommendation X.25.

With a *multipoint* circuit, any number of devices are connected using a single physical connection, as shown in Figure 5.4. With a multipoint circuit, one device acts as the master and is in control of the circuit, while the other devices act as slaves. Each slave receives all the transmissions of the master, and the master receives the transmissions of all the slaves. The slaves cannot communicate directly with each other; they can communicate directly only with the master. In the Data Link layer, however, DNA models a multipoint physical circuit as a collection of separate point-to-point links between the master and each of the slaves. Thus, the multipoint characteristics of the link are hidden from layers above the Data Link layer.

FIGURE 5.4   A multipoint circuit.

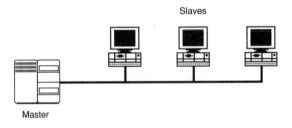

FIGURE 5.5   **A multiaccess circuit.**

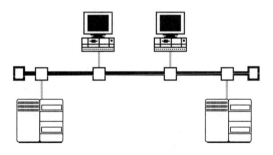

A *multiaccess* circuit has some similarities to a multipoint circuit in that any number of devices can be attached to a single physical circuit, as shown in Figure 5.5. However, with a multiaccess circuit, all devices act as peers, and there is no master/slave relationship between devices. Each device on the multiaccess circuit receives all the transmissions of all the others. The CSMA/CD form of local area network uses a multiaccess circuit to attach all devices to a common bus- or tree-structured transmission medium.

Synchronous versus Asynchronous Transmission

Data can be transmitted over a physical link in either an *asynchronous* or a *synchronous* fashion. With asynchronous transmission, sometimes called *start-stop*, a small number of bits, such as the 8 bits representing a single character, are sent at a time. Relatively simple equipment can be used because the two devices must be in synchronization only for the time it takes to transmit and receive a single character.

With synchronous transmission, bits are sent in a continuous stream. A block of perhaps hundreds or even thousands of bits can be sent at one time, and for the duration of the entire block the receiving device must stay in synchronization with the transmitting device. Box 5.1 provides brief descriptions of the characteristics of asynchronous and synchronous transmission.

Cable Plant Considerations

Work is being done in various standards bodies, with the Electronic Industries Association (EIA) playing a leadership role, in developing architectures to govern the way in which electrical and optical cables should be installed in buildings to support flexible network topologies.

BOX 5.1

Asynchronous and
Synchronous
Transmission

Asynchronous Transmission

Asynchronous transmission is well suited for slow-speed transmission, for example, with keyboard devices that do not have a buffer and with which the operator sends characters along the line at more or less random intervals. With asynchronous transmission, each transmitted character begins with a *start bit* and ends with one or more *stop bits*. The start bit indicates the beginning of a transmission, and there can be an indeterminate interval between transmitted characters. Characters are transmitted when the operator presses the keys. The receiving machine has a clocking device that starts when the start bit is detected and operates for as many bits as there are in a character. The receiving machine uses the clocking device to tell where each bit starts and ends. Asynchronous transmission often is used to communicate over short distances, for example, over the cable that attaches an inexpensive terminal to a terminal controller. Simple asynchronous transmission techniques also are sometimes used in computer networks where a high bandwidth is not required.

Synchronous Transmission

When machines transmit to each other continuously and with regular timing, *synchronous* transmission can provide more efficient transmission. Here the bits are strung together and are transmitted in a continuous stream. There are no start bits, stop bits, or pauses. The bit stream is divided into units called *frames*, and all the bits in the frame are transmitted at equal time intervals. The transmitting and receiving machines must remain in synchronization during the time it takes to transmit a complete frame. Devices using synchronous transmission employ a wide variety of frame lengths. The frame size may vary from a few bits to thousands of bits. A period of time is taken up between the transmission of one frame and the next, so the larger the frame length, in general, the higher can be the overall speed of transmission. On the other hand, the larger the frame, the higher the probability that an error will occur during transmission, which will require the frame to be retransmitted. A compromise between these two factors must be made.

Wiring Environments

The EIA technical report TR 48.1 describes one such standard that defines three different types of environment in which network cabling can be used:

- **Work Area Environment.** A work area environment consists of an open area within a building in which walls and cabling are not considered permanent. In any given work area, the distances spanned by cabling are relatively short and relatively few devices are installed. One type of work area might be a general office area in which typical network equipment consists of devices connected to some form of LAN and employed by end users. Typical devices installed in such a work area might be personal computers, file and print servers, and technical workstations. Another type of work area might be a computer room in which various types of host computer equipment are installed.

- **Building Environment.** A building environment is a building, or a collection of floors in a building, in which the walls and the wiring are considered relatively permanent. In a building environment, the distances spanned by cable runs are moderate, and relatively large numbers of devices are installed.

- **Campus Environment.** A campus environment involves a number of buildings connected by cable segments making up what is often called a *backbone* network. In a campus environment, distances are relatively great and cables are often permanently installed in underground tunnels.

Local area networks typically form the basis of network wiring in work area, building, and campus environments, with common carrier facilities most often linking multiple widely separated building and campus environments. Most early local area networks were installed in work area environments, where a relatively small number of network devices were connected in an ad hoc manner. In today's environment, building and campus environments are increasingly important as organization-wide networks are being created to link together all parts of an organization. Careful planning is of the greatest importance in building and campus environments because of the relative permanence of the wiring and its greater cost relative to the wiring installed in a work area environment.

Equipment Rooms

The EIA cable plant architecture defines three types of *equipment rooms,* which are those physical places in the three environments at which cables are physically terminated (see Figure 5.6). An equipment room is a dedicated space for facility wiring in which all types of wiring might be terminated, including wiring for data, telephone, electrical power, security, and fire alarms. Network cabling is terminated in each type of equipment room using various types of patch panels that facilitate documentation,

FIGURE 5.6   **Hierarchy of equipment rooms.**

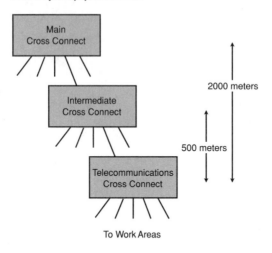

maintenance, and reconfiguration. Equipment rooms normally are kept locked and are accessed only by qualified service personnel.

The equipment room at the top of the hierarchy is called the *main cross connect* equipment room. A campus of buildings has a single main cross connect equipment room used to terminate cabling running to each individual building or collection of building floors in the campus environment. For each building or for each collection of floors making up an individual building environment, there is a single *intermediate cross connect* equipment room that terminates the cabling running from the main cross connect equipment room. Cabling is run from the intermediate cross connect equipment room to as many *telecommunications cross connect* equipment rooms as are needed to serve the needs of the building environment. Cabling runs from a telecommunications cross connect equipment room to the individual work areas it serves.

Physical Layer Standards

DNA Phase V supports a number of international standards that define the operation of the Physical layer. Standards are supported for the wide area networking environment as well as for the local area network environment. This chapter concentrates on standards that define the operation of wide area networking circuits. Physical layer standards for local area networks are also introduced in this chapter, but Physical layer details for LANs are deferred to the chapters in Part V. Chapters 22 and 23 in Part V describe the two major forms of LAN technology currently supported by DNA Phase V.

DTE-DCE Interface Standards

In the wide area networking environment, various international standards, all similar in function, define the way in which a computing device is attached to a signaling device, such as a modem. These standards define the concrete interface between a device in a class called *data terminal equipment* (DTE) and a device in a complementary class called *data circuit-terminating equipment* (DCE). The communication adapters in terminals and computers are common examples of devices containing DTEs; modems are common examples of devices containing DCEs. The important DTE-DCE interface standards for the wide area networking environment include:

- EIA-232-D
- CCITT Recommendation V.24
- EIA-422
- EIA-423
- EIA-449
- CCITT Recommendation V.35

EIA-232-D and Recommendation V.24

The EIA publishes standards analogous to some published by CCITT. A common EIA standard for the Physical layer is EIA-232-D. The EIA-232-D standard has CCITT counterparts—*Recommendation V.24* and *Recommendation V.28*—that together are equivalent to the EIA-232-D standard. EIA-232-D defines 25 *interchange circuits* that carry positive and negative voltages ranging from about 5 to 15 volts to connect a computing device (DTE) to a signaling device (DCE), such as a modem. Not all 25 circuits need be used. As few as 3 circuits can be used for communication between two devices and still be in conformance with the standard; however, many implementations use more than the minimum. CCITT Recommendation V.24 defines these same 25 circuits, and Recommendation V.28 defines the electrical characteristics of the signals. The standard defines the interface as suitable for serial transmission at speeds up to about 20,000 bits per second at a distance of typically 50 feet or less. In practice, the EIA-232-D standard is often used over distances up to a few hundred feet.

FIGURE 5.7   **EIA-232-D cable connector and circuits.**

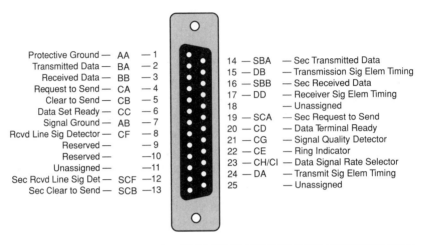

A 25-pin connector, such as that shown in Figure 5.7, is most often used for implementing an EIA-232-D connection. However, a 9-pin connector is used in many implementations, including many serial communications adapters installed in personal computers. Figure 5.7 also shows some of the commonly used functions of EIA-232-D circuits.

Figure 5.8 illustrates a typical long-distance implementation of a physical circuit between two computers. In this case, the computer on

FIGURE 5.8   **Two computers connected by two modems and a telecommunications link.**

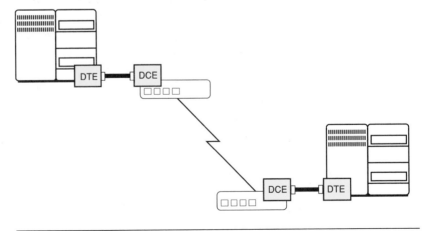

the left has circuitry that performs the functions of a DTE. It is connected via a short cable that uses two 25-pin EIA-232-D connectors to a complementary device with circuitry that performs the functions of a DCE. The computer on the right also implements a DTE connected by another EIA-232-D cable to a DCE. The DCEs are connected to each other by a telephone line of arbitrary length. In this example, the two computers each implement a DTE in a communication adapter, and the two DCEs are implemented in a pair of compatible modems.

Notice that there are three physical connections in this configuration. The DTE on the left is connected to its DCE by an EIA-232-D cable, the two DCEs are connected by a telephone line, and the DTE on the right is connected to its DCE by another EIA-232-D cable. The Physical layer is concerned only with the interface between the DTE and the DCE. The way in which the two DCEs (modems) exchange signals is governed by entirely different sets of international standards and is of no concern to DNA. As long as both modems use the *same* signaling scheme, the way in which they exchange signals is of no concern to the two DTEs.

A *null modem* cable is sometimes used to directly connect two DTEs over short distances using only the data interchange circuits. A null modem is a special cable or connecting device that crosses circuits to simulate the presence of a pair of modems between the two communicating devices. Figure 5.9 shows a possible null modem cable configuration for connecting two DTEs using the EIA-232-D standard.

FIGURE 5.9   **Typical null-modem cable.**

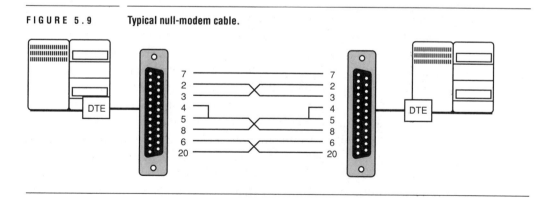

Other Physical Layer Standards   EIA-232-D is the most commonly used Physical layer standard for implementing relatively low-speed wide area networking circuits. The EIA also defines specifications for higher-performance circuits, including the following:

- **EIA-422-A.** The EIA-422-A standard is entitled *Electrical Characteristics of Balanced Voltage Digital Interface Circuits*. It specifies an alternative method to EIA-232-D for connecting a DTE to a DCE. The EIA-422-A standard specifies a more electrically stable method for generating balanced positive and negative voltages in the range of from 2 to 6 volts—the voltage level normally used in integrated circuits. The standard states these techniques can be used to implement equipment capable of transmitting and receiving data at up to 10 megabits per second. However, many implementations are limited to speeds much less than this.

- **EIA-423-A.** The EIA-423-A standard, entitled *Electrical Characteristics of Unbalanced Voltage Digital Interface Circuits*, is similar to EIA-422-A but specifies the use of unbalanced rather than balanced signals. As with EIA-422-A, this standard states that these techniques can be used to implement equipment capable of transmitting and receiving data at up to 10 megabits per second. However, as with EIA-422-A, many implementations are limited to speeds much less than this.

- **EIA-449.** The EIA-449 standard is entitled *General Purpose 37-position and 9-position Interface for Data Terminal Equipment and Data Circuit-Terminating Equipment Employing Serial Binary Data Interchange*. It defines signal characteristics, provides functional descriptions of interchange circuits, and specifies the characteristics of the physical connectors used to implement the EIA-422-A and EIA-423-A standards.

Modem Standards It is desirable that independent organizations be able to design and manufacture modems and data processing equipment with modems integrated into them. To permit this, various standards exist for modem design that permit modems of different manufacturers to communicate with one another. It is desirable that modem standards be internationally accepted and permit international transmission. To this end, CCITT has published a series of standards for modems in its V series of Recommendations. In addition to the international standards for modems, ad hoc standards for modems have arisen simply because certain types of modem are, or have been, widely used. As long as a modem manufacturer conforms to a standard in designing a modem, modems of different manufacturers can communicate with one another over any type of analog telecommunication link. Two types of standards are important for modems:

- the signals used for transmitting data between two compatible modems over the physical circuit

- the command set used by the computer to control the operation of the modem

Signaling System

As we have already introduced, the Physical layer is concerned only with the way in which a computer is attached to a modem and how the computer communicates with it, so the modems can implement any desired form of signaling between them as long as both modems implement the same type of signaling. Some commonly used signaling system standards have been set by AT&T. An obsolete AT&T modem, the Model 212A Data Set, implemented two alternative signaling systems to support data transmission at either 300 bits per second or 1200 bits per second. Modems compatible with the two signaling systems of the Model 212A modem are in common use today. The signaling system most often used by the manufacturers of 2400 bps modems in the United States is described by CCITT Recommendation V.26bis. Many manufacturers of high-speed modems for use over the switched telephone network conform to CCITT recommendation V.32, which specifies a data transmission rate of 9600 bits per second.

Command Set

A modem manufacturer can use any desired command set that the computer must employ in controlling the modem. However, many manufacturers of modems use the command set first introduced by the Hayes Corporation for its *Smartmodem* family of modems for personal computers. This command set, generally referred to as the AT command set, is now a de facto standard. The AT command set implements commands the computer can issue to perform such functions as setting the modem's data transmission rate, dialing the telephone number of the computer with which it would like to communicate, and controlling the modem's automatic answering features.

Recommendations V.25 and V.25bis

CCITT Recommendations V.25 and V.25bis are international standards for performing some of the functions implemented by the Hayes AT command set. These include dialing the telephone number of the modem with which a connection is desired and for controlling the automatic answering features of the modem.

Digital Circuits

The DNA Phase V Physical layer also supports the use of industry standard digital circuits for connecting communicating devices. In the United States, most common carriers provide digital circuits that support various data rates. Other countries provide such telecommunications services as well. When a digital circuit is used, modems are not required and devices called *digital service units* (DSUs) or *line drivers* provide the interface between the communicating device and the digital circuit. (See Figure 5.10.)

Physical Layer Specifications

As introduced in Chapter 4, DNA Phase V includes three architectural specifications that define Physical layer capabilities. No proprietary protocols are included in the Physical layer; only accepted international standards are used. The three Physical layer specifications are:

- Modem Connect
- CSMA/CD LAN
- FDDI LAN

There is a separate architectural specification for each of the above, and each is augmented by documents describing the associated ISO standards each specification incorporates. The DNA architectural specifications and the ISO standards often combine descriptions of both the Physical layer and the Data Link layer for a particular type of data link. An actual implementation of the Physical layer is closely tied to an implementation of the Data Link layer for a particular form of transmis-

FIGURE 5.10   A digital circuit.

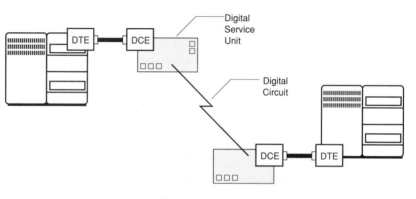

sion technology, and both are often implemented in hardware in the same device. The DNA specifications and ISO standards for the Physical layer typically contain information about service definitions, concrete interfaces, and protocol specifications.

Service Definitions

A Physical layer *service definition* defines the abstract interface between a Physical layer entity and a user of the Physical layer entity. This abstract interface defines the services a Physical layer entity provides to its user.

The international standards for local area networking technology (the IEEE 802/ISO 8802 family of standards) define the abstract interface between a Physical layer entity and its users in terms of *service primitives*. (Chapter 3 introduced the service primitives used in ISO standards to document abstract interfaces.) DNA architectural specifications for Modem Connect and the two forms of LAN describe the abstract services the Physical layer provides to its users in terms of *procedure declarations*.

Concrete Interfaces

In addition to the abstract interfaces described by service definitions, standards for the Physical layer also define *concrete interfaces*. These include specifications for physical connectors and cables and the characteristics of the various types of signals exchanged. They also define the characteristics of certain types of devices, such as the transceivers, concentrators, and repeaters used in constructing networks.

Protocol Specifications

A *protocol specification* for the Physical layer involves mechanical, electrical, functional, and procedural means for activating and deactivating physical circuits and for transmitting signals across them. Protocol specifications for the Physical layer are contained in the architectural specifications for Modem Connect and the two forms of LAN supported by DNA Phase V.

We continue by discussing each of the Physical layer architectural specifications that define the operation of the DNA Phase V Physical layer. This chapter includes details for Modem Connect. The two forms of LAN are introduced, but details concerning the Physical layer for CSMA/CD LANs are in Chapter 22, and details concerning the Physical layer for FDDI LANs are in Chapter 23.

Modem Connect

The *Modem Connect* specification defines how the DNA Phase V Physical layer operates over WAN telecommunication links. Modem Connect supports any type of modem or service unit for communication over a conventional analog telecommunications link or over a digital data service. Figure 5.11 shows the Modem Connect architectural model when HDLC is used in the Data Link layer and the DNA Phase V Network layer is the user of the Data Link layer service. A user of Modem Connect accesses its services via a port. A *port* is a data structure employed by a particular Modem Connect user. A port is assigned to a user upon request and remains associated with that user until it is explicitly released. Each user has its own port assigned, and many users can access the services of Modem Connect simultaneously, each through its own assigned port.

Modem Connect defines two types of ports: call control ports and data ports. The Network layer (and other Data Link service users) communicate directly with a Modem Connect entity through a *call control port*. A Data Link layer entity communicates with Modem Connect through a *data port*.

The following sections introduce the important services and functions provided by Modem Connect through the call control and data ports.

Call Control Port Services

The services accessed via a call control port are used to control and monitor the circuit establishment and circuit release functions for switched lines. A call control port allows higher layer entities to request the establishment of an outgoing call, such as over a dial-up line, to handle incoming calls, and to clear established calls. The call control services are

FIGURE 5.11   Modem Connect architectural model.

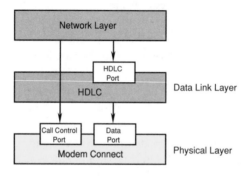

not used when a leased line is employed. The procedure declarations defining the Call Control services are listed in Box 5.2.

BOX 5.2

Modem Connect Call Control Service Interface Procedures

The following function and procedure declarations define the abstract interface between the Physical layer and a user of the Physical layer in terms of the call control services a Modem Connect entity provides to its users.

Port Control Functions

- **CcOpenPort.** Assigns system resources for a *call control port*, which is a data structure that defines an access point to the switched line call control service.

- **CcEnablePort.** Allows the user to gain access to a call control port that was previously disabled and then subsequently made available again through a network management action.

- **CcClosePort.** Frees up the system resources assigned to an existing call control port.

Call Control Functions

- **CcCallConnectedPoll.** Determines whether a call has come in on a switched line circuit.

- **CcHoldCall.** Attaches a call control port to a call so other users of the Modem Connect entity are unable to clear the call.

- **CcClearCall.** Requests that the call associated with the call control port be cleared.

- **CcInitiateCall.** Allows the user to employ a call control port to make an outgoing call to establish a switched line circuit.

- **CcCallState.** Returns the status of the call currently associated with a particular call control port. Possible status conditions include connecting, connected, disconnecting, disconnected, and disconnect pending.

- **CcDisconnectReason.** Obtains information about the reason an established call was disconnected or that an outgoing call request failed to connect.

Control Functions

- **PhCallConnectedPoll.** Determines whether a call has come in on a switched line circuit.

BOX 5.2

continued

- **PhAttachToCall.** Used only with switched lines to attach a data port to a connected switched line.
- **PhEnableTransmit.** Enables the transmitter component of a Modem Connect entity and activates the modem's Request to Send interchange circuit.
- **PhEnableTransmitPoll.** Determines whether an operation requested by the PhEnableTransmit function has been completed, either successfully or unsuccessfully.
- **PhDisableTransmit.** Disables the transmitter component of a Modem Connect entity and deactivates the modem's Request to Send interchange circuit.
- **PhDisableTransmitPoll.** Determines whether an operation requested by the PhDisableTransmit function has been completed, either successfully or unsuccessfully.
- **PhEnableReceieve.** Enables the receiver component of a Modem Connect entity.
- **PhTestForLoopback.** Used to perform a loopback test function.

Data Port Services

The services accessed via a data port allow a user of the Physical layer to transmit and receive data on either a leased or a switched circuit. They are also used to control line turnaround operations on half-duplex circuits. These services can be requested for both switched and nonswitched telecommunications facilities. For example, an HDLC data link might request these services in order to transmit and receive individual bits over a physical circuit. The data transfer services Modem Connect supplies are independent of characteristics of individual devices and physical circuits. The procedure calls defining the Data Transfer service are listed in Box 5.3.

Polled Interfaces

The procedure declarations that make up the service interface to Modem Connect, like all service interfaces defined for the layers of the DNA Phase V architecture, document a *polled interface*. To transmit data using a polled interface, the user makes a request to transmit and then follows that request with explicit requests to determine whether the operation has been completed. Actual implementations of the service inter-

BOX 5.3

**Modem Connect
Data Service
Interface
Procedures**

The following function and procedure declarations define the abstract interface between the Physical layer and a user of the Physical layer in terms of the data transfer services a Modem Connect entity provides to its users.

Port Control Functions

- **PhOpenPort.** Reserves system resources for a *data port*, which is a data structure that defines an access point to the data transmission services for a modem connect line.
- **PhClosePort.** Frees up the system resources assigned to an existing data port.
- **PhEnablePort.** Allows the user to gain access to a data port that was previously disabled and then subsequently made available again through a network management action.

Data Transfer Functions

- **PhTransmitBit.** Issued by a user of the Physical layer entity to enqueue a single bit of data for physical transmission.
- **PhReceiveBit.** Issued by a user of the Physical layer entity to read a single bit of the data received by a Modem Connect entity.

face, however, are much more likely to use interrupts rather than a polled interface. With interrupts, the user makes a request and then continues with other tasks. When the request has been satisfied, the user is notified with an interrupt.

Service interfaces are defined in the DNA Phase V architecture using polled interfaces because a polled interface is easier to describe than an interface using interrupts. As discussed in Chapter 3, abstract interfaces are intended to convey only the semantics of the services they describe. They are not intended to restrict the implementation of that interface to any particular set of techniques. An implementor is free to choose any desired method to build an implementation of the services defined by an abstract service interface.

Call References

Modem Connect assigns unique identifiers, known as *call references*, to incoming and outgoing calls. Call references are assigned via a counter maintained for each switched line. The counter is incremented for each incoming and outgoing call attempt made on a line, thus providing a unique call reference for each attempted call. Call references provide a means of tying together the call establishment and release phases with the data transfer phase. They also provide a means for correlating management information about the various phases of a call.

Call Sharing

The *call sharing* feature allows calls on a switched line to be accessed by more than one user of the Physical layer. For example, a network management entity and a DNA Network layer entity might share the same call and thus both use the same physical circuit. When the call sharing feature is used, the clearing of calls is coordinated by Modem Connect so that when one user requests that a call be cleared, the call will be retained if it is currently in use by some other user.

Modem Connect Operation

A detailed architectural model that illustrates how a Modem Connect entity controls a single physical circuit is shown in Figure 5.12. Requests made by a user of the Physical layer are handled by the *line handler* component. At the lowest level of the architectural model, the *interchange circuit interface* component provides access to the DTE-DCE interchange circuits. These are the physical circuits implemented in the cable

FIGURE 5.12   **Modem Connect functional components.**

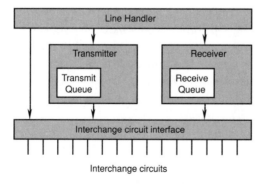

and connectors used to connect the DTE (computer) to the DCE (modem or other signalling device). The line handler uses the services of the *transmitter* and *receiver* components in providing each service to a user of Modem Connect. Modem Connect provides a bit-stream interface to its users in which data pass across the interface in 1-bit units.

A Modem Connect entity user *sending* data passes bits across the interface, one at a time, to the line handler. The line handler passes them to the transmitter component, which adds them to the end of the *transmit queue*. The transmitter concurrently removes bits from the front of the transmit queue and clocks them onto the transmit interchange circuit. To service a user receiving data, the *receiver* component clocks bits from the receive interchange circuit and adds them to the end of the *receive queue*. A user receiving data issues a request to the line handler for each bit. For each request, the line handler asks for a bit from the receiver component, which then removes a bit from the front of the receive queue. Both the transmitter and the receiver components operate autonomously from the service interface. The transmit and receive queues act as a buffer between the line handler component and the transmitter and receiver components.

CSMA/CD LANs

One form of local area network supported by DNA Phase V is the CSMA/CD form of data link. CSMA/CD stands for *carrier sense multiple access with collision detection* and refers to the way access to the communication medium is controlled. This is a LAN standard defined by the IEEE and is documented in IEEE 802.2 and IEEE 802.3. These standards are also published by ISO as ISO 8802-2 and ISO 8802-3. A CSMA/CD LAN typically uses coaxial cable or twisted-wire pair cable for transmission at a rate of 10 megabits per second. The CSMA/CD LAN data link also provides support for the *Ethernet Specification,* which describes the local area networking scheme jointly developed by Digital, Intel, and Xerox and used in DECnet networks for many years. Ethernet was used as the model for the development of the IEEE/ISO CSMA/CD standard. It is similar to IEEE/ISO CSMA/CD but uses a slightly different frame format. Ethernet is defined in DNA Phase V mainly for compatibility with Phase IV of the architecture. The CSMA/CD and Ethernet LAN data links are described in detail in Chapter 22.

In a CSMA/CD implementation of a local area network, a group of communicating devices are connected to a common cable, often using devices called *medium access units* (MAUs) (see Figure 5.13). A medium

FIGURE 5.13   **CSMA/CD form of local area network.**

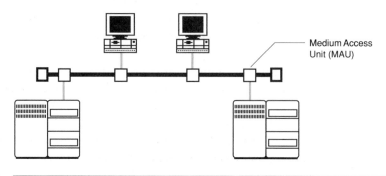

access unit is sometimes called a *transceiver*. When one device sends data, all the other devices on the cable receive the data. Thus, a CSMA/CD LAN implements a multiaccess form of physical circuit. Physical layer standards for the CSMA/CD form of LAN specify the characteristics of the signals broadcast over the communication medium and define the type of hardware used to connect a device to the communication medium and to connect individual cable segments with one another to form a bus- or tree-structured network.

A CSMA/CD LAN can be implemented using many different types of transmission mediums, including:

- original thick Ethernet cable
- less expensive thin Ethernet cable
- coaxial cable used for cable television distribution
- fiber-optic cable
- twisted-pair telephone cable

All the forms of transmission medium supported by DNA Phase V are compatible with one another and all support a data rate of 10 megabits per second. Additional information about the Physical layer for the IEEE/ISO CSMA/CD and Ethernet forms of local area network is provided in Chapter 22.

FDDI LANs   Another form of local area networking DNA Phase V supports is *Fiber Distributed Data Interface* (FDDI). The FDDI standard was initially developed by a committee of ANSI and is now an accepted international standard described by ISO 9314. An FDDI LAN uses a series of fiber-

FIGURE 5.14   A small FDDI network consisting of a dual ring of trees.

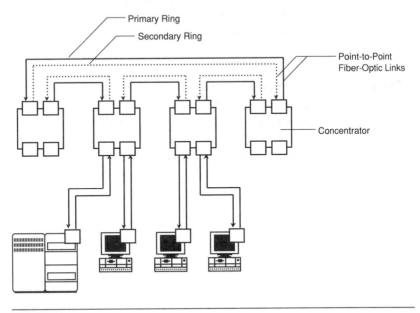

optic point-to-point circuits to form a logical ring configuration. The FDDI standard supports many configurations. A commonly used configuration is a *dual ring of trees*, in which devices called concentrators are connected to form a dual ring structure with a primary ring and a secondary ring. Individual stations are then connected directly to the concentrators to form tree structures. (See Figure 5.14.)

FDDI LANs support a data rate of 100 megabits per second and provide the ability to build very high speed backbone networks that can be used to interconnect slower CSMA/CD networks. FDDI LANs can also be used to support powerful workstations that must communicate with one another using very high transmission rates. Additional information about the Physical layer for the FDDI form of local area network is provided in Chapter 23.

Other Physical Layer Standards

The Physical layer of the DNA architecture is structured in a modular fashion so that as support is required for new forms of circuit, additional Physical layer specifications can be added to accommodate them. Of particular interest in today's environment is the emerging technology of *integrated services digital networks* (ISDN). Support can also easily be added for other types of LANs, including the token bus technology—commonly used in the factory automation environment and based on IEEE 802.4/ISO 8802-4—and the token ring standard, based on IEEE 802.5/ISO 8802-5.

Conclusion

The Physical layer implements the mechanisms required to provide circuits between network devices. But procedures must be provided that run on top of these circuits to allow them to be used for exchanging data in a reliable fashion. These procedures are implemented in the Data Link layer, the subject of Chapter 6.

CHAPTER 6

The Data Link Layer

The *Data Link layer* is responsible for handling data transmission from one network device to another and for shielding higher layers from any concerns about the physical transmission medium. The Data Link layer uses the point-to-point, multipoint, and multiaccess forms of physical circuit provided by the Physical layer to implement two fundamentally different types of data links: *nonbroadcast* links and *broadcast* links. A typical nonbroadcast link might be implemented by a simple point-to-point telecommunications circuit between exactly two devices. A typical broadcast link might be implemented by a local area network connecting hundreds of devices. A broadcast link might be implemented by a multi-access circuit, as in the case of a CSMA/CD LAN, or by a series of point-to-point circuits, as in the case of FDDI.

A critical function of the Data Link layer for all types of data links is to detect errors that occur during transmission, perhaps when a burst of noise obscures the signals representing one or more bits. Error detection is accomplished through the use of redundant data transmitted with each unit of data in the form of a *frame check sequence* (FCS) field. For broadcast data links to which many devices may be attached on a peer basis, the Data Link layer must perform additional functions, such as scheduling the use of the transmission medium and resolving contention.

Data Link Layer Services

The Data Link layer must provide a set of basic services to a user of the Data Link layer service and perform certain general functions in providing those services. The OSI model and the DNA Phase V architecture list the following services and functions of the Data Link layer:

- **Data Link Connection Establishment and Release.** Dynamically establishes, for a *connection-mode* Data Link service, a logical data link connection between two users of the Data Link service (typically Network layer entities) and releases the connection when it is no longer required. These functions are not provided for a *connectionless-mode* Data Link service, in which connections are not established or released. (Later in this chapter we discuss in detail the differences between a connection-mode Data Link service and a connectionless-mode Data Link service.)

• **Data-Link-Service-Data-Units.** Defines the data-link-service-data-unit (DLSDU) passed down from the user of the Data Link layer service to a Data Link layer entity in the sending device and up from a Data Link layer entity to the user of the Data Link layer service in the receiving device.

• **Framing.** Creates a single data-link-protocol-data-unit (DLPDU) from each DLSDU passed from a user of the Data Link layer service, marks the beginning and the end of the DLPDU when sending, and determines the beginning and ending of frames when receiving. The informal name most often used for the DLPDU exchanged between peer Data Link layer entities is *frame*.

• **Data Transfer.** Transfers frames over a physical circuit, extracts the DLSDU from each frame by removing the protocol-control-information (PCI), and passes DLSDUs up to the user of the Data Link layer service in the receiving device.

• **Frame Synchronization.** Establishes and maintains synchronization between the sending device and the receiving device. This means the receiving device must be capable of determining where each frame begins and ends.

• **Frame Sequencing.** Uses sequence numbers to ensure that frames are delivered in the same order in which they were transmitted (does not apply to a connectionless-mode Data Link service).

• **Error Detection.** Detects transmission errors, frame format errors, and procedural errors on the data link connection using redundant bits carried in the PCI in the frame.

• **Error Recovery.** Recovers from errors detected on data links using connection-mode operation (does not apply to a connectionless-mode Data Link service).

• **Identification and Parameter Exchange.** Performs a set of identification and parameter exchange functions, typically prior to the exchange of frames carrying user data. Some types of Data Link services allow parameter values to be negotiated.

• **Flow Control.** Controls the rate at which a user of a connection-mode Data Link layer service receives frames to prevent a user of the Data Link layer service from being overloaded (does not apply to a connectionless-mode Data Link service).

- **Physical Layer Services.** Uses the services of the Physical layer to transmit and receive data and to control the operation of the physical communication link.

- **Network Management.** Performs network management functions to control the operation of the Data Link layer. Management functions include setting data link layer protocol operating characteristics, enabling and disabling data link connections, monitoring the status of enabled connections, and performing a loopback test for testing the data link.

Architectural Model

A general architectural model of a Data Link layer entity is shown in Figure 6.1. This model shows how the Data Link layer uses the services of the Physical layer and how it provides services to a user of the Data Link layer service. Each specific type of Data Link layer service defines a somewhat different architectural model, but each is similar to that shown in Figure 6.1. A user of the Data Link layer service perceives both *stations* and *ports*:

- **Stations.** In many types of data link, a *station* corresponds to a particular instance of a Data Link layer entity and corresponds to a single Physical layer entity.[*] A station typically represents a physical point of attach-

---

[*] With an FDDI data link, a station can contain zero, one, or two Data Link layer entities, and a station can attach to either one or two full-duplex optical fiber cable segments. So an FDDI station is somewhat different from other types of data link station. The FDDI form of data link is described in Chapter 23.

FIGURE 6.1   **A typical Data Link layer architectural model.**

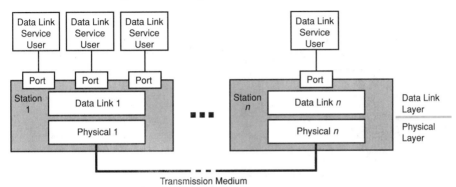

Transmission Medium

ment to the transmission medium. A particular node must implement at least one station to attach that node to the network. A station is identified by a *station address* that is unique among all the stations attached to the same data link.

- **Ports.** A Data Link layer *port* consists of a data structure that represents a particular user of the Data Link layer service. Each user of the Data Link layer has a port that it uses to request Data Link layer services. A particular station can implement any number of ports, and a user can simultaneously employ more than one port. However, a port can service only a single user at a time.

Service Definitions and Protocol Specifications

As introduced in Chapter 3, the ISO standards for the Data Link layer include both service definitions and protocol specifications. The relationship between the services the Data Link layer provides and the protocol governing its operation is shown in Figure 6.2. As shown there in the context of the OSI model, the data link protocol uses the services of the Physical layer to provide a defined set of services to a user of the Data Link layer service above it.

A user of the Data Link layer service in one node accesses the Data Link service via a *data-link-service-access-point* (DLSAP) and passes a DLSDU for delivery to the user of the Data Link layer service at the

FIGURE 6.2   **The relationship between the Data Link layer service definition and the Data Link layer protocol specification.**

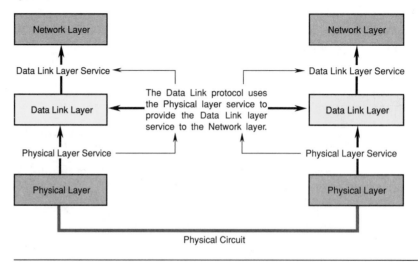

Physical Circuit

other end of the link. The Data Link layer entity adds PCI to the DLSDU in the form of a header and a trailer to create a data-link-protocol-data-unit (DLPDU), or *frame*, and uses the services of the Physical layer to transmit the frame across the data link. The Data Link layer entity at the other end of the link removes the PCI and delivers the enclosed DLSDU to the user of the Data Link layer service there. This process is summarized in Figure 6.3.

The standards for the layers above the Data Link layer make a clear separation between the service definition and the protocol specification, and each is published by ISO in a separate document. The intent is to have a single ISO service definition and one or more protocol specifications for each layer. Because the Physical and the Data Link layers are so tightly integrated in actual implementations, it is common for a single ISO standard to describe service definitions and protocol specifications for both the Physical layer and the Data Link layer. Many local area network standards documents take this approach. In the Data Link layer standards for protocols to support wide area network data links, there is often not a clear separation between the service definition and the protocol specification. The main reason for this is that many of the wide area

FIGURE 6.3   **The Data Link layer service.**

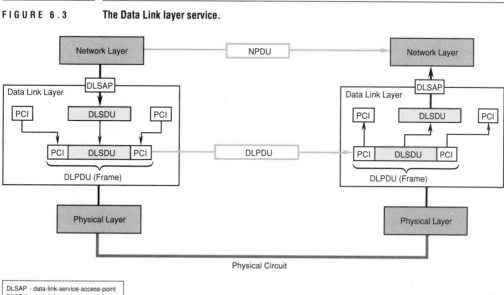

DLSAP - data-link-service-access-point
DLSDU - data-link-service-data-unit
DLPDU - data-link-protocol-data-unit
NPDU   - network-protocol-data-unit
PCI   - protocol-control-information

networking data link protocols were developed before work was completed on the OSI model.

<table>
<tr><td>

**Data Link Layer
Service
Definitions**

</td><td>

As with the standards for all the OSI model layers, a Data Link layer service definition describes an abstract set of services a user of the Data Link layer service can request. The service definition can be implemented in any desired way, and conformance to the standard is not based on any formal adherence to the service definition. However, it does define what types of service the Data Link layer must provide to users invoking its services. Many service definitions now exist for the Data Link layer. The discussion of the Network layer in Chapters 7, 8, and 9 shows how the Network layer makes use of widely differing types of Data Link technology in providing a unified interface to the Transport layer.

</td></tr>
</table>

Local Area Network Data Links

Data Link technology for local area networks implements a broadcast type of data link, in which many stations can be attached on a peer basis to a common transmission medium. All stations on the link receive the transmissions of all other stations, and mechanisms must be provided for determining when a station can transmit and which transmissions should be accepted.

Service definitions for the local area networking environment are defined by the IEEE/ISO LAN architecture documented in the IEEE 802/ISO 8802 family of LAN standards and by the standards for the FDDI form of data link. The IEEE/ISO LAN architecture and the ISO FDDI standard define a number of ways in which a local area network can be implemented (e.g., CSMA/CD bus, token bus, token ring, and FDDI timed token ring).

Figure 6.4 shows how the layering structure of the two lowermost layers of the OSI model have been evolving as LAN technology has matured. To present a unified LAN interface to users of the Data Link layer service, the IEEE/ISO LAN architecture divides the Data Link layer into two sublayers: the *Logical Link Control* (LLC) sublayer and the *Medium Access Control* (MAC) sublayer. The FDDI form of LAN can also use the IEEE/ISO LLC sublayer. Since all forms of LANs can share a common LLC sublayer, they can all present a similar interface to users of the LLC sublayer. The protocols operating in the LLC sublayer are based on those defined for HDLC and so share a similar frame format with the protocols used in the wide area networking environment. The LLC ser-

FIGURE 6.4   Comparison of the layers of the OSI model, the IEEE/ISO LAN architecture, and the FDDI form of LAN.

OSI Model	IEEE/ISO LAN Architecture	FDDI LAN Architecture
Application		
Presentation		
Session		
Transport		
Network		
Data Link	Logical Link Control (LLC)	Logical Link Control (LLC)
	Medium Access Control (MAC)	Medium Access Control (MAC)
Physical	Physical	Physical Layer Protocol (PHY)
		Physical Layer Medium Dependent (PMD)

(FDDI column also includes: Station Management (SMT))

vice definition is documented in IEEE 802.2 and ISO 8808-2. The way in which DNA Phase V implements the LLC service definition is described in detail in Chapter 21.

Differences in transmission technology are addressed in the MAC sublayer and in the Physical layer. Various forms of LAN also break the Physical layer into sublayers. For example, the FDDI form of local area networking defines a *Physical Layer Protocol* (PHY) sublayer and a *Physical Layer Medium Dependent* (PMD) sublayer. The FDDI standard also defines a Station Management (SMT) function that interfaces with the MAC, PHY, and PMD sublayers. The MAC sublayer and the Physical layer for the CSMA/CD and FDDI forms of LAN are described in Chapters 22 and 23.

LAN data links implement a broadcast form of data link, in which each station on the data link receives all frames transmitted by all the other stations. The broadcast data link can be implemented using a multiaccess circuit in which all stations immediately receive any frame transmitted. A broadcast data link can also be implemented by a collection of point-to-point circuits forming a ring configuration. With a ring structure, each frame is repeated from station to station around the ring, thus ensuring that all stations receive each frame. With a broadcast data link, a station can send each frame to multiple stations on the data link. A broadcast form of data link can provide a broad range of services that allow different types of users to employ simultaneously the services of the broadcast data link. Such services include the following:

- **Multiplexing.** This service makes it possible for more than one type of user to simultaneously use the Data Link layer service. Different types of users of the Data Link service might include DNA Phase V Network layer entities, TCP/IP users, and local area transport (LAT) users.

- **Address Filtering.** Each station on a broadcast data link receives the frames transmitted by all other stations on the data link. Each frame contains both a source and a destination station address. The address filtering function allows a station to specify the destination address value or values it will accept as being addressed to it.

- **Protocol Filtering.** This service allows a data link user to specify which types of frames it will accept based on data link addressing. For example, a user of the Data Link layer service might specify that it will accept only frames conforming to the Ethernet format and not those conforming to the IEEE/ISO CSMA/CD frame format.

- **Multicasting.** This service allows a station to send a frame to multiple destination stations on the data link.

The services associated with broadcast forms of data links are discussed further in Chapter 22 on the CSMA/CD form of local area data link and in Chapter 23 on FDDI.

Wide Area Network Data Links

Data link technology for wide area networking typically implements a nonbroadcast type of data link in which only two stations are attached using a point-to-point facility. Multipoint data links are also supported in some situations, although, as discussed in Chapter 5, a multipoint circuit is modeled in the Data Link layer as a collection of point-to-point links. The main data link protocol for the wide area networking environment is *High-level Data Link Control* (HDLC), which has its roots in IBM's *Synchronous Data Link Control* (SDLC), first described in the mid-1970s. HDLC predates the OSI model, and the ISO HDLC standard itself contains no separate service definition of the services the Data Link layer provides to the layer above. The reason for this is that the HDLC standard predates the OSI model and was standardized before there was such a clear distinction between a service definition and a protocol specification. The DNA Phase V documentation for HDLC does, however, contain a precise definition of the service interface between the Data Link layer and the layer above. The documentation of the DDCMP data link protocol also contains a precise definition of the Data Link layer service interface.

ISO 8886 Data Link Service Definition	In an attempt to unify the services and protocols defined for the Data Link layer, ISO has published ISO 8886, *Data Link Service Definition*. This service definition defines an abstract set of service primitives, each with a defined set of parameters, that defines the services a Data Link layer entity provides to a user of the Data Link layer service. The Data Link service definition defines both a connectionless-mode service and a connection-mode service. These services are similar to those defined by the IEEE/ISO LAN architecture service definition, described in Chapter 21.

The ISO Data Link service definition, however, is less useful than the service definitions defined for the other layers in the OSI architecture. |

NETWORK ARCHITECT

The Data Link service is much more of an architectural abstraction than, say, the Network layer service. This is because, in reality, the service the Data Link layer supplies is very dependent on the type of data link used. Frankly, ISO 8886 really exists only because of the feeling that every layer "ought to have" a single service definition.

To give a feeling for the type of service the Data Link layer provides, we next describe the ISO 8886 Data Link layer service definition. However, the DNA Phase V architectural specifications describe separately the service that each type of data link supplies to a user of that data link. The types of data link supported by DNA Phase V are introduced later in this chapter and are described in detail in the chapters in Part V.

Connectionless-Mode Data Link Service	We can think of a connectionless-mode Data Link service as a black box. The user of the Data Link layer service at one end of the data link inserts a DLSDU into the black box. If no error occurs during transmission to corrupt the data, an identical copy of the DLSDU emerges from the black box at the other end of the link, and the user of the Data Link layer service there accepts it. When a transmission error occurs, the Data Link service detects the error, discards the erroneous data, and nothing emerges from the other end of the black box.

The DL_UNITDATA Service

A connectionless-mode Data Link service defines a single data transfer service with the two service primitives listed in Box 6.1. The time-sequence diagram in Figure 6.5 shows the way in which the two service primitives are issued in providing the connectionless-mode Data Link service.

To send a DLSDU from one Data Link layer service user to another across a data link, the Data Link layer service user in the sending device issues a DL_UNITDATA.request primitive to a Data Link entity in the sending device. The Data Link entity transfers the DLSDU specified by the user_data parameter to the device defined by the destination_address parameter. The Data Link entity in the receiving device passes the DLSDU to the user of the Data Link layer service at the destination by issuing the DL_UNITDATA.indication service primitive. If something happens during frame transmission to corrupt the data in the DLSDU, the Data Link layer entity in the destination device detects this fact, discards the erroneous frame, and does not issue the DL_UNITDATA.indication primitive. Thus, when a transmission error occurs, the user of the Data Link layer service in the destination device has no knowledge that the delivery of a DLSDU was even attempted. Neither the source nor the destination station is aware that an error has occurred.

Connection-Mode Data Link Service With a connection-mode Data Link service, a logical connection between the sending and the receiving stations must be established before data transfer can begin. The logical connection must be maintained while

FIGURE 6.5   A time-sequence diagram for the **DL_UNITDATA service.**

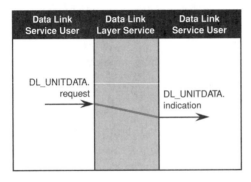

BOX 6.1

Connectionless-
Mode Data Link
Service Primitives

The DL_UNITDATA Service

```
DL_UNITDATA.request  (
                         source_address
                         destination_address
                         quality_of_service
                         user_data
                         )

DL_UNITDATA.indication  (
                         source_address
                         destination_address
                         quality_of_service
                         user_data
                         )
```

data transfer proceeds, and the connection is released after all data transfer operations have been completed. With a connection-mode Data Link service, the user of the Data Link service at one end requests a connection, the Data Link service and the user at the other end agree, and the Data Link service establishes the connection. We can think of the connection-mode Data Link service as a pair of pipes that connect two users of the Data Link layer service, one pipe for data flowing in each direction. A user of the Data Link layer service at one end inserts a DLSDU into the appropriate pipe, and an identical copy of the DLSDU emerges at the other end. The protocol that provides a connection-mode Data Link service attempts to correct any errors detected, most often by automatically retransmitting frames found to be in error. With a connection-mode Data Link service, an identical copy of each DLSDU emerges from the pipe for each DLSDU inserted, whether or not transmission errors occur. If an error occurs from which the Data Link service cannot recover, it releases the connection and informs the two Data Link layer service users of this fact.

For the connection-mode service, the Data Link service definition defines four services, each of which involves a separate set of service primitives. The service primitives for the connection-mode Data Link service are listed in Box 6.2 and are described below:

BOX 6.2

**Connection-Mode
Data Link Service
Primitives**

The DL_CONNECT Service

```
DL_CONNECT.request    (
                      called_address
                      calling_address
                      quality_of_service
                      )

DL_CONNECT.indication (
                      called_address
                      calling_address
                      quality_of_service
                      )

DL_CONNECT.response   (
                      responding_address
                      quality_of_service
                      )

DL_CONNECT.confirm    (
                      responding_address
                      quality_of_service
                      )
```

The DL_DATA Service

```
DL_DATA.request       (
                      user_data
                      )

DL_DATA.indication    (
                      user_data
                      )
```

The DL_DISCONNECT Service

```
DL_DISCONNECT.request    (
                         reason
                         )

DL_DISCONNECT.indication (
                         originator
                         reason
                         )
```

BOX 6.2

continued

The DL_RESET Service

```
          DL_RESET.request    (
                                reason
                              )
          DL_RESET.indication (
                                originator
                                reason
                              )

          DL_RESET.response

          DL_RESET.confirm
```

- **DL_CONNECT.** The DL_CONNECT connection establishment service is used to establish a logical link connection between two users of the Data Link layer service. The DL_CONNECT service is a confirmed service in which the service requester is informed of the success or failure of the attempt to establish a connection with a distant peer Data Link layer service user. The DL_CONNECT service is provided through the four DL_CONNECT service primitives. Figure 6.6 (page 122) includes time-sequence diagrams that show how service primitives are issued to provide the DL_CONNECT service.

- **DL_DATA.** The DL_DATA service is a data transfer service that can be used by two users of the Data Link layer service after a connection has been successfully established with the DL_CONNECT service. The DL_DATA service is provided by the two DL_DATA service primitives. Figure 6.7 (page 123) is a time-sequence diagram that shows the sequence in which the two DL_DATA data transfer service primitives are issued. Notice that the requester of the data transfer operation is not informed of the success or failure of the data transfer operation. However, the connection-mode data transfer service is a guaranteed delivery service because the Data Link layer service requester can assume delivery was accomplished as long as the connection is not released or reset.

- **DL_DISCONNECT.** The DL_DISCONNECT service is used to disconnect a connection previously established by the DL_CONNECT service.

FIGURE 6.6   Time-sequence diagrams for the DL_CONNECT service.

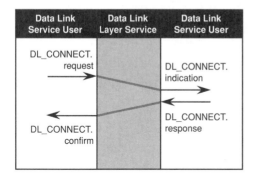

Successful Data Link connection establishment

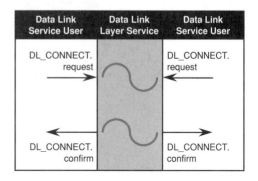

Data Link connection establishment collision

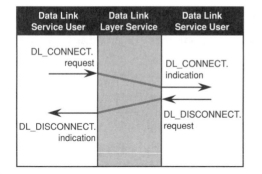

Data Link user rejection of an attempt to establish
a Data Link connection

Data Link service rejection of an attempt to establish
a Data Link connection

The DL_DISCONNECT service is provided through the two DL_DIS-
CONNECT service primitives. Figure 6.8 (page 124) includes time-
sequence diagrams that show ways in which a connection can be released using the DL_DISCONNECT service.

- **DL_RESET.** The DL_RESET service can be used to reset a link connection to its initial state while data is being transferred. The reset operation
  can be issued by either user of the Data Link layer service or by the Data
  Link layer entity on either end of the link. The DL_RESET service is provided through the DL_RESET service primitives. Although the standard

FIGURE 6.7   A time-sequence diagram for the DL_DATA service.

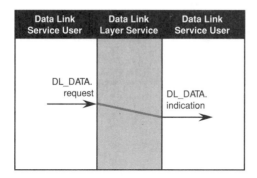

defines a reset service, it is not implemented in any actual data link implementation.

Connectionless-Mode versus Connection-Mode Service

At first glance it may appear that the connection-mode Data Link service is to be preferred because of its ability to handle error correction. However, each type of service has its own advantages and disadvantages, and both types of Data Link services are employed in DECnet Phase V networks. With local area network technology, the transmission medium is highly reliable, and the vast majority of transmitted frames do get through. Also, a local area network is a broadcast type of service in which any device on the network can communicate with any of the others. Any two users typically stay in communication only for a small fraction of a second due to the very high transmission speeds used. For these reasons most local area network implementations provide a connectionless-mode Data Link service. Recovery from the rare transmission errors that occur is left to higher layers.

When dial-up telecommunications facilities are used to connect two devices, however, the circuit is more error prone than a local area network circuit, and a connection-mode Data Link service is most often employed to handle retransmission of erroneous frames in the Data Link layer to provide a reliable Data Link service.

The two types of Data Link services are not incompatible and can co-exist in the same network. In a complex network, a connectionless-mode Data Link service might be used in a part of the network implemented using a LAN, and a connection-mode Data Link service might be used in

FIGURE 6.8   Time-sequence diagrams for the DL_DISCONNECT service.

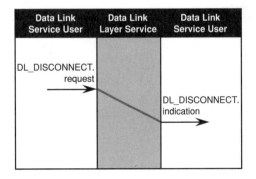

Data Link connection release requested by a Data Link service user

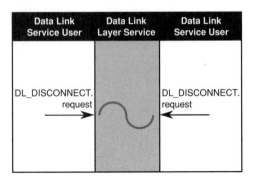

Data Link connection release requested simultaneously by both Data Link service users

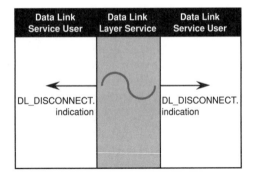

Data Link connection release requested by the Data Link service

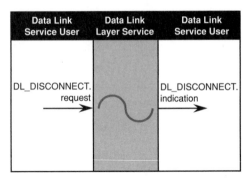

Data Link connection release requested simultaneously by a Data Link service user and the Data Link service

other parts of the network constructed using long-distance telecommunications facilities. Such a situation is illustrated in Figure 6.9.

Data Link Layer Protocol Specifications

The Data Link service definition describes the services a Data Link entity provides to a user of the Data Link layer service above it. A protocol specification for the Data Link layer, on the other hand, precisely defines the formats of the data-link-protocol-data-units (DLPDUs), or frames, peer entities in the Data Link layer exchange with each other. It also specifies the rules that govern the exchanges of frames that take place in

Combination of connectionless-mode Data Link service and connection-mode Data Link service.

supplying the Data Link service. The entity in each communicating device must employ exactly the same frame formats and must follow the same rules; otherwise, communication is not possible. Therefore, conformance to the ISO standards for the Data Link layer is based on exact adherence to a protocol specification. The interface between the Data Link layer and a user of the Data Link layer service defined in the service definition is abstract; it can be implemented in any desired way. But the frames that two peer Data Link layer entities exchange with each other are real; we can actually see the frames flowing over the wire if we use appropriate test equipment.

Many protocol specifications currently exist that define frame formats and procedures for exchanging frames in the Data Link layer. For example, the IEEE/ISO LAN standards documents describe protocol specifications for the local area networking environment; the documentation of HDLC describes the protocol specification for HDLC links; the documentation of X.25 protocols describes the protocol specification for the Data Link layer in the X.25 packet-switched data network environment; and DNA architectural documentation defines the protocol specification for DDCMP links. These various protocol specifications are described in the chapters in Part V.

The next sections describe general protocol mechanisms used in implementing the protocols the Data Link layer uses in controlling data link operation. When a connectionless-mode Data Link service is used, some of these protocol mechanisms may not be implemented in the Data

Link layer; instead, similar protocol mechanisms must be provided in higher layers to provide similar functions.

Error Detection

When a Data Link layer entity receives a DLSDU from a user of the Data Link layer service, it encapsulates the DLSDU in a frame. As part of the encapsulation process, the Data Link layer entity places the frame through an algorithm that calculates a cyclical redundancy check (CRC) value. This CRC value is then placed in the FCS field in the frame's trailer and transmitted over the Data Link as part of the frame. When the Data Link layer in a receiving station accepts a frame, it places the frame through an identical algorithm to calculate its own CRC value. If the calculated FCS field value matches the received FCS field value, the Data Link layer accepts the frame and assumes it has not been corrupted during transmission. It then extracts the DLSDU from the frame and passes the DLSDU up to the user of the Data Link layer service. If the values do not match, the Data Link layer assumes the frame has been corrupted, possibly through a transmission error, and discards it. Since this error detection mechanism is operating in the Data Link layer, the user of the Data Link layer service never receives the DLSDUs contained in corrupted frames.

Error Correction

With a connectionless-mode Data Link service, error correction is left to a higher layer. The connection-mode Data Link service, however, implements a mechanism that causes the missing frames resulting from transmission errors to be retransmitted. A sending station places a sequence number in each frame it sends. A receiving station checks the sequence numbers in the frames it receives to verify there are no missing frames. If the receiving station detects one or more missing frames, it notifies the sending station of that fact and the sending station retransmits the missing frame(s).

Flow Control

Flow control mechanisms control the flow of frames between a sender and a receiver to prevent the sender from transmitting frames faster than the receiver can accept them. One type of flow control mechanism uses a *window* to control the flow of frames. With this type of flow control, there is a limit to the number of frames the sender can transmit before it must wait for an acknowledgement. This value is known as the *window size*. The window size value that sending and receiving Data Link entities maintain prevents a sending station from sending more frames than the receiving station is able to accept at a given time. With some protocols, Data Link entities exchange control frames during link initialization to exchange window size values. When a Data Link layer entity sends the number of frames specified by the window size without receiving an acknowledgement, it stops sending until it receives an acknowledgement.

The window size limits the number of frames the sending Data Link layer entity transmits and thus prevents the receiving Data Link layer entity from being overloaded. If the Data Link layer entity in the receiving station waits for multiple frames to arrive, the number of frames allowed to accumulate before a response must be sent depends on the window size. The receiving Data Link layer entity can also use acknowledgements and control frames to control the rate at which it receives frames. In this way the receiving Data Link layer entity can ensure it does not receive more data than it has the resources to handle.

DNA Phase V Data Links

The Data Link layer in DNA Phase V includes support for several standards for the Data Link layer to handle the different types of data links used to construct a computer network. The Data Link layer protocols defined in the DNA Phase V architecture include protocols suitable for implementing local area network data links and wide area network data links.

Local Area Network Data Links

Local area networking protocols are most often used when two or more network devices are located relatively close together (generally less than a mile or two). As discussed earlier, local area networks implement a broadcast form of data link implemented using either a bus- or a tree-structured multiaccess circuit or a collection of point-to-point circuits forming a ring configuration. The LAN data links supported by DNA Phase V include the following:

- **CSMA/CD LAN.** This is a LAN standard defined by the IEEE and documented in IEEE 802.2 and IEEE 802.3. These standards are also published by ISO as ISO 8802-2 and ISO 8802-3. CSMA/CD stands for *carrier sense multiple access with collision detection* and refers to the way access to the communication medium is controlled. A CSMA/CD LAN typically uses a coaxial cable for transmission at a rate of 10 megabits per second. The CSMA/CD LAN data link is described in detail in Chapter 22. The CSMA/CD LAN data link also provides support for the *Ethernet Specification*, which describes the local area networking scheme jointly developed by Digital, Intel, and Xerox and which has been used in DECnet networks for many years. Ethernet was used as the model for the development of the IEEE/ISO CSMA/CD standard. It is similar to IEEE/ISO CSMA/CD but uses a slightly different frame format. Ethernet is defined in DNA Phase V mainly for compatibility with Phase IV of the architecture. The *Ethernet Specification* is also described in Chapter 22.

- **Fiber Distributed Data Interface (FDDI).** The *fiber distributed data interface* (FDDI) is a form of LAN that uses a series of point-to-point fiber-optic circuits forming a ring configuration. An FDDI LAN supports a data transmission rate of 100 megabits per second. The FDDI standard was developed by a committee of ANSI and has now also been accepted by ISO as an international standard (ISO 9314). It shares the same specifications for the Logical Link Control (LLC) layer as IEEE 802.2/ISO 8802-2 and so is compatible with the IEEE/ISO standards for local area networks. FDDI is described in detail in Chapter 23.

  Because the IEEE/ISO forms of local area network and FDDI can both use a common Logical Link Control sublayer and can present a similar interface to users of the Data Link layer service, the DNA Phase V architecture is capable of accommodating the other forms of local area network in common use, including the token bus form based on IEEE 802.4/ISO 8802-4 and the token ring form based on ISO 802.5/ISO 8802-5.

Wide Area Networking Data Links

Wide area networking protocols are most often used when two or more network devices must be connected using a relatively long-distance telecommunications facility, such as a leased telephone line or a private microwave or satellite circuit. Wide area networking protocols are used over distances ranging from a few miles to many thousands of miles. The wide area networking data links defined by DNA Phase V include the following:

- **High-level Data Link Control (HDLC).** This is a data link protocol described by international standards published by both CCITT and ISO. Many variations and modes of operation of HDLC have been defined.

DNA Phase V specifies the use of both the *normal response mode* (NRM) for data links operating in a half-duplex fashion and the *asynchronous balanced mode* (ABM) for full-duplex links. Normal response mode is essentially equivalent to IBM's *synchronous data link control* (SDLC) protocol used in SNA networks; asynchronous balanced mode is the preferred operating mode in DNA Phase V. HDLC is described in detail in Chapter 19.

- **Link Access Procedure—Balanced (LAPB).** This is a variant of HDLC that describes the operation of the Data Link layer in a packet-switched data network that implements CCITT Recommendation X.25. The DNA Phase V architecture includes support for the LAPB specification for compatibility with X.25. CCITT Recommendation X.25 is described in Chapter 18.

- **Digital Data Communications Message Protocol (DDCMP).** This is a Digital proprietary protocol that has been used in DECnet networks for many years. It is defined in DNA Phase V mainly for compatibility with Phase IV of the architecture. DDCMP is described in detail in Chapter 20.

Conclusion

In the DNA Phase V environment, a major user of the Data Link service is the Network layer. Whereas the Data Link layer is concerned only with transmitting data across a single data link between adjacent network devices, the Network layer is concerned with carrying data between any two devices in the network. Chapter 7 introduces the Network layer and describes the services it provides to the Transport layer above it; Chapter 8 describes the protocols the Network layer uses to supply the Network service; and Chapter 9 describes the protocols that control the way in which packets are routed through the network.

CHAPTER 7

The Network Layer

The purpose of the Network layer is to provide a means by which Transport layer entities operating in any two computing systems in the network can exchange data with one another as if they were directly connected. From the perspective of the Network layer, a DECnet network is made up of a collection of general-purpose computing systems and specialized devices, such as routers and nameservers. We will call all such devices *network nodes*, or *nodes*, as we have been doing in earlier chapters. As we introduced in Chapter 3, there are two types of node: *end nodes* are typically the source and the destination of user data, and *intermediate nodes* relay user data through the network when the two end nodes are not directly connected. Intermediate nodes are often called *routers*; this is the term we will often use in this book because it is more descriptive of their function.

| **Subnetworks** | The nodes making up the network are interconnected by *data links*. Nodes and data links together form *subnetworks*, where a collection of nodes are attached to a single virtual transmission medium so that each node is one hop from any other node. A *hop* is defined as a traversal from one node to an adjacent node across a single data link.* A subnetwork employing a broadcast form of data link technology, such as a |

---

* Traversing from one station to any other in a ring-structured LAN or in an extended LAN is viewed as a single hop, even though a data unit may be relayed many times from one device to another through the LAN. Relaying performed by stations, repeaters, or bridges in a LAN or extended LAN is a Data Link layer function and is hidden from the Network layer.

CSMA/CD LAN, can contain two or more nodes; a subnetwork employing a point-to-point form of data link technology, such as an HDLC
telecommunications link, has exactly two nodes. An X.25 packet-
switched data network (PSDN) is another example of a type of subnetwork that contains two or more nodes. In an X.25 PSDN, the internal
workings of the network are hidden from the individual computers attached to the network, and an X.25 PSDN appears as a single virtual
transmission medium, in which each node is a single hop from any other
node attached to the network.

**Services and
Protocols**

As with other OSI model layers, ISO standards for the OSI architecture
define the Network layer in terms of a service definition and a protocol
specification. The relationship between the services the Network layer
provides and the protocol governing its operation is shown in Figure 7.1.
As shown there, a Network layer protocol uses the services of the Data
Link layer to provide a defined set of services to the Transport layer
above it.

In a typical use of the Network layer service, illustrated in Figure
7.2, a Transport layer entity in one node accesses the Network layer service via a *network-service-access-point* (NSAP) and passes a network-
service-data-unit (NSDU) to the Network layer entity for delivery to the
Transport layer entity at the destination node. The Network layer entity
adds PCI to the NSDU in the form of a header to create a network-

FIGURE 7.1   **The relationship between the Network layer service definition and the Network layer protocol
specification.**

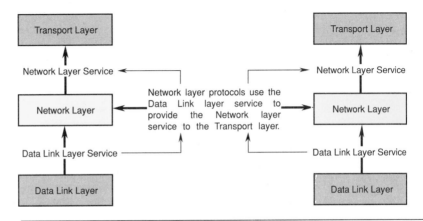

FIGURE 7.2   **The Network layer service.**

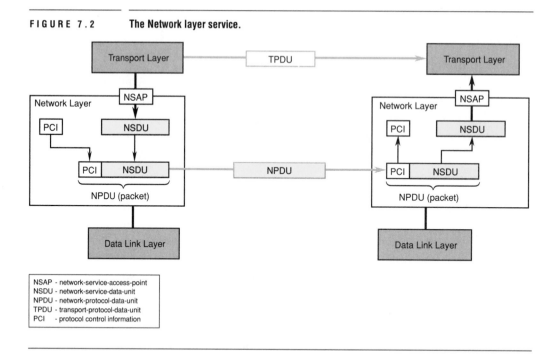

protocol-data-unit (NPDU) and then passes the NPDU to the Data Link layer in the form of a DLSDU.[*] We will typically use the informal term *packet* in the chapters on the Network layer to mean an NPDU. If there are one or more routers between two communicating end nodes, Network layer entities in the routers move the packet to the destination node. The Network layer entity in the destination node removes the PCI from the packet and delivers the enclosed NSDU to the Transport layer entity there.

Routing

A major function of the Network layer is to determine the best path for moving each packet to its destination based on the current topology of the network. This is called the *routing* function.[†] The network might be

---

[*] The Network layer supports a segmentation facility. If it is used, a single NSDU may be split into multiple pieces, each of which is carried in a separate NPDU with its own protocol control information.

[†] ISO standards for the Network layer use the spelling "routeing," but we use the more common spelling, "routing," throughout this book, even in the titles of the standards themselves.

made up of a large number of nodes interconnected in various ways. It is also likely, especially in a large network, that the topology of the network is constantly changing as new nodes and links are added, as existing nodes and links are removed, and as failures occur. To determine the best path for a packet at any given instant, the DNA Phase V Network layer uses a *distributed routing algorithm* to determine the route over which each packet travels in reaching its destination. The operation of the DNA Phase V routing algorithm is described in Chapter 9, and specific details concerning how the routing algorithm operates need not concern us here. Routers also perform a *relaying* function in moving each packet from one node to the next over the route it travels through the network.

Network Layer Service Definition

The Network layer service definition is described in the following international standards:

- ISO 8348, *Network Service Definition*
- Amendment 1, *Connectionless-mode Transmission*
- Amendment 2, *Network Layer Addressing*
- Amendment 3, *Additional Features of the Network Service*

With the Data Link layer, most experts agree there is a place for both a connectionless-mode and a connection-mode Data Link service. However, the world of computer networking has historically been divided into two camps regarding the *one* type of Network service a computer network should provide.

NETWORK ARCHITECT

The CLNS/CONS controversy was once a raging battle. Now it's more like an armed truce, since everyone realizes that nothing dramatic is going to happen very quickly. Everyone now is rather bored with it as well. It's kind of like North and South Korea.

A computer network typically offers users either a connectionless-mode Network service (CLNS) or a connection-mode Network service (CONS). Digital is in the CLNS camp, although it does provide support for the CONS. IBM and the telecommunications industry are mainly in the CONS camp. We shall have more to say about this division after we examine the characteristics of the two forms of Network service.

The Connectionless-Mode Network Service (CLNS)

The connectionless-mode Network service makes routing decisions *independently* for each packet, and each packet may flow over a different path through the network. A connectionless-mode Network service can be thought of as a black box. The Transport entity at one end inserts an NSDU into the black box. Then, if nothing goes wrong, an identical copy of the NSDU emerges from the black box at the other end and is received by the Transport layer entity there. Three things can go wrong during the operation of a connectionless Network service:

- **Lost Packets.** It is possible for the Network layer to lose a packet. For example, a transmission error may occur when the Network layer transmits, over a connectionless data link, a frame containing a packet. In such a case, the connectionless Data Link layer detects the error and discards the frame. When the Network service loses a packet, no NSDU emerges from the black box at the destination. The Transport entity is not explicitly notified of the error; the NSDU in the lost packet simply does not appear at the destination.

- **Out-of-Sequence Packets.** Each packet may take a different amount of time to arrive at its destination. So, if the Transport layer entity at one end inserts a number of NSDUs into the black box, they may appear at the other end in a sequence different from the sequence in which they were sent.

- **Duplicate Packets.** Duplicate packets can also be received. For example, a sending Transport entity uses a timer to help determine if an NSDU it has sent has been received. If the timer expires before the sending Transport entity receives an acknowledgement, the Transport entity sends the NSDU again. In some cases, the timer may expire while an acknowledgement is still in transit, thus causing duplicate NSDUs to arrive at the destination.

Because it is possible for some packets to be lost or to travel over different paths and thus delivered in a sequence different from the sequence sent or delivered more than once, a connectionless-mode Network service cannot be considered reliable. As we pointed out in Chapter 3, the word *reliable* in this context does not have a "good" or "bad" connotation. It simply means that a higher layer—typically the Transport layer—is responsible for detecting lost packets and requesting their retransmission, placing the packets into their proper sequence, and detecting and discarding duplicate packets.

A connectionless-mode Network service is often called a *datagram* service.

Connectionless-Mode Network Service Definition

Box 7.1 lists the service primitives defined in ISO 8348, *Network Service Definition, Amendment 1: Connectionless-Mode Transmission.* Figure 7.3 is a time-sequence diagram that shows the sequence in which the service primitives are issued. A Transport layer entity in the source node issues an N_UNITDATA.request primitive to the Network layer entity below it to hand an NSDU over to the Network layer. The Network layer entity encapsulates the NSDU in a packet for transmission through the network. The Network layer entities in the two end nodes and the Network layer entities in all the routers along the path the packet travels provide the Network layer service. They work together to transfer the

BOX 7.1

Connectionless-Mode Network Service Primitives

```
          N_UNITDATA.request  (
                              source_address
                              destination_address
                              quality_of_service
                              user_data
                              )

      N_UNITDATA.indication  (
                              source_address
                              destination_address
                              quality_of_service
                              user_data
                              )
```

FIGURE 7.3   **A time sequence diagram for the N_UNITDATA service.**

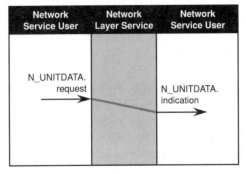

NSDU specified in the user_data parameter to the node whose network address is specified in the destination_address parameter at a quality of service described by the quality_of_service parameters. The Network layer entity in the destination node extracts the NSDU from the packet and passes it up to the Transport layer entity by issuing the N_UNIT-DATA.indication service primitive.

CLNS Interface Procedure Declarations

The DNA Phase V architecture also defines the abstract service interface between a Network layer entity and a Transport layer entity. The procedure declarations that define the services the Network layer provides to its user (most often a Transport layer entity) in supplying the connectionless-mode Network service are listed in Box 7.2.

Connection-Mode Network Service (CONS)

With the connection-mode Network service (CONS), a Network service user requests that a connection be established, the Network service and the user at the other end both agree, and the Network service establishes the connection, sometimes called a *virtual circuit*.

We can think of the connection-mode Network service as two pipes between a pair of Transport layer entities, one pipe for data flowing in one direction and another for data flowing in the opposite direction. The Transport entity at one end inserts an NSDU into the appropriate pipe. When all goes well, an identical copy of the NSDU emerges at the other end. In a network providing the CONS, all the physical resources required to support the pipe are typically assigned when the connection is established, and all packets flowing through the pipe typically flow over the same physical path. Once a connection has been established, full addressing information does not have to be included in each packet flowing over the connection; all that is needed is a reference to the connection a packet is associated with. The NSDUs that the Transport layer sends into the network always arrive in the same sequence in which they were sent, and the CONS attempts to ensure that no packets are lost or duplicated. If an error occurs that prevents a packet from being delivered, the connection is released and the two Transport layer entities are informed that the virtual circuit is no longer available.

The connection-mode Network service is considered to be a reliable service; failures are automatically corrected, if necessary, to ensure that NSDUs inserted into the pipe at one end emerge intact and in the same

BOX 7.2

CLNS Interface
Procedure
Declarations

The following function and procedure declarations define the abstract interface between the Network layer and a user of the Network layer in terms of the services a Network layer entity provides to a user requesting the connectionless-mode Network service (CLNS).

Port Control Functions

- **OpenPort.** Allocates a port for use by a Network service user. A port is a data structure that maintains pointers to its users, identifies the network addresses associated with a port, and identifies the entity using the port.
- **ClosePort.** Deallocates a port opened via the OpenPort function.

Data Transfer Functions

- **Transmit.** Causes an NSDU to be queued for transmission by the Network layer.
- **CheckTransmitBuffer.** Checks the status of a previously enqueued transmit buffer.
- **SupplyReceiveBuffer.** Provides a receive buffer for use by a Network layer entity.
- **CheckReceiveBuffer.** Determines whether any buffer supplied with a SupplyReceiveBuffer function has been filled with received data and returns the contents of the buffer to the Network service user if it contains a packet.

Miscellaneous Functions

- **ReadBlockSize.** Determines the maximum packet size the Network layer entity can transmit without having to segment the packet.
- **GetAddresses.** Determines the set of network addresses associated with a port.

sequence at the other end. As we pointed out in Chapter 3, the term *reliable* in this context does not necessarily have a "good" connotation. It simply means that appropriate error-recovery procedures are implemented in the Network layer. As with the connection-mode Data Link service described in Chapter 6, failures can occur to cause the connection to be released. However, when a failure occurs, the Transport entities both ends are notified that the connection was released. Experts at D tal, however, question whether the CONS, especially in a large and heterogeneous network, really does provide a reliable service.

NETWORK ARCHITECT

When connection-oriented X.25 networks began to be used, we quickly observed that they didn't really work reliably and that you still had to treat an X.25 Network service as an unreliable service. The people who were trying to sell X.25 as a service wanted something they could standardize, in order to create a bigger market for their services. So they put a whole bunch of things into X.25, which then evolved into the CONS. This myth of the CONS being reliable was started at that point because they were attempting to provide what they thought was a reliable service. As it turned out, they can't provide a reliable service because of congestion problems. Just as in the telephone service, a call gets disconnected every once in a while. But when people are talking on the telephone and that happens, they can recover. The X.25 people forgot that people do recover on an end-to-end basis with their conversations. So that's how computers should be programmed to operate. We don't have any problem with the concept of virtual circuits, providing the virtual circuits are provided by the Transport layer on an end-to-end basis between the two computers involved. But where the unreliability comes in is when you start stacking all the virtual circuits on top of each other, through all the intermediate machines, and end up having to trust the integrity of all those intermediate machines.

We will discuss further this issue of reliability later in this chapter when we examine the CLNS versus CONS controversy.

DNA Phase V and the CONS

DNA Phase V incorporates support for both the CLNS and the CONS. However, this should not be taken to mean that when an organization implements a DECnet Phase V network it can choose the style of Network service it prefers. A DECnet Phase V network always operates internally using a connectionless Network service. The Network layer in routers provides only the CLNS, and the DNA Phase V routing functions use only the CLNS in relaying user data through the network. The DNA Phase V routing algorithm is closely tied to the connectionless-mode Network service. It is interesting to note that, at the time of this writing, standards for routing exist only for connectionless-oriented routing. There are currently no standards—even de-facto ones—for connection-oriented routing.

The normal operating mode of the Network layer in an *end node* is also to use the CLNS. For example, a Transport entity in a DECnet Phase V node sends data to a Transport entity in another DECnet Phase V node via DECnet Phase V routers using the CLNS. The DNA Phase V Network layer in end nodes, however, does provide full support for the CONS as an alternative to the CLNS. But direct support for the CONS in the Network layer has a limited scope within the context of the DNA Phase V architecture. The CONS might be requested by a Transport entity in a DNA Phase V end node when it needs to communicate with a Transport entity in a non-DNA end node supporting only the CONS. This facility typically would be used when a DNA end node needs to communicate over an X.25 PSDN with an X.25 node supporting only the CONS.

Connection-Mode Network Service Definition

Box 7.3 lists the service primitives defined in ISO 8348, *Network Service Definition*, for the connection-mode Network service. The service primitives listed in Box 7.3 are issued in a manner similar to that of the connection-mode service primitives defined for the Data Link layer in Chapter 6. We do not describe these further here, since the CONS has limited use in a DECnet Phase V network.

CONS Interface Procedure Declarations

The procedure declarations defining the abstract service interface between the Network layer and a user communicating with another user over a PSDN conforming to CCITT Recommendation X.25 are listed in Box 7.4 (page 142).

The CLNS versus CONS Controversy

The proponents of the connection-mode Network service say the Network layer should provide a reliable service, and users should not have to worry about end-to-end controls above the Network layer; the network should do this work for them. It permits a much simpler Transport layer protocol to be used, since the Transport layer does not have to check for lost, out-of-sequence, or duplicate packets. In the CONS camp fall the common carriers who are used to supplying network services and charging for them.

The proponents of the connectionless-mode Network service, on the other hand, say the job of the Network layer is to move the bits from one end of the network to another and nothing else. This camp is represented

BOX 7.3

**Connection-Mode
Network Service
Primitives**

The N_CONNECT Service

```
N_CONNECT.request    (
                     called_address
                     calling_address
                     receipt_confirmation_selection
                     expedited_data_selection
                     quality_of_service, user_data
                     )

N_CONNECT.indication (
                     called_address
                     calling_address
                     receipt_confirmation_selection
                     expedited_data_selection
                     quality_of_service
                     user_data
                     )

N_CONNECT.response   (
                     responding_address
                     receipt_confirmation_selection
                     expedited_data_selection
                     quality_of_service
                     user_data
                     )

N_CONNECT.confirm    (
                     responding_address
                     receipt_confirmation_selection
                     expedited_data_selection
                     quality_of_service, user_data
                     )
```

The N_DATA Service

```
N_DATA.request       (
                     user_data
                     confirmation_request
                     )

N_DATA.indication    (
                     user_data
                     confirmation_request
                     )
```

BOX 7.3

continued

The N_DATA_ACKNOWLEDGE Service

```
N_DATA_ACKNOWLEDGE.request

N_DATA_ACKNOWLEDGE.indication
```

The N_EXPEDITED_DATA Service

```
N_EXPEDITED_DATA.request    (
                              user_data
                            )

N_EXPEDITED_DATA.indication (
                              user_data
                            )
```

The N_RESET Service

```
N_RESET.request   (
                   reason
                  )

N_RESET.indication (
                     originator
                     reason
                   )

N_RESET.response

N_RESET.confirm
```

The N_DISCONNECT Service

```
N_DISCONNECT.request   (
                         reason
                         user_data
                         responding_address
                       )

N_DISCONNECT.indication (
                          originator
                          reason
                          user_data
                          responding_address
                        )
```

BOX 7.4

CONS Interface
Procedure
Declarations

The following function and procedure declarations define the abstract interface between the Network layer and a user of the Network layer in terms of the services a Network layer entity provides to a user requesting the connection-mode Network service (CONS).

Port Control Functions

- **OpenPort.** Allocates a port for use by a Network service user. A port is a data structure that can be used later to establish a Network connection.
- **ClosePort.** Deallocates a port opened via the OpenPort function.

Connection Control Functions

- **MakeCall.** Establishes a Network connection and associates it with a port opened previously with the OpenPort function.
- **ReadAccept.** Obtains data about a connection established using the MakeCall function.
- **ListenForCall.** Adds a filter to the list of filters the Network service user maintains that determine the criteria for accepting calls.
- **StopListeningFor.** Removes a filter from the list of filters the Network service user maintains that determine the criteria for accepting calls.
- **Listen.** Determines whether an inbound Network connection request has been received.
- **TakeCall.** Indicates the Network service user intends to accept an inbound Network connection request. The connection request is then later accepted and bound to a port using the AcceptCall function.
- **CannotTakeCall.** Refuses an inbound Network connection request.
- **AcceptCall.** Accepts an incoming Network connection request and binds it to a port; issued after a TakeCall function.
- **ClearCall.** Disconnects an established Network connection.

Data Transfer Functions

- **TransmitData.** Causes an NSDU to be queued for transmission over an established Network connection.
- **TransmitPoll.** Checks for the completion of the transmission of a packet initiated by a previous TransmitData function.

BOX 7.4

continued

ReceiveData. Provides the Network layer entity with a buffer to receive the NSDU in an incoming packet. Where a received data unit is longer than the packet size established for the connection, the Network service user issues multiple ReceiveData functions and reassembles the original NSDU.

ReceivePoll. Checks for the completion of the previous ReceiveData function.

ShowPortStatus. Obtains information about a port and its associated Network connection.

Reset. Acknowledges that the Network layer entity has reset a Network connection. The Network service user determines that a Network connection reset has occurred by issuing the ShowPortStatus function.

by the Internet community, which has over 20 years of experience with a large, heterogeneous computer network. Digital falls into this camp as well, having much experience with DECnet networks, which have also always employed connectionless-mode Network service.

NETWORK ARCHITECT

The people who advocated the connection-mode form of Network service would just as soon have had no Transport layer. This controversy is, in a sense, the great religious divide. The champions of the connection-mode network service have always been the people that make their living from selling the network as a service, so they want to provide a complete service within the network itself. The telephone people have this network they say the computer people need, and they want to charge for that. The original champions of the connectionless-mode form of Network service, on the other hand, were those in the ARPANET world. They were people who were interested in using computers; they didn't care too much about how the service is provided. The problem is that the telephone people and the computer people have very different viewpoints.

Those in the connectionless camp say that experience has show that a Network layer service can never be regarded as completely rel able, no matter what types of reliability features are built into it, especially in a large and heterogeneous network. The Transport layer is the lowest layer that is required only in the two machines that are communicating. In a large network, there may be Network layer entities operating in many machines that are not under the control of the two communicating parties.

Imagine that you are using a global network to implement what must be absolutely reliable data transmission. The network uses many forms of data link technology, and each packet must travel through many routers, over many types of communication facilities, in many different countries, to arrive at its destination. In such a situation, the mechanisms operating in the Network layer in all the various routers are not under your control. It would be entirely understandable if you were unwilling to trust the claims of the operators of individual subnetworks that they never lose packets.

NETWORK ARCHITECT

The situation I try to make people understand is that the Network layer is inherently a multiparty situation, where there are not just multiple machines, but multiple organizations involved. If you have a Transport protocol that does not have robust error detection and error correction facilities, what you are saying is that, when you transmit data from your computer in one location to your computer in another location, you have total, absolute, and implicit trust in every organization that may touch those bits between your two computers. If you are a bank, or an insurance company, or anyone who cares anything about your data, you wouldn't make that assumption. You have to implement end-to-end controls in the Transport layer, because it is only there that you can place the mechanisms to recover from the failures of other people's equipment. The fundamental property of the Transport layer is that it's the lowest layer that needs to exists only in the two end systems that are communicating with one another. If you are the end system, then you've clearly got to trust the guy at the other end, because that's the guy whom you're communicating with. But it's the lowest layer in which that's the only person you've got to trust.

The main problem with depending on a reliable Network layer service and not performing error recovery in higher layers is that in a large network there may be too many places where something can go wrong. Suppose we are trying to transfer a long file from one computer to another over a complex network in which each packet must flow through a great many routers in reaching its destination. If the network is implemented using the CONS, a separate connection must be set up on each subnetwork over which the packets must travel. If any one of those connections is broken while the file is being transferred and we are not doing error recovery in any of the layers above the Network layer, then we don't know what has been delivered and what has not, and so we have to start the file transfer over from the beginning. In a large network, in which the chances are relatively high that at least one failure will occur that will cause a connection to be released before the file is completely transferred, it may never be possible to complete the file transfer operation.

In networks that use the CONS, it is useful to perform error recovery in the Transport layer (Class 4 Transport), even though error recovery processing is also being done in the Network layer. If we do this, then the two end systems keep track of what has been successfully transferred as the file transfer operation proceeds. If a particular Network layer connection is broken, Class 4 Transport can ask that a new connection be established, and the file transfer operation can pick up where it left off using the new connection. The file transfer operation will complete even though Network layer connections are being released and new ones are being established as the file transfer operation proceeds.

The main point here is that experience has shown that we must perform error recovery processing in the Transport layer whether or not we are doing it in the Network layer. If you are going to implement in the Transport layer all required end-to-end controls anyway, then a simple, datagram Network service is all that is required. It is difficult to justify the expense of providing a reliable Network service, especially in a large and heterogeneous computer network. Why place the reliability controls in both layers? This is exactly the point of view adopted by many in the connectionless camp, including Digital.

Box 7.5 summarizes some of the advantages and disadvantages of both the CONS and the CLNS. Keep in mind that each disadvantage listed for each form of service can be addressed through the use of additional mechanisms performed in the Network layer, so it remains extremely difficult for individuals in the two camps to convince each other that their way is best.

NETWORK ARCHITECT

Both the CLNS and the CONS have their disadvantages. We think the advantages of the connectionless Network service far outweigh the disadvantages. But there's no doubt they both have their disadvantages. What we really need is

BOX 7.5

**Advantages and
Disadvantages of
CONS and CLNS**

Connection-Mode Network Service

Advantages

- The path through the network that data packets take is ordinarily fixed for the duration of the connection, so less overhead may be associated with forwarding packets. The difficult decisions are all made during the connection-establishment phase.

- Router and data link resources to support a connection are reserved when the connection is established, so end nodes using the connection are less affected by other network traffic loads.

- Because there are definite connection establishment and connection release phases, it is easy to create accounting schemes that charge for connect time.

- Because errors are detected and corrected by Network layer protocols, the protocols in the Transport layer may not need to handle lost, duplicated, or out-of-sequence packets.

Disadvantages

- The connection establishment phase is quite complex, and the requirement for connection establishment may result in excessive overhead for applications that transmit only small bursts of data.

- The path that data packets travel over a connection ordinarily remains fixed for the duration of the connection. If a router or data link associated with the path fails or becomes congested, the connection must be released even though an alternate path through the network may exist.

- After a connection is established, resources associated with that connection remain allocated even when no data packets are being transmitted. It may not be possible to assign those resources to other users of the Network service, thus possibly reducing the efficiency of resource utilization.

- The establishment and maintenance of information concerning the connection and its associated resources, among many network components, is inherently complex and may lead to difficulties due to

BOX 7.5

continued

unforeseen situations or small errors or misjudgments in implementation details.

- The error detection and correction property of the CONS may be only illusory. Therefore, if the higher layers assume that the reliability attribute is real, they may experience failures; if the higher layers assume that the reliability guarantee is not real, they end up duplicating the work.

Connectionless-Mode Network Service

Advantages

- Since there is no connection-establishment phase, initial data transmission may begin more quickly than with the connection-mode Network service.

- There is no fixed path over which data packets must travel. Therefore, the connectionless-mode Network service can be made more robust than the connection-mode Network service and can allow alternative paths to be used when routers or data links fail.

- Because no router or data link resources need be reserved in advance and kept idle when not being used, network resources can be used more efficiently.

Disadvantages

- Because there is no fixed path for data packets, each router must determine the data link to use for the next hop independently for each data packet.

- The Transport layer protocols must support adequate congestion-avoidance procedures to avoid catastrophic failures when router and/or data link resources reach the saturation point.

- Since it is not possible to charge for connect time, it is more difficult to implement accounting schemes for charging for network usage than with a connection-mode Network service.

- Since the Network layer provides only a datagram service, the protocols that operate in the Transport layer are complex and must handle lost, duplicated, and out-of-sequence packets.

something that reduces the disadvantages of the connectionless service. The current buzzwords for it are lightweight connections or flows. This is something where there is a very small amount of state information associated with the communication. It doesn't require end-to-end synchronization, and it shouldn't require the assignment of dedicated processing or memory resources beyond very small amounts. Such a service would avoid the major disadvantage of the CLNS—that of requiring every single packet to be routed completely independently of all other packets. With the connectionless service, every packet has to carry around all the routing baggage, including full network addresses, and it has to carry that across every hop through the network. When you have a burst of several megabytes of these for a file that are following hard on each other's heels, you should be able to take advantage of that fact.

It is our feeling that Digital and those in the connectionless camp are justified in preferring the connectionless-mode Network service. The real controversy involves only where to place the complexity: in the Network layer or in the Transport layer. It makes better sense to us to place the end-to-end controls in the two machines that are communicating, even if this makes the software running in the end nodes a bit more complex. From our point of view, a major advantage of the CLNS is that it can be made more robust than the CONS. Since each packet is routed independently through the network, each can find its own optimal path, depending on network conditions, at the instant it is being transmitted. Since the connection-mode Network service generally establishes a fixed path for all packets flowing over a connection, it is possible that changing network conditions can cause the chosen path to become less than optimal as time passes. Also, if a resource along the path fails, the connection must be broken, even though other paths may exist at that time between the source node and the destination.

What is really unfortunate, however, is that the ISO committees were not able to agree on a single approach for the Network layer. In the Data Link layer it is appropriate to support both a connectionless-mode and a connection-mode style of operation, depending on the data link technology used. But the controversy that has caused support for both a connectionless-mode and a connection-mode service to be included in the Network layer has caused the OSI Network layer to be much too complex. The world of networking—both the connectionless and connection-mode camps—would probably have been better served in the long run had ISO adopted only one of the approaches in the Network layer rather than both. But many at Digital disagree with this view.

NETWORK ARCHITECT

If OSI had continued to define only the CONS, as in the original OSI model, OSI would have become the European networking standard, and the United States would have stayed with TCP/IP. Now what we were hoping to have was a single worldwide standard. We didn't want to have a U.S. standard and a European standard. Having two standards that are geographically different is much worse than having two standards that coexist worldwide. I think the most likely outcome of all of this is that both the CLNS and the CONS will exist to the end of the century. But the CONS will be something that will be pushed increasingly into a niche. It won't die; it will survive. But increasingly, migration to the CLNS will push the CONS more and more into the background. The explosion of TCP/IP usage, even in Europe, lends additional credence to this view.

Network Layer Protocol Specification

In some layers of the OSI model, the intent is to define a single international standard protocol specification that defines how the services of that layer should be provided. This is not possible in the Network layer because the Network layer must be able to provide the Network service using a wide variety of subnetwork technologies and interconnection strategies. So there will remain a family of Network layer protocols that will be used to provide the Network layer service. These protocols are described in a number of ISO documents and in the DNA Phase V architectural specifications.

Network Layer Protocols

There are five important ISO protocols the DNA Phase V architecture supports for the Network layer. Many Digital engineers played a major role in developing these international standards as members of ISO committees.

Protocols for Supplying the CLNS

Three ISO protocols work together to supply the connectionless-mode Network service:

- **ISO 8473, *Protocol for Providing the Connectionless-mode Network Service*.** The ISO 8473 protocol is often called the *ISO Internet Protocol*. End nodes use the ISO Internet protocol for exchanging user data with each other in supplying the CLNS to two peer Transport layer entities. It is designed to handle data transmission between end nodes connected by an arbitrary number of subnetworks of various types.

- ISO 9542, *End System to Intermediate System Routing Exchange Protocol for Providing the Connectionless-mode Network Service.* The *ISO ES-IS Routing Exchange Protocol*, for short, defines the procedures that allow end nodes and routers to communicate with one another for the purposes of exchanging information to control the routing function. This protocol allows an end node to automatically configure itself into the network by exchanging configuration information with a router.

- ISO 10589, *Intermediate System to Intermediate System Intra-Domain Routing Exchange Protocol for Use in Conjunction with the Protocol for Providing the Connectionless-mode Network Service (ISO 8473).* ISO 10589, often called the *IS-IS Routing Protocol*, is based on the distributed routing algorithm originally designed by Digital for DNA Phase V. Digital's routing protocol has been accepted by ISO for standardization and at the time of this writing is a draft international standard. This protocol defines the procedures that control how data packets and packets containing routing information are relayed between routers. The IS-IS routing protocol is examined in detail in Chapter 9.

Protocols for Supplying the CONS

Two protocols are used to supply the connection-mode Network service for communication with another node attached to an X.25 packet-switched data network. However, these two protocols have a different relationship from that of the protocols for supplying the CLNS:

- ISO 8208, *X.25 Packet-level Protocol for Data Terminal Equipment.* This is the ISO version of CCITT Recommendation X.25. Recommendation X.25 and ISO 8208 define the interface between a computer and a packet-switched data network. ISO 8208 is a protocol that predates the CONS and does not itself supply all the services required to provide the CONS.

- ISO 8878, *Use of X.25 to Provide the OSI Connection-mode Network Service.* ISO 8878 is a protocol that enhances the services provided by ISO 8208 to supply all the services required to provide the CONS. ISO 8878 can be viewed as a sublayer running on top of ISO 8208 that defines how the CONS is provided using the underlying X.25 packets and procedures.

The protocols for supplying the CLNS and the CONS are described further in Chapter 8.

We next discuss in detail the characteristics of network nodes to see how the Network layer protocols are implemented in the various types of node that can make up a DECnet Phase V network.

Node Types

The Network layer functions that a node is capable of performing depend on the node's role in the network. As we described at the beginning of this chapter, two major types of nodes are defined by the DNA Phase V architecture: end nodes and routers.

End Nodes

End nodes are computing systems that originate packets for transmission to other end nodes and that receive packets originating in other end nodes. End nodes are not capable of performing the routing function and do not implement the ISO 10589 IS-IS routing protocol. In most cases, an end node is attached to a single data link, such as a single local area network or a single point-to-point data link. End nodes can, however, be attached to more than one data link to provide better protection from failures. Three types of end node can be attached to a DECnet Phase V network:

- **Phase V End Nodes.** These end nodes support both the ISO 8473 Internet protocol and the ISO 9542 ES-IS protocol. This type of node can be attached to the network and will exchange the required information with the router to which it is connected to automatically configure itself into the network. A Phase V node also supports the CONS for communication with another end node supporting only the CONS.

- **Non-DNA End Nodes.** These end nodes support the ISO 8473 Internet protocol but not the ISO 9542 ES-IS protocol. This type of node can exchange data packets with other end nodes but must first be manually configured into the network using network management procedures.

- **Phase IV End Nodes.** These nodes implement the DNA Phase IV architecture and can communicate only with nodes whose network addresses map into the 16-bit network address space defined by the DNA Phase IV architecture. Support for such nodes is provided for backward compatibility with DNA Phase IV and for transition from a Phase IV to a Phase V environment.

Routers

Routers are devices that, in addition to being able to originate and serve as the final destination of packets, are able to perform the routing function and can relay packets from other source nodes to other destination nodes. Routers can be implemented in general-purpose computing systems, but they are more typically implemented as special-purpose devices that perform only the routing function. Two types of routers can function in a DNA Phase V network:

- **Phase V Routers.** These routers implement the ISO 8473 Internet protocol, the ISO 9542 ES-IS routing exchange protocol, and the ISO 10589 IS-IS routing protocol. Phase V routers also implement parts of the Phase IV routing algorithm to allow them to interoperate with Phase IV end nodes and routers.

- **Phase IV Routers.** These routers use 16-bit network addresses and implement the DNA Phase IV routing algorithm. They can participate in a DNA Phase V network, with certain restrictions, since Phase V routers also support the DNA Phase IV routing algorithm.

Phase V and Phase IV routers are classified as either *level 1 routers* or *level 2 routers* and use a hierarchical routing scheme designed to support large networks. The hierarchical routing scheme used by DNA Phase V is described next.

Hierarchical Routing

An individual DECnet Phase V network, consisting of a collection of end nodes, routers, and data links operated by a single organization, is called an *administrative domain*. The boundaries of an administrative domain are determined only by a network management policy, and an administrative domain is not an architecturally defined entity. An administrative domain can be subdivided into a number of routing domains. A *routing domain* is a set of end nodes and routers that share routing information, operate according to the same routing protocol, and are contained within a single administrative domain. Some routing domains in an administrative domain may not be DNA domains and may run a routing algorithm other than the DNA Phase V routing algorithm. On the other hand, an administrative domain can also consist of a single routing domain. Like an administrative domain, the boundaries of a routing domain are also determined by policy and not by architectural specifications.

To support very large routing domains, possibly containing a million or more nodes, DNA Phase V routing domains are themselves hierarchical. A large DNA routing domain can be partitioned into regions called *areas*, which are the largest subdivisions of a network defined by the architecture. Each node (end node or router) resides in exactly one area. The division of a large network into separate areas can improve network performance by reducing the amount of routing overhead compared to using a single area of the same size. It also allows interarea traffic to be confined to a particular set of routers and data links.

Level 1 and Level 2 Routing

Routing in a multiple-area routing domain is classified as either *level 1 routing* or *level 2 routing*:

- **Level 1 Routing.** Routing within an area is called level 1 routing and is handled by level 1 routers. A level 1 router routes network traffic directly toward destination nodes within its own area and toward a level 2 router when it determines a packet's destination node is in a different area.

- **Level 2 Routing.** Routing of network traffic between areas is called level 2 routing and is handled by level 2 routers. A level 2 router performs level 1 routing for traffic destined to nodes within its own area and level 2 routing for traffic destined for other areas. Level 2 routing also includes interdomain routing for traffic destined to other routing domains and to other administrative domains.

A routing domain divided into areas is shown in Figure 7.4. Keep in mind that the space limitations of the printed page make it necessary to

FIGURE 7.4   **A routing domain divided into four areas.**

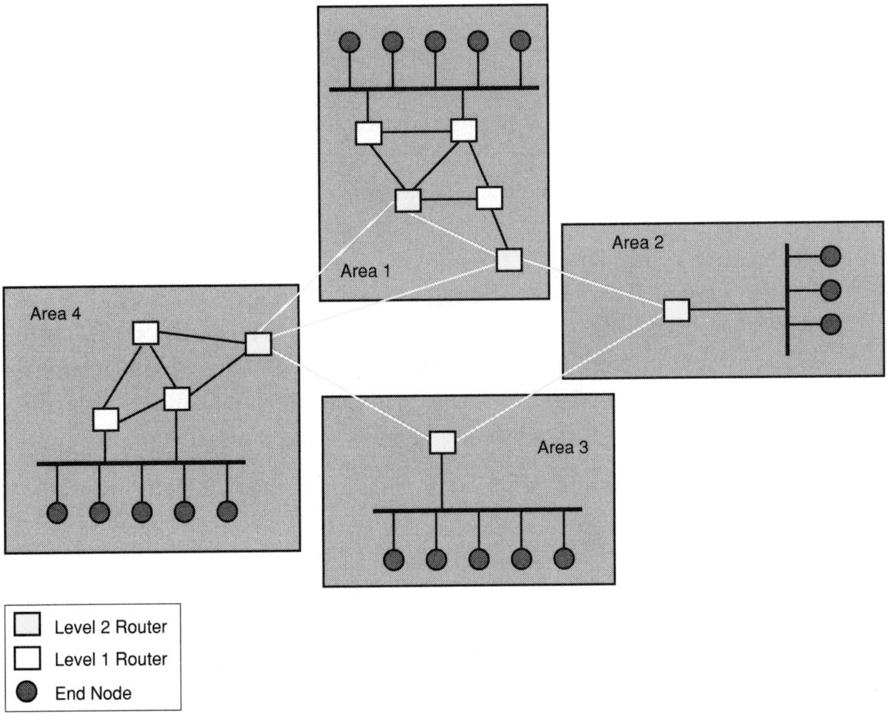

show an unrealistically small network. An actual network would typically be much larger than the network shown in Figure 7.4 before it would be advisable to divide the network into areas. Each end node in a routing domain that is divided into areas must be attached to either a level 1 or a level 2 router. If an end node originates a packet destined for a node in some other area, the end node transmits the packet to its router. If that router is a level 1 router, it sends the packet to the nearest level 2 router in its own area. That router then moves the packet to a level 2 router in the destination area. The level 2 router then transmits the packet via level 1 routing to the destination end node.

Interdomain Routing

Routing can also take place between individual routing domains, thus allowing individual DECnet routing domains and other types of networks to be interconnected to form even larger networks. Such interdomain traffic is handled using a technique called *static routing*, which uses tables of routing information maintained by level 2 routers using network management procedures. The level 2 routers at the boundaries between routing domains decide how traffic goes out to other routing domains and how it comes in from other routing domains. Because a routing domain administered by one organization can be connected to a routing domain administered by some other organization, it is important that the two networks do not merge when they are connected. The static routing technique used at the boundary between routing domains prevents this from happening. We will have more to say about this in Chapter 9 when we examine routing in detail.

An individual organization can also set up multiple routing domains of its own, each of which functions as a separate DECnet network. These can also be connected using interdomain routing facilities. An organization may choose to divide its own network into multiple routing domains for a number of reasons:

- **Reduction of Routing Traffic.** Only data traffic, and not routing traffic, is exchanged between the routing domains, thus reducing the amount of routing control traffic flowing through the network.

- **Very Large Networks.** Theoretically, the number of areas a routing domain can contain is unlimited. In practice, however, there will be limits to the size of a routing domain due to router implementation considerations. Networks of unlimited size can still be built by dividing the network into multiple routing domains.

- **Robustness.** Routing domains are isolated from each other, and each routing domain is protected from failures that might occur in the other routing domains. This allows failures to have an impact only on the routing domains in which they occur.
- **Interoperability with Other Routing Algorithms.** All the nodes in a routing domain must run the same routing algorithm. Constructing a network having multiple routing domains allows collections of nodes running entirely different routing algorithms to coexist in the same network.

The static routing information used to control interdomain routing consists of *reachable addresses* identified by lists of *address prefixes*. Lists of address prefixes are maintained, using network management procedures, by each level 2 router that communicates with another routing domain. Each reachable address in a level 2 router's address prefix list is associated with a circuit connecting that router to some other routing domain. If a level 2 router receives a packet having a destination address that matches one of its address prefixes, the level 2 router relays the packet out of its domain over the circuit associated with that address prefix. The level 2 router in the destination routing domain is then responsible for determining an optimal route and for relaying the packet to the next node along the path to its final destination. The static routing information required to reach end nodes in other routing domains is automatically distributed around the level 2 domain by the routing algorithm, just as all other routing information is distributed.

We can make an analogy between the notion of address prefixes and the system of telephone number area codes used in the United States. All the telephone numbers in northern Wisconsin have an area code of 715. In a similar manner, if all the computers in northern Wisconsin were in the same routing domain, which might consist of one or more areas, their network addresses would all begin with the same address prefix, say 1234. All level 2 routers in other routing domains that are capable of reaching the computers in the northern Wisconsin routing domain would then have a reachable address of 1234 in their address prefix lists and would be capable of routing traffic via static routing to the northern Wisconsin routing domain. In actual practice, the telephone area code analogy is not exact because the boundaries of a routing domain are not necessarily determined by geographic location, as telephone area codes are, but are determined by the organization administering the routing domain.

We next examine the format of the network addresses used to uniquely identify nodes in a network.

Network Addressing

Access to Network layer services, as in other layers, is through a service-access-point. *Network-service-access-point* (NSAP) addresses are the network addresses of end nodes and routers in a DECnet Phase V network. Unlike the small 16-bit addresses used in DNA Phase IV, which the Digital network architects freely admit was a mistake because it placed severe limitations on the sizes of networks that could be built, the ISO standard NSAP addresses used in DNA Phase V are very large—up to 160 bits in length. There are two ways in which we can view the network addresses that DNA Phase V uses. First, we can look at them from the viewpoint of a router that must interpret the NSAP address in making routing decisions. Second, we can look at them from the viewpoint of the ISO Network layer addressing standards that concern addressing authorities and network managers who must ensure that network addresses are assigned so each address is globally unique.

Router Address Interpretation

A router interprets an NSAP address as shown in Figure 7.5. The entire NSAP address must be at least 10 octets in length and can be no longer than 20 octets. The format of the last 9 octets is defined by the DNA Phase V architecture, which conforms to the format specified in the ISO 10589 routing protocol.

Addressing Authority Dependent Octets

The format of the initial octets of the NSAP address is defined by an addressing authority responsible for the assignment of the values for the initial octets of NSAP addresses for individual organizations. The assignment of values to the initial octets of the address is the mechanism by which NSAP addresses are guaranteed to be globally unique. But the way in which this value is assigned is beyond the scope of the DNA Phase V architecture. The addressing authorities that assign address values are discussed later in this chapter.

FIGURE 7.5   **A router view of a DNA Phase V network address.**

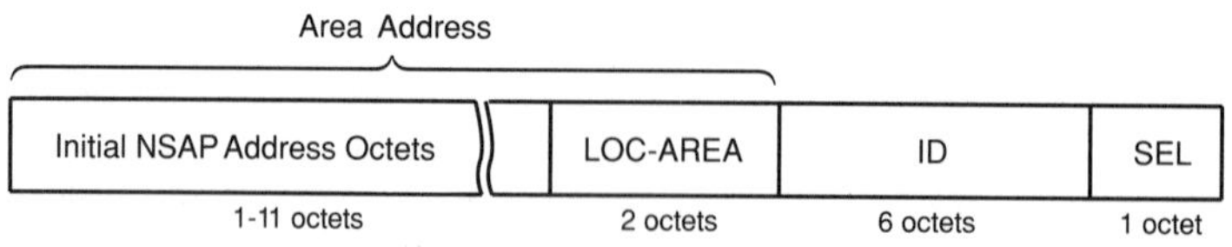

The LOC-AREA Field

The LOC-AREA field in the address is the first part of the NSAP address defined by the DNA Phase V architecture. It contains a 2-octet value set by the organization implementing the network. The value assigned to the initial octets of the address plus the LOC-AREA value (the entire address minus the last 7 octets) define the bounds of an area and together are called the *area address*. Some subset of the initial octets of the address plus the LOC-AREA field can be used to define address prefixes to group areas into routing domains. The actual lengths of address prefixes and the way in which areas are grouped into routing domains are strictly a matter of policy determined by network managers. The DNA Phase V architecture places no restrictions on how address prefixes are administered.

The large number of octets that can be used to uniquely define an area theoretically permits building an individual routing domain with an almost unlimited number of areas. But, as we have already stated, implementation considerations will typically limit the number of areas a routing domain can contain. However, a large network can still have an almost unlimited number of areas by dividing the network into multiple routing domains.

The ID Field

The ID field contains a 6-octet value that uniquely identifies a node within its area. The entire address, including a 1-byte SEL field value of binary 0, is called the *network entity title* (NET) of the node. The node's NET uniquely identifies the node in the OSI environment. The ISO 10589 routing protocol requires only that ID field values be unique within an individual area. However, the DNA Phase V architectural specifications for the Network layer recommend that the ID field value for each node be chosen using the IEEE local area network addressing plan, in which case the ID field values themselves are guaranteed to be globally unique. Each DECnet node is assigned a *nodeID* value during manufacture chosen according to the IEEE addressing plan. A node's DECnet nodeID value is ordinarily used as the ID value in the node's network address. The routing algorithm does not depend on a correspondence between ID field values and nodeID values. However, if the IEEE local area network addressing plan is used to generate the ID field value of a nodes's address, the node can be plugged into an OSI network anywhere in the world and be guaranteed of having a unique NSAP address.

The SEL Field

The SEL field is the last octet of the address. It contains a 1-octet value that acts as a selector to define the particular type of Transport layer entity that is to receive the packet. The SEL field values are not architecturally defined and are set by the sending Transport layer entity. The following values are two possible SEL field values used by Transport layer entities to identify the Transport entity within the node to which a packet is destined:

- **32.** A packet whose PCI contains this SEL field value is a data or control packet sent to an ISO Transport layer entity in a DNA Phase V node.
- **33.** A packet whose PCI contains this SEL field value is a data or control packet sent to an NSP Transport layer entity.

Other SEL field values are permitted to allow interoperation with nodes that do not follow the DNA Phase V addressing plan. The SEL field value is not required to uniquely identify a node. Thus, a node's NET is considered to contain a SEL field value of binary 0.

Automatic Configuration of End Nodes

The area addresses of a router must be set using an explicit network management function before the router is attached to the network. A network management action is required to set a value for a router's area address (the initial octets of the address plus the LOC-AREA field) because assignment of routers to routing domains and areas is inherently a policy matter that must be controlled by network managers. When an end node is attached to a DECnet Phase V router, the end node gets the value of its area address from the router to which it is attached, and it typically gets its ID field value from its own internal nodeID value. The SEL field value used in the address fields in a packet's PCI is assigned by the entity creating the packet. Thus, an end node is capable of generating its own complete NSAP address when it is attached to the network without requiring human intervention.

Multiple Area Addresses

In some circumstances it may be desirable for an area (and hence any of the nodes within it) to have more than one area address. For example, if the area is attached to public data networks via multiple connections, it may be useful to have network addresses that correspond to each point of attachment. However, all the routers in an area must have at least one area address common to each node adjacent to it. During normal operation, all the routers in an area must have the same area address or the same set of area addresses.

ISO Network Layer Addressing Standards

The structure of the NSAP addresses used in the DNA Phase V architecture conforms to the international standard addressing scheme defined by ISO 8348, *Network Service Definition, Amendment 2: Network Layer Addressing.* This addressing scheme defines methods by which the initial octets of the network addresses can be assigned so all the network addresses an organization generates are globally unique. Although network managers must be aware of the hierarchical structure of NSAP addresses as defined in ISO 8348, Amendment 2, this hierarchical structure is not known to routers. As discussed in the previous section, routers work only with area addresses, which are defined as the initial octets of the address plus the LOC-AREA field (the complete address minus the last seven octets.)

Amendment 2 to ISO 8348 makes clear distinctions among three concepts, illustrated in Figure 7.6, associated with describing the semantics of a network address:

- **Abstract Syntax.** The abstract syntax of network addresses is the means employed in ISO 8348, Amendment 2, to define the hierarchical structure of a network address and is used by addressing authorities to allocate and assign network address values. An abstract syntax defines information content without specifying how that information content is represented in a computer or encoded for transmission. The standard allows the abstract syntax of a network address value to be expressed in either decimal or binary form.

- **Encoding.** Encoding refers to the way in which a network address value is represented in the protocol-control-information attached to a packet and conveyed between nodes during Network layer protocol operation. The way in which address values are encoded has no relation to the ab-

FIGURE 7.6   **Network addressing concepts associated with address semantics and syntax.**

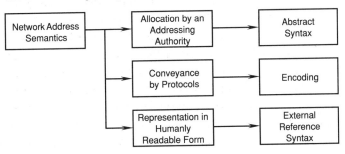

stract syntax that defines how address values are allocated and assigned. For example, the abstract syntax might define an address value as consisting of decimal digits. That address value might be encoded using a binary number to represent the decimal address value. Alternatively, some scheme might be used to individually encode each decimal digital of the address value. According to ISO 8348, Amendment 2, addresses can be encoded in any desired way, but the standard recommends certain preferred encoding methods. Other ISO standards for the OSI model and the DNA Phase V architecture specify that NSAP addresses be encoded using the ISO preferred binary encoding scheme, in which each digit of a decimal address is represented in a 4-bit semi-octet.

- **External Reference Syntax.** This is the syntax of a network address as it might be displayed in human-readable form in a printed report or on a display screen. The way a network address is externally represented can be different from both the abstract syntax and the encoding method. For example, the abstract syntax might define address values as being decimal, the encoding method might be the preferred binary encoding scheme, and the external reference syntax might use decimal numbers with punctuation added to separate the various fields of the address for ease of reading.

ISO 8348, Amendment 2, is concerned only with the abstract syntax of network addresses and for allocating and assigning address values. The ISO standard addressing scheme defines a hierarchical address, with the top level of the hierarchy being a number of *addressing domains*, each of which is associated with an *addressing authority*. An addressing authority can then allocate addresses within its own domain, or it can further subdivide its domain and assign an authority to each subdomain it creates. This process can be continued to an arbitrary extent, limited only by the maximum network address length. The uniqueness of addresses within a particular addressing domain must be ensured by the authority responsible for allocating addresses in that domain.

The addressing authority and network management view of a DNA Phase V NSAP address, which conforms to the ISO network addressing standard, is illustrated in Figure 7.7. According to the ISO addressing standard, the NSAP address is divided into two major parts, the *initial domain part* (IDP) and the *domain specific part* (DSP). We have already described the low-order nine octets of the DSP for DNA Phase V addresses.

The IDP makes up the beginning of an ISO network address and is further divided into an *authority and format identifier* (AFI) and an *initial domain identifier* (IDI). DNA Phase V supports any valid AFI and IDI. The abstract syntax of the IDP specifies that IDP values are allo-

Initial Domain Part (IDP)		Domain Specific Part (DSP)			
Authority and Format Identifier (AFI)	Initial Domain Identifier (IDI)	HO-DSP	LOC-AREA	ID	SEL
1 octet	variable	variable	2 octets	6 octets	1 octet

cated in the form of decimal digits. This does not indicate, however, that the IDP must be encoded as decimal digits. It only indicates that addressing authorities must allocate and assign IDP values in the form of decimal digits. As indicated earlier, the DNA Phase V architecture specifies that AFI and IDI values are *encoded* using a 4-bit semi-octet to encode each decimal digit.

Authority and Format Identifier (AFI)

The AFI contains a two-digit decimal number that defines the addressing authority responsible for allocating IDI values, defines the format of the IDI, and specifies whether the abstract syntax of the domain specific part (DSP) of the address is binary or decimal. DSP address values can be allocated and assigned using either values expressed as decimal numbers or values expressed as binary numbers. DSP values in DNA Phase V NSAP addresses use a binary abstract syntax, and DSP values are allocated and assigned in the form of strings of hexadecimal digits.

The Initial Domain Identifier (IDI)

Specific AFI values determine the format of the IDI. For example, AFI value 48 for a decimal DSP and AFI value 49 for a binary DSP specify that the IDI is a null value and 0 decimal digits in length. With this IDP value, the entire address is contained in the DSP. These are called *local* AFI values, and NSAP address values that are allocated using them cannot be guaranteed to be globally unique.

The other AFI values thus far defined can be divided into two categories: those associated with ISO-administered addressing plans and those associated with CCITT-administered addressing plans.

ISO Address Administration

With ISO address administration, each IDP value identifies a particular country or an international organization. An addressing authority in each country assigns one or more unique values for the high-order DSP (HO-DSP) field of the DSP to each organization applying for them. That organization then ensures that the HO-DSP field of the DSP for each network address it creates contains one of the values the addressing authority assigned it. The organization must then guarantee the value of the remaining bits in the DSP is different within that HO-DSP value. In this way an individual organization is guaranteed that each of its network addresses is globally unique.

For a DNA Phase V NSAP address using the ISO addressing scheme, an organization in the United States begins each of its NSAP addresses with the IDP value assigned to the United States and applies to an addressing authority in the United States for a value it can use for the HO-DSP field in the DSP. The organization then assigns a unique value to the LOC-AREA field of the address for each area it defines within that HO-DSP field value.

Unique AFI values are assigned to each of the following ISO-administered addressing plans:

- **ISO 3166 DCC.** With this scheme, the IDI consists of a three-digit code allocated according to ISO 3166. This is an ISO-defined geographically oriented addressing plan that assigns IDI values to countries and national areas independent of public data networks. This is the addressing scheme typically used to assign network addresses in DECnet Phase V networks.

- **ISO 6523 ICD.** The IDI consists of a four-digit international code designator (ICD) allocated according to ISO 6523. This is an ISO-defined nongeographic addressing plan that assigns addresses to certain types of international organizations, such as the United Nations, the Red Cross, and certain maritime and avionics networks that are nongeographical or multinational in scope.

CCITT Address Administration

With CCITT address administration, the values contained in the IDP identify not an entire country but an individual subscriber, in a similar manner to a telephone number.

Unique AFI values are assigned to each of the following CCITT-administered addressing plans:

- **CCITT X.121.** With this scheme, the IDI consists of a sequence of up to 14 decimal digits defined by CCITT Recommendation X.121. This is a

CCITT-defined addressing plan that assigns addresses to individual DTEs in X.21 and X.25 networks.

- **CCITT F.69.** The IDI consists of a sequence of up to 8 decimal digits defined by CCITT Recommendation F.69. This is the CCITT-defined addressing plan for the international telex network.

- **CCITT E.163.** The IDI consists of a sequence of up to 12 decimal digits defined by CCITT Recommendation E.163. This is the CCITT-defined addressing plan for the global telephone network.

- **CCITT E.164.** The IDI consists of a sequence of up to 15 decimal digits defined by CCITT Recommendation E.164. This is the CCITT-defined addressing plan for the global integrated services digital network (ISDN).

Conclusion

This chapter has introduced the function of the Network layer in the DNA Phase V architecture. Chapter 8 further describes the operation of the Network layer protocols used to supply the connectionless-mode Network service and introduces the protocols used to supply the connection-mode Network service.

CHAPTER 8

Network Layer Protocols

In Chapter 7, we introduced the five important ISO protocols the DNA Phase V architecture supports for the Network layer. In this chapter, we examine in detail the two protocols used in both end systems and routers to provide the connectionless-mode Network service (CLNS), and we introduce the two protocols end systems and routers used to provide the connection-mode Network service (CONS). Chapter 9 describes the ISO 10589 routing protocol implemented only in routers. Before we describe the specific protocols used in end systems and routers to provide the Network service, we must examine the characteristics of the underlying data links and subnetworks used to provide the Network service.

Data Links and Subnetworks

In Chapter 6, we saw that DNA Phase V permits the use of a wide variety of different types of data links to interconnect computing systems. Network layer entities must be able to use the services of all these different types of links in providing the Network layer service of moving a packet from a source node to a destination node. As we introduced in Chapter 7, a network is generally made up of a number of subnetworks, each of which consists of a collection of nodes connected to one another by a particular form of data link technology. The various types of data links used to construct subnetworks can be divided into two categories: broadcast data links and nonbroadcast data links. We describe each of these next.

Broadcast Data Links

A *broadcast data link* is one in which a given node's transmissions are received by all the other nodes attached to the link. Subnetworks implemented by local area network equipment typically use a broadcast form of data link technology. A broadcast data link can implement a subnetwork that contains two or more nodes. An important feature of a broadcast data link is that it allows a *multicast* facility to be implemented, in which a node can send a data unit to a group of other nodes on the data link. For example, an end node or a router might want to send a data unit to all the other routers on the data link. With a broadcast data link, it can do so in a single operation.

A broadcast data link supplies the IEEE 802.2/ISO 8802-2 Logical Link Control (LLC) sublayer service introduced in Chapter 6 and described further in Chapter 21. An IEEE/ISO form of LAN can supply either a connectionless-mode or a connection-mode Data Link service. With DNA Phase V, the Network layer makes use of only the IEEE/ISO connectionless-mode LLC sublayer service.

Nonbroadcast Data Links

The Network layer views *nonbroadcast data links* as networks that contain exactly two nodes. Examples of nonbroadcast links are HDLC and DDCMP telecommunication links and the virtual circuits provided by an X.25 packet-switched data network. A reliable, connection-mode Data Link service is generally provided over nonbroadcast links, although the service requester may not perceive the connection establishment or connection release phases of the service. There are three main types of nonbroadcast data link: permanent point-to-point links, dynamically established point-to-point links, and multipoint links.

Permanent Point-to-Point Links

Examples of *permanent point-to-point links* are private communication facilities, leased telecommunication links, and permanent virtual circuits provided by X.25 PSDNs. These are links that stay connected at all times unless a failure occurs. For a permanent link, the connection establishment and connection release phases of the connection-mode Data Link service are performed by network management; Network layer entities perceive only the data transfer phase of the service.

Dynamically Established Point-to-Point Links

With *dynamically established point-to-point links*, the data link is established when it is needed and released when it is no longer required. Examples of dynamically established point-to-point data links are dial-up telecommunications links and point-to-point links implemented by switched virtual circuits (SVCs) in X.25 PSDNs. The DNA Phase V Network layer supports two types of dynamically established point-to-point data links; they differ in how the connection establishment and connection release phases of the connection-mode Data Link service are performed.

- **Static Point-to-Point Links.** With a static point-to-point link, the Network layer entities work with the link as if it were a permanent point-to-point link. The connection is established by a network management action, and the connection typically remains established during network operation unless a failure occurs.

- **Dynamically Assigned Point-to-Point Links.** With a dynamically assigned point-to-point data link, the Network layer entities using it are involved in the connection establishment and connection release phases of the Data Link service. If a node receives a packet and then determines the packet must be sent over a dynamically assigned data link over which no connection currently exists, the Network layer entity establishes the connection. This may require that a telephone number be dialed or that an X.25 switched virtual circuit be established. The protocol attempts to use an already existing connection for transmission whenever possible to minimize the connection establishment overhead. Once a connection has been established, it is retained until a certain period of time has elapsed during which no traffic has flowed over the connection. After the time interval has elapsed, the connection is released.

Multipoint Data Links

With a *multipoint data link*, one of the nodes is designated as the *primary node*; all the other nodes are designated as *secondary nodes*. The primary node is in control of the link; a secondary node originates traffic only when the primary node grants it permission. The primary node can communicate with any of the secondary nodes, but a secondary node can communicate only with the primary node. Secondary nodes cannot exchange data directly with one another over the data link. DNA models a multipoint data link as a collection of point-to-point links, and so the multipoint characteristics of the link are hidden from Network layer entities. Network layer entities view a multipoint data link as if it were a set of point-to-point subnetworks, each of which connects the primary node with one of the secondary nodes.

Although the DNA Phase V architecture defines support for multipoint data links, they are rarely used today in computer networks having the primary goal of peer-to-peer communication among all nodes. They are often used, however, in other forms of network in which computers are connected to large numbers of simple terminals.

Network Example An example of a network that implements a number of subnetworks employing both broadcast and nonbroadcast data links is shown in Figure 8.1. To move a packet from node A, on the left, to node H, on the right, the packet must travel in the following manner:

1. The packet travels from node A to node B over the subnetwork implemented by a local area network (a broadcast data link).

FIGURE 8.1 A network employing broadcast and nonbroadcast data links.

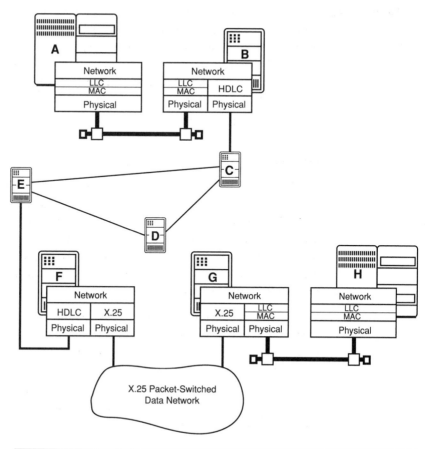

2. The packet travels from node B to node F over the subnetworks implemented by point-to-point data links.

3. The packet travels from node F to node G over an X.25 PSDN (another point-to-point data link).

4. The packet travels from node G to node H over the subnetwork implemented by a LAN (another broadcast data link).

To understand how various types of data link technologies are used to provide a unified Network service, it is necessary to understand how the Network layer is organized and how it accesses the services of the underlying Data Link layer.

Internal Organization of the Network Layer

The Network layer has a somewhat more complex organization than many of the other layers. One reason for its complexity is that it is possible for a network to be constructed with different types of subnetworks. As we have seen, some subnetworks may provide only a connectionless-mode Data Link service, others may provide only a connection-mode Data Link service, and some may provide both. In addition, many alternative forms of data link technology can be used to supply the Data Link service. All of these must together be used to provide a unified service to users of the Network layer.

Network Sublayers

The DNA Phase V architecture divides the Network layer into two sublayers: a *subnetwork independent layer* and a *subnetwork dependent layer*. An important reason for dividing the network layer into two sublayers is to make it possible to provide a consistent Network layer service using the facilities of a wide variety of different types of subnetworks using various types of data link. The following are the major functions of the two Network layer sublayers:

- **Subnetwork Independent Sublayer.** The major function of the subnetwork independent sublayer is to provide either the CLNS or the CONS on the request of a user of the Network layer service (typically a Transport layer entity).

- **Subnetwork Dependent Sublayer.** The major function of the subnetwork dependent layer is to access the underlying services of the Data Link layer on the request of the subnetwork independent sublayer.

Network Layer Protocol Roles

ISO has described the way in which the Network layer is organized in ISO 8648, *Internal Organization of the Network Layer*. This international standard describes three roles that a Network layer protocol can play in helping to provide the Network layer service. It is helpful to view the three protocol roles as operating within the two Network layer sublayers, as shown in Figure 8.2. Following are descriptions of the three Network layer protocol roles:

- **Subnetwork Independent Convergence Protocol Role (SNICP).** A protocol operating in the SNICP role operates to provide the requested Network service to a user of the Network layer service using a well-defined set of underlying capabilities. It interfaces directly with the Network layer service requester (typically the Transport layer) and is independent of the actual Data Link services used to provide the Network service.

- **Subnetwork Access Protocol Role (SNAcP).** A protocol operating in the SNAcP role directly accesses the services of the Data Link layer in helping to provide the requested Network service.

- **Subnetwork Dependent Convergence Protocol Role (SNDCP).** A protocol operating in the SNDCP role augments the functions provided by a protocol operating in the SNAcP role to provide the services the subnetwork independent sublayer requires to provide the requested Network service.

FIGURE 8.2   **Network layer sublayers and protocol roles.**

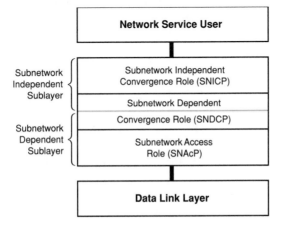

The SNICP role operates in the subnetwork independent sublayer, the SNAcP role operates in the subnetwork dependent sublayer, and the SNDCP role, when it is required, helps to interface between the two sublayers. A single protocol can provide one, two, or all three of the protocol roles. Generally the SNICP and SNAcP roles are always required, but the SNDCP role may be null in some cases. Let us look at some examples of how the three protocol roles work together to provide the Network layer service.

Suppose the Transport layer requests the CLNS and the underlying subnetwork uses a broadcast form of data link that provides a connectionless-mode Data Link service. In this case, a single protocol may play both the SNAcP role of accessing the underlying Data Link service and the SNICP role of providing the Network service to the Transport layer entity. Here, the Data Link service provides exactly the functions required to provide the CLNS, and the SNDCP role is null.

In a more complex case, the Transport layer may request the CLNS, and the underlying Data Link service may provide only a connection-mode service, possibly using an X.25 virtual circuit. In such a case, one protocol may play the SNAcP role of accessing the connection-mode Data Link service, and an entirely different protocol may play the SNICP role of providing the network service to the Transport layer. In that case, the characteristics of the underlying Data Link service are quite different from the Network service being requested. For example, the CLNS has no connection establishment and release phases. A third protocol (it may or may not be the same protocol operating in the SNICP role) is required operating in the SNDCP role. It defines the procedures for selecting an existing Data Link connection, establishing a new Data Link connection when required, transferring data over the connection, and determining when to release the Data Link connection when it is no longer required.

As a packet moves through the network, different protocols, operating in the various roles, may be used for each hop the packet takes over a data link. The protocols used for each hop are those appropriate for the Network service requested and the data link technology used on that link.

The remainder of this chapter describes the ISO protocols that operate in end systems and routers for providing both the CLNS and the CONS, beginning with protocols for providing the CLNS.

Protocols for Supplying the CLNS

The preferred operating mode of the DNA Phase V Network layer is to use the protocols that supply the CLNS. This is the Network layer service requested by the Transport layer most often in a DECnet Phase V network. The ISO 8473 Internet protocol supplies the CLNS and works in conjunction with the ISO 9542 ES-IS routing protocol and the ISO 10589 IS-IS routing protocol. (These three protocols were introduced in Chapter 7.) The next sections describe the ISO 8473 Internet protocol and the ISO 9542 ES-IS routing protocol; the ISO 10589 IS-IS routing protocol is described in Chapter 9.

ISO 8473 Internet Protocol

The ISO Internet protocol is described in ISO 8473, *Protocol for Providing the Connectionless-mode Network Service*. A major portion of ISO 8473 concerns the SNICP role in the subnetwork independent sublayer and specifies the procedures that end nodes use for exchanging user data with each other in supplying the CLNS to users of the Network service. A part of the Internet protocol also operates in the subnetwork dependent layer and is concerned with accessing the underlying Data Link services.

We will first discuss the functions of the ISO 8473 Internet protocol that operate in the subnetwork dependent sublayer; then we will look at the ISO 8473 functions performed in the subnetwork independent sublayer.

ISO 8473 Subnetwork Dependent Layer Functions

The functions of the ISO 8473 protocol that operate in the subnetwork dependent layer are concerned mainly with the SNDCP role of augmenting the underlying Data Link service to provide the service expected by the subnetwork independent sublayer. The SNDCP role of the ISO 8473 protocol is concerned with how the subnetwork dependent sublayer performs data link initialization, hop-by-hop segmentation over subnetworks with small maximum frame sizes, and connection establishment and release for dynamically established data links.

We will see that ISO 8473 defines specific SNDCP functions for accessing subnetworks implemented by local area networks, X.25 virtual circuits, and point-to-point data links.

ISO 8473 Subnetwork Dependent Sublayer Service Definition

The specification of the ISO 8473 Internet protocol includes a service definition of the interface between the subnetwork dependent sublayer and the subnetwork independent layer. Unlike the interfaces between layers, this service interface is not standardized and appears in the ISO standard only for descriptive purposes. As with other service definitions, this interface is defined in terms of a set of service primitives and service primitive parameters. These are listed in Box 8.1. Figure 8.3 is a time-se-

BOX 8.1

**Subnetwork
Dependent
Sublayer Service
Primitives**

```
SN_UNITDATA.request   (
                          source_address
                          destination_address
                          quality_of_service
                          user_data
                      )

SN_UNITDATA.indication  (
                          source_address
                          destination_address
                          quality_of_service
                          user-data
                      )
```

quence diagram that shows the sequence in which the service primitives are issued to transmit a packet across a single data link.

There is a difference between the service definition described here and the one presented in Chapter 7 that defines the services the Network layer provides to a user of the Network layer service. The service definition described in Chapter 7 defines the service the Network layer provides as a whole; the service definition described in Box 8.1 defines the service the subnetwork dependent sublayer provides to the subnetwork dependent sublayer.

In a typical use of the Network layer service, a Transport layer entity issues an N_UNITDATA.request primitive to hand an NSDU over to

FIGURE 8.3   **A time-sequence diagram for the SN-UNITDATA service.**

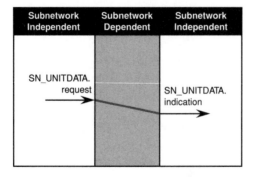

a Network layer entity for transmission through the network. A Network layer entity in the node at the final destination then issues an N_UNITDATA.indication primitive to pass the NSDU up to the destination Transport layer entity. With this service, the routing and relaying of packets between routers are hidden from the Transport layer entities. The roles of the subnetwork independent and subnetwork dependent sublayers in routing packets through the network is shown in Figure 8.4.

After the subnetwork independent sublayer receives an NSDU from a Transport layer entity, it encapsulates the NSDU in a packet and issues an SN_UNITDATA.request primitive to the subnetwork dependent sub-

---

FIGURE 8.4   **The roles of the subnetwork independent sublayer and the subnetwork dependent sublayer in routing data through different types of subnetworks.**

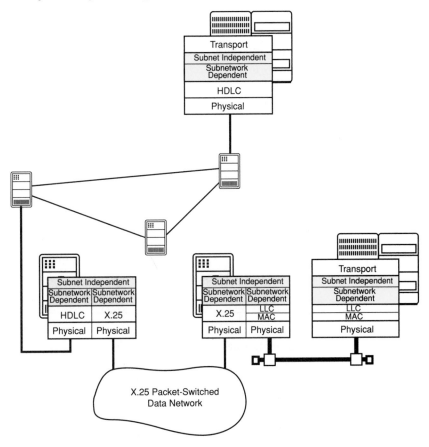

layer below to transmit the packet over a single subnetwork. The sub-network dependent sublayer entity provides the service of accessing a Data Link layer service to transfer the packet specified by the user_data parameter across a single data link. A subnetwork dependent entity in the receiving node then passes the packet up to the subnetwork inde-pendent sublayer in that node by issuing the SN_UNITDATA.indication primitive.

If the packet has reached a router and not the destination end node, the subnetwork independent sublayer in the router performs the routing function and issues another SN_UNITDATA.request primitive to relay the packet across the next subnetwork. This process continues until the packet reaches its final destination. The subnetwork independent sub-layer in the destination node then extracts the NSDU from the packet and issues the N_UNITDATA.indication primitive to pass the NSDU up to the destination Transport entity.

Subnetwork Dependent Service Interface Procedure Declarations

Like the interface between the Transport layer and the Network layer, the DNA Phase V architecture defines the interface between the subnet-work independent sublayer and the subnetwork dependent sublayer. The architectural specification for the Network layer uses the terms *circuit* and *adjacency* in defining this service interface. A *circuit* is a generic term that includes any type of link, including a local area network broadcast link, a point-to-point link, an attachment to a node on a DDCMP multi-point link, a dial-up link, or an X.25 virtual circuit. An *adjacency* repre-sents the combination of a circuit and a node attached to that circuit.

For example, a router attached to a LAN having 10 end nodes at-tached to it and no other routers perceives one circuit with 10 adjacen-cies. The procedure declarations that define the services a subnetwork dependent sublayer entity supplies to a subnetwork independent sub-layer entity are listed in Box 8.2.

ISO 8473 Subnetwork Dependent Sublayer Functions

As we have described, the subnetwork dependent sublayer provides the function of accessing a real Data Link layer service to provide the service of transmitting packets from one node to another. As we have seen, the subnetwork dependent sublayer is capable of working with many types of data links, some of which may offer a connectionless-mode and some of which may offer a connection-mode Data Link layer service.

The ISO 8473 Internet protocol functions running in the subnet-work dependent sublayer operate in the SNDCP role and perform the

BOX 8.2

**Subnetwork
Dependent
Sublayer Interface
Procedure
Declarations**

The following function and procedure declarations define the abstract interface between the subnetwork independent sublayer and the subnetwork dependent sublayer of the Network layer in terms of the services a subnetwork dependent sublayer entity provides to a subnetwork independent sublayer entity.

Circuit Control Functions

- **CircuitStatus.** Determines the status of a circuit.
- **Reinitialize.** Resets a circuit so previously received messages are discarded.
- **SupplyCircuitUpComplete.** Informs the subnetwork dependent sublayer that the update process of the routing algorithm recognizes that a circuit is up.
- **SupplyCircuitDownComplete.** Informs the subnetwork dependent sublayer that the update process of the routing algorithm recognizes that a circuit is down.

Adjacency Control Functions

- **AdjacencyStatus.** Determines the status of an adjacency.
- **SupplyBroadcastAdjacencyUpComplete.** Informs the subnetwork dependent sublayer that the update process of the routing algorithm recognizes that an adjacency on a broadcast circuit is up.
- **SupplyBroadcastAdjacencyDownComplete.** Informs the subnetwork dependent sublayer that the update process of the routing algorithm recognizes that an adjacency on a broadcast circuit is down.

Data Transfer Functions

- **Transmit.** Transmits the contents of a buffer containing an NSDU.
- **CheckTransmitBuffer.** Checks the status of a buffer whose contents previously were sent as a result of the Transmit function.
- **SupplyReceiveBuffer.** Provides a receive buffer for use by a subnetwork dependent sublayer entity.
- **CheckReceiveBuffer.** Determines whether any buffer supplied with a SupplyReceiveBuffer function has been filled with received data and returns the contents of the buffer to the subnetwork independent sublayer entity when a packet arrives.

subnetwork dependent convergence functions required to offer a uniform interface to the subnetwork independent layer, no matter what the actual characteristics of the underlying Data Link layer service are.

In some cases, the underlying Data Link layer service provides a connectionless-mode service. In such a case, the subnetwork dependent convergence function consists of a simple mapping to the Data Link service required to implement the SN_UNITDATA.request primitive. In other cases, the underlying Data Link layer service may provide a connection-mode service, such as that offered by an X.25 virtual circuit. In such a case, the subnetwork dependent convergence function consists of the specification of an actual protocol that uses an existing connection or establishes a new connection, if required, to relay the packet across the connection and then releases the connection at an appropriate time.

Subnetwork Dependent Convergence General Model

In general, when the subnetwork dependent sublayer receives a packet from the subnetwork independent sublayer as a result of an SN_UNITDATA.request primitive, it attempts to determine what it needs to transmit the packet to the next node along its path. It then transmits the packet to the appropriate node. If for any reason the subnetwork dependent sublayer entity is unable to transmit the packet to an appropriate next node, it discards the packet and generates, if so requested, an Error Report packet to be returned to the source.

ISO 8473 Subnetwork Dependent Convergence Functions

The ISO 8473 Internet protocol defines subnetwork dependent convergence functions for three types of subnetworks:

- **Point-to-Point Subnetworks.** These subnetworks are implemented by conventional wide area networking Data Link protocols. DNA Phase V supports both HDLC and DDCMP data links for point-to-point subnetworks. With an HDLC or DDCMP point-to-point link, the SNDCP role of the Data Link protocol consists of a simple mapping function.
- **Broadcast Subnetworks.** These subnetworks are implemented by local area networks that supply the Logical Link Control (LLC) service defined in IEEE 802.2/ISO 8802-2. The LLC service is exactly the service required to support the CLNS, so the SNDCP function consists of a simple mapping to the LLC service primitives.

- **X.25 Virtual Circuits.** These subnetworks supply a connection-mode Data Link service. An X.25 virtual circuit subnetwork is an example of a dynamically assigned point-to-point data link. The SNDCP function for X.25 virtual circuits specifies a protocol for choosing an existing connection, establishing a new connection when required, transferring data over a connection, and releasing the connection when appropriate. This protocol is augmented by additional policies and parameters described in the DNA Phase V architectural specification for the Network layer.

We next describe the functions of the ISO 8473 Internet protocol that operate in the subnetwork independent layer to provide the CLNS to a user of the Network layer.

ISO 8473 Subnetwork Independent Sublayer

As we introduced earlier, the subnetwork independent sublayer is responsible for the transmission of packets between any two end nodes in the network wishing to communicate with one another. The ISO 8473 protocol functions operating in the subnetwork independent layer are not concerned with the type of service provided by the individual subnetworks over which packets must travel; they are independent of the Data Link layer.

The functions of the ISO 8473 Internet protocol operating in the subnetwork independent sublayer play the SNICP role and supply the Network service directly to a user of the Network layer service. These protocol functions define the way in which two end nodes exchange packets with each other to provide the CLNS.

ISO 8473 Packets

The ISO 8473 Internet protocol defines two network-protocol-data-units (NPDUs), or packets, that are used to control its operation. Following are brief descriptions of the two ISO 8473 Internet protocol packet types:

- **Data Packet.** Carries NSDUs between users of the Network layer service in the two end nodes that are communicating using the Network service.
- **Error Report Packet.** Returned to the originating node when a Data packet is discarded because of a problem. It is generated by the node that discarded the packet if requested by the sender of the packet.

Packet Format Figure 8.5 shows the general format of a Network layer packet. It begins with a protocol identifier field that identifies the packet as one associated with the ISO 8473 Internet protocol. Following the identifier field is a length indicator, which contains a value indicating

FIGURE 8.5   **The general format of a Network layer packet.**

Protocol Identifier	Length	Header Fixed Portion	Header Variable Portion (optional)	Data

the length of the header portion of the message. After the length field is the fixed portion of the header, which has the same format for both Data and Error Report packets. Following the fixed portion of the header is an optional variable portion that contains additional parameters. Following the variable portion of the header is the data portion of the packet. In a Data packet, the data portion contains the NSDU passed from a user of the Network layer service for transmission by the Network service.

Packet Header Fields   Figure 8.6 shows the format of Data and Error

FIGURE 8.6   **Data packet and Error Report packet format.**

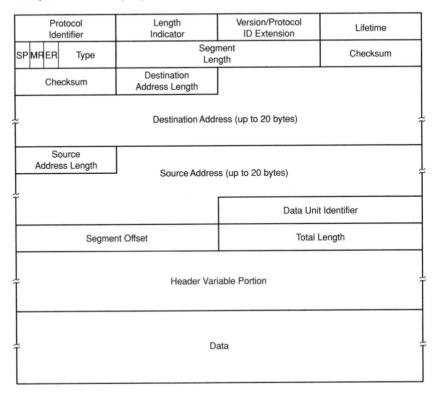

FIGURE 8.7 **Header variable portion parameter format.**

Parameter Code	Length	Parameter Value

Report packets. When a packet contains parameters in the variable portion of the header, each parameter is structured as shown in Figure 8.7. A parameter begins with a 1-octet code identifying the parameter's type, followed by a 1-octet field giving the parameter's length, and ending with one or more octets containing the parameter's value. The parameters that can be included in both the fixed and the variable portions of the header for Data and Error Report packets are listed in Box 8.3.

ISO 8473 Subnetwork Independent Protocol Functions

The procedures performed by the subnetwork independent layer of the Network layer and the mechanisms used in implementing these procedures are described in both ISO 8473 and the DNA architectural specification for the Network layer. The operation of the ISO 8473 Internet protocol is defined in terms of a set of *protocol functions* documented in ISO 8473. Not all functions need be supported by an implementation of ISO 8473. Box 8.4 (page 182) describes each protocol function described in the ISO 8473 protocol specification.

Protocol Function Subsets

ISO 8473 defines two subsets of the full protocol, each of which needs to implement only some of the protocol functions:

- **Inactive Network Layer Subset.** This protocol subset consists of a limited number of protocol functions that can be used when it is known that both the source and the destination end nodes are in the subnetwork.

- **Nonsegmenting Subset.** This protocol subset allows a simplified form of packet header to be used if it is known that it will not be necessary to segment packets over any of the subnetworks that connect the source and the destination nodes.

DNA Phase V provides the full protocol. The inactive Network layer subset is provided for compatibility with the equipment of other vendors that does not support the full protocol.

BOX 8.3

ISO 8473 Data and
Error Report Packet
Header Fields

Header Fixed Portion Fields

- **Network Layer Protocol Identifier.** Contains the value 129 and identifies the packet as being associated with the ISO 8473 protocol.

- **Length Indicator.** Contains a value giving the length of the header.

- **Version/Protocol ID Extension.** Contains the value 1.

- **Lifetime.** Contains a value specifying the remaining lifetime of the packet in units of 1/2 second.

- **Segmentation Permitted (SP).** Contains the value 1 if segmentation is permitted.

- **More Segments (MR).** Contains the value 1 if more segments follow this one.

- **Error Report (ER).** Contains the value 1 to request the return of an Error Report packet should this packet be discarded.

- **Type.** Contains the value 28 if the packet is a Data packet; contains the value 1 if the packet is an Error Report packet.

- **Segment Length.** Contains a value giving the length of the entire packet, including the header.

- **Checksum.** Used to contain a calculated checksum to detect corruption of the data in the packet's header. The use of this field is optional and is not recommended in DNA. When not used, both octets are set to values of 0.

- **Destination Address Length.** Contains a value giving the length of the destination address field that follows.

- **Destination Address.** Contains the network address of the node to which the packet is being sent.

- **Source Address Length.** Contains a value giving the length of the source address field that follows.

- **Source Address.** Contains the network address of the node originating the packet.

- **Data Unit Identifier.** Contains a unique identifier generated by the source node (included only in packets having the Segmentation Permitted field set to 1).

- **Segment Offset.** Contains a value indicating the relative position within the original PDU of this segment (included only in packets having the Segmentation Permitted field set to 1).

BOX 8.3

continued

- **Total Length.** Total length of the entire PDU before segmentation (included only in packets having the Segmentation Permitted field set to 1).

Header Variable Portion Fields

- **Padding.** Used to align the data portion of the PDU on some desired boundary.
- **Security.** Used to contain implementation-defined security information.
- **Source Routing.** Used to contain information about the route the packet should take through the network.
- **Route Recording.** Used to record information about the route the packet travels through the network.
- **Quality of Service.** Used to contain values describing quality-of-service parameters. This field contains the congestion experienced indicator used to implement congestion avoidance procedures.
- **Priority.** Used to contain a value specifying the relative priority of the packet.
- **Reason for Discard.** Used in Error Report packets sent after a node discards a packet to indicate the reason a packet was discarded.

Protocol Function Categories

The ISO 8473 protocol specification divides the protocol functions into three categories:

- **Type 1.** These are functions that all implementations of the full protocol must provide.
- **Type 2.** An implementation may or may not provide these functions. If a node receives a packet that selects a type 2 function that the node does not provide, the node discards the PDU and generates an Error Report packet.
- **Type 3.** An implementation may or may not provide these functions. If a node receives a packet that selects a type 3 function that the node does not provide, the node processes the packet as if the function had not been selected.

Figure 8.8 (page 184) lists the protocol functions, indicates each function's type, indicates the functions that must be provided by the full

BOX 8.4

**ISO 8473 ES-ES
Protocol Functions**

- **PDU Composition.** Constructs packets according to the rules governing the encoding of packets defined in the protocol specification.

- **PDU Decomposition.** Removes protocol-control-information from packets.

- **Header Format Analysis.** Analyzes information in the packet header and determines whether it is in the correct format.

- **PDU Lifetime Control.** Used to enforce a maximum lifetime for a packet so no packet can circulate endlessly through the network.

- **Route PDU.** Determines the node to which a packet should be forwarded and the underlying service that must be used to move the packet to that node.

- **Forward PDU.** Transmits a packet over a data link to the node determined as a result of the route PDU function.

- **Segmentation.** Breaks up a large packet for transmission over a data link into two or more smaller packets.

- **Reassembly.** Reassembles the original packet segmented using the segmentation function.

- **Discard PDU.** Discards a packet that cannot be processed because of a lack of resources, a protocol violation, or an error that occurred during its transmission.

- **Error Reporting.** Attempts to return an Error Report packet when the discard PDU function was used to discard a packet.

- **PDU Header Error Detection.** Performs a checksum calculation on the protocol-control-information to ensure that it has not been corrupted.

- **Padding Function.** Allows space to be reserved in a packet header to allow the data portion to be aligned on a convenient boundary, such as a word boundary in a computer.

- **Security.** Used to implement protection and data integrity controls. The standard does not specify how the protection is to be provided, only where in the packet header security information can be encoded. *(This protocol function is not provided by DNA Phase V.)*

- **Source Routing.** Allows the source node to specify the path through the network a generated packet should take. *(This protocol function is not provided by DNA Phase V.)*

- **Record Route.** Records the route traveled by a packet as it passes through each router on its way to the destination node.

BOX 8.4

continued

- **Quality-of-Service Maintenance.** Provides information to routers that can be used in making routing decisions where those decisions affect the quality of service the Network service provides to a user of the Network layer service.
- **Priority.** Allows a packet having a higher priority value in its header to be processed ahead of packets having lower priorities. *(This protocol function is not provided by DNA Phase V.)*
- **Congestion Notification.** Sets an indicator in a packet's header to indicate that congestion was experienced in transmitting the packet over a data link.

protocol and the two protocol subsets, and summarizes the protocol functions that the DNA Phase V implementation of ISO 8473 provides.

Subnetwork Independent Sublayer Protocol Mechanisms

The descriptions of the protocol functions in ISO 8473 precisely document all aspects of Network layer protocol operation for the CLNS. However, the descriptions are overly detailed for all but those who build products implementing the protocol. Full descriptions of the protocol functions used to provide the CLNS would fill a rather large book, so we cannot describe them here in detail. The following sections contain general descriptions of the various types of protocol mechanisms used in the DNA Phase V Network layer to implement ISO 8473. Here we provide a high-level overview of some of the more interesting aspects of the operation of the ISO 8473 Internet protocol.

Routing

The routing function determines the path over which a packet flows from the source node to the destination node. The routing function in a router extracts and interprets routing PCI from the packets it receives, forwards packets based on the destination address in the PCI, and finds an alternative route when nodes or data links fail. The routing function also receives reports from the subnetwork dependent layer concerning changes in the availability of the routers and the end nodes to which it is

FIGURE 8.8   Network layer protocol function support.

Function	Full Protocol	Nonsegmenting Subset	Inactive Subset	Supported by DNA Phase V
PDU Composition	Type 1	Type 1	Type 1	Yes
PDU Decomposition	Type 1	Type 1	Type 1	Yes
Header Format Analysis	Type 1	Type 1	Type 1	Yes
PDU Lifetime Control	Type 1	Type 1	n.a.	Yes
Route PDU	Type 1	Type 1	n.a.	Yes
Forward PDU	Type 1	Type 1	n.a.	Yes
Segmentation	Type 1	n.a.	n.a.	Yes
Reassembly	Type 1	n.a.	n.a.	Yes
Discard PDU	Type 1	Type 1	n.a.	Yes
Error Reporting	Type 1	Type 1	n.a.	Yes
PDU Header Error Detection	Type 1	Type 1	n.a.	Yes
Security	Type 2	Type 2	n.a.	No
Complete Source Routing	Type 2	Type 2	n.a.	No
Complete Route Recording	Type 2	Type 2	n.a.	No
Partial Source Routing	Type 3	Type 3	n.a.	No
Partial Route Recording	Type 3	Type 3	n.a.	Yes
Quality of Service Maintenance	Type 3	Type 3	n.a.	No
Priority	Type 3	Type 3	n.a.	No
Congestion Notification	Type 3	Type 3	n.a.	Yes
Padding Function	Type 3	Type 3	n.a.	Yes

attached and returns error reports to the user of the Network layer service when necessary. The ISO 8473 Internet protocol describes a routing protocol function but does not specify the algorithm that is to be used to perform it. As we have already discussed, routing in a DNA Phase V network is handled by the ISO 10589 IS-IS routing protocol, described in Chapter 9.

Segmentation and Reassembly

In some situations, packets may be too large to be transmitted by the Data Link layer in a single transmission frame, perhaps because devices having a limited frame buffer size are used to implement the data link. In such a case, a segmentation function breaks up the packet into smaller packets. Packets that are segmented remain so until they are received by the destination node. A reassembly function in the Network layer in the destination node reassembles the packet after receiving all the segments.

(Note that this function is different from the Transport layer function of breaking long messages into individual packets before passing them down to a Network layer entity in separate NSDUs.)

PDU Lifetime Control

PDU lifetime control places a limit on the amount of time a packet can remain in the network and thus ensures that a packet does not circulate endlessly through the network. This function is important to the Transport layer because the Transport layer requires that each packet is either delivered in a bounded amount of time or discarded. Packets that remain in the network too long can cause the Transport layer message sequence number mechanism to fail.

Congestion Avoidance

The congestion avoidance function keeps track of the available buffer resources in each router. When the average number of packets in the queue for a given data link exceeds some predefined value, the router sets a congestion experienced indicator in the packets it forwards over that data link. This information is used by the Transport layer congestion avoidance functions described in Chapter 10. If the queue continues to grow, the router begins to discard packets to prevent deadlocks. The congestion control function regulates the ratio of traffic being relayed by a node to traffic originated by that node.

We next examine the functions that are performed by the ISO 9542 ES-IS routing protocol.

ISO 9542 ES-IS Routing Protocol

The ISO ES-IS routing protocol is described in ISO 9542, *End System to Intermediate System Routing Exchange Protocol for Providing the Connectionless-mode Network Service*. This protocol allows end nodes and routers to communicate with one another for the purposes of exchanging information to control the routing function. This protocol defines how an end node exchanges routing control information with a router to automatically configure itself into the network. The 9542 ES-IS protocol works with two types of information: *configuration* information and *route redirection* information:

• **Configuration Information.** Configuration information allows end nodes and routers to learn of each other's existence and to determine if they are reachable. This information allows end nodes and routers to dynamically learn of their availability, thus eliminating the need for explicit network management actions when connecting a new end node to the network or when disconnecting an end node or router.

- **Route Redirection Information.** Route redirection information allows routers to inform end nodes of better routes to use when forwarding packets to a particular destination node. A better path could be another router on the same subnetwork as the source end node or the destination end node itself if it is on the same subnetwork as the source end node. Allowing the routers to inform end nodes of better routes minimizes the complexity of the routing decisions end nodes must make and allows end nodes to make use of more efficient routes when transmitting future packets. For example, a source end node need not check to see whether the destination end node is in its own subnetwork. The source end node simply sends the first packet to a router it knows about. If the router determines that the destination end node is in the same subnetwork as the source end node, it informs the source end node of that fact. The source end node can then forward all subsequent packets directly to the destination end node.

The following sections describe the formats of the packets defined by the ISO ES-IS protocol and list the procedures the protocol defines.

ISO 9542 ES-IS Protocol Packet Types

The ISO 9542 ES-IS protocol defines three packet types used to exchange routing information:

- **Redirect.** This packet is generated by a router when it receives a Data packet from an end node and determines that the end node could have forwarded the packet directly to the node to which the router is about to forward the packet. The Redirect packets provide the end node that originally sent the Data packet with the subnetwork address of the node to which it should forward future packets for the specified destination.
- **End System Hello (ESH).** This packet, called *Endnode Hello* in the DNA Phase V documentation, is generated periodically by each end node to inform all routers currently on the data link of the existence of the end node.
- **Intermediate System Hello (ISH).** This packet, called *Router Hello* in the DNA Phase V documentation, is generated periodically by each router on a data link to inform all end nodes on that data link of the existence of the router.

ISO 9542 Protocol Functions

The ISO 9542 protocol specification describes the operation of the ES-IS routing protocol in terms of a set of protocol functions. Not all functions need be supported by an implementation of ISO 9542. Box 8.5 describes each of the protocol functions defined in ISO 9542.

The remainder of this chapter introduces the protocols used in supplying the CONS.

Protocols for Supplying the CONS

Two protocols are used to supply the CONS: ISO 8208 and ISO 8878. Together they provide the CONS, but not in the same way as ISO 8473, ISO 9542, and ISO 10589 supply the CLNS. As described in Chapter 7, DNA Phase V end nodes support the CONS for communication with other nodes attached to an X.25 PSDN.

ISO 8208 X.25 Protocol

The specification of the main protocol used to implement the X.25 interface is described in ISO 8208, *X.25 Packet-level Protocol for Data Terminal Equipment*. The ISO 8208 protocol is a subnetwork dependent sublayer protocol that operates in the SNAcP role to access the underlying subnetwork service in an X.25 network. The ISO 8208 protocol is identical to the protocol described in the 1984 *Red Book* version of Recommendation X.25 published by CCITT. The 1984 version of X.25 defines a protocol rich enough in function that it provides all required facilities to directly provide the CONS. However, the X.25 and the CONS are defined in different ways.

The CONS, described by ISO 8348, *Network Service Definition*, is defined in terms of the following:

- service primitives that define actions and events
- service primitive parameters
- the interrelationships among valid sequences of actions and events

Recommendation X.25, on the other hand, is defined in terms of the following:

- procedures for establishing and using virtual circuits
- the formats of packets associated with virtual circuit procedures
- procedures for optional user facilities

BOX 8.5

ISO 9542 ES-IS
Protocol Functions

- **Protocol Timers.** Maintenance of timers used to trigger the execution of other protocol functions.
- **Report Configuration.** Used by end nodes and routers to inform each other of their existence and of their network addresses.
- **Record Configuration.** Used by a router to record configuration information obtained from end nodes and other routers to update the router's routing information database and by an end node to record the configuration of routers on a subnetwork.
- **Flush Old Configuration.** Used by a router or an end node to flush old configuration information from the router's routing information database after the expiration of a timer.
- **Query Configuration.** Issued to locate an end node when no router is currently reachable on the subnetwork.
- **Configuration Response.** Issued in response to the query configuration function.
- **Configuration Notification.** Used by end nodes and routers to transmit configuration information to a node that has become newly available.
- **Request Redirect.** Used by routers to provide an end node with a better path over which to forward Data packets.
- **Record Redirect.** Used by end nodes to handle Redirect packets received from routers issuing the request redirect function.
- **Refresh Redirect.** Used by end nodes to refresh redirection information when packets are received in order to increase the length of time a redirection persists without allowing it to persist indefinitely.
- **Flush Old Redirect.** Flushes redirection entries in the routing information database after the expiration of a timer.
- **PDU Header Error Detection.** Performs a checksum calculation on the protocol-control-information to ensure that it has not been corrupted.
- **Protocol Error Processing.** Discards packets found to contain protocol errors.

Because Recommendation X.25 was not originally designed for the purpose of supplying the CONS, it does not indicate exactly how X.25 procedures and packets should be used to supply the Network service. To supplement the information in ISO 8208 and Recommendation X.25, ISO has published ISO 8878.

ISO 8878 Provision of CONS Using X.25

The protocol defined in ISO 8878, *Use of X.25 to Provide the OSI Con-nection-mode Network Service*, is a protocol operating in the subnet-work independent sublayer. ISO 8878 operates in the SNICP and SNDCP roles and can be viewed as running in a thin layer on top of a lower sublayer in which the ISO 8208 protocol operates. The ISO 8878 protocol defines how X.25 packets and procedures are used to supply the various services defined in the service definition for the CONS.

ISO 8878 also defines a protocol operating in the SNDCP role that specifies how an older version of Recommendation X.25 can be used to supply the CONS. Many PSDNs are still operating using the procedures defined by the 1980 *Yellow Book* version of Recommendation X.25. The 1980 version does not provide a sufficiently powerful protocol to furnish all the services required to supply the CONS. The protocol specified in ISO 8878 defines procedures by which information concerning certain elements of the protocol is carried in the headers of 1980 X.25 packets, and other information concerning the protocol is carried in the data por-tion of special X.25 Data packets. The protocol generates these and transmits them along with Data packets that carry information passed down from the Transport layer.

Conclusion

Chapter 7 introduced the functions of the Network layer, and this chap-ter discussed the protocols that end nodes use to communicate with each other and to exchange information with routers. Another important Network layer protocol involves the procedures routers use in communi-cating with each other in choosing routes and relaying user traffic through the network. The ISO 10589 routing protocol is the subject of Chapter 9.

CHAPTER 9

Network Layer Routing

The routing function in a computer network must determine the path over which each packet travels from a source node to a destination node. Routing in computer networks is a very difficult problem, to which there does not exist today a totally acceptable solution. There is no known algorithm that always relays packets, over optimal routes, to their correct destinations in the face of an arbitrary network topology, an arbitrary amount of network traffic, and an arbitrary set of failures. However, the routing problem can be partitioned into two parts: routing *within* a single routing domain and routing *between* administrative domains.

As discussed in Chapter 7, an administrative domain includes all the end systems, routers, and subnetworks making up a network that is the responsibility of a single organization. The DNA Phase V routing algorithm solves the problem of routing within a single routing domain. The routing algorithm designed specifically for DNA Phase V has now been accepted as the basis for the international standard ISO 10589—*Intermediate System to Intermediate System Intra-Domain Routing Exchange Protocol for use in Conjunction with the Protocol for Providing the Connectionless-mode Network Service (ISO 8473)*. After we describe how the DNA Phase V routing algorithm handles intradomain routing, we will discuss the more difficult problem of interdomain routing.

Routing Algorithm Properties

In developing the routing algorithm for DNA Phase V, the DNA architects began by determining the desirable properties of a routing algorithm.

NETWORK ARCHITECT

First, the algorithm has to be robust; if a physical path exists between a source node and a destination node, then the routing algorithm should be able to find it. The algorithm must compute good routes; if there are multiple paths between two nodes, the system should use the one with the lowest cost. The algorithm must stabilize quickly; when changes occur in the network, new routes should be computed quickly, and the system should stabilize fast and should not oscillate. The algorithm has to be frugal; it should use minimum amounts of CPU cycles, memory, and network bandwidth. And the algorithm must be fault-tolerant; it should be able to survive data corruption and failures of hardware and communication links. It is difficult, to say the least, to achieve all of these objectives simultaneously.

We will next examine the types of routing algorithms that can be used in a computer network.

Types of Routing Algorithms

The ISO Technical Report TR 9575, *OSI Routing Framework*, provides a general discussion of routing in an OSI network and identifies five forms of routing that can be employed in a computer network. These are summarized in Figure 9.1 and are described in the following sections.

Static Routing

With *static routing*, all routing information for each node is precomputed and is provided to each router through a management action. Static routing has the advantage that sophisticated computational methods can be used for computing routes, since routes are not computed in real time. However, with static routing techniques, routing information must be recomputed and provided to the routers each time the network topology changes. Thus, static routing techniques are generally not well suited to large networks that may be constantly changing.

Quasistatic Routing

Quasistatic routing is similar to static routing except the routing information that is computed and provided to each node includes information about alternative paths that can be used when certain types of failures

FIGURE 9.1   Characteristics of five types of routing algorithms.

Method	Collection	Distribution	Computation	Adaptability
Static	Through network management.	Through network management.	Routes computed offline.	None in real time.
Quasistatic	Through network management.	Through network management.	Routes computed offline.	Limited adaptibility to failures.
Centralized	Routers report information about the local environment to a central facility.	Central facility distributes forwarding information to each router.	Routes computed by central facility.	Can adapt to any changes to the central facility, but routers have difficulty finding the central facility.
Distributed Distance Vector	Routers report current routes to each neighbor router.	Routers accept routing information from neighbor routers and redistribute their view of local neighborhood.	Routes computed individually by each router on receipt of information that changes their routing decisions.	Adapts to any changes that are reported by neighbors.
Link State	Routers collect globally provided information to obtain a map of the routing domain.	Routers globally distribute information about their local environments to all other routers.	Routes computed individually by each router upon receipt of information that changes their map of the routing domain.	Adapts to any changes that are reported in the link state information.

occur. Quasistatic routing techniques can handle certain types of topological changes, such as links becoming unavailable, but major changes to the network topology still require routing information to be recomputed offline for the routers.

Centralized Routing

With *centralized routing*, end nodes and routers report information about their local environments to a centralized facility. The centralized facility accumulates routing information from all the nodes in the network, computes routes, and sends to each router the information it needs to handle routing decisions. In effect, only the centralized facility has complete knowledge of the network topology. Although, in theory, a centralized routing scheme can respond to topological changes, it has two major drawbacks. First, a way must be found for relaying the routing information to the centralized facility after a topological change occurs. This is difficult because the routing information maintained by the centralized facility cannot be reliably used for this purpose after the network topology changes. Second, the delays inherent in propagating routing information to and from the centralized facility can cause the calculated routes to be different from the routes that should be used.

Distributed Adaptive Routing

With *distributed adaptive routing*, nodes dynamically sense their local environments and exchange this information with each other in a distributed fashion. Each node then periodically computes new routes for relaying packets from one node to the next. Distributed adaptive algorithms are robust, and they can quickly adapt to changing network topologies. There are two main types of distributed adaptive routing: *distance-vector* routing and *link state* routing. Each of these is discussed next.

Distance-Vector Routing   With a *distance-vector* routing algorithm, also sometimes called a *Bellman-Ford* algorithm, each node in the network learns about the network topology by exchanging routing information packets with its neighbors. In effect, each node learns what its neighbors think the network looks like. Each node then constructs a new description of the network topology and communicates this new picture to its neighbors. The process is repeated and eventually stabilizes when all the nodes learn they have the same description of the network topology. The routing algorithm defined by DNA Phase IV is a distance-vector algorithm.

A distance-vector algorithm is a relatively simple algorithm and is relatively easy to design and implement. A major problem with distance-vector routing, however, is that the computational complexity of the algorithm grows quite rapidly with the size of the network. It is well suited to networks having a maximum size of perhaps 64 areas with 1,000 nodes per area, but it does not scale well much beyond this limit. Another problem is that under certain circumstances, the algorithm can take many iterations to converge after topology changes occur. In a network containing routers having varying levels of performance, and links having varying bandwidths, the slowest routers in the network and the slowest links tend to become convergence bottlenecks. Problems that occur with distance-vector algorithms also tend to be difficult to diagnose because none of the routers see the actual original messages describing the topology of the network; they see only messages indicating what the network looks like to the router's neighbors. The information exchanged by routers consists basically only of distance information. Network management generally requires map and path information as well as distance information for effective troubleshooting.

Link State Routing   With a *link state routing algorithm*, which is the type of routing algorithm chosen for DNA Phase V, instead of a node learning about the topology of the network by asking its neighbors what they think it looks like, a router determines what *its* individual area of the network looks like and then broadcasts that information to all the other routers. With link state routing each router broadcasts information about its local environment, so it is eventually possible for all the routers to receive a complete description of the network topology. Each router then knows where all the other nodes are and what links interconnect them. In contrast with distance-vector routing, link state algorithms converge in a single iteration after a topology change. A link state algorithm also provides the map and path information network management requires for troubleshooting.

NETWORK ARCHITECT

We chose a link state algorithm mainly because it scales better and it converges faster. While a network's routing is unconverged, routing doesn't work, which means the network doesn't work. You want the network to stay out of the unconverged state as much as possible. Also, since every node has a map of the entire network topology, problems are easier to diagnose. You can look at any node's map of the network and determine if that map is the same as the maps maintained by other nodes. The main disadvantage of link state algorithms is that they are much more difficult to design and build than distance-vector algorithms.

Link State Algorithm Operation

The basic function of a routing algorithm is to determine the *paths* over which packets travel through the network. A path is a particular sequence of connected nodes and links between the node originating a packet and the packet's destination node. The DNA Phase V routing algorithm is a distributed algorithm, a component of which runs in every active router.

The Pseudonode

Special considerations must be given to broadcast links, such as those employed in local area networks. One way to implement the algorithm for a broadcast link would be to model the broadcast link as a set of separate point-to-point links between each node on the broadcast link to all of the other nodes—a full mesh topology. This causes the number of logical links to grow quadratically as the number of nodes grows, thus causing the computational complexity of the algorithm to grow much too quickly. This problem is solved by modeling the broadcast transmission medium itself as a node on the network (called the *pseudonode*). This converts the full mesh topology of the network into a logical star topology having many fewer logical links, as shown in Figure 9.2.

Routing Control Packets

The information contained in the packet types exchanged by the routers provides considerable insight into the operation of the DNA Phase V routing algorithm. Box 9.1 lists the packet types used to control the operation of the routing algorithm.

Link State Routing Processes

The DNA Phase V link state routing algorithm consists of four major processes:

- update
- forward
- decision
- receive

FIGURE 9.2   The pseudonode.

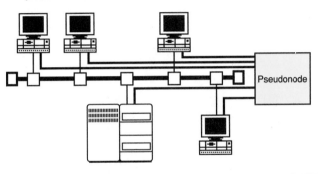

BOX 9.1

Routing Control
Packets

- **LAN Level 1 Router-to-Router Hello.** Broadcast over a local area network (LAN) subnetwork to discover the network addresses of all level 1 routers on that subnetwork.

- **LAN Level 2 Router-to-Router Hello.** Broadcast over a LAN subnetwork to discover the network addresses of all level 2 routers on that subnetwork.

- **Point-to-Point Router-to-Router Hello.** Transmitted by a router on a nonbroadcast data link in response to a Router Hello packet from an adjacent router to determine whether the adjacent router is a level 1 or a level 2 router.

- **Link State Packet, Level 1.** Generated by level 1 and level 2 routers and propagated to all routers in an area. The contents of a level 1 Link State packet describe the topology of the network in the immediate neighborhood of the router that generates it.

- **Link State Packet, Level 2.** Generated by level 2 routers and propagated to all level 2 routers in a private subnetwork. The contents of a level 2 Link State packet describe the topology of the network with respect to the level 2 routers (in a private subnetwork) in the immediate neighborhood of the level 2 router that generates it.

- **Complete Sequence Numbers Packet, Level 1.** Generated periodically by a designated level 1 router attached to a broadcast link. It provides adjacent routers with information about the designated router's LSP database. This information allows routers to ensure that their level 1 routing information is synchronized.

- **Complete Sequence Numbers Packet, Level 2.** Generated by level 2 routers in a manner similar to that of Complete Sequence Numbers packets, level 1.

- **Partial Sequence Numbers Packet, Level 1.** Sent over point-to-point links by a level 1 router to acknowledge received LSPs. Also sent when a router determines that some other router has one or more level 1 LSPs that are more up-to-date than those in its LSP database and serves as a request for the more up-to-date LSPs.

- **Partial Sequence Numbers Packet, Level 2.** Generated by level 2 routers in a manner similar to that of Partial Sequence Numbers packets, level 1.

- **XID Message.** Used for compatibility with DNA Phase IV in conjunction with DDCMP data links.

Figure 9.3 shows how these four major processes relate to each other and to the routing information maintained by routers. The following sections describe the operation of the four main functions of the routing algorithm.

The Update Process

The update process is a distributed algorithm in which all routers in the network participate. Its operation is based on much research that has been done on routing algorithms over the years. [1, 2, 3, 4] In running the update process, each router in the network packages the adjacency information determined by the subnetwork dependent layer into a routing control packet called a Link State packet (LSP), which describes the router's local environment. The LSP contains information about the reachability and identity of the router's immediate neighbors. By "imme-

FIGURE 9.3 **A functional model of DNA Phase V routing algorithm.**

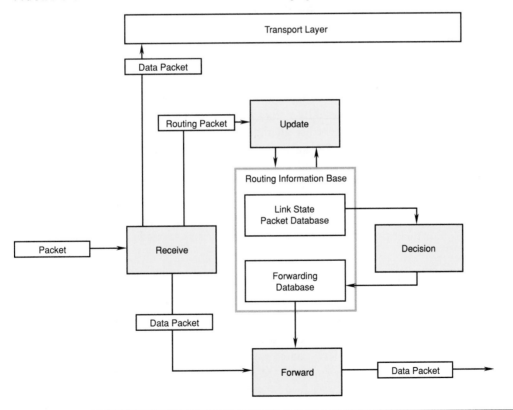

diate neighbors" we mean all those nodes currently reachable from the router over a single link.

Link State Packets

A router's LSP contains the following information:

- **Router Identification.** Identifies the router that generated the LSP.
- **Sequence Number and Lifetime Indicator.** Used to allow the update process to determine the relative age of the LSP.
- **Checksum.** Used to detect LSP corruption.
- **Link Entries.** Includes a separate entry for each of the links attached to the router. Each entry contains the following information:
  —**Link Status.** Contains information about the status of the link.
  —**Node Identification.** Contains information about the identification of all the neighbor nodes that can be reached via the link. For a point-to-point link this describes a single node. For a broadcast link, this describes all the nodes that can be reached via that link.
  —**Link Cost.** Contains a locally determined indication of the cost of using the link.

Level 1 and Level 2 Routers

The information contained in an LSP differs depending on whether the LSP was generated by a level 1 router or a level 2 router. LSPs generated by level 1 routers list all that router's neighbors, both end nodes and other routers. LSPs generated by level 2 routers do not list end nodes—they list neighbor nodes that are other level 2 routers and nodes in other routing domains reachable from that level 2 router. Information about reachable nodes in other routing domains consists of static routing information that must be entered for level 2 routers using network management procedures. Interdomain routing is discussed later in this chapter.

Flooding

The update process in each router is also responsible for propagating LSPs throughout the network using a technique called *flooding*. Each router sends out its own LSP over each of its links so all its neighbor routers receive it. A router sends its LSP over a point-to-point link only if there is another router at the other end of the link. For a broadcast link, a router multicasts its LSP to all the routers on the link. Each router propagates its LSP both periodically and whenever there is a change in any of that router's links. A level 1 router does not send LSPs outside its area, and a level 2 router propagates LSPs only to other level 2 routers in the routing domain. A level 2 router does not propagate LSPs outside its routing domain.

When a router receives an LSP from another router, it determines if it has ever received an LSP from that router before. If not, it stores the LSP in its local *link state database*. It then propagates the received LSP using the same procedure it uses to propagate its own LSP, except that it does not send the LSP to the router from which it received the LSP. If a router receives an LSP identical to one it already has in its link state database, it acknowledges receipt of the LSP but does not propagate the LSP.

Since LSPs are forwarded from router to router throughout the network, it is possible for a router to receive an LSP older than one it already has in its link state database. When this occurs, the router does not forward the LSP it received (the older LSP). Instead, it sends a copy of the newer LSP (the one it is currently holding) to the router from which it received the older LSP. In the absence of topological changes, the algorithm converges quickly. After convergence, each level 1 router contains a complete topological map of its area, and each level 2 router contains a topological map of the relationships among areas. Routers use these topological maps to compute least-cost routes from any source node to any destination node.

Sequence Number Packets

A key responsibility of the update process is to make sure that the latest LSPs eventually reach every router in the network. To ensure that the update process is reliable, routers send control packets, called *Sequence Number packets* (SNPs), that inform adjacent routers of the current contents of their LSP databases. There are two types of Sequence Number packets: *Partial Sequence Number packets* (PSNPs) and *Complete Sequence Number packets* (CSNPs). A router attached to a point-to-point link uses a PSNP to explicitly acknowledge each LSP it receives. The PSNP contains the router's node ID and information identifying the LSP that the PSNP acknowledges, including the LSP's sequence number. A router attached to a broadcast link does not individually acknowledge each LSP received. Instead, through an election process, one of the routers on each broadcast link is elected the *designated router*. The designated router on a broadcast link periodically multicasts over that link information about all the LSPs currently in its own LSP database. A router multicasts this information in the form of a set of CSNPs that indicate the sequence numbers of all the LSPs in the router's LSP database. The set of CSNPs a router multicasts contains enough information to allow routers receiving it to determine whether the receiving router's and sending router's LSP databases are synchronized. If a router determines that some other router has more up-to-date LSPs, it sends a PSNP to that router as a request for the more up-to-date LSPs.

LSP Checksums

An interesting part of the update process concerns the checksum values the update process places in the Link State packets it generates. The checksum values contained in LSPs are calculated only by the routers that initially generate the LSPs; they are not regenerated as the LSPs are flooded through the network. This makes it possible for any router to detect an LSP that has been corrupted, by either a transmission error or a problem in one of the routers. In this way, no router can inadvertently change the information in an LSP without one of the other routers detecting it.

LSP Sequence Number Space

Another interesting aspect of the update process is the system of sequence numbers used to sequentially number LSPs. In most protocols that depend on a system of sequence numbers, a relatively small, circular sequence number space is used. The network architects determined that a small, circular sequence number space would not be suitable for LSPs. If the sequence numbers are allowed to wrap around, then the sequence number space must be large enough so an old LSP will time out before a new LSP having the same value as the previous one is generated. But a large, circular space causes problems when dealing with router failures. If a router fails, it does not know with which sequence number to begin numbering its LSPs, because it does not know what values are in the LSPs already in the network. This could be solved by having the router wait for a period of time equal to the LSP timeout value. But if the network is set up so LSPs time out after, say, 30 minutes, a failed router would have to wait 30 minutes before coming back up. There would then have to be a difficult tradeoff between how much bandwidth is consumed sending out new LSPs to keep them from dying out when the router is up and how long a router has to wait to come back up after a failure.

The solution was to use a 32-bit, linear sequence number space that does not wrap around. A router continually increases the sequence number value as it generates LSP values, and the value does not wrap around. Instead, if a router runs out of numbers, it shuts itself down. However, with a 32-bit sequence number, a router generating a new LSP every 20 seconds would be able to stay in operation for over a thousand years before running out of numbers.

With a linear sequence number space, a router that starts up, either initially or after a failure, always numbers its first LSP with a sequence number value of 0. Let us say router A fails, restarts, and sends out an LSP having a sequence number value of 0. Router B receives that LSP and determines it already has an LSP from router A. The sequence number in the LSP held by router B will have a sequence number higher than the one in the LSP just received from router A. This causes router B to send the LSP back to router A. In this way, router A learns the sequence number that was contained in the LSP it issued to everyone else before it failed. It can then add one to that number and go on from there. Theoretically there may be a problem if a router manages to stay up for a thousand years, but from an engineering perspective this is good enough.

The Decision Process

The decision process uses the link state database generated through operation of the update process to determine the least-cost path to each router in the routing domain. The decision process does this by running a *shortest path first* (SPF) graph minimization algorithm to find the best path through the network to any destination. [5] This information is used to create a *forwarding database*, from which the forward process can determine the least-cost next hop for each Data packet it receives. The SPF algorithm uses the link state database to construct a *spanning tree* of the network topology—a graph structure in which redundant paths and loops have been eliminated. The SPF algorithm essentially finds the shortest path to each destination node, starting with the router itself as the root of a shortest-path tree, and records the neighbors on the shortest path to each destination. It also computes an *adjacency set* for each destination node, which is a representation of all the equal-cost paths for the next hop to each destination. Adjacency sets allow traffic to be split across these equal-cost paths.

The Forward Process

The forward process decides for each Data packet received which link to forward that Data packet over. This process inspects the destination NSAP address of each Data packet it receives and uses the forwarding database generated by the decision process to determine the correct link over which to forward the packet. It then queues the packet for transmission over that link. If the forwarding database indicates there are multiple equal-cost paths to the destination, the forward process performs a load-splitting function and transmits successive Data packets over different links to evenly distribute the traffic over the adjacency set.

When the forward process is unable to deliver a Data packet, it discards the packet. If the discarded packet requested an error report in its protocol-control-information, the forward process returns an Error Report packet to the source node. The Error Report packet specifies the node at which the error occurred and the nature of the error.

When the forward process forwards the Data packet onto the same subnetwork from which it was received, it also sends a Redirect packet to the packet's source node to inform the source node that it could have sent the packet directly to the destination node. Subsequent Data packets generated by that node can then be sent directly to the node identified in the Redirect packet without further involvement of the router.

Router Resource Shortages

An interesting aspect of the forward process is the way in which the algorithm is designed to handle situations where routers run out of resources. Each router maintains an attribute called the *hippity cost.*

NETWORK ARCHITECT

The most significant cost associated with traversing a subnetwork is associated with the hops, or the cost of crossing a data link between two nodes. But there is a cost associated with the processing a node performs before making the next hop. So in going from node A to node B to node C, we say hippity-hop, hippity-hop. So the hippity cost is the cost that applies to the node between two hops.

The hippity cost is a routing metric that defines the relative cost of a packet traversing a router. The algorithm is carefully designed so when a router runs out of resources, it keeps running but sets its hippity cost attribute to infinity and notifies network management it has run out of resources. Other routers then route traffic around that router if they can. This is useful because the worst-case memory requirements for a router can be much more than their average-case memory requirements. Transient conditions can occur in which the memory required is many times the average memory requirement. It is not practical to design a router to handle the worst-case condition that may persist for only a few seconds, so the algorithm is designed to deal with these worst-case conditions.

Router Failure Example

As an example, let us suppose we have a broadcast subnetwork with 1000 end nodes and several routers. The designated router, operating on behalf of the link's pseudonode, constructs a Link State packet that reports a link to each of the nodes attached to the broadcast link. Thus, the designated router's LSP is very large—it contains entries for all 1000 end nodes and all the other routers. The designated router sends this LSP to the other routers, so they maintain this large LSP in their memory as well. With such a large number of nodes on the link, the routers might be tight on memory.

Let us suppose now that the designated router fails. Through an election process, one of the other routers will become the new designated router. It will, on behalf of the pseudonode, build its own LSP reporting a link to each of the nodes on the data link. But since the original LSP will not yet have timed out, the router will have to store both the old one and the new one. If the router was already tight on memory, it will run out of memory. The algorithm is designed to handle such a situation. The router signals an out-of-memory condition and changes its hippity cost value to a value of infinity. This effectively causes the router to stop routing until the problem resolves itself. As soon as the original LSP times out, the router will discard it, thus making room for the new LSP. The router will then quickly go back into normal operation.

The Receive Process

The receive process analyzes the protocol-control-information accompanying each packet to decide the action it should take for that packet. The receive process takes one of four actions for each packet it receives:

- **Pass the Packet to Transport.** If the packet is a Data packet and the NSAP address indicates the packet is addressed to this node, the packet is passed up to a Transport layer entity.

- **Pass the Packet to the Forward Process.** If the packet is a Data packet and the NSAP address indicates it is not addressed to this node, the packet is passed to the forward process, which forwards it over one of the router's data links.

- **Pass the Packet to the Update Process.** If the packet is a Routing Control packet, the packet is passed to the update process.

- **Discard the Packet.** The packet is discarded if its PCI does not correspond to any of the packet types handled by the routing algorithm, if the lifetime control process determines its lifetime is up, or if congestion has made it necessary to discard the Data packet.

Interdomain Routing

As we stated earlier in this chapter, the DNA Phase V routing algorithm is designed to provide an automated solution to the problem of intradomain routing. DNA Phase V now provides only a partial solution to the more complex problem of interdomain routing when the network may be made up of multiple administrative domains run by different organizations.

NETWORK ARCHITECT

The problems of routing in the interdomain environment are very different from the problems of routing in the intradomain environment. Within a single routing domain, the routing problem is one of optimizing the communications that take place among the various nodes, and the routing problem can be described relatively simply. We just have to take an arbitrary set of nodes and subnetworks and set things up so any node can reach any other node. And in the absence of failure, we'd like the data to take an optimal path through the network. When we connect together the networks of two or more different organizations, the problem becomes one not of optimization but one of causing the networks to interact in a very controlled way. In such an environment, the problem of routing is to provide a means for controlling and restricting the traffic flows that occur between the networks. The concern becomes one of who can talk to who via who. Routing between administrative domains is more concerned with implementing policy than it is with optimizing the routing.

Policy Concerns

A simple interdomain routing scenario provides an example of possible policy constraints. Figure 9.4 shows three administrative domains run by Waterloo University, the University of British Columbia (UBC), and the University of Wisconsin. A Canadian law states that data traffic flowing between two locations both physically in Canada cannot flow outside of Canada. Therefore, with the topology shown in Figure 9.4, if the link between UBC and Waterloo fails, the routing algorithm must not allow

FIGURE 9.4   **An interdomain routing example.**

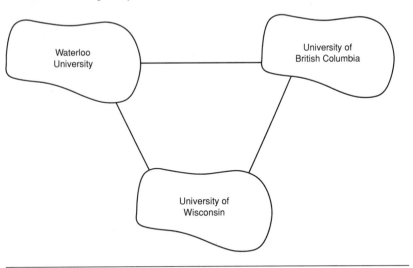

UBC to send traffic to Waterloo through the Wisconsin network. But if
the link between UBC and Wisconsin fails, the routing algorithm can
allow Wisconsin to send traffic to UBC through Waterloo.

A routing algorithm designed to run in a single administrative domain typically would be designed to automatically respond to any link
failure and to find an alternative route. A routing algorithm designed for
routing between administrative domains must provide for policy decisions to be made regarding which routes are legal and which are not.

Private Policy Information

A second source of complexity in routing between administrative domains concerns the fact that the policies governing routing decisions may
not themselves be public knowledge in the network. For example, each
organization may want to keep its own policies private. So what is
needed is a scheme in which only *routes* are disseminated and not the
policies used to determine those routes. This can be done, but it makes
the routing problem more difficult. Routing algorithms typically avoid
creating loops, around which packets circulate endlessly, by having
sufficient knowledge about the network topology to prevent loops from
occurring. But if policies are not known throughout the network, individual routers may not have enough information to detect loops. What is
needed is a routing scheme capable of detecting loops without having

total topology information. Such a routing scheme eventually will be worked out, but this is still the subject of research and controversy.

The DNA Phase V routing algorithm currently uses static routing information to control the flow of traffic from one administrative domain to another when interdomain routing is required. The problem with static routing is that it does not allow the network itself to suppress loops. Loops are, in effect, suppressed in the network administrator's head.

Conclusion

The Network layer provides important services for choosing routes for user traffic and for relaying that traffic through the network. These services are used by the Transport layer to provide a reliable end-to-end data transfer service that processes running in end nodes can use for communicating with one another. The functions performed by the Transport layer are the subject of Chapter 10.

References

1. J. McQuillan, et al., "The New Routing Algorithm for the Arpanet," *IEEE Transactions on Communications*, May 1980.

2. E. C. Rosen, "The Updating Protocol of Arpanet's New Routing Algorithm," *Computer Networks,* vol. 4, no. 1, 1980.

3. E. C. Rosen, "Vulnerabilities of Network Control Protocols: An Example," *Computer Communication Review*, July 1981.

4. Radia Perlman, "Fault-tolerant Broadcasting of Routing Information," *Computer Networks 7*, 1983.

5. E. W. Dijkstra, "A Note on Two Problems in Connexion with Graphs," *Numerische Mathematik 1*, 1959.

CHAPTER 10

The Transport Layer

The main role of the Transport layer of the OSI model, and in the DNA Phase V architecture, is to handle the end-to-end exchange of data between two users of the Transport service. The Transport layer in DNA provides a reliable, sequential data transfer service between users. Again, "reliable" in this context means that the destination node either receives all messages sent or receives an indication that an error has occurred. "Sequential" means that the Transport layer delivers messages to the receiver in the same sequence in which they are sent. Another function that the OSI Transport service provides is *multiplexing*, that is, a user can establish multiple concurrent connections to one or more other Transport service users.

Users of the Transport layer service normally consist of either an OSI Session layer entity or a DNA Session Control layer entity, depending on which higher-layer protocol stack the two communicating users are employing. The Transport layer provides an end-to-end data transmission service using protocols to enhance the inherent characteristics of the underlying Network service. The Transport layer is the lowest layer required *only* in the machines running user processes. This relationship is shown in Figure 10.1. Although not shown in Figure 10.1, the Transport layer is also present in routers for use by network management.

There are two architectural specifications for the Transport layer of the DNA Phase V architecture. The preferred form of transport is defined by the *OSI Transport* specification, which incorporates ISO standards for the Transport layer of the OSI model. The other Transport layer specification describes Digital's own proprietary network service protocol (NSP). The NSP transport protocol is provided mainly for compatibility with DNA Phase IV. Class 4 of the OSI transport protocol had its roots in Digital's NSP protocol, and there are a great many simi-

FIGURE 10.1   **The Transport layer is the lowest layer required only in the computers that are communicating.**

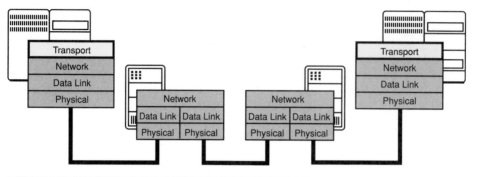

larities between them. Class 4 of OSI transport is essentially an enhancement and refinement of Digital's proprietary NSP protocol. The various OSI transport classes are described later in this chapter.

OSI Transport

As with other OSI model layers, the ISO standards that define the Transport layer include both a service definition and a protocol specification. The relationship between the services the Transport layer provides and the protocol governing its operation is shown in Figure 10.2. As shown there, the Transport layer protocol uses the services of the Network layer to provide a defined set of services to a user of the Transport service.

FIGURE 10.2   **The relationship between the Transport layer service definition and the Transport layer protocol specification.**

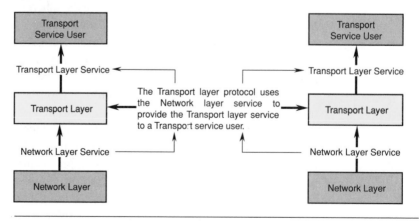

The Transport layer can use either the connectionless-mode Network service (CLNS) or the connection-mode Network service (CONS) (described in Chapter 7). However, when the DNA Session Control layer uses the services of the Transport layer, only the CLNS is used; the CONS is supported only for the OSI upper-layer protocol stack. In a typical use of the Transport layer service, a Transport service user in one node accesses the Transport service via a transport-service-access-point (TSAP) and passes a transport-service-data-unit (TSDU) to the Transport layer entity for delivery to the Transport service user in the destination node. The transmitting Transport layer entity adds PCI to the TSDU in the form of a header to create a transport-protocol-data-unit (TPDU). The Transport layer then uses the services of the Network layer to transmit the TPDU through the network to the destination node. The Transport layer entity at the destination removes the PCI and delivers the enclosed TSDU to the Transport service user there. This process is summarized in Figure 10.3. As we will discuss later, and which is not shown in Figure 10.3, a Transport layer entity can segment a TSDU for transmission in the form of multiple TPDUs, and it can also group multiple TPDUs for transmission in the form of a single packet.

FIGURE 10.3   **The Transport layer service.**

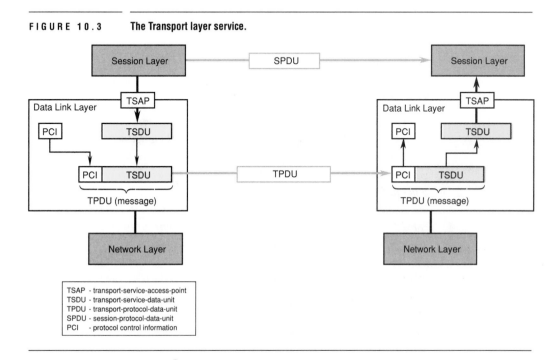

**OSI Transport
Service Definition**

As with other layers of the OSI model, the ISO standards for the Transport layer define both a connection-mode Transport service and a connectionless-mode Transport service. By far the greatest number of today's networking applications require a reliable Transport service, so the DNA Phase V architectural layers above the Network layer provide a connection-mode service. The connectionless-mode services defined in the ISO standards for the Transport, Session, Presentation, and Application layers are not currently addressed by DNA Phase V, although support for connectionless-mode services could easily be added to the architecture should connectionless applications become more prevalent.

The OSI transport protocol specification defines five classes of Transport layer protocols that can be used to supply the Transport service: classes 0, 1, 2, 3, and 4. Box 10.1 describes the five classes of OSI transport protocols. DNA Phase V supports three of these: classes 0, 2, and 4. (Classes 1 and 3 are implemented very infrequently throughout the industry, and support for them is not included in DNA Phase V.) Classes 0 and 2 are designed to be run only over the connection-mode Network service (CONS); class 4 transport can be run over either the CONS or the connectionless-mode Network service (CLNS) and is the preferred transport protocol class. Class 4 transport is the only allowable class when the DNA Session Control layer uses the Transport service. Classes 0 and 2 are provided for use only by the OSI upper-layer protocol stack.

NETWORK ARCHITECT

The CLNS versus CONS controversy in the Network layer carries over into the Transport layer. What has happened is that the world is developing two distinct ways of doing the Transport service. One uses the connectionless Network service and class 4 transport. Class 4 transport is designed to recover from anything bad the Network layer is going to do to it, including loss, duplication, mis-sequencing, and so on. The other camp is designed around a connection-oriented Network service together with a trivial transport protocol—class 0 or 2—which do nothing other than a bit of addressing.

Our feeling at Digital is that class 4 transport is the only one that really works in heterogeneous networks because class 4 is the only one that can deal with anything going wrong. Classes 0 and 2 basically assume that nothing goes wrong in the Network service. And classes 1 and 3 have kind of fallen by the wayside—no one uses them. None of the classes other than class 4 adds substantial value to the underlying Network service. Class 4 transport was really

BOX 10.1

Five Classes of OSI Transport Protocols

- **Class 0: Simple Class.** This class was developed initially by CCITT for teletext applications. It is sometimes mandated for use with the CCITT X.400 messaging systems, although this is not technically necessary. Class 0 is the simplest form of transport protocol and assumes that most required protocol mechanisms for supplying a reliable Transport connection are supplied by the Network layer. Class 0 transport requires the connection-mode Network service (CONS). DNA Phase V supports class 0 transport.

- **Class 1: Basic Error Recovery Class.** This class was also initially developed by CCITT and is designed for use with a Network service using the X.25 protocols for packet-switched data networks. The main difference between class 1 and class 0 is that class 1 employs sequence numbers so limited error recovery is possible; class 0 does not use sequence numbers. Class 1 transport operates only over the CONS. DNA Phase V does not support class 1 transport.

- **Class 2: Multiplexing Class.** Class 2 is also an enhancement of class 0 and permits multiple Transport connections to be created using a single Network connection. It also requires the CONS. DNA Phase V supports class 2 transport.

- **Class 3: Error Recovery and Multiplexing Class.** This class effectively combines the capabilities of class 1 and class 2. It also requires the CONS. DNA Phase V does not support class 3 transport.

- **Class 4: Error Detection and Recovery Class.** This is the only transport class that operates over the connectionless-mode Network service (CLNS). It performs in the Transport layer all required protocol mechanisms to provide a reliable Transport connection running on top of either the CLNS or the CONS. Class 4 transport is the recommended transport protocol and is expected to be the most widely used in a DECnet Phase V network.

designed to run over the CONS, but it happens to have the property that it is also perfectly happy to run over the CLNS. This is different for all the other classes, which can't run over the CLNS at all.

So we spent a lot of effort getting the class 4 transport protocol to work efficiently, but we also included support for class 0 and class 2. For example, some public X.400 messaging services mandate the use of class 0 transport. But our basic philosophy is that in the normal mode of operation, a DECnet Phase V network will use class 4 transport.

With the connection-mode Transport service, the user of the Transport service at one end requests a connection, both the Transport service itself and the Transport service user at the other end agree, and the Transport service establishes the connection. We can then think of the Transport service as a set of two pipes connecting the two transport users—one pipe for messages flowing in one direction and the other for messages flowing in the opposite direction. The user at one end inserts a message into the appropriate pipe, and an identical copy of the message emerges at the other end. Messages inserted into the pipe emerge from the other end in the same sequence in which they were sent. The protocol providing the connection-mode Transport service corrects any errors detected by automatically retransmitting frames that are either missing or found to be in error. With the connection-mode Transport service, either an identical copy of each message emerges from the pipe, in the proper sequence, for each message transmitted, or the connection is released and the two Transport layer users are informed of the failure.

The Transport layer service definition for the connection-mode Transport layer service is described in ISO 8072, *Transport Service Definition*. This international standard defines a number of services, each of which involves a set of service primitives. The service primitives for the connection-mode Transport service are listed in Box 10.2 and are described in the following sections.

BOX 10.2

OSI Transport Service Primitives

The T_CONNECT Service

```
        T_CONNECT.request      (
                                called_address
                                calling_address
                                expedited_data_option
                                quality_of_service
                                user_data
                               )

    T_CONNECT.indication       (
                                called_address
                                calling_address
                                expedited_data_option
                                quality_of_service
                                user_data
                               )
```

BOX 10.2

continued

```
        T_CONNECT.response  (
                            quality_of_service
                            responding_address
                            expedited_data_option
                            user_data
                            )

        T_CONNECT.confirm   (
                            quality_of_service
                            responding_address
                            expedited_data_option
                            user_data
                            )
```

The T_DATA Service

```
            T_DATA.request   (
                              user_data
                              )

            T_DATA.indication   (
                              user_data
                              )
```

The T_EXPEDITED_DATA Service

```
    T_EXPEDITED_DATA.request   (
                              user_data
                              )

    T_EXPEDITED_DATA.indication   (
                              user_data
                              )
```

The T_DISCONNECT Service

```
        T_DISCONNECT.request   (
                              user_data
                              )

        T_DISCONNECT.indication   (
                              disconnect_reason
                              user_data
                              )
```

The T_CONNECT Service

The T_CONNECT connection establishment service is used to establish a connection between two users of the Transport service. A Transport connection consists of a virtual circuit in the Transport layer between two users of the Transport service. A Transport connection must be established before two Transport service users can exchange data. The process of connection establishment allows the users of the Transport service to negotiate mutually acceptable characteristics for the connection, such as selecting the class of protocol to be used and determining whether messages should carry checksums to detect errors that might otherwise be undetected by the underlying Network service.

The T_CONNECT service is defined by four T_CONNECT service primitives. The T_CONNECT service is a confirmed service in which users of the Transport service are informed of the success or failure of the attempt to establish a Transport connection. Figure 10.4 contains time-sequence diagrams that show how the four T_CONNECT service primitives are issued in three situations: successful connection establishment, rejection of the connection request by the peer Transport service user, and rejection of the connection request by the Transport service itself.

The T_DATA Service

Once connection establishment has been successfully performed, the Transport connection enters the data transfer phase, which provides the two users of the Transport service with a full duplex path for the exchange of data. The two Transport service users employ the two T_DATA service primitives to exchange data units. Figure 10.5 is a time-sequence diagram that shows the sequence in which the two T_DATA data transfer service primitives are issued. Notice the T_DATA service is a nonconfirmed service, and the requester of the Transport service data transfer operation is not explicitly informed of its completion. However, the T_DATA service provides for reliable data transfer. If a data unit is delivered successfully, all previous data units will also have been delivered, in the order sent, without duplication or omission. Either a data transfer operation is successful or transport informs the user of the failure by releasing the connection.

FIGURE 10.4   **Time-sequence diagrams for the T-CONNECT service.**

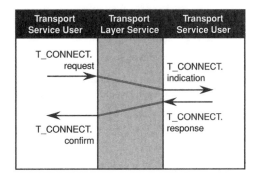

Successful Transport connection establishment

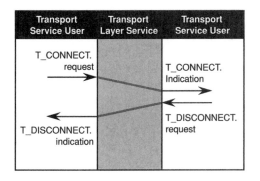

Transport service user rejection of an attempt to
establish a Transport connection

Transport service rejection of an attempt to establish
a Transport connection

FIGURE 10.5   **Time-sequence diagram for the T-DATA service.**

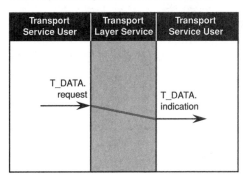

The T_EXPEDITED_DATA Service

OSI transport classes 2 and 4 provide an additional data transfer service called T_EXPEDITED_DATA. This service permits a single, short data message to be transmitted that will bypass any blockages in the normal flow of traffic over the Transport connection. However, an Expedited data message is not necessarily transferred any faster than normal data messages. Figure 10.6 is a time-sequence diagram showing the sequence in which the two T_EXPEDITED_DATA data transfer service primitives are issued.

FIGURE 10.6   Time-sequence diagram for the T-EXPEDITED-DATA service.

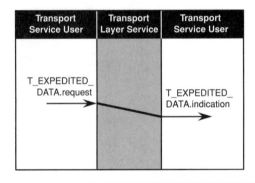

The T_DISCONNECT Service

The T_DISCONNECT service is used to release a connection previously established by the T_CONNECT service. The T_DISCONNECT service is provided through the two T_DISCONNECT service primitives. Either Transport service user can issue a T_DISCONNECT.request service primitive to request the release of a connection. The Transport service itself also can, for some internal reason, release a connection by issuing the T_DISCONNECT.indication primitive. Figure 10.7 includes time-sequence diagrams that show ways in which a Transport connection can be released. If a connection is released by one user of the Transport service, the Transport layer entity issues the T_DISCONNECT.indication

FIGURE 10.7   Time-sequence diagrams for the T-DISCONNECT service.

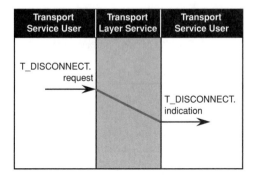

Transport connection release requested by a
Transport service user

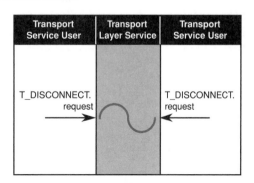

Transport connection release requested simultaneously
by both Transport service users

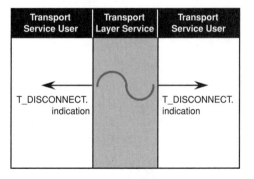

Transport connection release requested by the
Transport service

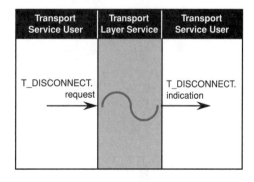

Transport connection release requested simultaneously
by a Transport service user and the Transport service

primitive to the other user. If both users simultaneously release the connection, neither user may receive the indication. If the Transport layer entity itself releases the connection, both users receive the indication. If a transport user and the Transport service simultaneously release the connection, the other user receives the indication. The reason parameter in the T_DISCONNECT.indication primitive contains values that describe the reason for the connection release and identify the entity that initiated the disconnect request.

OSI Transport Service Interface Procedure Declarations

The DNA Phase V architectural specification for OSI transport also defines the abstract interface between a Transport layer entity and a user of the Transport layer service. The procedure declarations defining the services a Transport layer entity provides to a Transport service user are listed in Box 10.3.

BOX 10.3

OSI Transport Service Interface Procedure Declarations

The following function and procedure declarations define the abstract interface between the Transport layer and a user of the Transport layer in terms of the services a Transport layer entity provides to a user.

Port Control Functions

- **OpenIncoming.** Allocates a port in the Transport layer used to accept an inbound request for a connection.

- **OpenOutgoing.** Allocates a port in the Transport layer used later to establish an outbound connection.

- **Close.** Deallocates a port allocated with either OpenIncoming or OpenOutgoing.

Connection Control Functions

- **ConnectTransmit.** Requests an outbound connection using a port allocated with OpenOutgoing.

- **OutgoingConnectPoll.** Obtains the results of a previously issued ConnectTransmit.

- **IncomingConnectPoll.** Issued after OpenIncoming to determine whether an inbound connection request was received.

- **Accept.** Initiates the acceptance of an inbound Transport connection.

- **AcceptPoll.** Checks for the completion of a previously issued Accept call.

- **DisconnectTransmit.** Requests the disconnection of a Transport connection.

- **DisconnectReceive.** Determines whether the peer Transport layer entity has disconnected the Transport connection and obtains information about the reason for the disconnection.

Normal Data Transfer Functions

- **DataReceive.** Associates a receive buffer with a port that can be used to accept a received normal (not expedited) Data message over the Transport connection.

BOX 10.3

continued

- **DataReceivePoll.** Checks for the completion of a previously issued DataReceive call and returns a buffer containing a message if it has completed.
- **DataTransmit.** Queues a transmit buffer for the transmission of a normal (not expedited) Data message over the Transport connection.
- **DataTransmitPoll.** Retrieves a previously queued transmit buffer for which a DataTransmit operation has been completed.

Expedited Data Transfer Functions

- **ExpeditedReceive.** Associates a receive buffer with a port that can be used to accept a received Expedited data message over the Transport connection.
- **ExpeditedReceivePoll.** Checks for the completion of a previously issued ExpeditedReceive call and returns a buffer containing an Expedited data message if it has completed.
- **ExpeditedTransmit.** Queues a transmit buffer for the transmission of an Expedited data message over the Transport connection.
- **ExpeditedTransmitPoll.** Retrieves a previously queued transmit buffer for which an ExpeditedTransmit operation has been completed.

Miscellaneous Functions

- **ReadAddress.** Requests the Transport layer entity to supply a list of the network addresses currently being used to support the transport protocol.
- **State.** Returns the status of a port.
- **Status.** Determines the status of a specified protocol and obtains the minimum receive buffer size.

NETWORK ARCHITECT

Both the ISO standards and the DNA specifications define the Transport layer service interface in terms of a single TSDU passed across the interface as a unit. One way to implement the interface is to pass the whole TSDU across the interface in a single operation. But it is also possible to allow a user to pass the TSDU across the interface in pieces and to then pass a bit across the interface signalling when the last piece of the TSDU has been passed. One way to handle this in the receiver is to have the receiver ask for some number of octets to be passed across the interface, rather than having to receive the whole TSDU in a single piece. This is a good example of how ingenuity can be applied to the implementation of a standard. A software designer does not have to blindly implement the standard in the most obvious way. The obvious thing to do is not always the best thing.

OSI Transport Protocol Specification

The OSI transport protocol specification is documented in ISO 8073, *Connection Oriented Transport Protocol Specification.* As described earlier, DNA Phase V supports classes 0, 2, and 4 of the OSI transport protocol, with class 4 being the recommended class. By supporting the OSI transport protocol, users of the Transport service running in computing systems that implement DECnet Phase V software can communicate not only with one another but with transport users running in any type of computing system implementing class 0, 2, or 4 of the OSI transport protocol and the appropriate lower layers. The DNA Transport layer integrates the three supported classes of OSI transport protocol with the proprietary NSP protocol and offers a single, consistent service interface to the Transport service user. The choice of protocol to be used is made when the Transport layer receives a request for a Transport connection.

OSI Transport Protocol Messages

The OSI transport protocol defines 10 different TPDUs to control the operation of the protocol. Unlike DLPDUs (generally called *frames*) and NSDUs (often called *packets*), there is no generally accepted informal name for TPDUs. Where no confusion will result, we will sometimes call TPDUs *messages*.

TPDU Types

All but one of the 10 TPDU types are used to support class 4 transport; classes 0 and 2 employ other subsets of the 10 TPDU types. Box 10.4 gives brief descriptions of the 10 TPDU types defined by the OSI transport protocol specification.

TPDU Format

Figure 10.8 shows the general format of an OSI transport TPDU. It begins with a length field giving the length of the header portion of the message. Following the length field is the fixed portion of the header, which has a different format for each of the different types of TPDUs.

BOX 10.4

Transport Protocol Data Units

- **Connection request (CR).** Carries a request for a new Transport connection to be established between a source Transport layer entity and a destination Transport layer entity.

- **Connection confirm (CC).** Carries confirmation of acceptance of a request for the establishment of a Transport connection.

- **Data (DT).** Carries normal user data between transport entities over a Transport connection.

- **Expedited data (ED).** Carries expedited user data between transport entities over a Transport connection.

- **Acknowledgment (AK).** Acknowledges the receipt of one or more data TPDUs and/or allocates credit to permit the transmission of additional messages. (The concept of *credit* is described when we discuss the flow control procedures of the transport protocol.)

- **Expedited acknowledgment (EA).** Acknowledges the receipt of an Expedited data TPDU.

- **Reject (RJ).** Used only by transport classes 1 and 3 and so is not used by DNA Phase V.

- **Error (ER).** Sent by a Transport layer entity receiving a message constituting a protocol violation.

- **Disconnect request (DR).** Carries a rejection of a request for Transport connection establishment or a request that a Transport connection be released.

- **Disconnect confirm (DC).** Acknowledges the receipt of a Disconnect request TPDU.

Following the fixed portion of the header for some types of TPDUs is a variable portion of the header optionally containing additional parameters. Following the variable portion of the header is the data portion of the TPDU. In a Data TPDU, the data portion contains all or part of the TSDU passed to the Transport layer entity by the Transport service user for transmission over the Transport connection.

FIGURE 10.8   **General format of a Transport layer TPDU.**

Length	Header Fixed Portion	Header Variable Portion (optional)	Data

FIGURE 10.9   **Data TPDU format for class 4 transport.**

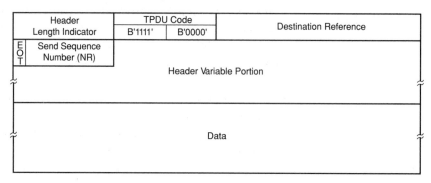

TPDU Header Fields

Figure 10.9 shows the format of a Data TPDU for class 4 transport. When a message contains parameters in the variable portion of the header, each parameter included is structured as shown in Figure 10.10. A parameter begins with a 1-octet code identifying the parameter's type, followed by a 1-octet field giving the parameter's length, and ending with one or more octets containing the parameter's value. The parameters that can be included in both the fixed and the variable portions of the header are listed in Box 10.5 (pages 224–225). Each TPDU has a different header format, and not all the parameters are carried in all the TPDUs. The DNA Phase V architectural specifications and the ISO standards for the Transport layer contain detailed specifications of the format of the header for each individual TPDU.

OSI Transport Elements of Procedure

We next discuss the mechanisms that class 4 transport uses to create and support the connection between Transport layer entities. The specific protocol mechanisms the OSI transport protocol defines are called *ele-*

FIGURE 10.10   **Header variable portion parameter format.**

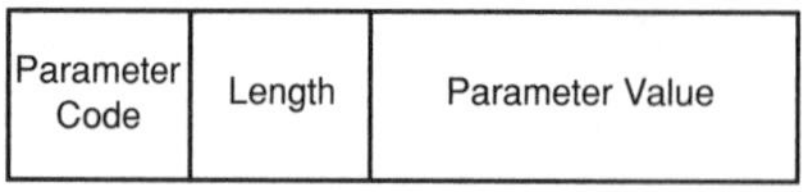

Parameter Code	Length	Parameter Value

ments of procedure in the OSI transport protocol specification. The elements of procedure precisely document the Network layer service primitives involved and the exchanges of TPDUs occurring during operation of the transport protocol. The OSI transport elements of procedure are augmented by additional documentation in the DNA Phase V architectural specifications, where Digital has gone beyond what is required by the ISO standards in documenting the operation of the transport protocol. To fully understand how the DNA Phase V version of the OSI transport protocol operates, read the OSI transport protocol specification in conjunction with the DNA Phase V documentation for the Transport layer. The elements of procedure defining the operation of the OSI transport protocol are briefly described in Box 10.6 (pages 226–227).

OSI Transport Protocol Mechanisms

The following sections contain general descriptions of the various types of protocol mechanisms the OSI transport protocol uses. Here we provide a high-level overview of some of the more interesting aspects of OSI transport protocol operation.

Connection Establishment

Upon request of a Transport service user (typically an OSI Session layer entity or a DNA Session Control layer entity), the source OSI Transport layer entity transmits a Connection request (CR) message to the destination Transport layer entity to establish a connection. This begins a procedure in which the class of protocol operation is chosen and other characteristics of the connection are negotiated. The Connection request message indicates the preferred transport protocol class, any acceptable alternative classes, and various other characteristics of the desired connection, such as the maximum message size. The destination Transport layer entity receiving the Connection request analyzes the information it contains and, if it determines it is able to comply with the connection request, responds with a Connection confirm (CC) message. The Connection confirm message specifies the protocol class that will actually be used and other characteristics of the connection.

Normal Data Transfer

The transport protocol implements a full duplex path between a pair of communicating Transport service users and uses Data TPDUs to transfer data from transmit buffers in one Transport layer entity to

BOX 10.5

TPDU Header
Parameters

TPDU Header Fixed Portion Parameters

- **Length Indicator.** Length of the header in octets, excluding the length indicator field itself.
- **TPDU Code.** Code identifying a message's TPDU type.
- **Credit.** Credit allocation used to implement flow control procedures.
- **Source Reference.** A value identifying the Transport connection within the source Transport layer entity's node.
- **Destination Reference.** A value identifying the Transport connection within the destination Transport layer entity's node.
- **Class.** A value used during Transport connection negotiation indicating which of the five transport classes is preferred.
- **Option.** Specifies whether normal or extended flow control fields are used. Normal flow control fields use 7-bit sequence numbers and 4-bit credit fields; extended flow control fields use 31-bit sequence numbers and 16-bit credit fields. A DECnet Phase V network normally uses extended flow control fields.
- **Reason.** A value that describes the reason for requesting the release of a connection or for rejecting a request for connection establishment.
- **EOT.** Indicates the last TPDU in a TSDU.
- **TPDU-NR.** Send sequence number for a Data message.
- **EDTPDU-NR.** Send sequence number for an Expedited data message.
- **YR-TU-NR.** Send sequence number of the next normal Data message the destination Transport layer entity expects to receive.
- **YR-EDTU-NR.** Send sequence number of the next Expedited data message the destination Transport layer entity expects to receive.

TPDU Header Variable Portion Parameters

- **Calling TSAP Identifier.** Identifies the transport-service-access-point (TSAP) used by the source Transport service user.
- **Called TSAP Identifier.** Identifies the transport-service-access-point used by the destination Transport service user.
- **TPDU Size.** Maximum allowable TPDU size in octets.

BOX 10.5

continued

- **Version Number.** Specifies the version number of the transport protocol being used. This parameter is provided in anticipation of future versions of the transport protocol being developed.

- **Security.** A user-defined parameter that specifies information about security procedures.

- **Checksum.** The result of passing the message through a checksum algorithm. Used only for class 4 transport.

- **Additional Option Selection.** Used to select various options to be used during protocol operation.

- **Alternative Protocol Class.** Indicates one or more alternative protocol classes that can be used if the destination Transport layer entity is not able to run the requested protocol class or elects to use some other protocol class.

- **Acknowledge Time.** Provides an estimate of the amount of time a Transport layer entity will take to acknowledge a Data message.

- **Throughput.** A set of values specifying the transport user's throughput requirements in octets per second.

- **Residual Error Rate.** A set of values specifying target and minimum rates of unreported user data loss.

- **Priority.** A value indicating the priority of the Transport connection.

- **Transit Delay.** A set of values indicating the target and the maximum values for the amount of time it should take to transmit a Data message between transport entities.

- **Reassignment Time.** A value indicating how long transport should wait for a response when trying to reassign the Transport connection to another Network connection.

- **Additional Information.** Implementation-defined information related to releasing a Transport connection.

- **Subsequence Number.** A sequence number assigned to an Acknowledge message to ensure that Acknowledge messages are processed in the correct sequence.

- **Flow Control Confirmation.** Used to echo the parameter values contained in the last Acknowledge message received.

- **Invalid Message.** Used to specify the bit pattern of a rejected message.

BOX 10.6

**OSI Transport
Protocol Elements
of Procedure**

- **Assignment of Network Connections.** When the OSI transport protocol uses the connection-mode Network service (CONS) it either assigns the Transport connection to an existing Network connection or requests a new Network connection.

- **Transport-Protocol-Data-Unit Transfer.** Used in all classes of OSI transport to carry messages between Transport entities.

- **Segmenting and Reassembling.** Allows large TSDUs to be broken into multiple TPDUs for transmission.

- **Concatenation and Separation.** Allows multiple TPDUs to be transmitted in a single packet (NSDU). OSI transport allows TPDUs from different connections to be carried in a single packet. DNA Phase V does not concatenate TPDUs from different connections but does handle the receipt of packets containing concatenated TPDUs from different Transport connections.

- **Connection Establishment.** Used to create a new Transport connection.

- **Connection Refusal.** Used to refuse a request for the establishment of a Transport connection.

- **Normal Release.** Used to release a Transport connection.

- **Error Release.** Used only in transport classes 0 and 2 to release a Transport connection as a result of the release or reset of an underlying Network connection.

- **Association of TPDUs with Transport Connections.** Used to interpret as TPDUs the NSDUs passed up from the Network layer entity in the destination node and to associate each one with the appropriate Transport connection.

- **Data TPDU Numbering.** Assigns a send sequence number to each TPDU for the purposes of recovery, flow control, and resequencing functions.

- **Expedited Data Transfer.** Used to transfer Expedited data TPDUs between Transport entities.

- **Reassignment After Failure.** Defined by OSI transport for use with the CONS to attempt to recover from the release of a Network connection by establishing a new Network connection. This procedure is defined only for class 3 transport and so is not implemented by DNA Phase V. However, an alternative method for reestablishing Network connec-

BOX 10.6

continued

tions is provided when class 4 transport is run over the CONS.

- **Retention Until Acknowledgment of TPDUs.** Copies of certain TPDUs are retained after transmission until they are acknowledged, to permit their retransmission should they fail to be delivered correctly. Supported by class 4 transport only.

- **Resynchronization.** This element of procedure applies only to classes 1 and 3 transport and so does not apply to DNA Phase V.

- **Multiplexing and Demultiplexing.** Used only for Transport connections operating over the CONS to allow multiple Transport connections to share the same Network connection.

- **Explicit Flow Control.** Used to regulate the flow of TPDUs over the Transport connection independent of the flow control mechanisms operating in other layers.

- **Checksum.** Implements an algorithm to calculate the checksum used to detect corruption of TPDUs by the Network service provider, a lower layer, or a hardware failure.

- **Frozen References.** Prevents the reuse of a connection reference while TPDUs associated with the old use of the connection reference may still exist in the network.

- **Retransmission on Timeout.** Used with class 4 transport to detect TPDUs the Network service provider loses and does not inform the Transport layer entity of the loss.

- **Resequencing.** Used with class 4 transport by a destination Transport layer entity to place TPDUs into the sequence in which they were sent by the source Transport layer entity.

- **Inactivity Control.** Used with class 4 transport operating over the CLNS to detect apparent loss of network connectivity between communicating nodes.

- **Treatment of Protocol Errors.** Procedures for handling TPDUs that constitute protocol violations.

- **Splitting and Recombining.** Used by class 4 transport to allow a Transport connection to concurrently use multiple Network connections. DNA Phase V does not support the splitting function for source nodes but does support the recombining function for destination nodes.

receive buffers in another Transport layer entity over an active Transport connection. An underlying connectionless-mode Network service or connection-mode Network service is used to perform the data transfer.

Expedited Data Transfer

Classes 2 and 4 transport provide the expedited data transfer service, allowing short data messages to be transmitted that bypass blockages caused by normal flow control procedures. Class 0 transport does not provide the expedited data transfer service.

Error Detection and Retransmission

The Transport layer provides detection and recovery from loss, duplication, corruption, and misordering of data units that might occur in lower layers. It employs send sequence numbers and an acknowledgment mechanism to ensure that messages are delivered and an optional checksum capability to detect message corruption. The class 4 transport protocol also employs a retransmission timer to detect lost messages. The timer is started when a Data message is transmitted and is stopped when the message's acknowledgment is received. If the timer expires before the sending Transport layer entity receives the acknowledgment, the sending Transport layer entity assumes the message has been lost and retransmits it.

NETWORK ARCHITECT

The retransmission timer function is an example of where the ISO standard gives no direction. The standard says there must be a value for a time limit determining after what time interval a message will be retransmitted. But the standard says nothing about how this timer should be set. This timer value could be a network management parameter set by a network manager. The number could be set small for a small network to give better performance and bigger for a large network to ensure a message is retransmitted only if it is really lost. But we decided to develop an algorithm in the protocol itself that adjusts the timer automatically.

We use an adaptive algorithm that maintains an average estimate of the round-trip delay on each Transport connection. This algorithm allows the Transport service to set the interval of the retransmission timer so it is short enough to ensure that lost messages are detected quickly but not so short that it is likely for the message to still be in transit. The timer interval is thus automatically adjusted depending on current conditions in the network rather than depending on manual assignment.

This is an example of where we have gone beyond what is specified in the ISO standards to provide enhanced function. This goes along with the philosophical attitude we have about network management—we feel that algorithms for optimizing network performance should run in the networking protocols themselves rather than in a network manager's head.

Another area in which DNA improves on the ISO standard is the way in which acknowledgments are sent. According to the ISO standards, a user could send an individual acknowledgment for each message received. However, this would ordinarily result in inefficient use of bandwidth. The DNA specification for the transport protocol allows transport to delay the sending of acknowledgments as a way of reducing the amount of computation required in the end systems to operate the transport protocol and to reduce the number of messages that have to be propagated through the network. For example, when an end system receives a packet that is not the last packet in a TSDU, transport might wait until all the packets have been received before sending an acknowledgment rather than acknowledging each packet individually.

Flow Control

The transport protocol also uses acknowledgments to implement flow control procedures to balance the relative speeds of the sender and the receiver. The Transport service recovers from messages being lost or duplicated by lower layers and ensures that messages are passed to the receiving Transport service user in the same order in which they were transmitted. Classes 2 and 4 transport also assign send sequence numbers to Data messages in order to provide reliable, sequenced message delivery. As Data messages arrive at their destination, the destination Transport layer entity returns an acknowledgment message to the source Transport layer entity indicating the sequence number up to which Data messages have thus far been successfully received. Class 0 transport does not implement explicit flow control, nor does it number Data messages or send acknowledgments. Instead, procedures in the CONS are used to provide flow control facilities with class 0 transport.

Although the OSI transport protocol defines a comprehensive scheme to provide end-to-end flow control and defines a number of rules for correct behavior, it does not make entirely clear what each rule is meant to achieve within the overall flow control procedure. The DNA Phase V architectural specification for the Transport layer augments the ISO protocol specification by providing a detailed description of the flow control algorithm. It also presents a detailed example of a possible implementation as an aid to implementors. The flow control procedures defined by the DNA Phase V architecture go much further than simply implementing the ISO standard and thus are able to perform flow control in a highly efficient manner.

The transport protocol implements flow control based on the concept of *credit*. This means, in effect, that the destination Transport layer entity tells the source Transport layer entity how many messages it is prepared to receive. The source transport is then able to transmit only that many messages, after which it must wait until it is granted additional credit. Flow control operates in conjunction with the sequence numbering scheme. The way in which credit is granted to a source Transport layer entity by a destination Transport layer entity is done in a carefully designed manner. It is not enough for the destination Transport layer entity to say simply, "You can send me another eight messages." The Network service may at any given time contain an unknown number of Data messages in transit. So the credit granting mechanism uses the Data message sequence numbering scheme in granting credit. A destination Transport layer entity grants credit based on the directive: "You can send all Data messages up to the message whose sequence number is n." Such a scheme leads to the concept of a flow control *window* that slides up the sequence numbering space and defines the range of Data messages a destination Transport layer entity is prepared to receive.

NETWORK ARCHITECT

This idea of assigning credits in flow control is an example of where we take advantage of an ambiguity in the ISO protocol specification to achieve enhanced performance. The ISO scheme is very simple. It says we should send credits telling the other user how many messages it can send to us. But deciding how many credits to send is not covered in the standard. If we have only one buffer, and we implement the ISO flow control algorithm in a simple-minded manner, we might send the user a single credit. That would allow the other user to send only one message before it must wait for another credit allowing it to send the next message. This might result in long delays if the two users are far apart. With our scheme, even if we have only one buffer, we might send the other user a lot of credits because we know we can process the data very fast.

This allows the other user to send a large number of messages, and as long as we're able to process them rapidly, we're OK.

The flow control algorithms in our version of transport implement various dynamic schemes allowing us to determine how many credits we can send to the other side, independent of the buffer resources we have available. This is an example of where we have applied significant ingenuity to provide good performance.

Class 4 transport can use either normal flow control fields or extended flow control fields. *Normal* flow control fields specify the use of 7-bit sequence numbers and 4-bit credit fields; *extended* flow control fields specify the use of 31-bit sequence numbers and 16-bit credit fields. A DECnet Phase V network normally uses extended flow control fields. This is because in a very high speed network, it is possible for a 7-bit sequence number space to wrap around before an old TPDU having a given sequence number has disappeared from the network. This can cause two different TPDUs to have the same sequence number value, thus violating one of the reliability guarantees of class 4 transport.

Congestion Avoidance

Congestion occurs when a network or part of a network is overloaded and has insufficient communication resources for the volume of traffic it is experiencing. A congested network exhibits all sorts of undesirable behavior, such as excessive transit delay. The goal in a computer network should be not only to recover after congestion occurs, but to stop congestion from occurring in the first place. The DNA version of OSI transport contains mechanisms designed to achieve this goal by attempting to reduce the load on the Network service to prevent congestion from occurring. This idea of reducing the load to reduce or prevent congestion is an important characteristic of the DNA Phase V congestion avoidance scheme.

NETWORK ARCHITECT

It's important to point out that the scheme we picked for dealing with congestion has the property of controlling congestion without introducing any additional traffic or load on the network. This is unlike many other congestion control schemes, which do absolutely the wrong thing. When the network becomes congested, many schemes—the one used in SNA being one example—cause more traffic to be sent into the network to signal congestion is occurring. So when you're near the cliff, and you get congested, the congestion messages send you over the cliff.

Class 4 transport implements two algorithms concerned with congestion. One is a congestion avoidance algorithm that attempts to prevent congestion from occurring; the other is a congestion recovery algorithm designed to recover from congestion if the first algorithm fails. The changeover from one to the other occurs when transport determines the Network service has lost a message. As long as the Network service does not lose messages, transport assumes the first algorithm is working. Once the Network service begins to lose messages, transport assumes congestion is occurring and invokes the congestion recovery algorithm. Following are descriptions of the operations of these two algorithms:

- **Congestion Avoidance Algorithm.** The congestion avoidance algorithm operates in conjunction with the Network service. It employs the congestion experienced indicator the Network service sets in the PCI attached to packets when the traffic across a data link increases beyond a predetermined point. If during any sampling period the number of messages encountering congestion reaches a certain threshold, the Transport layer entity reduces the size of its flow control window, thus reducing the amount of traffic flowing over the Transport connection. This reduces the number of messages the Network service needs to handle and reduces the load on the network accordingly. When congestion abates, each Transport entity independently begins to gradually increase its flow control window size to increase the message flow.

- **Congestion Recovery Algorithm.** The congestion recovery algorithm is invoked whenever a Transport layer entity determines that the Network service has lost a message. When this occurs, the Transport layer entity detecting the lost message assumes the Network service is experiencing congestion and dramatically reduces the flow of new Data messages into the network. It does this by initially setting its flow control window to a value of 1, permitting only the lost message to be retransmitted. The value of the window is then increased by 1 each time the number of Data messages for which acknowledgments have been received since the last change becomes greater than the current value of the local credit window. As long as no further messages are lost by the Network service, the local credit window gradually grows until it reaches the value originally assigned by the peer Transport layer entity.

Reassignment After Failure

When the class 4 protocol operates over the CONS, DNA attempts to maintain the Transport connection even if the underlying Network connection fails. The Transport service does this either by reassigning the Transport connection to some other appropriate existing Network connection or by requesting the establishment of a new Network connection to support the Transport connection. The Transport service user is not aware of the reassignment operation.

Segmentation and Reassembly

OSI transport permits the OSI Session or DNA Session Control user to transmit extremely large messages. If the underlying Network service is unable to accept a single message of the desired size, the Transport layer entity divides that large TSDU into a number of smaller TPDUs for transmission. The receiving Transport layer entity reconstructs the original TSDU after it has received the final segment and passes it to the destination Transport service user. Note that the segmentation and reassembly function is different from the notion described earlier of passing a single TSDU across the interface to transport in multiple pieces. Here, the Transport layer itself is transmitting a single TSDU in multiple TPDUs.

Multiplexing

Classes 2 and 4 of transport implement a multiplexing function, introduced earlier, allowing a user to set up any number of Transport connections between the same pair of users or between different pairs of users. Multiplexing allows multiple Transport connections to be assigned to a single Network connection. Each Transport connection in the network is independent of any other Transport connection. When a connection is established, the two Transport entities exchange 16-bit reference numbers that are assigned to the connection. These numbers are assigned so they are unique among all the Transport connections controlled by a given Transport layer entity. Messages carried over a given connection carry the reference number associated with the destination Transport layer entity. Some messages also carry the reference number associated with the source Transport layer entity as well. Each end of the connection has its own reference number, and these reference numbers are assigned independently. This is quite different from earlier protocols, such as X.25, where the two ends agree on a single identifier. Using a single identifier leads to various protocol complexities, such as collisions in reference number assignment.

Concatenation

A Transport layer entity may group together TPDUs in order to pass them to the Network service in the form of a single packet for transmission through the network. Concatenation is sometimes called *piggybacking* and, especially with very small messages, can increase the efficiency of the Transport and Network services. The concatenation function is especially useful to group Data and Acknowledgment messages in a single packet when they are traveling in the same direction over the same connection.

NETWORK ARCHITECT

The architecture allows a Transport entity to receive messages from the same Transport connection or from different Transport connections that are grouped together in the same packet. However, DECnet implementations will use concatenation only to group TPDUs from the same Transport connection and won't attempt to group TPDUs from different Transport connections. The latter is simply much harder to do than it's worth.

Connection Release

As introduced earlier, a Transport connection can be released on the request of either transport user entity or the Transport service itself. A transport user can request the release of a connection at any time. However, if the user wants to ensure that all messages it has sent have arrived at their destination, the user is responsible for determining this before releasing the Transport connection; the Transport layer does not provide this as a service. When the Transport service user requests the connection release, it must ensure that any messages in transit have been successfully received before requesting the connection release. For class 2 and class 4 transport, a Transport layer entity releases the connection by transmitting a Disconnect request (DR) message to its peer. The Transport layer entity receiving a Disconnect request message acknowledges its receipt by sending a Disconnect confirm (DC) message. With class 0 transport, a Transport layer entity releases the Transport connection by requesting the underlying CONS to release the Network connection.

NSP Transport	The second architectural specification for the DNA Phase V Transport layer describes the Digital proprietary network services protocol (NSP). NSP was designed specifically for DNA and has been a part of DNA since its inception. It can be used for communication between two users of the NSP Transport service running DECnet Phase V software, but its main purpose is for backward compatibility with DNA Phase IV. The NSP transport protocol has many similarities to class 4 of OSI transport.
NSP Transport Service Interface Procedure Declarations	The interface between a DNA Session Control layer entity and an NSP Transport layer entity is defined by essentially the same procedure declarations listed in Box 10.3. The architectural specification for the NSP transport protocol documents any minor differences.
NSP Transport Protocol Messages	Fourteen types of messages can flow over an NSP Transport connection to convey user data between two users of the NSP Transport service and to control the operation of the NSP transport protocol. These 14 types can be divided into three categories: *Data* messages, *Control* messages, and *Acknowledgment* messages. Box 10.7 contains brief descriptions of the 14 NSP transport protocol messages.
NSP Transport Protocol Mechanisms	As with the OSI transport protocol, the NSP transport protocol involves a great many procedures, many of which are similar to those employed by OSI transport. A detailed understanding of the NSP transport protocol procedures is required only by those who build products that implement the NSP transport protocol. Complete descriptions of the procedures are contained in the architectural specification for NSP Transport. The following sections provide a high-level overview of the more interesting aspects of NSP transport protocol operation. We concentrate here on those aspects of the NSP transport protocol that are different from OSI transport.

Connection Establishment

NSP establishes, maintains, and releases NSP Transport connections by exchanging control messages with a peer NSP entity. An established connection implements two separate data subchannels, each carrying messages in both directions:

BOX 10.7

**NSP Transport
Messages**

Data Messages

- **Data Segment.** Carries a message or a portion of a message passed down to an NSP Transport layer entity by a DNA Session Control layer entity.

- **Expedited.** Carries urgent data originating in a higher DNA layer.

- **Data Request.** Carries information used to control the NSP transport flow control algorithm.

- **Expedited Request.** Carries expedited flow control information.

Control Messages

- **Connect Initiate.** Carries information about a request for the establishment of an NSP Transport connection.

- **Connect Confirm.** Carries information about the acceptance of a request for the establishment of an NSP Transport connection.

- **Disconnect Initiate.** Carries information about the rejection of a request for the establishment of NSP Transport connection or a request for the release of an established NSP Transport connection.

- **No Resources.** Sent by an NSP Transport layer entity when it receives a Connect Initiate or Retransmitted Connect Initiate message and the entity has no resources available to establish a new port.

- **Disconnect Complete.** Acknowledges the receipt of a Disconnect Initiate message.

- **No Link.** Sent by an NSP Transport layer entity when it receives a message referring to a nonexistent NSP Transport connection.

- **No Operation.** Has no function and is included for compatibility with a previous version of the NSP transport protocol.

Acknowledgment Messages

- **Data Acknowledgment.** Acknowledges receipt of one or more Data Segment messages or, optionally, Connect Confirm, Expedited, Data Request, or Expedited Request messages.

- **Other Data Acknowledge.** Acknowledges receipt of one or more Connect Confirm, Expedited, Data Request, or Expedited Request messages.

- **Connect Acknowledgment.** Acknowledges receipt of a Connect Initiate message or a Retransmitted Connect Initiate message.

- **Normal-Data Subchannel.** This subchannel carries normal Data messages between two NSP entities.
- **Other-Data Subchannel.** This subchannel carries expedited Data messages and messages related to the NSP flow control algorithm.

Data Transfer

The DNA Session Control layer passes data units to an NSP Transport layer entity for transmission over an NSP Transport connection. User data units are transported between NSP entities in Data Segment messages. Like OSI transport, NSP can handle the transmission of very large messages between Transport layer entities. If NSP needs to handle a message larger than the maximum packet size supported by the Network service, it breaks the message into segments and passes each segment to the Network service in the form of a separate Data Segment message. Each Data Segment message contains a message sequence number and other control information. The destination NSP entity uses Data Segment sequence numbers to reassemble the segments. NSP segments only normal data. Expedited data messages have a limited size that is always smaller than the packet size supported by the Network service.

Flow Control

The flow control mechanisms that NSP implements ensure that messages are not lost because of limited buffering capability at the destination NSP entity and that deadlocks do not occur. Flow control mechanisms operate independently over both the normal-data and the other-data subchannels. When an NSP Transport connection is established, each NSP Transport layer entity informs its peer entity of the method to be used for flow control for messages flowing to it. Two types of flow control are supported by NSP. With the first method, called *on/off only*, the destination NSP Transport layer entity explicitly tells the source NSP Transport layer entity when to stop and when to start sending data. With the second method, called *segment with on/off*, the destination NSP Transport layer entity sends the source NSP Transport layer entity a *request count*, which indicates the number of segments it can accept. In addition, the destination entity can always tell the source entity either to stop sending data unconditionally or to start sending data under the normal request count conditions. The receiver also controls the flow of messages over the other-data subchannel with an *other-data request count*.

Data Retransmission

The NSP Transport entities at each end of a Transport connection positively acknowledge received Data messages. If a source NSP Transport layer entity fails to receive a positive acknowledgment within a predetermined time interval, it automatically retransmits the message. As with class 4 OSI transport, the time interval is adjusted dynamically based on the round-trip delay determined by the source NSP Transport layer entity.

Congestion Avoidance

While the flow control mechanisms protect against an NSP Transport layer entity having a shortage of buffer resources, they do not handle problems associated with resource shortages in other parts of the network. NSP employs congestion avoidance mechanisms similar to those of OSI transport to adapt to changing traffic loads. A difference between NSP and OSI transport is that in NSP the congestion information is not used by the receiver to control credits. Instead, the information is forwarded by the receiver to the transmitter in Acknowledgment messages. The transmitter then adjusts the maximum number of Data Segment messages sent but not acknowledged it is allowed to have outstanding. This reduces the number of Data Segment messages flowing across the NSP Transport connection, thus reducing the load on the network.

Connection Release

An NSP Transport connection can be released at any time. The connection can be released by either one of the communicating Transport service users or by one of the peer NSP Transport entities.

Conclusion

The Transport layer provides a general-purpose data transfer service that all types of users can employ for reliable communication. The layers above the Transport layer add value to this basic data Transport service. Chapter 11 introduces the DNA Session Control layer that forms one of the two major higher-layer protocol stacks the DNA Phase V architecture provides above the Transport layer.

CHAPTER 11

The DNA Phase V
Session Control Layer

The Session Control layer is the layer of one of the upper-layer protocol stacks of DNA that presents an interface to programs using a DECnet Phase V network. By programs, we mean all types of applications, including those written by users and those supplied by Digital. Programs that implement components of DNA, such as those making up network management and the naming service, also use the services of the Session Control layer for communication. The Session Control layer provides services that allow programs to communicate with one another and requests services of the Transport layer in providing its services. The relationship between the services the Session Control layer provides and the protocol governing its operation is shown in Figure 11.1. As shown

FIGURE 11.1   The relationship between the Session Control layer service and the Session Control layer protocol.

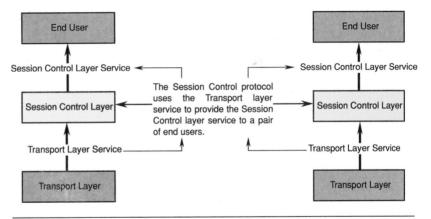

there in the context of the OSI model, the DNA Session Control layer protocol uses the services of the Transport layer to provide a defined set of services to a user of the Session Control layer. The DNA Session Control layer provides an alternative method to the three upper OSI layers—the Session layer, the Presentation layer, and the Application layer—for accessing Transport layer facilities.

The major purpose of the Session Control layer is to form a bridge between applications using a Transport connection for communication and the Transport layer itself. The Session Control layer provides a set of enhanced functions needed by an application program running under the control of an operating system. Many of the functions of the Session Control layer protocol consist of a relatively simple mapping to the basic communication services provided by the Transport layer. Among the functions the Session Control layer performs are:

- matching each incoming Transport connection establishment request with the appropriate user of a Session Control layer entity
- managing Transport connections on behalf of users of the Session Control layer entity
- enforcing access control policies to restrict communication between users of the Session Control layer
- using the naming service to maintain information about the protocols supported by the node on which a local object resides and the address of that node[*]
- accessing the services of the naming service to perform a name lookup operation to retrieve information about the protocols supported by a remote object and the address of the remote node
- selecting sets of appropriate communications protocols supported in common between the two Session Control layer users attempting to communicate over a Transport connection
- selecting the specific set of addresses and communication protocols to be used in an attempt to set up a Transport connection between the node in which the local object resides and the node in which the remote object resides

---

[*]We use the term *object* to refer to anything the naming service can maintain a name for and store information about. A *local object* is one residing in the same node as the Session Control layer entity itself; a *remote object* is one residing in some other node.

Session Control Layer Components

A Session Control layer entity implements three major components. The relationship among these functional components and their relationship with the naming service are shown in Figure 11.2. The arrows indicate the flows of information between components. The lower components provide services to the components above them. Notice that the address resolution component of the Session Control layer also interfaces directly with the clerk component of the naming service. The functions of the naming service clerk are introduced in this chapter and are described in detail in Chapter 16. The major functions of the three Session Control layer components and the naming service clerk are as follows:

- **Naming Service Clerk.** Provides the services of retrieving attribute information associated with objects and maintaining attribute information associated with local objects.

- **Connection Control.** Accesses Transport layer communication services on behalf of an object residing on the local node (such as a local application program). Also accesses Transport layer services on behalf of the ad-

FIGURE 11.2   **Session Control layer functional components.**

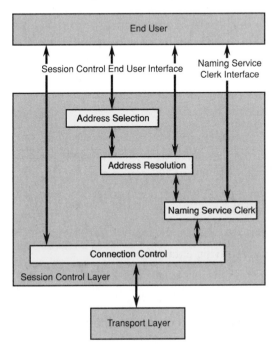

dress selection component of Session Control and on behalf of the naming service.

- **Address Resolution.** Accesses the naming service clerk to determine, given the name of an object (possibly residing in a remote node) all the various sets of communication protocols and associated addressing information that can be used to support communication between the local object and the remote object.

- **Address Selection.** Determines, given the name of an object, the specific set of protocol and addressing information, from among all the possible sets found by the address resolution component, that may be used for communication. The selected set of protocols and addressing information is used to attempt to establish a Transport connection.

Notice that the user of the Session Control layer can access any of the three Session Control layer components, as well as the naming service clerk itself. The specific component the user accesses depends on how much is known about the remote object with which the user wishes to communicate. The following sections discuss in detail the functions of each of the three components of the Session Control layer.

The Connection Control Component

The *connection control* component is concerned with functions related to establishing, maintaining, and releasing Transport connections. The connection control component also enforces access control policies defined by the installation. The services the connection control component provides using the underlying Transport layer communication services include the following:

- requesting an outbound Transport connection to an object based on the communication protocols and associated addressing information specified in the request

- receiving an incoming Transport connection request from the Transport layer

- validating access control information

- sending and receiving data

- monitoring a Transport connection

- releasing a Transport connection

Each of the above connection control component functions is described next.

Requesting a Connection by Destination Address

To directly use the services of the connection control component, the user must already have access to all required information concerning the communication protocols and associated addressing information required to establish communication between the local object and a remote object. There are three possible users of the connection control component:

- **A User of the Session Control Layer.** When a user of the Session Control layer, such as a DNA application program, already knows the specific communication protocols and associated addressing information required for communicating with the remote object, the user can access the connection control component directly, thus bypassing the address selection and address resolution components of Session Control.

- **The Address Selection Component.** The address selection component of the Session Control layer can access the connection control component to establish Transport connections on behalf of users of the Session Control layer.

- **The Clerk Component of the Naming Service.** The naming service clerk may also need to access connection control to set up Transport connections it uses to communicate with nameserver components of the naming service. Nameservers are the components of the naming service that maintain attribute information for names.

In performing its functions, the connection control component formats the data associated with each request for the establishment of a Transport connection it receives, issues a connection establishment request to the Transport layer, and starts an outgoing connection timer if the user requested it. If the timer expires before the remote Transport layer entity accepts or rejects the connection establishment request, the Session Control layer entity releases the Transport connection.

Receiving a Connect Request

The Session Control layer provides a major value-added service over and above the basic communication services that the Transport layer provides. When the connection control component receives an *incoming request* from the Transport layer for the establishment of a Transport connection, it begins by analyzing the information associated with the incoming connection to obtain descriptors of the source and destination objects and access control information. It then validates the access control information it receives using functions determined by the specific system implementing the local node. That information can be either an explicit access control string (including a password) or a request to invoke a *proxy* on behalf of the requesting user.

Proxy mapping is a mechanism by which a user on one node in the network can be given access to accounts on another node in the network without knowing the access control information of the target accounts. This is accomplished by setting up an association on the target node between the remote user and the proxy accounts on the local node. When the connection control component receives a request for connection establishment that references a proxy account name, it selects the appropriate proxy account and verifies that the user requesting access is permitted to use that account.

Once access control information has been validated, the connection control component next identifies, activates, or creates a destination application context using an algorithm defined by the particular system implementing the local node. This algorithm determines if an existing application in that node corresponds to the destination application specified in an incoming request for a Transport connection. The algorithm may include an interface to the local operating system that creates a new user context in which to run the application. Once the local application context has been identified or created, the connection control component delivers the incoming connection establishment request to the appropriate application and starts an incoming timer. If the timer expires before the application accepts the connection establishment request, the Session Control layer entity issues a reject to the Transport layer.

Sending and Receiving Data

The sending and receiving of data are system-dependent functions that are passed directly to the Transport layer. The Session Control layer can handle requests by users of the Session Control layer to exchange data with each other in a number of different ways. The Session Control layer can handle two forms of buffering and three different data transfer interfaces.

The two buffering techniques that the Session Control layer provides include one technique in which the end user handles buffering and one technique in which the Session Control layer itself performs the buffering function:

- **End User Buffering.** With this buffering technique, the sending end user passes entire buffers of data to the Session Control layer and then polls the Session Control layer to determine when transmission of the data in the buffer has been completed. In a similar manner, a receiving Session Control user passes an empty buffer to Session Control and then polls Session Control to determine when the buffer has been completely filled.
- **Session Control Buffering.** With this buffering technique, a sending end user requests transmission of the data in a buffer. Session Control either accepts or rejects the request. If Session Control accepts the request, the end user can reuse the buffer immediately. When a receiving end user passes Session Control a buffer to be filled with received data, Session Control either replies with a no data indication or immediately completely fills the buffer with received data.

The three data transfer interfaces the Session Control layer supports include techniques for working with *messages*, *segments*, and *streams* of data:

- **Message Interface.** This interface allows end users of the Session Control layer service to send and receive individual messages of any desired size. Senders and receivers work with messages contained in buffers using either the end user buffering or Session Control buffering technique.
- **Segment Interface.** This interface allows end users of the Session Control layer service to send messages limited in size to the maximum allowable transport-protocol-data-unit (TPDU) size. Senders and receivers work with messages contained in buffers using either the end user buffering or Session Control buffering technique.
- **Stream Interface.** This interface allows end users to view data as a continuous stream of octets, in which an occasional "end-of-message" marker may be inserted. The stream interface is similar to the segment interface, but the buffer size is not restricted by the maximum allowable TPDU size. The stream interface requires the use of the Session Control buffering technique.

Monitoring a Transport Connection

If requested by the user of the Session Control layer entity, the connection control component will monitor the Transport connection and will release the Transport connection if it detects the Transport layer has detected a probable network disconnection between the two communicating nodes or when it detects a failure to respond to a request for the establishment of a Transport connection.

Disconnecting or Aborting a Transport Connection

If an application requests the release of a Transport connection, the Session Control layer waits until all previously transmitted messages have been acknowledged and then issues to the Transport layer entity a request for the release of the Transport connection. If an application issues a request for a Transport connection abort, the Session Control layer immediately issues a disconnect request to the Transport layer. In such a case, previously transmitted but unacknowledged data may not be delivered to the remote application. Notification of a Transport layer connection release or abort initiated by the remote Transport layer entity is passed directly to the application along with any data associated with the request for the release or abort of the Transport connection.

We next examine the functions performed by the address resolution component of the Session Control layer.

The Address Resolution Component

The *address resolution* component of the Session Control layer performs three important functions. One function is associated with local objects (objects residing in the same node as the local Session Control layer entity), the second is associated with remote objects (objects residing in other nodes in the network), and the third is associated with performance.

Local Objects

The Session Control layer accesses the services of a naming service clerk to determine information about communication protocols and associated addressing information associated with objects, such as application programs, accessible via the network. An important responsibility of the address resolution component is to periodically update the protocol and addressing information stored in the naming service for local objects. Objects may move from one node to another and addresses may change. It is one responsibility of the address resolution component to ensure that the information stored in the naming service for local objects is up to date.

Remote Objects

A second important function of the address resolution component is to accept the name of the remote object with which a local object is attempting to communicate and to retrieve protocol and addressing information for that object. In doing this, the address resolution component uses the services of the naming service clerk to acquire information about all the communication protocols and associated addressing information through which it may be possible to communicate with the remote object. The address resolution component then attempts to identify communication protocols mutually supported by *both* the local node and the remote node.

Previous versions of Session Control (as in DECnet Phase IV networks) required tables maintained via explicit network management procedures that specified associations between node names and node addresses for those nodes with which local users might need to communicate. The size of the table, and consequently the number of node names known to a particular Session Control entity, was limited by the storage available in the local node. Furthermore, the information in the table was sometimes out of date, thus resulting in messages sometimes being delivered to the wrong destinations. With DNA Phase V, all Session Control layer entities have access to the naming service, which provides access to attribute information for all objects known to the network. By using a global naming service to maintain the association between object names and their addresses, the number of names to which a given node has access is no longer limited by the resources installed in the node itself. Since the address resolution component in each node is responsible for periodically updating the information in the naming service concerning local objects, attribute information stored for remote objects is more likely to be up to date.

Caching

A third function the address resolution component performs is related to performance. Whenever the address resolution component locates protocol and addressing information for a remote object, it stores that information in a local cache for possible later reference. The protocol and addressing information for frequently accessed objects tends to remain in the cache, thus eliminating the need to access the naming service to retrieve attribute information for frequently accessed objects.

The address resolution component performs its functions through the use of data structures called *protocol towers*, or simply *towers*. Towers are a unique feature of DNA Phase V, which we describe next.

Towers

In previous versions of DNA, there was no choice of the protocol that operated at each layer below the application itself, and each node had a single unique Network layer address. With DNA Phase V, a node can support multiple transport protocols (for example, both NSP and OSI transport) and also may have multiple Network layer addresses. For applications to communicate, they must agree on the protocols both will employ and they must agree on a compatible set of operational parameters for those protocols. In addition, two communicating users must have information about the addresses that indicate to each layer where to deliver data. This information is collected in a *tower*. A tower is a data structure, maintained in the naming service, which contains protocol and addressing information for each object that can be located via the network. An object's DNA$Towers attribute contains the object's tower data structure.

A tower consists of a *protocol sequence* along with associated address and protocol-specific information. A protocol sequence is an ordered list of *protocol identifiers*, each of which consists of an octet string naming a particular protocol. Some protocol identifiers are defined by Digital; others can be defined by network managers.

Associated with each protocol identifier in a tower is a component of the address and other protocol-specific information applying to the specified protocol. The address information indicates the access point through which this layer provides service to the next higher layer protocol in the sequence. Other protocol-specific information may be included in this field. Figure 11.3 illustrates the structure of a tower. Typically, a tower will extend from the DNA Application layer to the Network layer. An object often will have multiple towers associated with it.

Establishing Protocol Sequences for Communication

We next walk through a typical use of the address resolution service in which an application program in one node wants to communicate with an application program in another node. The user of the address resolu-

FIGURE 11.3   Tower structure.

Layer *i*+1 Protocol Identifier	Layer *i*+1 parameters and address data that select layer *i*+2 protocol
Layer *i* Protocol Identifier	Layer *i* parameters and address data that select layer *i*+1 protocol
Layer *i*−1 Protocol Identifier	Layer *i*−1 parameters and address data that select layer *i* protocol

tion component—in this case, the address selection component of the Session Control layer—begins by passing to the address resolution component the tower associated with the local application program and the name of the remote application program with which the local program is attempting to communicate. The address resolution component then searches the local cache to see if the tower associated with the remote program is currently available. If it is not, the address resolution component accesses the naming service clerk and retrieves the DNA$Towers attribute associated with the name of the remote program.

After the address resolution component has access to the towers for both the local and the remote programs, it matches up the protocol sequences in the local and remote towers. A pair of protocol sequences are said to match if the protocol identifiers in one member of the pair are identical to, are in the same order as, and map one-to-one with those in the other member. The address resolution component passes to its user the results of this matching operation, which consists of the protocol sequences and associated addressing and protocol-specific information supported by both the local and the remote nodes. This constitutes information about all the protocols through which it may be possible to establish communication between the two application programs.

The algorithm matching up the two towers may result in no common protocol sequences, in which case communication is not possible between the two programs. Alternatively, it may result in a single matching protocol sequence or in multiple matching protocol sequences. Each matching sequence found is returned to the address resolution component user along with the address and other protocol-specific information from both the local and the remote towers. The user of the address resolution component service may then select the specific protocols and addresses to be used in attempting to establish a Transport connection between the local program and the remote program.

As we have already discussed, to improve performance, protocol sequences and address pairs are cached for future use. An application may request that the information cached about a name be discarded and new protocol sequences and address pairs generated. An application program might request this in the event a request for the establishment of a connection fails.

Maintenance of Towers

Because each end node automatically generates its Network layer address when it is attached to the network, the addresses associated with protocols below the Session Control layer may change with time. For example, if a node is disconnected from its router, moved to another part of the network, and plugged into some other router, its network address will automatically be changed as the node is reconfigured into the network. The address resolution component includes a function an application program can request to maintain the protocol and address information stored in the naming service for local objects.

Using information about the higher layers the application program passes to the Session Control layer and information about the lower layers the Session Control layer obtains from the underlying Transport layer entities, the address resolution component uses the naming service to update the information stored in the DNA$Towers attribute for each local object, thus ensuring that the information stored in the tower for each object is up to date.

We next examine the functions performed by the address selection component of the Session Control layer.

The Address Selection Component

The *address selection* component allows a local program to establish a Transport connection with a remote program based only on the name of the remote application program. By using the address selection component, the local user is relieved of the responsibility for knowing the addresses associated with the remote object and about the protocols supported by the remote node. The address selection component accesses the services of the address resolution component to obtain the addresses and protocol sequences associated with a remote object. It also uses the services of the connection control component to establish a Transport connection with the remote application program once protocol and address information has been obtained.

For compatibility with DNA Phase IV, an application program can alternatively request the establishment of a Transport connection by specifying the name of the node on which the remote application program resides and information about higher layer protocols and addresses. For compatibility with existing applications, the address selection component accepts a six-character node alias and converts it to the full DNA Phase V node name. The Session Control layer then uses the services of the address resolution component to locate information about Transport and Network layer protocols and associated addressing information.

Ordering the Protocol Sequences

As we discussed earlier, the address resolution component attempts to find the set of all protocol sequences and associated addressing information mutually supported by both the local and the remote objects. The address selection component uses a system-specific algorithm to place the elements of this set into a specific sequence. It then uses the services of the connection control component to attempt to establish a Transport connection with the remote object using the first protocol sequence in the set. If the address resolution component fails to establish a Transport connection using the first element of the protocol sequence set, it tries again using the second element of the set. It continues to step through the protocol sequence set until one of the following situations occurs:

- A Transport connection is successfully established.
- The reason for the failure indicates that further attempts would be futile.
- The protocol sequence set is exhausted.

End User Interface The end user interface to the DNA Session Control layer is defined in a manner similar to that of the interfaces to the lower layers, in terms of a series of procedure declarations. These procedure declarations are listed in Box 11.1. Many of the calls request specific Session Control services, and others request services of the Transport layer. The Session Control layer passes requests for Transport layer services directly to the Transport layer. Note that the procedure declarations listed in Box 11.1 include no procedures for performing data transfer functions over the underlying Transport connection. As discussed earlier, the interface between end users and the Session Control layer is implementation dependent. The Session Control layer supports end user and Session Control layer buffering techniques and the message, segment, and stream data transfer interfaces in an implementation-dependent manner.

Conclusion The DNA Session Control layer provides users with an important point of entry into a DECnet Phase V network. Of increasing importance in the future will be the higher-layer protocol stack the DNA Phase V architecture provides as an alternative to the DNA Session Control layer: the OSI Application, Presentation, and Session layers. The OSI upper layer architecture defined by DNA Phase V is introduced in Chapter 12.

BOX 11.1

**DNA Session
Control Layer End
User Interface
Procedures**

The following function and procedure declarations define the
abstract interface between the Session Control layer and a user of the
Session Control layer in terms of the services a Session Control layer
entity provides to its users.

Name and Address Conversion Functions

- **NodeNameToInternal.** Passes a naming service external format node
  name to the naming service clerk for conversion to internal format.
  If the name is a node name synonym, the name is first converted to
  the node's full name before passing it to the naming service clerk.

- **NameToAddress.** Maps the name of an object to a set of protocol
  sequences supported by both the local system and the remote system
  on which the named object resides and returns the addresses of the
  service-access-points identifying the sending and receiving entities.

- **KeepMeHere.** Requests the DNA$Towers attribute of a named
  object to be periodically updated on an ongoing basis with current
  protocol and address information.

- **RemoveFromHere.** Halts the updating of the DNA$Towers attribute
  for a named object.

- **EnumerateLocalTowers.** Returns the set of local towers available at
  the end user interface to the Session Control layer.

Transport Connection Functions

- **ConnectAddress.** Requests a Transport connection by specifying
  explicit protocol and address information for both the source and
  the destination nodes.

- **ConnectNodeAddress.** Requests a Transport connection by specifying explicit protocol and address information for the destination
  node.

BOX 11.1

continued

- **ConnectObjectName.** Requests a Transport connection by specifying the name of the remote object and protocol information for the Session Control layer and above.

- **ConnectNodeName.** Requests a Transport connection by specifying the DNA Phase IV node name of the node on which the remote object resides. This function is provided for compatibility with Phase IV of DNA.

Port Control Functions

- **OpenIncoming.** Opens a port into the Session Control layer and waits for a matching incoming request for a connection.

- **IncomingPoll.** Polls a Session Control layer port for incoming data.

- **VerifyNodeName.** Verifies the remote node name for an incoming connect request if this function was deferred.

- **Accept.** Accepts or rejects an incoming request for a connection.

Transport Connection Release Functions

- **DisconnectTransmit.** Requests that a Transport connection be released.

- **DisconnectReceive.** Issued in response to the receipt of a Disconnect-Transmit request to obtain disconnect data.

Port Status Functions

- **PortStatus.** Requests information concerning the services available at the indicated Session Control layer port.

- **TPModuleStatus.** Requests information concerning the services available at the underlying Transport layer port.

CHAPTER 12

OSI Upper-Layer Architecture

The three upper layers of the OSI model provide an alternative means to the DNA Session Control layer that an application program can use to request communication services in a DECnet Phase V network. This chapter describes the functions of the three upper OSI model layers and describes how the DNA Phase V OSI upper-layer architecture implements them.

The four lower layers of the OSI architecture handle the end-to-end transfer of streams of octets—raw data. The lower-layer infrastructure is concerned with the network machines and the communication links connecting them. The Transport layer and the layers beneath it together provide a reliable end-to-end data transfer service that application programs running in end nodes use for communication. In contrast, the services provided by the three upper layers of the OSI model are concerned with the application programs themselves. They define how application programs transfer meaningful information using the services of the underlying communication infrastructure. The intent of the developers of the upper three layers of the OSI model was to provide a rich set of application-oriented services for creating distributed computing applications.

The Application layer provides OSI communication support directly to distributed applications. Unlike the lower layers, many protocols for the Application layer are specific to a particular distributed application, and the functions performed in the Application layer are dependent on that application. The Presentation layer is concerned with the information content of the data units that application programs exchange and with how that information content is encoded for transmission through the network. The Session layer is responsible for organizing the dialog between two application programs and for managing the data exchanges between them.

DNA Phase V
OSUL Architecture
The DNA Phase V specifications for the three OSI upper layers are contained in a single document that describes the OSI upper-layer (OSUL) architecture. The OSUL architecture defines an implementation model for the OSI Application, Presentation, and Session layers. The delineation between the layers is not as clearly defined in the OSUL architecture as it is for the lower four layers in the DNA Phase V architecture.

NETWORK ARCHITECT

In the lower layers, you will find that our implementation tends to be structured very much like the reference model, with appropriate interfaces closely resembling the service interfaces defined in the ISO standards. If you look at the upper layers, it is very difficult to build an efficient, practical implementation that accurately reflects the layering structure. The Application, Presentation, and Session layers turn out to be so closely related that the best thing to do is to have one big state machine for all three layers rather than implementing a separate state machine for each. So, in the upper layers, we feel the layering structure of the OSI model is not quite right; I think you'll find very few people who disagree with that. Nevertheless, it's something we have to live with because we realize it would be impossible at this point to make radical changes to the OSI model.

We now begin an examination of the three layers that make up the OSUL architecture in DNA Phase V, continuing to work from the bottom up.

The Session Layer
The Session layer provides services to structure the interaction between two application programs. The standards for the Session layer define two types of dialogs: two-way, simultaneous interaction, where both programs can send and receive concurrently, and two-way, alternate interaction, where the programs take turns sending and receiving. In addition to organizing the dialog, Session layer services include the establishment of synchronization points within the dialog, which allows a dialog to be interrupted and to be resumed from a synchronization point.

There is some controversy in the OSI community surrounding the services the Session layer provides.

NETWORK ARCHITECT

The way the standards for the Session layer were created worked something like this. Say I call you in and say I'd like you to build me a workshop. And you say, sure, what are some things you want to do? And I say, how about metalworking; that would be really interesting. But then electronics would be interesting as well, and so would woodworking. In the end, I give you a blank check, and a year later you come back and say here's your workshop.

I start out by going into it and try to make a table. I find this pile of wood, go to the lathe, and start building. But I find that I need a chisel, and there aren't any chisels. Then I decide to build a radio instead. I go to the electronics bench and start to build the radio but immediately discover that everything is there that I need, except for a soldering iron.

This is what the Session layer is like. There are lots of useful, general mechanisms. But when you actually begin to use them, you sometimes find they don't do quite what you need them to do. Or, because of the Session layer's position in the layering structure, it really doesn't work the way you want it to work. What is essentially happening now is that we are working hard on the standards for the Application layer, and we are finding that most of the new protocols being developed simply don't use many of the features originally designed into the Session layer. If we were to start over again, we would probably not have a separate Session layer. Instead, we might define the Session synchronization services in a separate Application layer standard.

Services and Protocols

As with the other OSI model layers, ISO standards for the Session layer include both a service definition and a protocol specification. The relationship between the services the Session layer provides and the protocol governing its operation is shown in Figure 12.1. The Session layer protocol uses the services of the Transport layer to provide a defined set of services to a user of the Session layer service. Note, however, that even though the Presentation layer is above the Session layer in the OSI model, the actual user of Session layer services is an entity in the Application layer. Each service the Session layer provides is mapped to a corresponding service of the Presentation layer. The Presentation layer then adds value to some of these Session layer services and provides additional services of its own to an Application layer entity.

FIGURE 12.1   The relationship between the Session layer service definition and the Session layer protocol
specification.

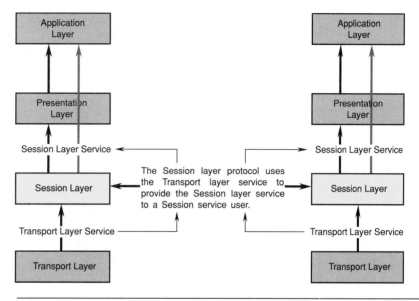

Session Layer Service Definition

The service definition for the Session layer is documented in ISO 8326, *Session Service Definition*. The functions provided by the Session layer are divided into a number of *functional units*. The functional units employed by a pair of users of the Session layer service are negotiated when the Session connection is established. Many of the services defined in functional units for the Session layer require the entity requesting the service to own a *token*, which grants that entity the right to request that service. Some of the services defined for the Session layer consist of requesting a particular token from the partner entity and passing a token to the partner upon request. Box 12.1 lists the services provided by all Session layer functional units.

The following are brief descriptions of the functional units included in the Session layer, all of which are supported by the OSUL architecture:

- **Kernel.** The kernel functional unit allows the use of basic session services that must be provided by any implementation of the Session layer.

- **Negotiated Release.** This functional unit allows the use of services that restrict the release of the Session connection to the partner who owns the Release token. Also, it allows a partner Session layer entity to reject a re-

BOX 12.1

Session Layer
Services

Kernel Functional Unit

- **Session Connection Establishment.** Requests the establishment of a Session connection.
- **Normal Data Transfer.** Transfers data over a Session connection.
- **Session Connection Release.** Requests the orderly release of a Session connection.
- **User Abort of a Session Connection.** Issued by a Session service user to request the immediate release of a Session connection.
- **Provider Abort of a Session Connection.** Issued by a Session layer entity to request the immediate release of a Session connection.

Negotiated Release Functional Unit

- **Requesting an Orderly Negotiated Release.** Requests a negotiated release of a Session connection in which the partner can either accept or reject the request. This service can be issued only by the partner who currently owns the Release token.
- **Requesting the Release Token.** Requests the Release token from the partner who currently owns it.
- **Passing the Release Token.** Passes the Release token to the other partner.

Half-Duplex Functional Unit

- **Requesting the Data Token.** Requests the Data token from the partner who currently owns it.
- **Passing the Data Token.** Passes the Data token to the other partner.

Activity Management Functional Unit

- **Starting an Activity.** The partner issuing this service must own the Major/Activity token. If the functional units concerning the Data token or the Synchronize-minor tokens are in effect, the partner must own these tokens as well.
- **Ending an Activity.** The partner issuing this service must own the Major/Activity token. If the functional units concerning the Data token or the Synchronize-minor tokens are in effect, the partner must own these tokens as well.
- **Interrupting an Activity.** The partner interrupting the activity may resume it later. The partner issuing this service must own the Major/Activity token.
- **Resuming an Interrupted Activity.** The partner issuing this service

BOX 12.1

continued

must own the Major/Activity token. If the functional units concerning the Data token or the Synchronize-minor tokens are in effect, the partner must own these tokens as well.

- **Discarding an Activity.** The partner issuing this service might discard an activity for any of a number of defined reasons. To discard an activity, the partner must own the Major/Activity token.

- **Requesting the Major/Activity Token.** Requests the Major/Activity token from the partner who currently owns it.

- **Passing the Major/Activity Token.** Passes the Major/Activity token to the other partner.

- **Passing Control to the Other Partner.** This service might be issued by a partner who currently owns all tokens and wishes to pass ownership of them to the other partner. This service could be performed by using the services of passing tokens to the other partner and is included in the Session service for compatibility with an older Session protocol.

Minor Synchronize Functional Unit

- **Establishing a Minor Synchronization Point.** This service can be issued only by the partner entity currently owning the Synchronize-minor token.

- **Requesting the Synchronize-Minor Token.** Requests the Synchronize-minor token from the partner who currently owns it.

- **Passing the Synchronize-Minor Token.** Passes the Synchronize-minor token to the other partner.

Major Synchronize Functional Unit

- **Establishing a Major Synchronization Point.** This service can be issued only by the partner entity currently owning the Major/Activity token.

- **Requesting the Synchronize-Major Token.** Requests the Synchronize-major token from the partner who currently owns it.

- **Passing the Synchronize-Major Token.** Passes the Synchronize-major token to the other partner.

Exception Reporting Functional Unit

- **User Exception Reporting.** Reporting of exceptional conditions by a Session layer user.

- **Provider Exception Reporting.** Reporting of exceptional conditions by a Session layer entity.

quest for the release of a Session connection, in which case the Session connection remains established.

- **Half-Duplex.** This functional unit allows two-way alternate interactions to take place over the Session connection. When the Half-duplex functional unit is chosen, data can be sent over the Session connection only by the partner currently in possession of the Data token. The services defined for the Half-duplex functional unit are concerned with requesting and passing the Data token. Both the Half-duplex and Duplex functional units cannot be in effect for the same Session connection.

- **Duplex.** This functional unit allows two-way simultaneous interactions to take place over the Session connection. When the Duplex functional unit is in effect, data can be sent over the Session connection by either partner at any time, and possession of the Data token is not required. Both the Half-duplex and Duplex functional units cannot be in effect for the same Session connection.

- **Expedited Data.** This functional unit allows the use of a single expedited data transfer service allowing a single short data unit to be sent over the Session connection. The expedited data transfer service allows blockages in the data transport service to be bypassed.

- **Typed Data.** This functional unit allows the use of a single typed data transfer service allowing data to be exchanged outside the normal flow of data over the Session connection. When the half-duplex functional unit is in effect, an entity can send data using the typed data transfer service even though it does not currently own the Data token.

- **Activity Management.** This functional unit allows the use of application exchanges in which an *activity* is divided into a number of restartable *dialogs*, each of which can be divided into smaller restartable units using one or more *checkpoints*.

- **Minor Synchronize.** This functional unit allows use of the dialog control services defined in the Session layer. Dialog control services consist of two types of synchronization points in the data stream flowing between two users of the Session layer service. A minor synchronization point marks a checkpoint within a dialog, and a major synchronization point separates individual dialogs from one another. The Minor Synchronize functional unit consists of services for establishing checkpoints within a dialog.

- **Major Synchronize.** This functional unit allows a dialog to be ended by establishing a major synchronization point. The Major Synchronize functional unit consists of services for establishing a major synchronization point.

- **Resynchronize.** This functional unit allows the use of a single resynchronize service requesting a dialog to be reset to a synchronization point.
- **Capability Data Exchange.** This functional unit can be chosen only when the Activity Management functional unit has also been chosen. It allows the use of a single capability data exchange service for transferring data concerning the capabilities of application programs.
- **Exceptions.** This functional unit allows the use of services for reporting exceptional conditions.

Amendments to the ISO Session Layer Service Definition

As of the time of this writing, ISO has published three amendments to ISO 8326, *Basic Connection Oriented Session Service Definition*:

- **Amendment 1, *Session Symmetric Synchronization for the Session Service*.** This amendment defines an optional Session Symmetric Synchronization functional unit, which allows two full-duplex users of the Session service to independently identify minor synchronization points on their sending data flows. It also allows users to resynchronize on one or both directions of flow. As of the time of this writing, the OSUL architecture does not support session symmetric synchronization since there currently are no OSI applications that require this functional unit.

- **Amendment 2, *Unlimited User Data*.** In ISO 8326, some session services limit user data to 512 octets, while others do not specify a user data parameter. This amendment defines a new version of the Session protocol that allows the use of an arbitrarily large user data parameter with all Session layer services. The OSUL architecture supports unlimited user data.

- **Amendment 3, *Connectionless Mode Transmission*.** ISO 8326 defines a connection-mode Session layer service. This amendment defines a connectionless-mode Session layer service. Support for this amendment is not included in the OSUL architecture. As of the time of this writing, the DNA Phase V architecture supports only connection-mode services in the Transport layer and above.

Session Layer Protocol Specification

The protocol specification for the Session layer is documented in ISO 8327, *Session Protocol Specification*. The protocol mechanisms to supply the optional services defined in the amendments to 8326 are described in the amendments to ISO 8327. Because of the many different types of services the Session layer provides, the protocol controlling its operation is relatively complex. However, the Session protocol accesses the underlying Transport layer services in a straightforward manner. Each Session layer service primitive causes one or more session-protocol-data-units (SPDUs) to be generated. The Session layer uses a Transport connection to carry these SPDUs over the network. The ISO standards for the Session layer define three possible mappings between Session connections and Transport connections:

- **One-to-One.** With a one-to-one mapping, a Session connection causes a Transport connection to be established. The Transport connection is then released when the Session connection is released.

- **One-to-Many.** With a one-to-many mapping, a single Session connection employs several Transport connections, one after the other. This capability is useful if Session layer entities wish to be able to recover from the release of Transport connections, possibly due to network failures.

- **Many-to-One.** With a many-to-one mapping, a single Transport connection is reused and supports two or more Session connections, one after the other. The OSUL architecture does not support this form of mapping and does not permit a Transport connection to be reused.

The Session protocol supports segmentation and concatenation functions. To allow the use of unlimited user data parameters, a single session-service-data-unit (SSDU) can be segmented into multiple SPDUs, each of which is carried over the network in a separate transport-protocol-data-unit (TPDU).

Multiple SPDUs can also be concatenated and carried in a single TPDU to reduce the number of network interactions required to support the Session protocol. For example, a Give Token SPDU can be concatenated with a Data Transfer SPDU, both of which can be carried together in a single TPDU. ISO 8326, *Session Protocol Specification*, specifies the types of SPDU that can be combined and defines both a basic and an extended form of concatenation. Basic concatenation is more restrictive than extended concatenation as to the types of SPDUs that can be combined in the same TPDU. The OSUL architecture supports basic concatenation but not extended concatenation.

NETWORK ARCHITECT

We felt that supporting extended concatenation would complicate buffer handling and increase processing overhead while not significantly reducing network traffic.

We next examine the services the Presentation layer provides to an Application layer entity.

The Presentation Layer	In the OSI environment, an application program sends data to another application program in a distributed system by using a data transfer service provided by the Presentation layer. The Presentation layer also provides services for negotiating the way in which data elements are to be encoded for transmission through the network and services that allow its users to access the services provided by the underlying Session layer.

The unit of data the user of the Presentation layer service passes down to a Presentation layer entity is the *presentation-service-data-unit* (PSDU). A PSDU can contain one or more *presentation-data-values* (PDVs). A PDV can be a complex data structure, and in many cases a PSDU will consist of a single PDV. A PDV typically consists of an application-protocol-data-unit (APDU) or a part of an APDU. An Application layer protocol defines the information content of the PDVs that the two communicating programs exchange with each other and the procedures governing the exchange of those PDVs. Consider a distributed personnel application: one of the PDVs exchanged by the programs in such a system might be a particular type of record containing elements of information about an employee.

To the layers below the Presentation layer, the data units exchanged consist simply of strings of octets. The lower layers are concerned with ensuring that the string of octets received by a receiving entity is identical to the string of octets transmitted. The Presentation layer, on the other hand, is concerned with preserving the information content of the data contained in the PDVs exchanged by application programs. The aim of the OSI architecture is to allow information systems to be interconnected with a minimum of agreement outside the ISO standards for the OSI model themselves.

One of the functions of the Presentation layer is to allow users of the Presentation layer service to unambiguously exchange PDVs with each other without requiring one open system to have knowledge of the form of data representation used by the other open system. A program running in open system A should be able to transmit numeric information over the network to a program running in open system B without having to know how open system B represents numeric values. To this end, the definition of a presentation-data-value is concerned only with the information content of the PDV and not with the way the information it contains is represented in a computer or the way in which it is encoded for transmission over the network.

As with the other OSI model layers, ISO standards for the Presentation layer include both a service definition and a protocol specification. The relationship between the services the Presentation layer provides and the protocol governing its operation is shown in Figure 12.2. The Presentation layer protocol uses the services of the Session layer to provide a defined set of services to a user of the Presentation service.

Data Syntax

The Presentation layer is concerned with three data syntax types that can be used to describe and represent data (see Figure 12.3):

- **Abstract Syntax.** An *abstract syntax* formally defines the information content of all the PDVs sent during the operation of a particular Application layer protocol. An abstract syntax is concerned with information content only and not with how that information content is represented in a computer or how it is encoded for transmission. For example, an abstract syntax might define a data type called CheckingBalance, values of which consist of integers. It does not specify whether a value of the CheckingBalance data type is represented by decimal digits, binary numbers, or any other form.

- **Local Concrete Syntax.** A *local concrete syntax* defines how a particular PDV is represented in a computing system. The local concrete syntax used

---

FIGURE 12.2   **The relationship between the Presentation layer service definition and the Presentation layer protocol specification.**

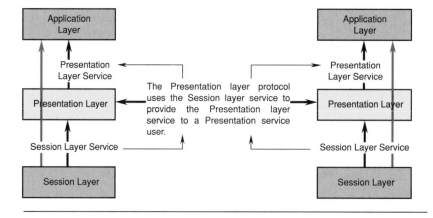

FIGURE 12.3   **Converting from system A's local concrete syntax to transfer syntax and from transfer syntax to system B's local concrete syntax.**

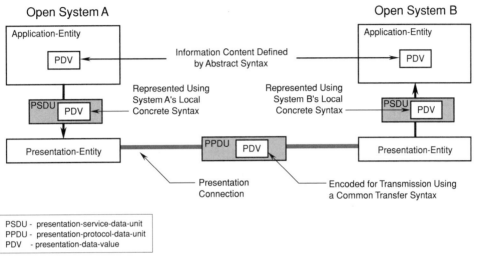

PSDU - presentation-service-data-unit
PPDU - presentation-protocol-data-unit
PDV - presentation-data-value

in the sending open system might be different from the local concrete syntax used in the receiving open system. For example, one system might represent a value of the CheckingBalance type as a 32-bit binary number using 2's complement notation; another system might represent a CheckingBalance value as a string of decimal digits, where each decimal digit is represented by a 4-bit binary number (packed-decimal notation).

- **Transfer Syntax.** A *transfer syntax* defines how a particular PDV is encoded for transmission over the network. For example, a value of the CheckingBalance type might be transferred over the network using some encoding scheme that identifies a particular value as being of the CheckingBalance type, specifies that it consists of an integer, and encodes that integer's value using a minimum number of bits. The two Presentation layer entities must agree on a particular transfer syntax to be used to transfer the PDVs defined by each abstract syntax employed by the two users of the Presentation layer service.

Abstract Syntax   A set of definitions of the information content of all the PDVs that can be exchanged during the operation of an Application layer protocol is called an *abstract syntax*. Each abstract syntax is assigned a name known to the two users of the Presentation layer service. For two Presentation layer users to communicate successfully, they must agree on the names of one or more abstract syntaxes they intend to use. As the communication proceeds, the two Presentation layer service users can modify their agreement by adding the names of new abstract syntax definitions to the set of abstract syntaxes they intend to use, or they can delete the names of abstract syntax definitions from this set. In other words, they can change the set of PDVs they intend to exchange as communication proceeds.

Consider our hypothetical distributed personnel system. An abstract syntax would consist of formal definitions of the information content of the records exchanged between a pair of programs supporting the distributed personnel system.

Abstract Syntax Notation   An abstract syntax is defined with an abstract syntax notation. An *abstract syntax notation* provides a means for defining data types without specifying how values of those data types will actually be represented internally in a computer or how they will be encoded for transmission through the network.

Standards for the various layers of the OSI model do not require the use of any particular abstract syntax notation for describing data structures. In fact, ISO standards are specifically designed for great generality and allow an abstract syntax to be specified in any desired manner. However, there is an ISO standard that defines an abstract syntax notation commonly used in the OSI environment for defining abstract syntaxes: ISO 8824, *Abstract Syntax Notation One* (ASN.1).

Abstract Syntax Notation One (ASN.1)

ASN.1 is supported by the OSUL architecture for defining abstract syntaxes. ASN.1 can be used for two related purposes: to define data types and to express values of those data types.

ASN.1 Data Type Assignments   One use of ASN.1 is as a standard notation for describing the information content of the PDVs that two users of the Presentation layer service exchange with each other. ASN.1 defines a number of primitive data types that can be used to construct more complex data structures. Examples of primitive types defined by ASN.1 follow:

INTEGER	an integer of arbitrary length
BOOLEAN	a data type containing a TRUE or FALSE value
BIT STRING	a list of 0 or more binary digits
OCTET STRING	a list of 0 or more 8-bit octets
SEQUENCE	an ordered list of other data types
SET	an unordered list of other data types

ASN.1 also includes a number of additional predefined types. For example, ASN.1 includes definitions of a number of data types that can contain characters from particular character sets. For example, the PrintableString type can contain characters that include the upper- and lower-case letters, the 10 digits, space, and the 11 special characters ()'+-.,/:=?.

An example of a data type used to represent a simple employee record expressed in ASN.1 data type notation follows:

```
Employee ::= SEQUENCE
    {
    name       PrintableString,
    empNumber  INTEGER,
    salary     INTEGER,
    hireYear   INTEGER
    }
```

The above ASN.1 code defines the *Employee* data type as an ordered list made up of a PrintableString data type called *name* followed by three integer data types called *empNumber*, *salary*, and *hireYear*. ASN.1 also allows default values to be assigned to values in a SET or SEQUENCE data type. A data value equal to the default value does not have to be transmitted.

Tags Each data type defined as part of ASN.1 (INTEGER, PrintableString, etc.) has an identifying *tag* associated with it consisting of a number. Tags can also be explicitly assigned to defined types to differentiate them from one another. We will see how the tags are used to distinguish one data type from another when we examine how a value of an ASN.1 data type is encoded. ASN.1 defines four different classes of tags:

- **UNIVERSAL.** UNIVERSAL tags are those assigned to the simple data types defined in the ASN.1 specification.

- **APPLICATION.** APPLICATION tags are meant to be assigned to data types defined in international standards and have universal meaning within a particular ASN.1 module.

- **PRIVATE.** PRIVATE tags are assigned to data types defined by an individual enterprise and have universal meaning within that enterprise. Digital does not recommend the use of PRIVATE tags, since they must have universal meaning among all the abstract syntaxes defined by a given enterprise.

- **Context Specific.** Context Specific tags are used to provide identification for the data types within some other data type. Digital recommends the use of Context Specific tags wherever possible to distinguish one data type from another within a data structure.

The ASN.1 specification defines the tags associated with the UNI-VERSAL data types. For example, all SEQUENCE data types have a tag of 16, PrintableString data types have a tag of 19, and INTEGER data types have a tag of 2. In the Employee data type defined above, tags are assigned as follows:

Employee	tag 16
name	tag 19
empNumber	tag 2
salary	tag 2
hireYear	tag 2

When a value of a particular type is encoded for transmission, the value's class and tag value are encoded along with it. In this manner, a Presentation layer entity receiving an encoded value can determine its type by examining its tag.

Tags can also be explicitly assigned to the data types in an ASN.1 data type definition to distinguish one data type from another. For example, suppose we change our Employee example to the following:

```
Employee ::= SET
    {
    name       PrintableString,
    empNumber  INTEGER,
    salary     INTEGER,
    hireYear   INTEGER
    }
```

By defining Employee as a SET data type, it would be possible for the four data types that make up the set to be arranged in any sequence. With the above definition it would be possible to distinguish a name value from values of any of the three integer types because the name data type is the only one in the set having a PrintableString tag. But it would not be possible to distinguish an empNumber value, say, from a salary value. We can solve this problem by assigning a different Context Specific tag to each of the three integer data types, as in the following example:

```
Employee ::= SET
    {
    name        PrintableString,
```

```
empNumber  [0]  INTEGER,
salary     [1]  INTEGER,
hireYear   [2]  INTEGER
}
```

When values of any of the three integer types are now encoded, the value's Context Specific tag accompanies it, thus distinguishing each of the three integer types from the others. An *empNumber* value would have the Context Specific tag 0 included with it, a *salary* value would have the tag 1 included with it, and a *hireYear* value would have the tag 2 included with it.

With the above ASN.1 definition, *empNumber, salary,* and *hireYear* values would also include a UNIVERSAL tag of 2 to indicate that they are integer data types. When Context Specific tags are defined for a data type, it is often not necessary for the UNIVERSAL tag to be carried with encodings of those data types. This is because when the receiver sees a value of a data type including a Context Specific tag, the Context specific tag is all the receiver requires to determine the value's type. For example, if the Context Specific tag identifies a value as a *salary* value, the receiver implicitly knows from the ASN.1 abstract syntax definition that the *salary* value is an integer, and so the UNIVERSAL tag of 2 is redundant. The ASN.1 definition can specify that the UNIVERSAL tag be omitted from the encoding by including the IMPLICIT keyword. In the following example, the IMPLICIT keyword indicates that values of the *empNumber, salary,* and *hireYear* types are implicitly of the integer type, as in the following example:

```
Employee ::= SET
   {
   name       PrintableString,
   empNumber  [0]  IMPLICIT INTEGER,
   salary     [1]  IMPLICIT INTEGER,
   hireYear   [2]  IMPLICIT INTEGER
   }
```

With the above abstract syntax definition, only the Context Specific tags and not the UNIVERSAL tags are included in encodings of *empNumber, salary,* and *hireYear* values.

ASN.1 Data Value Assignments Another way in which ASN.1 can be used is to express, in a human-readable manner, the value of a particular instance of a data type. A particular value of the *Employee* data type might be specified in ASN.1 value notation as:

```
jamesMartin employee ::=
   {
    "James Martin",
    123456,
    72000,
    1972
   }
```

We next discuss ways in which PDVs defined by an abstract syntax are represented in a real open system and how they are encoded for transmission.

Local Concrete Syntax

As we have stated previously, definitions of the PDVs that users of the Presentation layer service exchange constitute an abstract syntax specifying information content only. The way in which the information content of a PDV value is actually stored in a computer is called a *local concrete syntax*. The sending open system may use a local concrete syntax different from the local concrete syntax used by the receiving open system to represent a particular PDV value.

The following are just a few ways in which local concrete syntaxes can be different:

- The sending system might represent a PrintableString data type using the EBCDIC character code; the receiving system might use ASCII.

- The sending system might represent an INTEGER data type using a packed-decimal format in which each decimal digit is contained in a semi-octet with the final semi-octet representing the integer's sign; the receiving system might represent an INTEGER data type as a binary value stored in a 32-bit word.

- The sending system might represent an INTEGER data type using 1's complement notation; the receiving system might represent an INTEGER data type using 2's complement notation.

- The sending system might represent a floating-point value using one format; the receiving system might use another.

In addition to the above differences, which ordinarily can be handled using straightforward conversions, two users of the Presentation layer service might exchange PDVs that contain complex data structures consisting of values of many different data types, some of which may be optional in the data structure. The question then becomes one of how the Presentation layer entity in the receiving system parses the data structures contained in a PDV to determine the meaning of each data value contained in it.

Transfer Syntax

The information content of a PDV must be sent over the network in a way that preserves that information content. To do this, some method must be used for encoding the information content defined by a PDV into a string of octets that can be sent over the network. The receiving open system must then be able to decode the octet string it receives to completely recreate the information content of the original PDV. The set of rules used to encode and decode the information content of a PDV for transmission results in a *transfer syntax*. Each transfer syntax is given a name known to the two Presentation layer entities and to the two users of the Presentation layer service.

To set up a Presentation connection, two users of the Presentation layer service must agree on the set of abstract syntaxes they intend to use during communication, and they must inform their associated Presentation layer entities of the names of those abstract syntaxes. The job of the Presentation layer in establishing a Presentation connection is to negotiate a common transfer syntax for each abstract syntax the two communicating users of the Presentation layer service intend to use. The standards for the Presentation layer do not specify any particular transfer syntax that must be used. In fact, a Presentation layer entity might be able to use any number of transfer syntaxes to transfer PDVs defined by a given abstract syntax. The two peer Presentation layer entities must agree on the one common transfer syntax they intend to use to transfer PDVs defined using each abstract syntax.

ISO 8825, *Specification of Basic Encoding Rules for ASN.1*, defines a set of rules for encoding and decoding values of data types defined using ASN.1 notation. If a particular abstract syntax definition is expressed in ASN.1 notation, then application of the basic encoding rules (BER) produces a transfer syntax for a PDV defined by that abstract syntax definition. In practice in the OSI environment, the basic encoding rules are typically used to produce transfer syntaxes.

The basic encoding rules use a type/length/value (TLV) form of encoding. An *empNumber* value of 123456 from our hypothetical personnel record would be encoded using 5 octets, as shown in Figure 12.4. The

FIGURE 12.4   Basic encoding rules transfer syntax encoding of an *empNumber* value of 123456 in binary and hexadecimal.

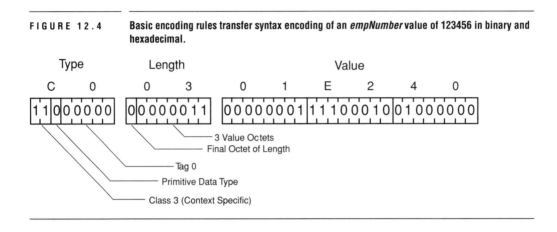

first octet defines the value's type. The first two bits contain the binary value 11 (decimal 3), which indicates that the value is of a Context Specific data type; the 0 in the next bit indicates that the value is a primitive data type and is not made up of other data types; and the final five bits contain a tag value of binary 00000 (decimal 0) indicating the data type's tag is 0, indicating an *empNumber* value. The second octet contains the number of octets used to contain the value, in this case, 00000010 (decimal 3). The first bit position is used to indicate the final octet of the length field, thus allowing for an unlimited length value. A 0 in the first position of the length field indicates that no more length octets follow. A value is encoded using the minimum number of octets required to encode that value, in this case, 3. The third, fourth, and fifth octets contain the decimal value 123456 in binary using 2's complement notation.

Presentation Contexts

The association of the name of an abstract syntax with the name of a particular transfer syntax is called a *presentation context*. Each presentation context is given a name known to the two users of the Presentation layer service. The set of the names of all the presentation contexts, and thus all the abstract syntaxes, that can be used over a Presentation connection is called the *defined context set* (DCS). Presentation layer services are defined for modifying the defined context set by adding presentation context names to it and deleting them from it. There is also a *default context*, which names a presentation context to use when the defined context set is empty.

Transformation to and from Transfer Syntax

The OSI model specifies that a function of the Presentation layer is to transform each PDV being sent from the local concrete syntax to the transfer syntax and to transform each PDV received from the transfer syntax to the local concrete syntax. However, these conversions are purely internal functions of the Presentation layer entity and have no effect on the operation of the Presentation layer protocol. The Presentation layer conversion function can, therefore, be implemented in any desired way.

In some cases, no conversion is even necessary. For example, if two users of the Presentation layer service are running in similar computing systems using the same local concrete syntax, the transfer syntax might specify that the data units be exchanged as is, without any conversion to a different transfer syntax. In such a case, the Presentation layer would perform a null function in converting from local concrete syntax to transfer syntax in the sending system and from transfer syntax to local concrete syntax in the receiving system.

Where conversion is required to and from the transfer syntax, the place in the layering structure where the conversion is performed can vary. When a Presentation connection is established, transfer syntaxes are negotiated and the two users of the Presentation layer service are given information about the defined context set. The defined context set provides each user with information about the transfer syntax to be used for each abstract syntax identified in the defined context set. Therefore, in a particular implementation of the OSI upper layers, the *user* of the Presentation layer service (in the Application layer) can be given the responsibility for encoding each PDV sent and for decoding each PDV received. Since the encoding and decoding of PDVs is an internal function that has no effect on the Presentation layer protocol, it does not really matter where the conversion is performed. This, in fact, is how the DNA Phase V OSUL architecture implements the conversion function to and from transfer syntax. The user of the Presentation layer service is responsible for encoding and decoding PDVs sent and received. The Presentation layer is responsible for encoding and decoding only its own protocol-control-information (PCI) and not user data.

NETWORK ARCHITECT

Standards for the OSI model define only abstract services and a protocol specification for each layer. It is important to realize that the OSI model is not necessarily an implementation model. Since the actual conversion process itself doesn't have any effect on the Presentation protocol, it doesn't really matter, from the viewpoint of conformance to the standards and whether two implementations will interoperate, where the conversion is performed. There are two primary reasons for making the conversion the responsibility of the application itself rather than the Presentation layer—efficiency and simplicity. It turns out that there is a real performance advantage to having the encoding and the decoding done by the application program rather than by the Presentation layer. This way, the encoding and decoding can be done directly between the application memory and the message buffers, which is the way we have chosen to do it. By making the conversion the responsibility of the application, the conversion routines can also be more efficient than a general-purpose set of conversion routines. For example, some values can be preencoded at compile time, saving the encode/decode overhead. Requiring the application to handle the conversion is also a much more simple approach to the conversion. The OSUL interface treats the user data as a stream of octets held in a sequence of buffers. With this approach, there is no need for a complicated and general interface to return user data in local concrete syntax.

Making the user of the Presentation layer service responsible for the encoding and decoding of PDVs seems at first glance to appear as if something has been left out of the Presentation layer. However, this is just one of those cases where the DNA Phase V architects have achieved performance advantages by interpreting and implementing the standards in a way that might not be immediately obvious.

Presentation Layer Service Definition

The service definition for the Presentation layer is documented in ISO 8822, *Presentation Service Definition*. Like the Session layer, the Presentation layer service definition divides services into functional units. The functional units themselves are grouped into two collections: *Session* functional units and *Presentation* functional units. Box 12.2 lists the services provided by the Presentation functional units in DNA Phase V.

Session Functional Units   The Session functional units define the services that the Presentation layer maps to services actually provided by the underlying Session layer (we described these earlier in this chapter). Each functional unit defined for the Session layer has a corresponding functional unit in the Presentation layer. The Session services that the Presentation layer can make available to a Presentation layer service user depend on which functional units are supported by the underlying Session layer.

Kernel Functional Unit

- **Connection Establishment.** Establishes a Presentation connection.
- **Normal Data Transfer.** Transfers data over a Presentation connection.
- **Connection Release.** Requests the orderly release of a Presentation connection.
- **User Connection Abort.** Issued by a Presentation service user to request the immediate release of a Presentation connection.
- **Provider Connection Abort.** Issued by a Presentation layer entity to request the immediate release of a Presentation connection.

Context Management Functional Unit

- **Alter Context.** Adds or deletes the name of a presentation context in the defined context set.

Presentation Functional Units   The service definition for the Presentation layer defines three Presentation functional units:

- **Kernel.** If the use of the kernel functional unit is chosen during Presentation connection establishment, only the default presentation context and those presentation contexts in the defined context set negotiated when the Presentation connection was established can be used during the life of the Presentation connection. This means the Presentation layer must have knowledge, at the time the connection is established, of all the PDVs that will be exchanged during the life of the Presentation connection. The contents of the defined context set cannot be modified during the life of the Presentation connection if only the kernel functional unit is chosen.

- **Context Management.** If the context management functional unit is chosen, the two entities are able to modify the defined context set during the life of the Presentation connection. Support for this functional unit means that users of the Presentation layer service can inform the Presentation layer of additional abstract syntaxes used to define the PDVs exchanged over the Presentation connection while the connection is in operation. When an abstract syntax is added, the two Presentation entities negotiate a common transfer syntax for that abstract syntax to add a new presentation context to the defined context set.

- **Context Restoration.** If the context restoration functional unit is chosen, the state of the defined context set can be restored after a resynchronization occurs in the Session layer. The DNA Phase V OSUL architecture does not support the context restoration functional unit.

NETWORK ARCHITECT

We feel that there are serious defects in the definition of context restoration in the existing ISO standards for the Presentation layer, making them unimplementable. In any case, context restoration is not needed by applications and imposes unnecessary overhead. With activities that are interrupted but not terminated, it is necessary to remember the defined context set for an arbitrary long time in case the activity is ever resumed.

Presentation Layer Protocol Specification

The protocol specification for the Presentation layer is documented in ISO 8823, *Presentation Protocol Specification*. Some of the mechanisms in the Presentation layer protocol are concerned with negotiating transfer syntaxes during connection establishment and for maintaining the defined context set. Other mechanisms consist of a straightforward mapping to the services provided by the Session layer. These services map directly to an analogous service provided by the Session layer, with the exception of resynchronize. The Presentation protocol allows the defined context set to be modified when resynchronizing and hence defines specific presentation-protocol-data-units (PPDUs) for this service. Each service primitive requesting a Presentation layer service results in the generation of a specific PPDU that is passed down to the Session layer in the form of a session-service-data-unit (SSDU).

The Application Layer

The structure of the Application layer is quite complex, and a number of terms must be introduced to explain its organization. Thus far, we have been describing communication in the OSI environment as that taking place between *application programs* running in end systems. The ISO 7498 definition of the OSI model is more abstract than this and describes communication between open systems in terms of interactions taking place between *application-processes* operating in open systems.

Application-Processes

An *application-process* represents a set of resources, including processing resources, within an open system that can be used to perform information processing activities. An *invocation* of an application-process is a particular use of the resources defined by an application-process to perform a particular information processing activity. An application-process is identified by an *application-process-title*. An application-process-title must be unambiguous throughout the OSI environment, giving each application-process a globally unique name.

It is helpful to think of an application-process as an application program and an application-process-invocation as one execution of that application program. The purpose of the OSI model is to allow an application-process-invocation in one open system to exchange information with an application-process-invocation running in another open system (see Figure 12.5).

During the time since the OSI model was first defined in ISO 7498, additional work has been done on the Application layer, and this work is documented in another international standard, ISO 9545, *Application Layer Structure*. This international standard defines the following:

- the nature of the standards for the Application layer and the relationship among those standards

- the architectural framework in which individual standard protocols for the Application layer are developed

- categories of identifiable Application layer elements necessary for the specification and operation of Application layer protocols

- how distributed information processing activities are related to Application layer standards

Distributed applications are constructed of multiple application-processes all cooperating to perform information processing activities. Cooperation between pairs of application-processes takes place via rela-

---

FIGURE 12.5   **Communication between application processes running in open systems.**

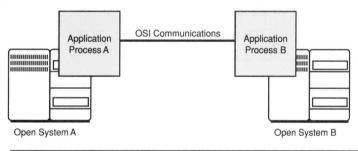

tionships established among invocations of those application-processes. Each invocation of an application-process is responsible for coordinating its interactions with other application-process-invocations.

Application-Entities

Application-processes normally represent resources associated with OSI communication and also resources not associated with communication. Therefore, part of an application-process can be viewed as residing in the OSI Application layer, and part of it is outside the scope of the OSI architecture, as shown in Figure 12.6. The OSI model defines the term *application-entity* (AE) to represent the part of an application-process that provides resources for OSI communication. Each application-entity describes a set of Application layer capabilities used for a specific purpose. Those parts of the application-process not associated with OSI communication may call on one or more application-entities in the application-process for the purposes of communication. Like application-processes, application-entities have names, called application-entity-titles, that must be unambiguous in the OSI environment. An application-entity-title is made up of its associated application-process-title plus an application-entity-qualifier.

FIGURE 12.6   **Relationship between application processes and the OSI model.**

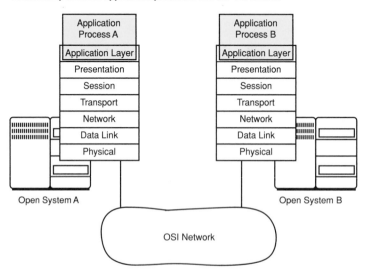

An application-process can include one or more application-entities, each representing a different set of resources used for OSI communication. An application-entity provides a particular component of a distributed application with access to the OSI communication facilities it needs to communicate with another component of the distributed application.

This notion of different types of application-entities is a distinguishing feature between the Application layer and the other layers of the OSI model. In the lower layers, each layer can be viewed as implementing a single entity type. For example, the functions performed by the Presentation layer can be viewed as being performed by a single presentation-entity type (see Figure 12.7). Similarly, a single entity type is defined for all the other OSI model layers.

Application-Service-Elements   An application-entity can be further broken down into a collection of *application-service-elements* (ASEs), each of which provides a set of OSI communication functions for a particular purpose (see Figure 12.8). There are a number of international standard ASEs, each of which is defined by a service definition and a protocol specification. An ASE's service definition describes the abstract services the ASE provides to its users; an ASE's protocol specification describes the formats of the application-protocol-data-units (APDUs) used by the ASE and specifies the rules by which these APDUs are exchanged.

An ASE defines a particular set of functions associated with OSI communication capabilities. Those parts of an application-process not directly associated with OSI communication use the services of an application-entity, which consists of one or more ASEs, to request OSI communication functions. In performing its functions, an ASE can also call on the services of other ASEs in the application-entity. An ASE can also use the services provided by the Presentation layer in carrying out communications functions.

FIGURE 12.7   **The Application layer and multiple application-entities.**

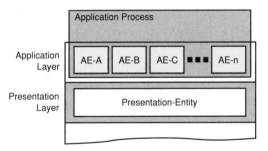

FIGURE 12.8   **An application-entity can comprise multiple application-service-elements.**

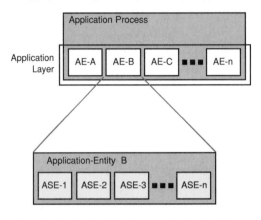

The OSI model itself does not specify the types of ASEs that will be defined for the Application layer. This has deliberately been left open-ended so the services provided by the Application layer can be extended indefinitely as new uses for OSI networking are developed. There is one ASE, however, that each application-entity must contain: the *association control service element* (ACSE). Support for ACSE is included in the DNA Phase V OSUL architecture.

In addition to general-purpose ASEs, likely to be used in many application-entities, many specific application-oriented ASEs will be defined. These are ASEs that support specific types of networking applications. An example of a standard for an application-oriented ASE is ISO 8571, *File Transfer, Access, and Management* (FTAM). FTAM is described in Chapter 14.

Association Control Service Element

Since there is no layer above the Application layer in the OSI model, there can be no notion of *connections* between application-entities as there are between entities in the lower layers. However, for meaningful communication to take place, there must be a relationship formed between two application-entities. For an application-entity-invocation in one open system to exchange information with an application-entity-invocation in another open system, there must be one or more application-associations between them. An *application-association* is a logical binding between two application-entity-invocations, one of which is called the *initiator* and the other the *responder*.

In effect, the ACSE provides the service of binding an application program executing in one open system with an application program executing in another open system for the purpose of exchanging information between them. ACSEs are responsible for establishing and releasing application-associations. (See Figure 12.9.)

Since no meaningful communication can take place in the OSI environment unless an association is formed between a pair of application-entity-invocations, support for ACSE must be included in each application-entity defined. Support for only an ACSE is sufficient to allow for communication to take place. The two communicating application-entity-invocations each use the services of an ACSE to establish an application-association and then call on the services of the Presentation layer to transmit APDUs between them. This is shown in Figure 12.10. As we will see later in this chapter, the OSUL architecture provides services that application programs can use to communicate in this manner.

Application-Contexts

An *application-context* defines a common set of rules shared by a pair of communicating application-entity-invocations, each including a set of ASEs (possibly only an ACSE) and an association between them. An application-context defines a particular set of communication capabilities

---

FIGURE 12.9   **An application-association between two application processes.**

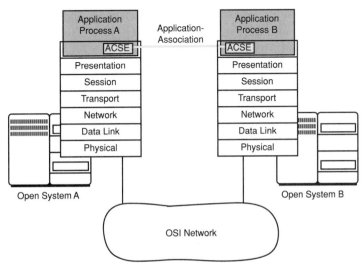

FIGURE 12.10   **The ACSE is the only ASE necessary for OSI communications.**

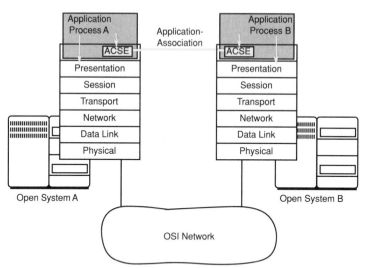

for two communicating application-entity-invocations. Each application-association has only one application-context.

Association-Control-Functions

The Application layer structure standard defines *association-control-functions*, which coordinate associations and ASEs. There are two types of association-control-functions: *single-association-control-functions* (SACFs) and *multiple-association-control-functions* (MACFs). An SACF is associated with a single association and thus a single application context; an MACF is associated with an entire application-entity-invocation. Figure 12.11 shows an example of three application-entity invocations and four application-associations. The MACF maps each service the application-entity-invocation provides to one of the associations and coordinates the interactions taking place on these associations.

ACSE Service Definition

The ACSE defines four straightforward services other ASEs in the application-entity and in the application-process itself can invoke for establishing and releasing application associations. The services defined in the ACSE service definition are listed in Box 12.3.

FIGURE 12.11   Three application-entities and four application-associations showing the single-application-control-functions (SACFs) and multiple-application-control-functions (MACFs).

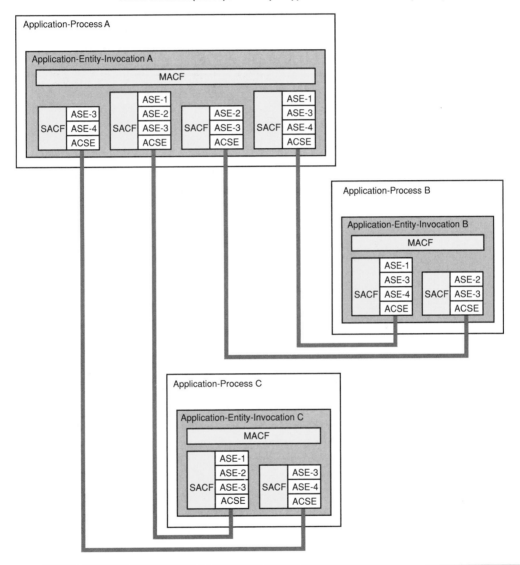

ACSE Protocol Specification

The protocol specification for the ACSE describes the operation of the ASCE in providing the services just described and also specifies the formats of the application-protocol-data-units (APDUs) exchanged in es-

BOX 12.3

ACSE Services

- **Association Establishment.** This service causes a new application-association to be established between an initiator application-entity-invocation and a responder application-entity-invocation. A great many parameters are associated with this service, but most are mapped to the Presentation layer and Session layer entities beneath ACSE. Each association established causes a connection to be established by the Presentation layer; there is always a one-to-one relationship between an application-association and a Presentation layer connection. Parameters passed when this service is invoked also contain information about the required underlying Session layer services. This is a confirmed service, and the responder application-entity-invocation can reply either negatively or positively to the request to establish an application-association.

- **Association Release.** This service can be issued by either of the application-entity-invocations to request the release of an existing application-association. This is a confirmed service, and the responder application-entity-invocation can reply either negatively or positively to the request to release an application-association. This service provides for graceful association release without the loss of information in transit, whether the responder replies positively or negatively.

- **User Association Abort.** This service can be issued by either of the application-entity-invocations to cause the abnormal release of an existing association. It is a nonconfirmed service and always causes the association to be released without requiring a response from the partner application-entity-invocation. Invoking this service may result in information in transit to be lost.

- **Provider Association Abort.** This service is issued by ACSE itself to signal that the association has been released, possibly due to a failure in the network. Invoking this service may cause information in transit to be lost.

tablishing and releasing associations. In general, a set of APDUs is defined for each of the four ACSE services described previously. Each of the service primitives included in the service definition has its own unique APDU defined for it, and the invocation of each service primitive causes a single APDU to flow to the partner application-entity. Box 12.4 lists the APDUs used in providing the ACSE services listed in Box 12.3.

There is a tight binding between the ACSE and the connection management services provided by the Presentation and Session layers. There

BOX 12.4

ACSE APDUs

- **A-Associate-Request.** The A-Associate-Request (AARQ) APDU is sent to request the establishment of an application-association.
- **A-Associate-Response.** The A-Associate-Response (AARE) APDU is used as a response to an AARQ APDU in performing the application-association establishment service.
- **A-Release-Request.** The A-Release-Request (RLRQ) APDU is sent to request the release of an application-association.
- **A-Associate-Response.** The A-Release-Response (RLRE) APDU is used as a response to an RLRQ APDU in performing the application-association release service.
- **A-Abort.** The A-Abort (ABRT) APDU is sent to request the abort of an application-association.

is a one-to-one mapping between an application-association and a Presentation connection and a one-to-one mapping between a Presentation connection and a Session connection. Establishing an application-association causes a Presentation connection to be established, which causes a Session connection to be established. Releasing an application-association causes the Presentation connection to be released, which causes the Session connection to be released.

OSUL Interfaces

The DNA Phase V OSUL architecture defines two abstract interfaces: an interface between OSUL and a user of OSUL services and an interface between OSUL and the Transport layer service. The services the Transport layer provides to OSUL are described in Chapter 10; this chapter describes only the services OSUL provides to an application-entity-invocation.

As with the other layers in the DNA Phase V architecture, access to OSUL services are provided through a port. An OSUL port is a data structure that represents an actual or potential application-association. A port must be referenced in each request for an OSUL service. An application-entity-invocation can open an OSUL port as either an initiator or as a responder:

- **Initiator.** A port opened as an initiator allows an application-entity-invocation to initiate the establishment of an application-association with another application-process-invocation.

• **Responder.** A port opened as a responder tells OSUL that the application-entity-invocation is prepared to receive a request for the establishment of an application-association.

Box 12.5 lists the procedure declarations documenting the services an application-entity-invocation can request of OSUL. The services are divided into four groups:

• services provided by ACSE for the establishment and release of application-associations

• services provided by OSUL for the management of buffers used during data transfer operations

• services provided by the Presentation layer for presentation-context management and data transfer

• services provided by the Presentation layer that map to services provided by the Session layer

Note that the OSUL service interface procedures compare quite closely to the ACSE, Presentation, and Session services defined in the ISO standards

---

BOX 12.5

OSUL Service Interface Procedure Declarations

The following procedure declarations define the abstract interface between OSUL and an application-entity-invocation in terms of the services OSUL provides to an application-entity-invocation.

Port Management Functions

• **OpenInitiator.** Allocates an OSUL port enabling the OSUL user to initiate the establishment of an association with another application-entity-invocation.

• **OpenResponder.** Allocates an OSUL port enabling the OSUL user to accept incoming requests for the establishment of an association with another application-entity-invocation.

Buffer Management Functions

• **GetEvent.** Prepares a port to receive an incoming request for an OSUL service.

• **GiveBuffers.** Passes temporary ownership of a buffer to OSUL.

• **SendMore.** Passes subsequent segments of user data to OSUL for an outbound service request.

BOX 12.5

continued

ACSE Functions

- **Associate.** Initiates the process of establishing an association with another application-entity-invocation and optionally passes one or more PDVs to the peer application-entity-invocation.
- **AssociateAccept.** Accepts an incoming request from another application-entity-invocation for the establishment of an association.
- **AssociateRefuse.** Rejects an incoming request from another application-entity-invocation for the establishment of an association.
- **ExceptionReport.** Generates an exception report concerning events not serious enough to terminate an application-association.
- **Release.** Requests the orderly termination of an association.
- **ReleaseReply.** Replies to a request for the orderly termination of an association.
- **Abort.** Requests the immediate termination of an association.

Presentation Service Functions (Provided by Presentation Layer)

- **Data.** Sends PDVs to the peer application-entity-invocation using a Transport connection over the normal flow.
- **TypedData.** Sends PDVs to the peer application-entity-invocation in the form of Session service typed data.
- **ExpeditedData.** Sends PDVs to the peer application-entity-invocation using a Transport connection over the expedited flow.
- **CapabilityData.** Sends PDVs to the peer application-entity-invocation in the form of Session service capability data.
- **CapabilityDataReply.** Sends PDVs to the peer application-entity-invocation in the form of Session service capability reply data.
- **AlterContext.** Sends to the peer application-entity-invocation lists of additions and deletions to be made to the Presentation service-defined context set and, optionally, a set of PDVs.
- **AlterContextReply.** Sends to the peer application-entity-invocation lists of accepted and rejected additions and deletions to the defined context set and, optionally, a set of PDVs.

Presentation Service Functions (Provided by Session Layer)

- **ActivityStart.** Requests the beginning of a Session service activity.
- **ActivityStartReply.** Replies to a request for the beginning of an activity.
- **ActivityEnd.** Requests the end of a Session service activity.

BOX 12.5

continued

- **ActivityInterrupt.** Requests interruption of a specified Session service activity.

- **ActivityInterruptReply.** Replies to a request for the interruption of an activity.

- **ActivityResume.** Requests resumption of a specified activity.

- **ActivityDiscard.** Requests a specified activity to be discarded.

- **ActivityDiscardReply.** Replies to a request to discard an activity.

- **TokenGive.** Relinquishes control of the specified Session service tokens to the peer application-entity-invocation.

- **TokenPlease.** Requests the peer application-entity-invocation to relinquish control of the specified Session service tokens.

- **GiveControl.** Relinquishes control of all currently owned Session service tokens.

- **SynchMajor.** Establishes a Session service major synchronization point.

- **SynchMajorReply.** Replies to a request for the establishment of a major synchronization point.

- **SyncMinor.** Establishes a Session service minor synchronization point.

- **SynchMinorReply.** Replies to a request for the establishment of a minor synchronization point.

- **Resynchronize.** Resets an application association to conditions associated with the specified synchronization point.

- **ResynchronizeReply.** Replies to a request for resynchronization.

OSUL Interface Style

The OSUL architecture does not restrict the number of simultaneous application-associations that can be formed between application-entity-invocations. OSUL achieves this by having no resources of its own that are specific to a particular application-association. Instead, an application-entity-invocation passes to OSUL the resources—such as the buffer resources—required to establish an application-association.

This style of interface makes it possible for an application-entity-invocation to implement its own flow control procedures. An application-entity-invocation passes temporary ownership of buffers to OSUL for the purposes of sending and receiving APDUs. An application-entity-invocation can temporarily stop receiving APDUs by not providing OSUL with a buffer.

Unlimited User Data

OSUL supports the use of unlimited user data fields in Presentation service primitives through the use of a segmented interface. All inbound and outbound requests for data transfer services include a *more flag*. If a request for an outbound data transfer service includes a more flag that is false, OSUL knows there are no more segments of user data to transmit. When the operation completes, OSUL returns ownership of the buffer to the application-entity-invocation. When the more flag is true in a request for an outbound data transfer service, OSUL expects the application-entity-invocation to pass subsequent segments of user data by issuing Send-More functions.

Inbound user data segments are handled through the use of a GetEvent function. GetEvent is used to receive each segment of inbound user data. If the more flag is false, the inbound service request is complete. If the more flag is true, the next user data segment is received by the issuing of another GetEvent function. For efficiency reasons, user buffers are passed directly to the Transport layer entity for both inbound and outbound data.

Conclusion

This chapter concludes our discussion of the functional layers that make up the DNA Phase V architecture. The two chapters in Part III introduce the uses to which a DECnet Phase V network can be put: Chapter 13 introduces applications that employ the DNA Session Control layer for communication, and Chapter 14 introduces applications that use OSUL for communication.

PART III

Network Applications

CHAPTER 13

DNA Applications

The chapters in Part III discuss the applications to which a large hetero-geneous computer network can be put. Distributed computing applications will become increasingly important in the 1990s as we bring the power of multiple computing systems to bear on a single problem. Client-server operations will be employed everywhere, with software in desktop computers interacting with software in larger server computers. Particularly important forms of distributed computing applications will involve the transmission of information to computers in other organizations—sometimes within the same enterprise, sometimes in a different enterprise. Direct communication between computers in separate enterprises is one of the primary ways to improve business efficiency. The term *electronic data interchange* (EDI) is used to describe such systems. This chapter begins by describing examples of the innovative applications that can be built using a sophisticated networking infrastructure.

Goodyear has implemented a worldwide EDI system in which computers in their supplier locations interact directly with the computers they use for planning production. Quality checks on supplier materials are performed at supplier sites before the materials are shipped, and the results are transmitted to the computer that schedules the manufacturing process. If the material is inadequate for the batches of work currently planned, it is not shipped. When the material is usable but of variable quality, the computer-to-computer interaction permits it to be appropriately allocated to the production process. This computer-to-computer interaction saves money, gives Goodyear early warning of problems, and enables them to find alternate suppliers, usually without delaying the production schedule. Navistar cut its inventories by nearly $200 million by building computer-to-computer links to its suppliers and implementing just-in-time inventory control. The General Motors EDI payment

293

system handles transactions totaling half a billion dollars in value every month.

The chapters in Part III divide applications into two categories. We define DNA applications—described in this chapter—as those applications that request communication services using the DNA Session Control layer. OSI applications—described in Chapter 14—are those that request communication services using the three upper layers of the OSI model protocol stack (the OSUL architecture).

Figure 13.1 shows the architectural layers of the DNA Phase V architecture and how DNA applications request networking services. DNA applications are provided by Digital, offered by many third-party vendors specializing in developing application software for the Digital environment, and written by end users themselves. Digital provides a wide range of networking applications, from general-purpose network-wide applications, such as file transfer programs, to highly specific distributed applications written to meet the needs of specific customers.

FIGURE 13.1   The relationship of a DNA application program to the DNA Phase V architecture.

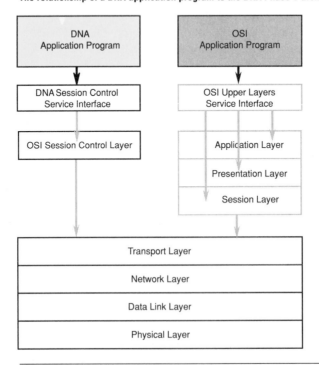

Digital Field Service Application

A distributed computing application that is being developed by the Digital field service organization is an example of the kind of distributed application that can be built when sophisticated networking mechanisms are available to interconnect the computer networks of different organizations.

In fixing a hardware problem at a customer's site, a field service representative often must be dispatched twice: the first time to do the diagnosis and a second time to do the repair if the required part is not available on site. The goal of Digital's field service organization is to place a computer *on each customer's computer network* that constantly monitors that customer's equipment. The monitoring computer will gather preventative maintenance data and transmit it to Digital's own computer network, where the data will be forwarded to one of a number of analysis centers around the world.

At these analysis centers, complex expert systems will analyze the preventative maintenance data and attempt to predict when field-replaceable devices are about to fail. The expert systems at the analysis centers will communicate with a distributed inventory system to locate the required field-replaceable parts. The distributed inventory application will then communicate with a logistics application that will pull field-replaceable units from inventory and communicate with the network of a shipping company to schedule the shipping of the items to the customer's site. When the logistics application on the Digital network receives confirmation from the shipper's network that the item has arrived at the customer's site, the logistics application will notify a field engineering scheduling application, which will handle the dispatching of a field engineer.

This system will be driven entirely by computer-to-computer communication. People are not involved until the very end of the process, when an engineer is actually dispatched to the customer's site to install the replacement part. The idea is that the entire distributed system is driven by machines and directed by computation.

**Digital DNA
Applications**

The remainder of this chapter describes four general-purpose networking applications, provided by Digital, that use the DNA Session Control layer for communication: virtual terminal mechanisms, electronic mail, computer conferencing, and remote file access. These applications are used by a great many of Digital's customers.

Virtual Terminal Mechanisms

The virtual terminal mechanisms in DNA Phase V allow a terminal user to communicate with an application running on any host processor attached to the network. These mechanisms define a client/server functional model for communicating between a *client* node running an application program and a *server* node to which a terminal is directly attached.

Virtual Terminal Facilities   The DNA Phase V virtual terminal mechanisms provide the following facilities:

- Distribution of terminal handling functions between the client node and the server node.

- Support for heterogeneous client systems that may run different operating systems. The operating system running in the client node can manage a terminal in its own way, regardless of which operating system runs in the server node.

- Functions operating at the operating system level to provide terminal input/output and management functions, including accepting input even if the program has not issued a read request (typeahead), taking action on certain characters immediately as keys are struck, recognizing ANSI standard escape sequences on input and output, and reading and setting terminal device characteristics.

Virtual Terminal Protocols   Virtual terminal mechanisms are provided through the use of two protocols:

- **Command Terminal (CTERM) Protocol.** The *Command Terminal* (CTERM) protocol implements a model of a terminal that provides a common mode of access to command language processors such as the Digital Command Language (DCL). The CTERM protocol uses the services of the Foundation protocol.

- **Foundation (FOUND) Protocol.** The *Foundation* (FOUND) protocol provides a basic set of connection management facilities and a transparent data transport capability over which a number of terminal usage models can run.

The goal of the CTERM and FOUND protocols is to allow a host-based application to treat all terminals in exactly the same manner, whether they are directly attached to the host or communicate with the host over a DECnet network.

Electronic Mail

Electronic mail systems are without a doubt among the most important networking applications in use today. Certainly the very large Digital internal network is used quite heavily by people for exchanging electronic messages. Almost everyone in the worldwide Digital organization now has access to a terminal or workstation connected to the internal network and can send and receive electronic messages. Almost all of Digital's customers that have extensive DECnet networks installed use them at least partially for electronic messaging applications.

Digital markets a wide range of products that provide electronic mail capabilities. Most of these products fall under the umbrella of the *MAILbus* family of products. The MAILbus product family provides facilities for the creation, transmission, reception, and management of electronic messages in a heterogeneous, distributed computing environment. In the MAILbus environment, a message can consist of a combination of text and data files of various types. The MAILbus product family consists of a number of products that together provide message handling services and directory services across a broad range of hardware and software systems.

The *VAX Message Router* product is Digital's main software system for providing a basic network-wide, store-and-forward message transport service and a descriptive directory service. The message transport service provides an application-independent mechanism for reliably relaying messages from an application on one computer system to an application on another computing system without requiring a direct end-to-end connection between the two. The message transport is accomplished by storing messages at one or more points along the path between the communicating applications. The Message Router supports both electronic mail and nonmail applications and provides an application programming interface users can employ for developing user-written messaging applications.

The descriptive directory service provided by the Message Router provides access to directory entries that allow users to locate other users of the system given possibly incomplete descriptive information. The information contained in such directory entries includes users' names, organizations, locations, and electronic mail addresses.

A variety of products can be used with the Message Router to allow messages to be exchanged between users in the following environments:

- DECnet Phase IV networks
- DECnet Phase V networks

- Messaging systems conforming to CCITT Recommendation X.400
- IBM Professional Office Systems (PROFS) networks
- IBM Systems Network Architecture Distribution Services (SNADS) networks

The Message Router and its related products can be used with a number of software systems to provide end users with access to electronic mail applications. For example, Digital's ALL-IN-1 office automation application provides end users with access to electronic messaging facilities as well as other office automation functions.

Computer Conferencing

A DNA application called *Notes* allows users throughout a DNA network to participate in round-table discussions using their terminals or workstations. Any number of Notes computer conferences can be established in a network. Conference participants use the Notes client software installed on their own nodes. The Notes client software communicates with Notes server software using a DNA Application layer protocol allowing access to conferences located anywhere in the network. Users employ Notes client software to read and write conference entries, called *topics* and *replies*. Any user can create a new topic. Other users can read the topics other users have created and can then post replies to them. New users joining a conference can view the existing notes and all the replies already posted to them. They can then reply to existing notes. Users can also create new topics of their own, to which all other conference members can post replies.

The Notes software allows users to conduct meetings with people in different geographic locations in which not all the meeting participants need to be online at the same time. Participants can join in a discussion from their own terminals or workstations at times convenient to them. Notes also offers the advantage of keeping a detailed record of the proceedings of a meeting, which can be searched by a variety of criteria, such as the name of participant, a specific subject, or a keyword. Notes can be used for a variety of purposes, such as to create an electronic bulletin board, to support the collaborative writing of a document, or to conduct an internal seminar. Notes is particularly useful when a group of people need to discuss issues and make decisions when it is not possible for all the participants to meet face to face.

Ease-of-Use Features   Users can request listings of topics posted by author, title, and date and the number of replies posted to each topic. Users can read notes either sequentially or at random and can request that only those notes and replies that the user has not already seen be displayed. The Notes software provides a number of facilities that make it easy for a user to access computer conferences:

- **Notebook.** Notes maintains a *notebook* for each user containing the user's own personal list of conferences of interest. Users can add or delete conferences from their notebooks. The notebook allows users to define personal names for conferences and allows remote conferences to be accessed without requiring the user to know on what node the conference is running. When a user accesses a conference, the notebook can optionally show whether new entries have been made since the last time the user accessed the conference. The notebook also keeps track of what notes and responses the user has already read and maintains a profile of user preferences, including personal name, editor choice, and default printer specifications.

- **Markers.** Users can create user-defined names, called *markers*, that point to entries in a conference. Markers can be used as special reminders of things to do or to flag notes of special interest.

- **Keywords.** Users can define *keywords* to group notes that are concerned with a particular subject or that do not have other attributes (such as title, author, or time of entry) in common. Keywords are useful for grouping notes that may not have the keyword in the note text or title but that do address the subject the keyword represents.

- **Imported Text.** The Notes software allows notes and replies to be created outside of Notes using any desired editor and later imported to the conference.

Moderators   A *moderator* is a person responsible for creating and managing one or more computer conferences. The Notes software supports both public and private conferences. For private conferences, the moderator can restrict access to a specific group of participants by specifying names and network locations. Public conferences have no restrictions on who may participate. The moderator can send announcements of new conferences to participants and can also create special notices displayed for all participants each time the conference is accessed. The moderator of a conference has special capabilities for controlling the discussion, including the following:

- deleting or hiding notes the moderator deems inappropriate to the discussion or which require further clarification
- changing the titles of topics or replies to topics to improve the organization of a conference
- creating keywords that can be associated with notes in the conference
- designating additional conference moderators

Remote File Access

In most computer networks there is a requirement for providing programs with access to the files residing on other nodes in the network. For example, it might be necessary to transfer files from one computer system to another when the computer systems involved in the file transfer operation may not conform to the same hardware architecture or run the same operating system. It also may be necessary to allow an application program to issue read and write requests for files residing on other nodes in the same manner as if the file resided on the user's own local node. Such file operations in a heterogeneous network environment are supported in the DNA Phase V environment by an architecture called the *Data Access Protocol* (DAP). Implementation of DAP provides the following functions and features:

- supports heterogeneous file systems
- retrieves a file from an input device, such as a disk file or a terminal
- sends a file to an output device, such as a disk file, a magnetic tape file, or a printer
- transfers files between systems in a heterogeneous environment
- supports the creation, deletion, and renaming of files stored on remote computing systems
- lists the directories of the file systems on remote computing systems
- recovers from transient errors and reports fatal errors to the user
- allows multiple data streams to be sent to the same remote file
- allows users to submit and execute remote command files
- permits sequential, random, and indexed access to records stored in the file systems of remote computer systems
- supports wildcard file specification for sequential file retrieval, file deletion, file renaming, and command file execution
- permits the optional use of a file checksum facility to ensure file integrity

DAP is designed to minimize protocol overhead. For example, the file transfer mode eliminates the need for DAP Control messages after a file transfer operation has begun. Also, small file records can be blocked together and sent in one protocol message. When two cooperating processes exchange DAP messages, one of the processes operates as the client and the other as the server. The input/output (I/O) commands issued by the client are mapped into equivalent DAP messages and transmitted via a Transport connection to the server at the remote system. The server interprets the DAP commands and performs the file I/O on behalf of the client. The server then returns status information and file data to the client.

Implementations of DAP—such as in VAX VMS—typically allow users to employ the same programming statements (e.g., READ and WRITE) and operating system commands (e.g., COPY) to access local files and remote files.

Conclusion

By the year 2000 the world will be laced with intercorporate networks, over which the computers in one corporation will interact directly with the computers in other corporations to form powerful distributed computing applications. Many of the decisions of commerce will be made at computer speed, in an optimal fashion, on a worldwide basis. Once this electronic interaction becomes a basic infrastructure of commerce, executives will wonder how they ever managed without it.

A great many such distributed computing applications exist and will be written using the DNA Session Control layer for communication. Of increasing importance in the world of networking, however, will be applications conforming to the architecture defined by the OSI upper layers: the Application, Presentation, and Session layers. Network applications that use the OSI upper layers for communication are the subject of Chapter 14.

CHAPTER 14

OSI Applications

As we discussed in Chapter 12, the Application layer is made up of a number of application-entities, each describing a particular set of OSI communication capabilities. An application-entity is in turn made up of a collection of application-service-elements (ASEs), each of which is defined by a service definition and a protocol specification. The service definition for an ASE describes the abstract services the ASE provides to its users, and an ASE's protocol specification describes the formats of the application-protocol-data-units (APDUs) used and specifies the rules by which they are exchanged by application entities in providing the ASE's services.

An ASE defines a particular set of functions associated with OSI communication capabilities. Those parts of an application-process not directly associated with OSI communications use the services of an application-entity, which consists of one or more ASEs, to request OSI communications functions. In performing its functions, an ASE can call on the services of other ASEs in the application-entity and can also use the services provided by the Presentation layer in providing communications functions.

User-Written OSI Applications

Chapter 12 described the OSUL architecture, which defines how the three upper layers of the OSI model are integrated into the DNA Phase V architecture. The OSUL architecture provides support for the association control service element (ACSE). The OSUL architecture also includes support for the OSI Presentation and Session layers. User-written application programs gain access to the OSI environment by requesting the services provided by the service interface defined by the OSUL architecture. An implementation of the OSUL architecture provides an application programming interface (API) that implements the abstract interface defined in the OSUL architecture. The OSUL abstract interface, defined through a series of procedure declarations, was described in Chapter 12. An application program uses the API defined by an implementation of the OSUL architecture to establish and release application-associations using the functions provided by the ACSE. It also uses the API to request the data transfer and dialog management services provided by implementations of the OSI Presentation and Session layers. The relationship between a user-written OSUL application program and the DNA Phase V architecture is shown in Figure 14.1.

International Standard OSI Applications

As described in Chapter 12, there will be many international standards for the Application layer. As just described, each of these standards takes the form of an ASE. Some ASEs, such as the association control service element (ACSE), are general-purpose ASEs that provide services to other ASEs and to an application-process. Implementations of general-purpose

FIGURE 14.1   **The relationship of an OSI application program to the DNA Phase V architecture.**

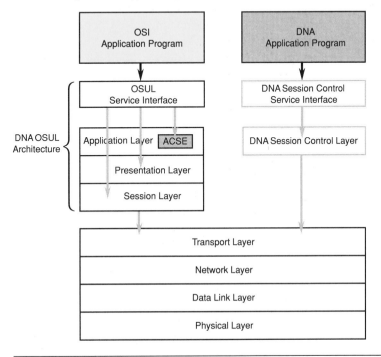

ASEs—such as ACSE—generally provide only application programming interfaces that allow other ASEs and application programs to request their services. They do not provide services directly to human users.

There will also be many international standards developed for more application-specific ASEs designed to provide specific types of services, sometimes directly to human users. International standards for distributed computing applications that use the services of ASEs will also be developed. This chapter examines an application-specific ASE—often implemented in the OSI environment—for which Digital provides an implementation: File Transfer, Access, and Management (FTAM) for providing remote access to data files. It also examines an international standard for a distributed computing application: the X.400 Message Handling System for electronic mail applications. Another important international standard for a distributed computing application is the X.500 Directory. The X.500 Directory provides naming services in the OSI environment and is introduced in Chapter 16.

In the remainder of this chapter, we examine the characteristics of the FTAM ASE and the X.400 distributed computing application.

File Transfer, Access, and Management

File Transfer, Access, and Management (FTAM) is an international standard, documented in ISO 8571, that defines an ASE for the Application layer of the OSI model. The FTAM ASE defines the functions required to support a remote file system in the OSI environment. The broad aim in the standardization of a file service is to allow file users on open systems to be able to transfer, access, or manage information held on any type of system that behaves as if it stores data files. Such a system is called a *virtual filestore* in the FTAM environment.

Master-Slave Relationship

The actions supported by FTAM take the form of master-slave relationships. Each activity is started by one of the two file service users having some objective to achieve. This user is called the *initiator*. The other user is the *responder*, which takes a passive role and reacts to requests made by the initiator. The act of transferring data from the file at the initiator to the file at the responder (either a record at a time or the entire file) can be viewed conceptually as being performed by a copying application having local access to one filestore and remote access to the other (see Figure 14.2). Whenever file data records are being transferred from one

FIGURE 14.2   A conceptual view of a file transfer operation using FTAM.

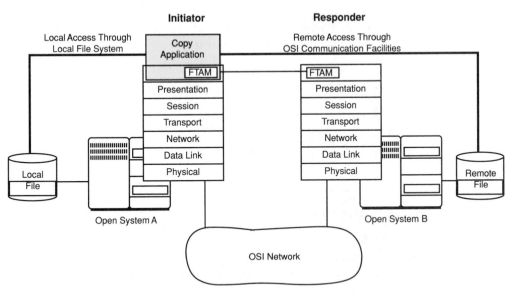

filestore to another, one of the users is the *sender* and the other is the *receiver*. An initiator or a responder can be either the sender or the receiver in any particular data transfer operation.

The Virtual Filestore

The virtual filestore in FTAM describes a conceptual model of a file service that might be implemented in any desired way in an open system. The virtual filestore is an abstraction that can be emulated by the file service existing in a real computing system. A virtual filestore consists of a collection of files, each of which has a unique name. A fundamental FTAM concept is that an FTAM user accesses a single file at a time, which is called the *selected* file. Each file in a filestore has two components:

- **Attributes.** Attributes specify information about the file, such as the file's name, the actions permitted on the file, the file's size, and so on.

- **Contents.** The contents make up the information stored in the file and any data describing the file's structuring (pointers, indexes, etc.).

Document Types

Different types of files are defined in the FTAM standard to support different types of processing. These are described as *document types*. FTAM currently defines five document types:

- **FTAM-1.** Unstructured text.
- **FTAM-2.** Sequential text.
- **FTAM-3.** Unstructured binary.
- **FTAM-4.** Sequential binary.
- **FTAM-5.** Simple hierarchical file.

FTAM Functional Units

FTAM defines a broad range of functions to support file operations. Not all implementations of FTAM will necessarily support all the functions defined in the international standard. The FTAM standard defines two ways in which subsets of these functions can be defined. At the most basic level, FTAM functions are grouped into *functional units*. To be in conformance with the standard, an FTAM implementation must support a functional unit either completely or not at all.

FTAM Service Classes

At a higher level, the standard defines a number of service classes, each of which supports broad categories of use. These classes are as follows:

- **Transfer Class.** This service class allows for the transfer of files or parts of files between open systems using a relatively simple protocol.
- **Management Class.** This service class allows control of the virtual filestore, such as renaming and deleting files, but does not include file transfer functions.
- **Transfer and Management Class.** This service class combines all the functions included in the transfer class and the management class.
- **Access Class.** This service class allows an initiating user to perform file access operations on individual units of data in the remote filestore, such as reading and writing individual records.
- **Unconstrained Class.** This service class allows the designer to choose the functional units to be implemented.

The following sections describe the file operations that can be performed for the transfer and management classes, the most commonly implemented FTAM service classes.

Transfer Class An open system implementing the transfer class and operating as the initiator can copy a file from a remote filestore residing on some other open system in the OSI environment to the local system or it can copy a file from the local system to a remote filestore. If the remote system also supports limited file management functions, the initiator can also *move* files in either direction. A move operation is different from a copy in that the original file is deleted after the operation is completed. An open system operating in the role of the responder can respond to requests made by other systems for file copy and move operations.

Management Class An open system implementing the management class and operating in the role of an initiator can create files, delete files, and read the attributes of files in a filestore on a remote system. If the remote system supports full file management operations, the system can also modify file attributes of files stored in a filestore on the remote system. As a responder, a system responds to requests made by a remote system to create files, delete files, read file attributes, and modify file attributes.

Services Used by FTAM

FTAM uses three specific services in the OSI environment (see Figure 14.3):

- **Association Control Service Element (ACSE).** FTAM employs the ACSE to establish the application-associations required to establish communication between file service users to support file transfer and management

---

FIGURE 14.3 **Services used by FTAM.**

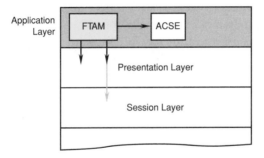

activities. At any instant, the file protocol operates so there is only one file activity in progress over a particular association; if more than one file activity is necessary, more than one association is established.

- **Presentation Layer Services.** FTAM uses the services of the underlying Presentation layer to transfer data between Application layer entities to support file transfer and management operations.

- **Session Layer Services.** The Session layer services that FTAM requests via the Presentation layer include the control of the dialog between the initiator and the responder and the creation of synchronization points to support file checkpointing and recovery operations.

FTAM Implementations

As an international standard for an ASE, FTAM is described in terms of a service definition and protocol specification in the same manner as for other ISO international standards for the OSI architecture. The FTAM service definition defines the semantics of FTAM services but does not specify any particular user or application programming interface that should be used to implement FTAM services. Therefore, it is likely that different implementations of FTAM may look very different to users and to application programs. However, if the protocol specification is adhered to, different implementations of FTAM will interoperate in the OSI environment.

X.400 Message Handling System

The main objective of the X.400 message handling system is to allow users to exchange messages on a store-and-forward basis. X.400 defines a number of standard message handling services useful in creating systems that implement electronic mail services. Recommendation X.400 does not specify information about how an electronic mail facility should be built, nor does it specify anything about what the user or application programming interface to such a system should look like. Rather it concentrates on the specification of aspects of message handling systems that allow one electronic mail system to interwork with other electronic mail systems conforming to the X.400 protocol specifications.

Digital products provide electronic mail services through the MAILbus family of products that run on various Digital processors. The MAILbus product family was initially introduced before the X.400 message handling system was accepted as an international standard, and

MAILbus products do not currently use the X.400 standard for exchanging messages among themselves. However, the MAILbus products fully conform with the X.400 in the way they interwork with other X.400 implementations.

Recommendation X.400 documents a service definition and a protocol specification. It uses the services of the ACSE and the services of the Presentation layer in performing communication functions. (See Figure 14.4.)

We next describe the major components of the X.400 message handling system architectural model.

User Agents

Users of the message handling system access X.400 services through an intermediary called a *user agent* (UA). A user called an *originator* employs a user agent to send a message to one or more other users called *recipients*. The user agents are in turn interconnected using facilities collectively called the *Message Transfer System* (MTS). The architectural model defined by the X.400 standard is shown in Figure 14.5.

Message Transfer Agents

The message transfer system is itself composed of *message transfer agents* (MTAs) interconnected using OSI communication facilities, as shown in Figure 14.6. MTAs physically exchange messages with one another using OSI Presentation layer facilities.

A message originator creates messages using the assistance of a user agent. A user agent is an application-process that can communicate di-

---

FIGURE 14.4   **Services used by X.400.**

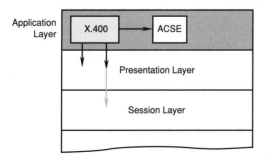

FIGURE 14.5   OSI X.400 message handling system architectural model.

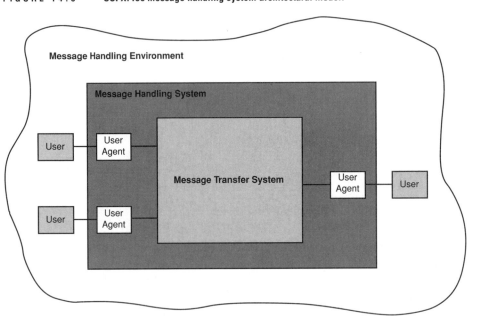

rectly with a message transfer agent to submit messages on behalf of a single user. The message transfer system uses message transfer agents to deliver to one or more recipient user agents the messages submitted to it. The message transfer system can also return *notifications* to a message originator. A user agent can accept delivery of messages directly from the message transfer system, or it can use the capabilities of a *message store* to receive delivered messages for subsequent retrieval by a user agent.

Message Stores

According to the X.400 standard, a user agent accepting messages directly from a message transfer agent must be available at the time a message is delivered. However, it is possible to implement a user agent on a different computing system from the message transfer agent with which it interacts. For example, a user agent might be implemented in the user's own computing system—possibly a personal computer or workstation—in which case, the user agent may not be available at all times. In such a situation, it is likely that a particular user agent will be active for only a very short time each day, during which all message

FIGURE 14.6   Message transfer agents in the message transfer system.

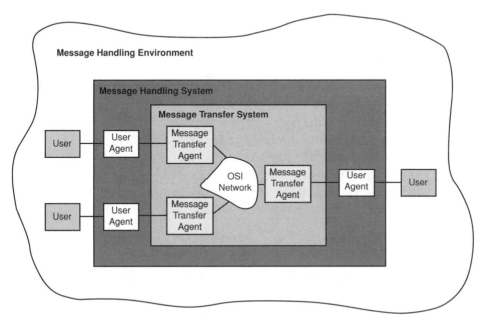

traffic is exchanged. X.400 provides message stores (MSs) that handle the common situation where the user agent may not be attached to the message handling system when a message arrives.

A message store acts on behalf of a user agent and provides a secure, continuously available storage medium a message transfer agent can use to store messages for later retrieval by a message agent. A message store is associated with a single user. When a message store is implemented, all messages destined for a particular user agent are delivered to the message store. If the user agent is active at the time a message is received, that user can receive an alert indicating a message has been received and has been placed into that user's message store. The message transfer system considers a message to have been delivered when it is accepted either by a user agent or by a message store. A user can direct his or her message store to forward received messages to some other destination in the message handling system.

A message store can be implemented in the same computer system implementing a user agent, it can be located in the same computer system as a message transfer agent, or it can be implemented in a computer system different from either the user agent or the message transfer agent.

The most common configuration is to implement a user agent's message store in the same computer system as the message transfer agent serving that user agent.

X.400 Messages

A message in the X.400 environment can be viewed as being made up of an envelope and its contents. The *envelope* carries information accessed by message transfer agents as they are transmitting the message through the message transfer system. The message's content consists of the information the originating user agent is using the message transfer system to deliver to one or more recipient user agents. Message transfer agents do not examine or modify the content of messages as they move messages through the message transfer system.

Message Transfer System Operation

The message transfer system implemented by a set of interconnected message transfer agents provides a general-purpose, store-and-forward message transfer service independent of any particular application. It provides the means by which user agents exchange messages with each other.

Message Transfer System Interactions

Two basic interactions can take place between message transfer agents and user agents or message stores:

- **Submission.** The *submission* interaction provides the means by which an originating user agent passes a message to a message transfer agent.
- **Delivery.** The *delivery* interaction provides the means by which a message transfer agent moves a message to its destination(s).

The originator's user agent uses the Submission interaction to pass a message to the message transfer agent serving that user agent. The originator's message transfer agent then uses the delivery interaction to transfer the message from one message transfer agent to the next until the message reaches the message transfer agent serving the recipient's user agent. That message transfer agent then passes the message to the recipient's user agent or to the message store serving the recipient.

Notifications   The message transfer system can implement two types of notifications: *delivery* and *nondelivery.* When a message transfer agent determines that a message cannot be delivered, it generates a nondelivery notification, which is sent back to the user agent originating the nondeliverable message. A message originator can also request a delivery notification, which serves as a positive acknowledgment of message delivery.

Conclusion

This chapter and the previous one provided a brief introduction to the types of applications for which a DECnet Phase V network can be used. As computer networks become ubiquitous, the variety of networking applications will increase. The chapters in Part IV introduce an important set of related architectures and networking mechanisms that support the functional layers of the DNA Phase V architecture. Chapter 15 begins Part IV by examining the *distributed computing services* that are used by components of the DNA architecture and that can also be employed by users of a DECnet Phase V network.

PART IV

Related Architectures and Mechanisms

CHAPTER 15

Distributed Computing Services

Applications that use the network for communication and various components of the networking software itself require certain common services. It is desirable that the network infrastructure provide these services rather than each application and each component of the networking software being forced to provide them for itself. With respect to these common services, the network infrastructure can in many ways be viewed as a *distributed operating system*. An operating system, typically running on a single computing system, provides the application programs it controls with a broad range of useful services, including, but not limited to:

- providing the date and the time of day
- providing security services
- allowing one procedure to invoke the execution of some other procedure
- assigning unique identifiers to objects such as programs and files
- locating computing system objects, such as programs and files, based on names users have assigned to them

DNA Phase V includes a collection of architectures that define how many of these same services can be supplied to users on a network-wide basis. This chapter examines architectures for an important set of *distributed computing services*:

- **Digital Time Service Architecture.** This architecture defines services and algorithms for maintaining and providing, in all network nodes, a consistent, correct date and time of day.

- **Distributed Authentication Security Service Architecture.** This architecture defines a subset of a comprehensive framework for security that Digital is developing. It is an architecture—related to DNA Phase V as well as to other architectures—that defines a comprehensive set of security services that can be used in implementing distributed systems.

- **Remote Procedure Call Architecture.** This architecture defines services by which a procedure executing in one computing system can pass control to a procedure residing in some other node of the network using a simple procedure call mechanism.

- **Unique Identifier Architecture.** This architecture defines a service that distributed systems and the DECnet software itself can use to obtain an identifier guaranteed to be globally unique over space and time.

Another important distributed computing service is provided by the *DNA Phase V naming service*. The naming service allows users to assign names to objects that mean the same thing anywhere in the network and to maintain a set of attribute values associated with each name, including the address of the node on which the object resides. The naming service accepts an object's name from a user and passes back the set of attributes associated with that name. The naming service is such an important part of DNA Phase V that we examine it separately in Chapter 16.

The time service, the remote procedure call service, the unique identifier service, and the naming service can be viewed as running in a layer between the DNA Session Control layer and the application programs (both Digital-developed and user-developed) employing the network for communication. This layer is sometimes called the *Network Applications* layer, as shown in Figure 15.1. These services are called by user applications and sometimes by each other as well. Some of the distributed computing services implement distributed algorithms, components of which are executed in each node in the network. The various components of these distributed algorithms must communicate with

FIGURE 15.1   Distributed computing services residing in a Network Applications layer.

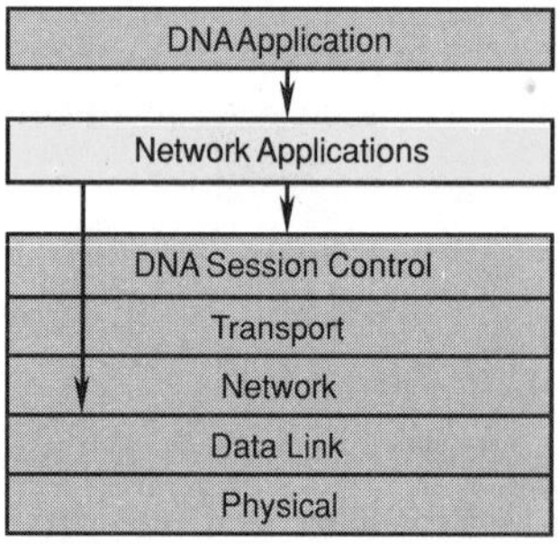

each other using protocols in performing their functions. This communication is handled through the use of DNA Session Control connections and/or Data Link layer services.

We will examine each of the four distributed computing services in detail.

Time Service Architecture	The notion of time is taken for granted in most of today's centralized computer systems. However, the mechanisms used to provide time in these systems are inadequate when applied to distributed systems. Even if all the computers in the network have accurate clocks, we cannot expect a diverse group of computer operators to all set the clocks correctly on a large number of computers. So in the distributed environment, new mechanisms are required for consistently setting the clocks on all the computers and for maintaining their accuracy. A single, global notion of time is necessary to coordinate the operation of a sophisticated distributed system. There are three major uses for time values in a distributed computing environment:

- **Time Ordering of Events.** Given two events occurring either at the same or at different places in the network, it is often useful to be able to determine which event took place first.

- **Measuring Time Intervals.** Given two events occurring either at the same or at different places in the network, it is often useful to be able to determine the length of the time interval elapsed between the times the two events occurred. Accurate performance measurements in a distributed system require this ability.

- **Scheduling of Events.** It is often useful to be able to specify that an event—or a set of distributed events—should take place either before or after a specified time.

To be able to use time values for the above purposes, a time service must be available that allows users to obtain consistent time values no matter where they reside in the network. This is not possible if each node in the network is responsible for independently maintaining its own internal clock. The DNA Phase V time service is a distributed algorithm, a component of which runs in every network node, responsible for synchronizing all the clocks in the network. Any user in the network can obtain a time value by requesting it from the time service. A major goal of the time service is to provide a time value on request with a minimum probability of the time value being incorrect. This is a difficult goal to accomplish because, unlike other services where faults or errors can be de-

BOX 15.1

Goals of the Time
Service

- **Correctness.** The architecture is designed to minimize the probability of a user obtaining an incorrect time value.
- **Client-Server Model.** The architecture conforms to the client-server model in which clients query servers for time values and in which the complexity of the architecture centers in the servers rather than in the clients.
- **Simplicity.** The architecture provides a simple and conventional view of time values and uses a single generally accepted standard for representing time.
- **Quality.** A component of each time value consists of a value that places a bound on the possible inaccuracy associated with that time value. The actual inaccuracy that can be associated with a time value is not specified in the architecture. Inaccuracy depends on the accuracy of the physical components used to maintain time values and on the network resources available for synchronizing clocks in the network.
- **Fault Tolerance.** The architecture is designed to withstand and compensate for a small number of servers that may be maintaining incorrect time values.
- **Scale.** The architecture is designed to accommodate network growth and can function correctly in networks of any size.
- **Auto Configuration.** The architecture allows clients and servers to be added to the network with little or no management intervention. In addition, clients and servers are able to initialize their clocks with no human intervention.
- **Performance.** The architecture is designed so the algorithms used consume a minimum amount of network resources in performing their functions.
- **Monotonicity.** The architecture is designed so that, except in dealing with extreme failures, clocks never run backward and forward adjustments in clock values are made gradually.

tected immediately, faulty time values are difficult to detect. Moreover, in a distributed system, faulty time values may lead to undetected incorrect operation of other distributed algorithms, such as the naming service.

In addition to providing time values with a minimum probability of providing the incorrect time, the time service has a number of other goals. These goals are listed in Box 15.1.

Time Values

We begin our discussion of how the time service meets its goals by examining the types of time values the time service is designed to maintain. Historically, time values have been based on the rotation of the earth about its axis. A time value based on this standard is called Universal Time (UT) and is the basis of our international and civil time standards. Universal Time corresponds with Greenwich Mean Time (GMT), the time of day in Greenwich, England, when Greenwich is on standard time. With Universal Time, a second is defined as 1/86400 of a mean solar day. A problem with Universal Time is that the earth's rotation is gradually slowing. So for precise scientific work, in 1964, the International Congress on Weights and Measures redefined the second to be 9,192,631,770 vibrations of the characteristic frequency of an atomic clock based on the cesium atom. Unlike the earth, the cesium atom is not gradually slowing and thus provides a much more precise measure of time. This time is called *Coordinated Universal Time*, often designated by the acronym UTC. Coordinated Universal Time is maintained by an international organization called the International Time Bureau. The DNA Phase V time service is based on Coordinated Universal Time.

Since Universal Time is continually slowing with respect to the vibration of the atomic clock used to maintain Coordinated Universal Time, the International Time Bureau periodically adjusts the atomic clock through the use of leap seconds to bring Coordinated Universal Time into coordination with Universal Time. The International Time Bureau announces these adjustments in advance and always performs the adjustment during the last minute of the month in which the correction is necessary. When such adjustments are necessary, it is possible for the last minute of the month to contain 61 seconds instead of 60 seconds. (Actually, the rules for leap seconds also allow for removing one second; thus, theoretically, the last minute of a month might have only 59 seconds. However, since the earth is slowing down and is not expected to speed up, it is unlikely that a minute of Coordinated Universal Time will ever have 59 seconds.)

A value can be obtained for Coordinated Universal Time, via a telephone call, radio, or satellite link in many parts of the world through various organizations. For example, in the United States the radio stations WWV in Colorado and WWVH in Hawaii broadcast values for Coordinated Universal Time throughout the day.

Since Coordinated Universal Time corresponds to Greenwich Mean Time, it is often modified by a factor called the *time differential factor*

(TDF). A TDF value is added or subtracted from a UTC value to obtain a time representation corresponding to the local time in some other time zone. For example, to obtain the standard time in the Eastern time zone of the United States, we would subtract a TDF value of 5 hours from the UTC value.

Time Value Inaccuracy

A characteristic inherent in the measurement of time is that a time value can never be said to be completely accurate. This is because no clock can be kept perfectly in synchronization with UTC. Four factors relate to how well a clock keeps time:

- **Inaccuracy.** A clock's inaccuracy represents how far its time value deviates from Coordinated Universal Time. The inaccuracy of a clock can never be known exactly, but it is possible to determine an upper bound for its inaccuracy.
- **Drift.** The inaccuracy of a clock is not constant but increases over time. Drift is a measure of the rate at which the inaccuracy of a clock is increasing. Like inaccuracy, drift can never be determined exactly, but we can place an upper bound on a clock's drift.
- **Skew.** Skew is a measure of the difference between a clock's value and the value for UTC at any instant. The upper bound of a clock's skew is a factor of the upper bound on a clock's inaccuracy and the upper bound on the clock's drift.
- **Resolution.** Clocks used in computer systems generally are digital and measure time in discrete *ticks*. A clock's resolution is a measure of the time interval between ticks.

Since a clock can never represent time completely accurately, the value the time service provides includes both an estimated value for UTC and an *inaccuracy value*, which is an upper bound on how inaccurate that time value is. Therefore, it is possible to determine only that the exact value for UTC at any instant falls somewhere between the estimated time value minus the inaccuracy and the estimated time value plus the inaccuracy (see Figure 15.2). When algorithms use the time values the time service provides—for example, in attempting to determine which of two events occurred first—the inaccuracy values the time service returns must be taken into account in comparing the two time values. If the two events occurred relatively close together in time, it is possible for the time ranges representing the times at which they occurred to

FIGURE 15.2   **A time value, consisting of an estimated UTC value and an inaccuracy value.**

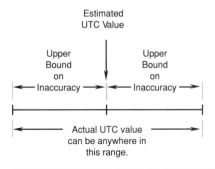

intersect, as shown in Figure 15.3. When such a situation occurs, although one of the events may have occurred earlier than the other, the order in which the two events occurred cannot be determined.

Time Value Representation

The time values that the time service works with and represents in interfaces and protocol messages consist of two types: binary absolute time and binary relative time. *Binary absolute time* contains an estimate of an

FIGURE 15.3   **If two events occur at the times indicated by these time values, the order in which the two events occurred cannot be determined.**

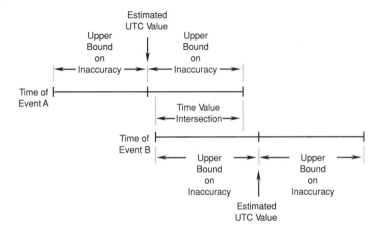

actual UTC value; *binary relative time* contains an estimate of an elapsed time interval. These two types of time values are represented with identical formats. The four components that currently make up a time value in the time service architecture are shown in Figure 15.4 and described below:

- **Version.** This field represents the version of the time service architecture being used. It must contain the value 1.

- **Time Differential Factor.** This field can be used to modify the value in the Coordinated Universal Time Estimate field to convert that value to the time in some other time zone. This field is present in an expression of binary relative time, but, since a TDF value is meaningless in a relative time value, it must contain the value zero in an expression of a relative time value.

- **Inaccuracy Value.** This field places an upper bound on the inaccuracy value inherent in the Coordinated Universal Time Estimate field.

- **Coordinated Universal Time Estimate.** This field estimates the time elapsed since midnight of October 15, 1582, the time at which the Gregorian calendar was officially adopted. This number can be used to obtain an estimate of the calendar date and an estimated value for UTC.

The exact format of the time values the time service works with may change over time as certain international standards that are currently being developed mature.

Time Service Architectural Model

The two major components that implement the distributed algorithms defined by the architecture are time service *clerks* and time service *servers*. Some of the servers may have access to a *time provider*, a device that obtains an accurate value for UTC from a service using a telephone line, radio communication, or satellite link. Each network node implementing the DNA Phase V architecture contains either a clerk or a server but not both. Both clerks and servers implement clocks that maintain

---

FIGURE 15.4   **Format of a Coordinated Universal Time (UTC) value.**

Version	Time Differential Factor	Inaccuracy	Coordinated Universal Time Estimate

values for the date, Coordinated Universal Time, inaccuracy, and a TDF value. A user of the time service makes a request of the time service for a time value. If that user's node implements a time service server, the server provides the time value; if the node implements a time service clerk, the clerk provides it. The time service defines clerks and servers to minimize the amount of synchronization that must take place to maintain the correct time in all nodes. Most nodes implement clerks, and servers are implemented in only some nodes. The complexity of synchronizing time values is handled mainly by the servers.

A clerk keeps its clock in synchronization by obtaining time values from some minimum number of servers, defined by a management attribute. The clerk then runs an algorithm that computes the intersection of all time values it obtains to calculate a "correct" time value. The algorithm defined in the time service architecture is designed so the clerk obtains the correct time even if somewhat fewer than half of the servers queried return incorrect time values.[*] The clerk then uses the time value it computes to adjust the time value it maintains in its own internal clock to improve its accuracy. The clerk adjusts its time value gradually so no user experiences discontinuities in the time values it obtains and so the clock never runs backward. However, the architecture has a provision for a clerk to make a step adjustment in the clock's value if the clerk determines its clock is wildly out of synchronization with UTC.

In an implementation of the time service, it is desirable that at least some of the time service servers have access to a time provider that provides an accurate value for UTC. To synchronize its clock, a server with access to a time provider periodically obtains an accurate time value from its time provider. Servers without access to a time provider periodically synchronize their clocks by obtaining the time from other servers in a manner similar to that of clerks.

Local and Global Sets

The time service assumes that in most networks most of the nodes are connected to local area networks having relatively short communication delays and that individual local area networks may be connected by

---

[*] The function that determines how many time servers can be faulty is $int((n-1)/2)$. This means, for example, that 4 out of 9 or 4 out of 10, but not 5 out of 10, servers can be faulty and the time service will still provide the correct time.

wide-area-networking links that may have a much longer communication delay. Each local area network implements a set of time servers known as the *local set*. It is possible for the local set to be empty for any given local area network. If there are enough servers in a given local set, all the clerks obtain time values only from servers in the local set, thus reducing communication delays and improving the accuracy of the time values maintained by the clerks.

Even though there may be enough servers to satisfy the needs of all the clerks attached to a given local area network, it is possible that none of these servers implements a time provider. To handle this situation and also the situation where there are not enough servers available in the local set, another set of servers is designated as a *global set*. These servers are available throughout the network. It is desirable that one or more of the servers in the global set have access to a time provider that servers can use as a source of accurate Coordinated Universal Time. The time service can function, however, even if no server has access to a time provider. In the absence of a time provider, a network manager must from time to time mimic a time provider on at least some of the servers and must provide those servers with accurate values for UTC. Choosing the global set requires a network management action. A server is made a part of the global set simply by registering its name with the naming service.

When a local area network does not have a server with access to a time provider, one of the servers in the local set is designated as a *courier server*, whose responsibility it is to import an accurate time value from one of the global servers. The use of a courier reduces the message traffic so not all of the servers on the local set need to import the time from a global server.

Advertisement and Solicitation Protocol

Servers periodically announce themselves to other servers attached to the same data link by sending multicast messages. A server must advertise on all the data links to which it is connected. Servers receive these advertisement messages and build lists of all the servers with which they can communicate. Clerks discover the servers in the local set by multicasting solicitation messages on all the data links to which the clerk is connected. (A server also does this when it first comes up.) A server replies to a solicitation message from a clerk by sending back its list of local servers. This allows a clerk to determine which servers are available to it. A server responds to a solicitation message not with a multicast message but with a message sent individually to the sender of the solicitation message.

Representative Inaccuracy Values

As discussed earlier, the inaccuracy value maintained by a clock increases in value as time goes on. Specific goals for maximum inaccuracy values are not defined by the architecture, but an appendix to the architectural specification contains some calculations showing what kinds of inaccuracy values implementations should be capable of providing. Accuracy values maintained by a clerk are functions of the following:

- the inherited inaccuracy in the time value a server provides
- the communication delay over the data links used to synchronize time values with servers
- the resolution of the clerk's clock
- the maximum value for the drift of the clerk's clock

The time service specification shows that for typical hardware the inherited inaccuracy of the time value provided by a server will be 10 ms, a typical computer system's clock has a resolution of 10 ms, a typical clock has a drift of one part in 10^{-4}, and a typical communication delay across a local area network is 20 ms. With these figures, the initial inaccuracy in the clerk's clock at the time of synchronization is 30 ms.* In 15 minutes after synchronization, the inaccuracy will be 120 ms; an hour after synchronization, the inaccuracy will be 390 ms. If the clerk must synchronize with a server across a wide area networking link with a delay of 500 ms, the initial inaccuracy will be 270 ms, the inaccuracy 15 minutes after synchronization will be 360 ms, and the inaccuracy an hour after synchronization will be 630 ms.

The specification then goes on to show that with optimized hardware using inexpensive crystal clocks and high-speed local area network links, the inherited accuracy can be reduced to 2 ms, the clock resolution can be reduced to 1 ms, the clock's drift can be reduced to 1 part in 10^{-6}, and the communication delay can be reduced to 2 ms. With this kind of optimized hardware, the initial inaccuracy of a clerk's clock immediately after synchronization would be reduced to 4 ms. Fifteen minutes after synchronization, the inaccuracy would increase to only 5 ms, and a full hour after synchronization the inaccuracy would still be only 8 ms.

---

* Since the communication delay contributes 20 ms to the width of the interval, it contributes only 10 ms to the inaccuracy; these examples, therefore, assume that the communication delay contributes only half its value to the inaccuracy.

Distributed Authentication Security Service Architecture

At the time of this writing, a task force at Digital is developing a comprehensive plan for security in distributed systems called the *Distributed System Security Architecture* (DSSA). The intent of DSSA is to define a comprehensive security framework and a set of protocol specifications that will enable users and systems to interact with one another in a secure fashion in a highly decentralized and distributed computing environment. Unlike more specific architectures, such as DNA for networking, a security architecture is much more pervasive and affects hardware, operating systems, networks, and both Digital-developed and user-developed applications. Therefore, DSSA will have effects on many architectures outside the scope of DNA Phase V.

DSSA Security Categories

The DSSA framework breaks the broad topic of security in distributed systems into five major components, which are introduced in Box 15.2. As one step along the long-term journey toward completing the design of the overall DSSA security framework, the *Distributed Authentication Security Service* (DASS) defines an implementation model for most of the requirements of the authentication component of DSSA and also addresses a portion of the requirements for the *delegation* and *secure channels* components.

Principals and Objects

Digital's security architectures discuss security in terms of *principals* that access *objects* in a distributed system. A principal can be either a human user or a program, such as one running on a node or a server in a distributed system. Both principals and objects have names known throughout the distributed system. As such, the security architectures depend on having access to a global directory service, such as that provided by the naming service described in Chapter 16.

Network Login

Many earlier security systems have been designed around a system of *user accounts* that individuals have on computer systems. A person that wants to access 10 computers would have to register a user account on each of them. Such a system on a large, possibly global, distributed system would be cumbersome at best. Instead of establishing accounts on individual computer systems, DASS defines the notions of *global identity* and *network logins*. Each principal has a name known globally and recognized on every node in the network. This means a user can use the same authentication procedures to login to any node without having to first set up a new account on that node. It is important to note that a user is not necessarily able to access the resources of any node in the network. Each node recognizes users by their names and has a policy concerning which users are allowed to access its resources.

Mutual, Strong Authentication

The authentication scheme defined by DASS provides for authentication that is both mutual and strong. *Mutual* authentication means that *each* of two communicating parties can learn the other party's name. Not only is it necessary for a server to know who a client is, but the client must also know that it is talking to an authentic server. For example, users who are accessing a file server would like to know the server is authentic before entrusting it with their files. *Strong* authentication means that in the exchange of information taking place during the authentication, neither party obtains any information it might subsequently use to impersonate the other party to someone else. The requirement for mutual authentication is relatively easy to meet and simply calls for authentication procedures to take place in both directions. But the requirement for strong authentication is more difficult to satisfy.

Cryptography

Many forms of cryptography can be used to encipher data for transmission over a network to protect the data from eavesdropping. A system of cryptography is often called a *cryptosystem*. Some cryptosystems depend on keeping secret the algorithms used to encipher and decipher messages. Such a system is of little use in computer systems because it is difficult to keep the algorithm secret. Once the system has been broken and the algorithm divulged, all users of the algorithm are compromised, and all computer systems using that algorithm have to be changed. Cryptosystems better suited to computer applications use algorithms that are public and that depend on the use of a *cryptographic key* that is kept secret. Users might know the algorithm used to decipher a message but cannot decipher it unless they also have knowledge of the unique key required to decipher it.

BOX 15.2

DSSA Security
Components

- **Authentication.** Authentication is the process whereby one user (either a person or a node) verifies the identity of another user. The classic way in which authentication is accomplished in computer systems is through systems of user IDs and passwords. However, there are a number of disadvantages to passwords, and the authentication component of DSSA provides procedures that overcome those disadvantages and are easier to use than current methods.

- **Secure Channels.** Because the network must be assumed to be an inherently public medium, data that must be kept private must be protected from eavesdropping while in transit. This is most often accomplished with cryptographic techniques in which messages are enciphered before transmission and deciphered after receipt. A channel using a cryptography mechanism is called a *secure channel*. Cryptography also protects data integrity because an intruder cannot modify, replay, or suppress data in transit without the receiver detecting it.

- **Installing and Loading.** Software often will have to be downline loaded across the network from one computing system to another. A method of attacking the security of a network is to install a *Trojan horse*, typically a piece of software that is not easily detectable and that can have some desired effect. For example, an unauthorized party who desires to gain access to the files stored on a particular computing system might arrange to add a Trojan horse to the software normally downline loaded to that computing system. The Trojan horse might implement functions, such as storing away files the computing system has access to, allowing the unauthorized person access to those files. This part of DSSA defines procedures using cryptographic techniques to verify the correctness of the software downline loaded across the network and executed in network machines.

- **Access Control.** The access control part of DSSA is related to, but different from, authentication. Authentication verifies the identity of a user; access control provides a means of specifying what that user is able to do after gaining access to the network. For example, a human user performs the authentication process once, at the beginning of the session. Then access control functions determine what operations are valid for that user during the life of the session. Access control procedures are based on two types of principals: users and

BOX 15.2

continued

systems. A user is an abstraction of the person who uses systems and resources and requests access to objects. A system is an abstraction of a computing system running a particular piece of software. A system is usually a DECnet network node. Groups are names representing some collection of users and/or systems. The principal method for defining who can do what in a distributed system is based on access control lists that define access rights to defined objects.

- **Delegation.** Delegation is the process by which one party authorizes a second party to act as its representative in the distributed system. For example, when a human user performs the authentication process at a workstation, that user delegates to the workstation the right to act as a surrogate for that user in the distributed system. This delegation might be expressed in the form of a certificate a user "signs" during the authentication procedure. The delegation certificate, in effect, tells the remote system that the user trusts the workstation to accurately reflect that user's requests.

NETWORK ARCHITECT

Strong authentication can't be done with passwords alone. Mutual authentication can be done with passwords by having a sign and a countersign the two parties must say to assure one another of their identities. But whichever party speaks first reveals information that can be used by the second party to impersonate it to a third party. Longer sequences (often seen in spy movies) cannot solve the problem in general. Further, anyone who can eavesdrop on the conversation can impersonate either party in a subsequent conversation, unless passwords are used only once. Cryptography provides a means by which one party can prove the knowledge of a secret without having to reveal the secret to the other party.

Symmetric Cryptography Algorithms Most cryptosystems in use at the time of this writing employ symmetric algorithms, in which both the sender and the receiver require knowledge of the key used to encipher the message. That same key is then used to decipher the message. With a symmetric crypto system, a sender enciphers a message by putting it through an algorithm, using a particular cryptographic key value, to transform the message so it is unreadable by ordinary means. The enciphered message is then transmitted to the receiver. The receiver places the enciphered message through a complementary algorithm, using the identical cryptographic key value, to obtain a copy of the original message.

A commonly used public cryptography algorithm was adopted in the United States in 1981 as ANSI X3.92-1981, *American National Standard Data Encryption Algorithm* (DES). The DES form of cryptography enciphers data in 64-bit blocks using a 56-bit cryptographic key. The DES algorithm has proven over the years to be very secure and, to our knowledge, no one has yet been able to decipher a message enciphered with the DES algorithm without knowing the cryptographic key. The DES algorithm is widely used in the banking industry. DASS uses the DES algorithm for most of the cryptography it does, especially where large quantities of data are involved. The DES scheme is used because the algorithm is simple, and data can be enciphered using the DES algorithm much more quickly than with other schemes.

The DES algorithm has a number of disadvantages, however, for certain applications. With the very high speed computer systems that are today possible, it is becoming conceivable that a very fast computer—or a set of distributed systems working collectively—could break the code by searching through all possible 56-bit keys. Another disadvantage of the DES algorithm is that both the sender and the receiver must be in possession of the same cryptographic key value, which must be kept secret.

Symmetric algorithms do not provide adequate protection if there is a high probability that an intruder could learn the value of the cryptographic key. In a large distributed computing environment, the requirement that every node know a secret key for every other node becomes unmanageable. Also, prior knowledge of keys does not work for applications such as electronic mail, where there is a requirement for sending mail securely to users all over the world. It would be desirable for the sender to change the cryptographic key often and to inform the receiver of the key value it is using. But how can cryptographic key values be sent over the network in a secure manner? An eavesdropper that obtains the cryptographic key will be able to decipher any message enciphered using that key. Until about the mid-1970s, the commonly used method for sending cryptographic keys over a network in a secure manner consisted of obtaining cryptographic key values from a trusted third party, with which both parties already share a key. But in 1978, three researchers named Rivest, Shamir, and Adleman developed a scheme that eliminated the need for relying on a trusted third party.

Asymmetric Cryptography Algorithms   An asymmetric cryptography algorithm is one in which the key used to decipher a message is different from the key used to encipher it. It must not be possible to derive the key that must be used to decipher the message from the key used to encipher it. Because the key used to encipher the message cannot be used to decipher it, it does not matter who knows its value, and the value of such a key can be made public with no compromise of security. Cryptosystems using asymmetric algorithms are often called *public key* systems. The algorithm described by Rivest, Shamir, and Adleman is generally called the *RSA public key* cryptography system. [1] Rivest, Shamir, and Adleman built on the preliminary work of Diffie and Hellman on public key cryptography. [2]

With the RSA public key cryptosystem, the cryptographic key used to encrypt a message can be sent over the network without compromising a message enciphered using that key. Such a crypto system can be made much more secure than one using a symmetric algorithm. In setting up for the transmission of an enciphered message, the intended receiver generates two key values: a private key, which the receiver keeps secret, and a public key, which the receiver sends to the sender. The sender then enciphers the message using the public key and transmits the enciphered message to the receiver. The receiver then deciphers the message using the private key it has kept secret. With such a system, knowing the value of the public key does an eavesdropper no good because it cannot be used to decipher the message. Deciphering the message requires knowledge of the private key, which is not transmitted over the network. The system works in the opposite direction as well. A message enciphered with the private key can be deciphered with the public key.

DASS Strong Authentication

The facilities provided by the RSA public key crypto system are exactly what is needed to provide a strong authentication facility. Node A can prove to node B that it has knowledge of a secret without actually divulging that secret to node B. Without such a facility a system of passwords is not secure. The DASS authentication scheme uses RSA public key cryptography. It is feasible to use RSA public key cryptography for authentication, even though it requires far more resources than the DES algorithm, because a relatively small amount of information is exchanged during the authentication procedure.

A strong authentication system using RSA public key cryptography might work something like this:

1. Each node in the network chooses a public key/private key pair. It then keeps the private key value secret and publishes the public key value.

2. Node A authenticates to node B by sending it a message containing an identifier both unenciphered and enciphered using its secret private key.

3. Node B obtains node A's public key value.

4. Node B deciphers the identifier it received from node A in enciphered form using node A's public key value.

5. If the deciphered identifier matches the identifier it received in unenciphered form, node B knows that node A is authentic because only the real node A knows the private cryptographic key that had to have been used to encipher the information.

Mutual authentication can be accomplished with the above system by using the same procedure to authenticate node B to node A. The system works, of course, only if each node can keep its own private cryptographic key secret. But because private cryptographic key values never have to be transmitted over the network, methods can be devised for keeping them secure. The actual cryptographic techniques the DASS authentication scheme uses are a good bit more complex than just described in order to deal with a variety of problems and security threats. We discuss some of these next.

Certificates

A flaw in the strong authentication scheme described in the preceding section is that each node must have a way of determining another node's public cryptography key. A ubiquitous service, such as the naming service, could be used to maintain public key values, but this would represent a point in the system that could be compromised. To avoid the necessity of one user requiring the other user's public key value, a system of *certificates* is used in DASS for authentication. With the DASS authentication scheme, each new principal must register its name with a *certification authority* (CA). A new node would go to the CA, present its public key value, and prove it has a particular name. The mechanism for this depends on the level of security to be provided. The CA then issues the node a certificate, which consists of a message containing an identifier and a public key value, both enciphered using the CA's private key. Now, when node A authenticates to node B, node A includes its certificate in the authentication message it sends to node B. Node B can determine node A's public key value by deciphering the certificate using the CA's public key value, which everyone knows.

An important characteristic of certificates is that their use does not require the CA to be available at the time authentication takes place. The CA need be available only when a new principal requires a certificate, thus making it much easier to keep the CA safe from compromise. (One possible plan for keeping the CA safe is to implement it on a small computer that could be locked away in a safe and taken out only when a principal needs to apply for a certificate.) However, since a certificate issued by the CA is likely to be used by a principal for a relatively long period of time, perhaps months, the system must include procedures for revoking certificates should private key values fall into the wrong hands. The DASS specification discusses methods for handling certificate revocation.

Timestamps

The authentication scheme we have been discussing allows for positive authentication, but only if the message is accepted only once. If an eavesdropper were listening in on an authentication exchange between node A and node B, it could make a copy of the certificate and then use it to impersonate node A to node B. To avoid the possibility of this happening, two additional requirements must be met. The authentication message (containing the certificate) that node A sends to node B must be acceptable only to node B and not to any other principal. It is also necessary for node B to accept an authentication message only once.

DASS solves the first problem by including in the authentication message not only a name that identifies node A but also a name that identifies node B. Node A enciphers both its own identifier and node B's identifier. Then when node B deciphers the authentication message, it will accept the message as authentic only if it sees its own name in it. This prevents an eavesdropper from using the authentication message to authenticate to some other node. An eavesdropper could still impersonate node A to node B, however, by using an identical copy of the authentication message. To prevent this from happening, the enciphered authentication message also contains a timestamp indicating the time the authentication took place. Node B then keeps track of all authentication messages it receives over a short period of time, say five minutes. If it receives the same message twice over a five-minute period, it rejects the second one. Then once the five-minute period is up, it discards the me sages it has been keeping and simply rejects any authentication messages it receives having a timestamp more than five minutes old.

Delegation

The scheme just described provides a means by which one principal can authenticate itself to another principal. In a distributed system, however, such one-to-one authentication is not enough. When a human user logs onto a distributed system, the user wants to use the distributed system to access resources on his or her behalf. This requires the user to give the node at which the desired service is performed the right to represent that user in the system for the purposes of gaining access to resources on behalf of that user. For one principal to represent another principal, the first principal must provide the second principal with access to the RSA private key value to use in subsequent authentication procedures. DSSA provides mechanisms for allowing one principal to pass a secret to another principal for a limited amount of time for the purposes of delegation. Secrets passed over the network are always encrypted so eavesdroppers cannot learn them.

Authentication of Human Users

As we have seen, the strong authentication system defined by DASS is based on RSA public key cryptography, which is computationally complex. Since human users would find it difficult to perform cryptography calculations in their heads, it is not possible for a human to strongly authenticate to the node at which he or she logs in. So the first link between the human user and the login node can represent a weak link in the authentication chain.

Smart Cards

The use of smart cards to handle the initial login can allow strong authentication procedures to be implemented on behalf of human users. A smart card is essentially a credit-card-sized computer a user carries around to handle the details of gaining access to a distributed system. Because smart cards currently are too expensive to be used in general-purpose network authentication schemes, the DASS architecture accommodates but does not require the use of smart cards for login. In the future, smart cards will become less expensive and will begin to play a more important role in providing secure access by human users to distributed systems.

Remote Procedure Call Architecture The idea behind providing a remote procedure call (RPC) facility in a network architecture is that procedure calls are a well-understood mechanism for transferring control and data from one procedure to another in a computer program. Almost all standard programming languages, such as FORTRAN, C, and COBOL, have such a mechanism, and procedure call semantics for these languages are well defined. It is therefore of great utility to extend the procedure call mechanism from a set of procedures in a single-computer environment to the distributed system environment. An RPC mechanism provides an excellent tool for implementing the client/server paradigm in a distributed system.

NETWORK ARCHITECT

The idea of the remote procedure call is of strategic importance to application developers in a distributed computing environment. Basically, it turns writing distributed applications from something akin to rocket science to something more like placing an overseas telephone call.

Figure 15.5 shows the basic concept behind a procedure call mechanism. Procedure A executes a CALL statement, possibly referencing some parameters, which passes control to procedure B. While procedure B executes, procedure A waits. When procedure B finishes its processing, it executes a RETURN statement. The RETURN statement causes control to be passed to the statement immediately after the CALL statement in procedure A. In most language/operating system environments, procedure calls can be nested to any desired level, as where procedure A in Figure 15.5 calls procedure C, which in turn calls procedure D.

The idea behind a remote procedure call facility is to allow the procedure call mechanism to work when the calling procedure and the called procedure reside in different computing systems connected by a communications network. Ideally this should be done so the calling procedure can call a remote procedure using exactly the same technique it would use to call a procedure residing on the same computing system. In other words, the mechanisms the RPC facility employs should be hidden from both the calling and the called procedures. The problems associated with creating an RPC facility lie in three major areas:

- **Locating the called procedure.** The RPC facility must provide a means for locating the called procedure in the network.

FIGURE 15.5   **Procedure call mechanism.**

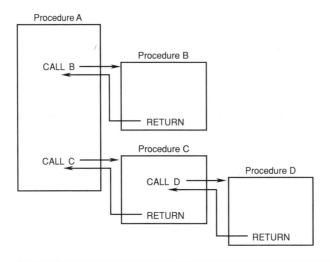

- **Passing parameters.** With the procedure call mechanism implemented in traditional language environments, communication between the two procedures is based on a shared address space. Parameter values are generally passed by *reference*, which means the calling procedure passes the called procedure *pointers* to the parameter values. When the two procedures reside on different computing systems, there is no common address space. Therefore, an RPC facility must be able to handle the passing of parameters in both directions.
- **Binding the called procedure to the calling procedure.** With a conventional procedure call mechanism, many techniques can be used for binding. With early binding, a linking mechanism is used to construct a single program module containing both the calling and the called procedure. Both the calling and the called procedures are then loaded into storage at the same time. With late binding, the procedure call mechanism implemented by the operating system may allow the called procedure to be dynamically loaded into computer storage at the time the CALL is executed. With a remote procedure call facility, binding is even more complex because it involves finding the server containing the desired procedure.

Remote Procedure Call Functional Model

A simplified functional model of an RPC facility is shown in Figure 15.6. The RPC facility serving the calling procedure may use a global naming service to determine on which node in the network the called procedure resides. The server is found before the actual call executes. The process of finding the server's address is called *importing*. In this functional model, a calling procedure executes a procedure call in the same manner as if it were executing a procedure call to a local procedure. A module called a *stub* in the local node mimics the presence of the actual procedure to which the calling procedure is attempting to pass control. There is a unique stub for each set of procedures using the RPC facility in the client. The stub in turn requests the services of the RPC facility.

The RPC facility uses the services of the communication network to transmit parameter information, in the form of RPC-protocol-data-units (RPC-PDUs), to and from the RPC facility in the remote node. When the RPC facility in the remote system receives the RPC-PDUs generated as a result of the procedure call, it determines whether the requested called

FIGURE 15.6   RPC facility functional model.

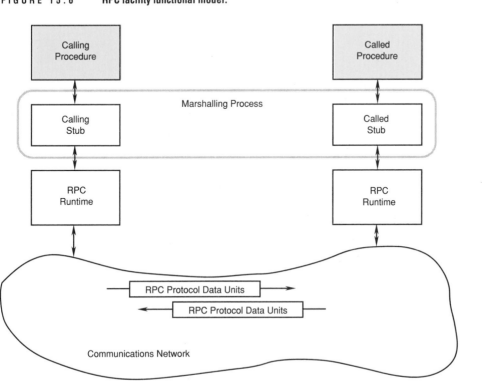

procedure already resides in computer storage there. If it does not, a facility in the remote node loads the program module containing the requested procedure and passes control to it, again using a stub unique to that procedure. The called procedure then passes parameter information back to the calling procedure and passes control back to it using a process similar to that described for the calling procedure.

The process of converting the parameter information in the local node into RPC-PDUs and performing the same process in the opposite direction is called *marshalling*. The marshalling process is straightforward if the two procedures represent parameter values using the same data representation. On Digital operating systems almost all programming languages use the same data formats. But this may not be true in other computing environments. To be useful in a heterogeneous environment, it is necessary for an RPC facility to handle the situation where the calling procedure and the called procedure use different formats, so data conversion must be done by the marshalling routines.

DNA Phase V RPC Architectural Model

The architecture for the DNA Phase V remote procedure call facility provides support for a heterogeneous computing system environment. The architectural model for the DNA Phase V RPC facility is shown in Figure 15.7. Like other distributed computing services, the RPC architecture uses a client/server model. The calling procedure is the client, and the procedure being called is the server. Both the client procedure and the server procedure execute as though they both resided in the same computing system.

Packages and Binding

Server procedures are grouped together in units called *interfaces*. An interface consists of the externally visible characteristics of a set of procedures. An interface is defined using an *interface definition language* (IDL). The interface definition defines the procedures, parameters, and error conditions of the interface. Each interface is assigned a unique *interface identifier*. This interface identifier is known to both the client and the server stubs. The client uses the interface identifier to find a server supporting the desired interface. In many applications there will be more than one such server.

To execute a remote procedure through the RPC facility, the RPC facility in the node executing the client procedure must learn what inter-

FIGURE 15.7   **DNA Phase V RPC architectural model.**

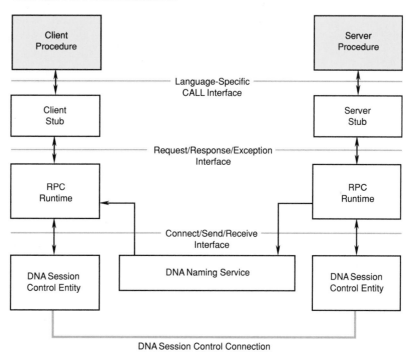

face the desired procedure is a part of. The RPC facility in the node executing the calling procedure then performs an *address resolution*, or *importing*, procedure using the naming service to determine where in the network the package resides. After a successful importing procedure, the RPC facility performs a *binding* operation that sets up a communication path, using a DNA Session Control connection, between the RPC runtime module serving the client procedure and the RPC runtime module in the server procedure's node. The binding operation takes place at the time the first call in the interface is executed using that interface. The RPC facilities in both nodes then use this connection for the purposes of requesting remote procedure invocation between the client procedure and the server procedure and transmitting the results of the invocation.

Unique Identifier
Architecture

The *Unique Identifier* (UID) architecture defines a service any user can employ to obtain an identifier that is unique over space and time. There is a very high probability that the identifier obtained through this service is different from any other identifier assigned by the UID service operating anywhere in a possibly global network. The UID architecture is unique in that it is designed to provide its service without requiring the setting of any management information and without requiring any communication between nodes in the distributed system. The algorithm providing the UID service in a given node is completely self-contained and requires no external communication.

The UID service is designed to be used by other distributed computing services. For example, the naming service uses the UID service to obtain unique identifiers it attaches to objects it stores attributes for. Network management also uses unique identifiers to control its operation. User-written applications can use the UID service to obtain unique identifiers they can use to unambiguously label objects, processes, events, and entities. Once the UID service has assigned an identifier, the process requesting it is ensured that there is an extremely low (but not zero) probability that the same identifier will be assigned by some other invocation of the UID service either in that node or in any other node in the network. Duplicate identifiers can occur only if the UID service is operating incorrectly, if node identifiers migrate, or if time runs backward on the clock in a node.

The UID service assigns unique identifiers whose components are based on the node's node ID, a value for Coordinate Universal Time (UTC), and other values that are used to ensure that there is a very high probability of the identifiers being unique over both space and time. However, even though a value for UTC is currently a part of the identifier, identifiers assigned by the UID service must be used only to ensure uniqueness and not for the purpose of time ordering events. This is because future versions of the architecture may use means other than UTC values, such as large random numbers, to achieve uniqueness.

UID Properties

The following are the properties of the unique identifiers the UID service assigns:

- **Uniqueness.** There is a very high probability that each UID value the UID service generates on any DNA Phase V node is different from any other UID value.
- **Immutability.** A UID value, once assigned, is guaranteed never to be changed as long as it is manipulated only by the UID service.

- **Lexical Ordering.** There exists a specific lexical ordering of any set of UIDs.
- **Lack of Temporal Ordering.** The architecture does not specify a means of placing a set of UIDs into the sequence in which they were created.

UID Service Operations

The UID service allows users of the service to request three different types of operations:

- creating a new UID
- testing two UIDs for equality
- sorting a set of UIDs based on their values

Users of the UID service should perform operations on UIDs using only these three operations in order to preserve the immutability property of UIDs.

UID Internal Structure

We will examine the internal structure of a UID next to provide some insight into the lengths to which the architecture goes to ensure that the probability of two UIDs being the same is extremely small. A unique identifier assigned by the UID service currently consists of the four components shown in Figure 15.8 and described below:

- **Node ID.** Each node in the network must be assigned at least one 48-bit node address assigned from the IEEE 802 address space. It is a requirement of the DNA Phase V architecture that each node must be assigned a 48-bit node ID even if it does not have a local area network interface adapter. The node address field in a UID guarantees that the UIDs generated by one node will be different from UIDs generated by any other node, anywhere in the world. The remainder of the UID is used to guarantee that a single node never generates the same UID value twice.

FIGURE 15.8   **General format of a UID.**

Node ID	Clock Sequence No.	Version	Adjusted Coordinated Universal Time

- **Clock Sequence Value.** It is possible for a node to have a clock that lacks the property of *monotonicity*, which means it is possible under some circumstances for a clock to run backward. For example, a system might fail, reboot, and reinitialize its clock to some value lower than the value it contained when the failure occurred. To provide a unique UID value even when such an event occurs, the UID service maintains a *clock sequence number* it changes whenever the UID service detects that the clock has run backward or that it is *possible* the clock may have run backward. Also, if the UID service loses the current clock sequence number, for example, after a catastrophic system failure, it reinitializes the clock sequence number using a random number before assigning new UID values.

- **Version Number.** This field identifies the version of the UID service architecture in effect at the time the UID was created. A version number is necessary because UIDs often are attached to objects having very long lifetimes. It is possible for a UID attached to an object to be processed in the future by a system implementing subsequent versions of the UID architecture. To ensure correct operation, it is necessary for the UID service to determine that the UID was created using an implementation of a previous version of the architecture.

- **Adjusted Time Value.** A UID contains a UTC value field. In most implementations of the UID service, this value is obtained using the time service described earlier in this chapter, although the architecture allows a value for UTC to be obtained using any desired means. Because it is possible on a very fast processor for multiple users to request UIDs within the same system clock tick, the UID service adjusts the UTC time value it generates by adding a different value to it for each new UID it assigns within the same tick of the system clock. In this way, the UID service assigns a different time value for each UID it generates.

Although we show the internal structure of the UID as it is defined by the version of the architecture current as of the time of this writing, the architectural specification warns that the means by which UIDs are generated and the internal structure of the UID may change in subsequent versions of the architecture. Changes may be necessary to bring the UID service into conformance with international standards now under development or to accommodate changes in requirements for the UID service. Therefore, users should regard the value the UID service assigns to a unique identifier as an opaque data structure whose internal structure is hidden.

Conclusion

This chapter introduced the important distributed computing services used by components of the DNA Phase V architecture and by users of a DECnet Phase V network. As discussed in this chapter, an extremely important distributed computing service implements a naming function that can be used to assign names to objects and to retrieve attributes associated with those names. The DNA Phase V naming service requires a chapter of its own, and its operation is described in Chapter 16.

References

1. Whitfield Diffie and Martin E. Hellman, "New Directions in Cryptography," *IEEE Transactions on Information Theory*, vol. IT-22, no. 6, November 1976.

2. R. L. Rivest, A. Shamir, and L. Adleman, "A Method for Obtaining Digital Signatures and Public-key Cryptosystems," *Communications of the ACM*, vol. 21, no. 2, February 1978.

CHAPTER 16

The Naming Service

Computer networks in many organizations are providing an ever growing and ever more sophisticated set of services to their users. To permit growing numbers of users to use these services effectively, they must be easy to locate and easy to use. A growing problem in computer networking—especially with large networks—involves identifying, locating, and accessing network devices, the people who use them, and the application programs running on them. In some cases, the resources provided by computer networks are underutilized simply because the users of the network are unaware of the facilities the network provides or are unable to find them. Many of the difficulties associated with locating network resources arise from the lack of an easy-to-use directory service for naming resources and for locating them using their assigned names. The *naming service* in DNA Phase V is Digital's solution to the directory problem.

NETWORK ARCHITECT

In Phase II of DNA, each node had a node name. There was no routing, so you could only talk to your neighbor nodes. When we put routing in, we assigned an address to each node. The question then became one of how to map between node names and node addresses, because we didn't want to require users to work with node addresses. We looked at the problem of translating node names to node addresses in a reliable, robust fashion, and we quickly concluded that it was a very hard problem. We decided not to try to solve it in Phase III or even in Phase IV. We provided each node with its own database that it used to translate node names into node addresses. That database simply consisted of a file that users updated and shipped around the network. In effect, the way we dealt with node name databases was outside the scope of the architecture. We couldn't deal with the naming problem in Phase III or Phase IV because it was simply too hard a problem to solve given the resources we had available. It ended up taking us a long time and a lot of resources to adequately solve the naming problem, and we have included this solution in Phase V of the architecture.

Objects and Names

Conceptually the main function of the naming service is very simple: it accepts a name and passes back the set of attributes associated with that name (see Figure 16.1). The naming service can be used to store attribute values for any type of named object the user of the naming service finds useful, including network devices and application programs. An important attribute that can be associated with a named object is the address of the node on which the object resides. An object's address consists of a set of towers that describe all the ways in which communication can be established with the named object. (Towers are described in Chapter 11.) The naming service allows network users to create a global *namespace* containing the names of all the objects that can be referenced, anywhere in a possibly global network.

The naming service is an integral part of the infrastructure of a DECnet Phase V network and is central to the network's operation. The services provided by the naming service are available at all times to all nodes in the network. For this reason, the DNA Phase V architects built into the naming service a variety of features to make it a highly robust, highly available network facility. A key concern during the design of the naming service was scalability—the naming service had to serve the needs of very large networks.

NETWORK ARCHITECT

We went to tremendous lengths, even beyond what we did in routing, to make the naming service scale indefinitely. We recognized that users might want to carve networks up for the purposes of autonomy and to serve the varying needs of different organizations. But we also realized that from the viewpoint of nam-

FIGURE 16.1   **Function of the naming service.**

ing things, the boundaries between networks become highly artificial and inconvenient. Organizations really need the ability to develop a single, global namespace in which anyone anywhere can name things in a consistent fashion. So we went to great lengths to make sure the naming service could provide that capability. Initial implementations of the naming service will be able to store enough names to serve the needs of networks as large as a million or so nodes. The architecture itself is scalable, so implementations will eventually be capable of storing hundreds of millions of names to give the naming service the capability of implementing something as large as a worldwide directory of computer network resources.

Naming Service Requirements and Design Goals

The DNA Phase V naming service was designed to meet a number of technical goals to support the directory services required in modern computer networks. The following are the most important of these requirements and design goals:

- **Homogeneity.** The naming service should be available as a service on all DNA Phase V network nodes.

- **Compatibility.** The naming service should be compatible with the naming services provided by DNA Phase IV.

- **Decentralizability.** Management of the naming service should be done in a decentralized fashion to avoid the inefficiencies associated with centralized management of network resources.

- **Predictability.** The naming service should be able to uniquely identify named objects in a large network so there is a very low probability of two objects having the same name.

- **Location Independence.** The naming service should permit a named object to be moved from one location to another in the network without requiring its name to be changed.

- **Stability.** The naming service should allow two isolated networks, each with its own private namespace, to be merged into a single network having a single namespace without requiring names to be changed.

- **Simplicity.** The naming service should be easy to understand, easy to use, easy to implement, and easy to manage. It must be able to adapt itself to changes that occur in the network to limit the amount of effort necessary to set up the naming service and to keep it running.

- **Extensibility.** The naming service should allow new functions to be added without disrupting existing functions.

- **Robustness.** The naming service must be at least as reliable and available as any of the resources whose names it stores. The objective is that the inability to communicate with a resource should never be solely due to a fault in the naming service.

- **Efficiency.** The process of looking up the attributes associated with a name must be fast and efficient so users are able to use the naming service to locate resources without paying a performance penalty.

- **Flexibility.** The naming service should be adaptable to naming a wide variety of objects, including nodes, files, users, application programs, devices, and the internal objects the naming service itself uses to maintain the namespace.

- **Security.** The naming service should ensure the privacy and integrity of names by preventing unauthorized disclosure, modification, insertion, or deletion of the naming information it maintains.

Kinds of Names

Before discussing the characteristics and features of the naming service, it will be helpful to describe the sorts of names a directory service might store. Basically four types of names can be used to identify resources in a computer network: addresses, routes, primitive names, and descriptive names.

Addresses

An *address* is a form of name that identifies a resource by its location in the network. Previous phases of DNA used this sort of name to identify resources. Although network resources in DNA Phase IV can be identified using an arbitrary string of characters, the use of a character string to identify a resource is really no more than a user convenience—the character string simply stands for the resource's address. The node address is derived by using a simple table lookup procedure on the local node. As a network grows, the relationships between nodes and the resources residing on them become increasingly complex and arbitrary. There are problems associated with using addresses to name objects when the objects are replicated in the network and frequently moved from one node to another. Names can become invalidated as resources are reconfigured and as new nodes are added and old nodes deleted.

Routes

A *route* names a resource by enumerating the exact path that must be traversed from the user to the resource in question. Routes are even more problematic than addresses as a means of identifying network resources. Route names depend on who is accessing a resource as well as where that resource is located—different users will use different routes. What is even worse, network reconfiguration can cause the names of resources to change over time.

Primitive Names

A *primitive name* is a character string that uniquely identifies a resource. An important feature of primitive names is that they are unambiguous— no two objects in the network can have the same primitive name. Primitive names can be constructed in any desired manner, and there is no particular relationship between a primitive name and any of the attributes associated with the name. Primitive names are the types of names the naming service processes. In a DNA Phase V network, a user name might look something like ENG.NAC.DaveOran. If Dave Oran is on one node today and some other node tomorrow, the address attribute of his name can be changed, so that other users can still refer to him by the name ENG.NAC.DaveOran without having to be aware that his node address changed.

Descriptive Names

A descriptive name is a name that identifies an object by specifying information about the attributes of that object. A descriptive name might refer to no objects, to a single object, or to more than one object. An example of a descriptive name might be "the mailbox of the person with signatory responsibility for the engineering cost center." A descriptive name uniquely identifies an object only if enough attribute information is included to differentiate the named object from all other objects. The above descriptive name uniquely identifies a particular mailbox as long as there is one and only one person with signatory responsibility for the engineering cost center.

Directory services that manipulate descriptive names are potentially the most powerful; however, they are also the most demanding of computing resources and are difficult to distribute among multiple computer systems.

CCITT Recommendation X.500, also called the OSI Directory, documented in ISO 9594—is an international standard for a naming service that has some descriptive naming capabilities. The OSI Directory is introduced at the end of this chapter. Digital is developing products to provide the services of the OSI Directory using the DNA Phase V naming service as a base.

Namespace Logical Structure

In creating a naming service that stores and manipulates primitive names, the namespace can be structured in a number of ways. The following are characteristics of some possible ways in which a namespace might be structured.

Flat Structure

The simplest namespace organization has a *flat structure* in which the names consist of arbitrary strings of symbols. A flat structure is easy for users to understand and places no restriction on the ways in which new names could be assigned (except possibly character set and length constraints). However, assigning unique names in a flat namespace becomes increasingly difficult as the size of the network, and hence the size of the namespace, increases.

Tree Structure

A *tree* is a graph structure in which each node has exactly one *parent* and any number of *children*. The bottommost nodes in the tree are called *leaf nodes*. A line connecting a parent node to a child node is called an *arc* of the graph. (See Figure 16.2.) Many existing computer file systems use a tree-structured naming system. Such file systems generally use a *rooted* tree structure, in which a single node is an ancestor of all other nodes.

Trees permit the use of a decentralized approach to naming that provides a natural, hierarchical scheme for organizing the namespace. Each user or group of users is free to organize a given portion of the namespace in any desired manner. A problem with a tree-structured namespace is that each object is permitted to have only one name because each node under the root has only one parent.

Directed Graph Structure

A *directed graph* is similar to a tree, but a given node can have any number of parent nodes (see Figure 16.3). A directed graph can be a *rooted*

FIGURE 16.2   Tree structure.

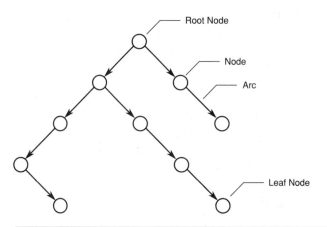

directed graph, in which one node is the ancestor of all other nodes, or it can be *unrooted*, in which there is no such common ancestor. Computer file systems that permit *alias names*, in which a given file can have more than one name, often implement a rooted, directed graph structure. A problem with a namespace structured as a directed graph is that endless cycles are possible. A name containing an endless loop is of little use, so most naming systems employing a directed graph structure contain mechanisms to prevent cycles from occurring. The structure of such a namespace is termed an *acyclic, rooted, directed graph*. This is the type of namespace structure employed by the naming service.

FIGURE 16.3   Acyclic, rooted, directed graph structure.

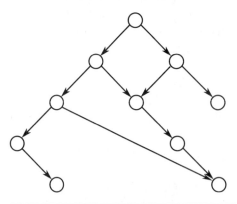

Simple Names and Full Names

The underlying structure used to create the namespace is that of a tree. Each arc of the tree is assigned a *simple name*, which consists of a string of octets having no internal structure. A complete name, called a *full name*, consists of a concatenation of all the simple names assigned to a set of arcs that begins at the root of the tree and ends with the object in question.

The underlying tree structure permits the use of simplified algorithms for namespace maintenance. The tree structure is augmented by allowing a given node to have arcs from more than one parent node. These additional arcs allow a given object to have more than one name (i.e., there can be more than one collection of arcs from the root of the graph to a particular node). Allowing a node to have more than one parent allows users to view the underlying tree structure as if it were a directed graph.

Characteristics of Names

We next examine the characteristics of names. We discuss the concept of referential transparency and then examine the semantics and the syntax of the primitive names the naming service stores and manipulates.

Referential Transparency

An important property of the names maintained by the naming service is that of *referential transparency*. This means that a full name always refers to the same thing no matter which user provided the name, and that the name can be freely passed outside the naming service (for example, on pieces of paper) from one user to another without the possibility of confusion.

Name Semantics

The naming service maintains full names. To the naming service, a full name consists of the concatenation of the simple names of a set of arcs beginning at the root of the namespace. Each full name in a namespace begins with a simple name containing a unique identifier called the *namespace creation timestamp* (NSCTS). The NSCTS is assigned to the namespace at the time the namespace is first created. This unique identifier ensures that each full name in the namespace is different from the full names stored in any other namespace. By assigning a unique identifier to each namespace, it is possible to merge together any collection of namespaces without requiring changes to any of the names in those namespaces. The naming service provides facilities so users themselves do not have to supply the NSCTS value when working with the naming service.

Name Syntax

Two syntaxes are employed by the naming service for representing names: an external syntax and an internal syntax. The *external syntax* refers to names in human-readable form; the *internal syntax* refers to names passed across the application programming interface to the naming service and maintained internally in the namespace database. The external syntax is designed for readability, while the internal syntax is designed to be convenient to encode in programs, protocols, and databases.

External Names

An external name consists of two parts: a *namespace nickname* and a *concatenation of simple names*. The namespace nickname is translated locally by the naming service into the NSCTS value uniquely identifying the namespace. If a namespace nickname is omitted from an external name, the naming service chooses a preselected NSCTS value.

The namespace nickname and the concatenation of simple names making up a full name are an ordered list of strings of letters, digits, and certain punctuation characters from the ISO Latin-1 character set. The case of each string is preserved by the naming service: when retrieved, a name registered with a mix of upper- and lowercase characters will appear exactly as it was entered. Lookups, however, are case-insensitive. The strings "jamesmartin," "JAMESMARTIN," and "JamesMartin" all refer to the same simple name.

The naming service also allows binary simple names to be used, in which the characters %x or %X are followed by a string of hexadecimal digits. Binary names allow users and application programs to work with names made up of data that cannot be expressed using the allowable character set.

The simple names in a full name are separated by periods (.). For a period or any other punctuation mark to be used as part of a simple name, the simple name must be enclosed in double quotation marks. The following are examples of full names:

- `Parts.widgets.left-handed.SMOKESHIFTER`
- `ENG.NAC.JamesMartin`

- Government:Treasury.Bills.CurrentSeries

- ENG:Engineering.Networks.Arch.Specs

- ENG.NAC.MARTIN.%xFA01E700FC

- ULTRIX.Sources."OSITransport.c"

Internal Names

While users generally work with external names, the naming service it-self works only with internal names. All names must be converted to in-ternal form before being passed across the interface to the naming ser-vice. This conversion generally is performed in software that directly interfaces with the naming service on behalf of an end user or an appli-cation program. An internal name consists of an NSCTS value followed by a sequence of fields each containing a simple name. The NSCTS and simple name values are encoded using a scheme defined in the naming service architecture. All programs interfacing directly with the naming service treat internal names as opaque data structures and must process them using the procedures described in the naming service architecture.

Attributes

The naming service stores values for a set of attributes associated with each name in the namespace. Values can be stored for two types of at-tributes: single-valued attributes and set-valued attributes. A *single-val-ued attribute* can take on only one value at a time; a *set-valued attribute* can take on any number of values, including zero values (an empty set).

Attribute Operations

The operations that can be performed on attributes were carefully specified to permit efficient, relatively simple mechanisms to be designed to perform those operations in a highly distributed and replicated envi-ronment. This is discussed further when we see how update operations are performed on the namespace database.

Two operations are defined for single-valued attributes:

- **Read.** Reads the attribute value.
- **Replace.** Replaces the attribute value.

Notice that no other update operation other than a complete re-placement is defined. The distributed update mechanisms would have been extremely difficult to design had an update operation been specified, for example, allowing a value to be added to or subtracted from an attribute containing a numeric value.

Three operations are defined for set-valued attributes:

- **Full Lookup.** Reads all existing values in the set.

- **Redundant Insert.** Inserts a new value into the set. A value is added to the set only if that value does not already exist in the set. (A set-valued attribute is a true *set* and not a *bag*, which allows duplicate values.)

- **Redundant Delete.** Deletes an existing value from the set. No error condition is returned if the value does not exist in the set.

Attribute Names

Each different type of attribute that can be stored for a name itself has a name. Users of the naming service can assign attribute names to any type of attribute they wish to associate with a named object. However, the naming service architecture and other parts of the DNA Phase V architecture assign names for certain attributes useful for many types of objects. Attribute names assigned by Digital always have at least one $ character in them to distinguish them from names created by users.

There are two general categories of attributes: global attributes and class-specific attributes. *Global attributes* are attributes defined by the naming service architecture itself. The meaning of a global attribute is defined by the architecture and is the same for any name with which it is associated. *Class-specific attributes* are attributes whose definition depends on the value assigned to the *Class* attribute, one of the global attributes.

We will defer a detailed discussion of the global attributes until after we have examined the objects the naming service uses to maintain the namespace graph structure.

Directories

In the naming service, the nodes of the underlying tree structure of the directed graph represent *directories*, each having a unique name, which is itself maintained by the naming service. Each directory has a number of attributes associated with it, including certain of the global attributes defined by the architecture, and contains zero or more *directory entries*.

Figure 16.4 shows a simple namespace in which each of the directories making up the namespace is represented by a circle. The entries

FIGURE 16.4   **Directory structure of a simple namespace.**

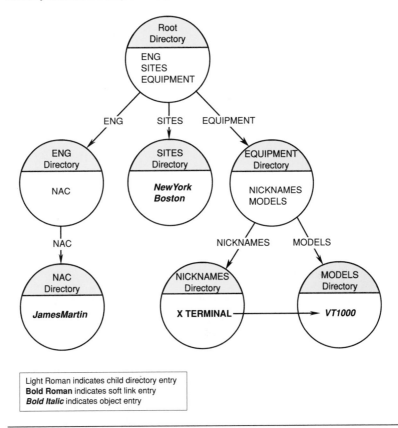

Light Roman indicates child directory entry
Bold Roman indicates soft link entry
Bold Italic indicates object entry

stored in a directory are shown at the bottom of the circle. The simple name of the arc leading to each directory is shown at the top of the circle. Each directory has a full name made up of a concatenation of the names of the arcs leading to it in the tree structure. The *root directory* stores the highest-level directory entries making up the namespace and is considered to be unnamed. There is a single root for the entire namespace, and all the directories can be located under the root. The entries in the directories are linked together to form an acyclic, rooted, directed graph structure.

Types of Directory Entries

Each of the entries stored in a directory has a simple name and a set of attributes. Some of the attributes stored for directory entries consist of the global attributes defined by the architecture. Entries for simple names stored in directories can be of three types:

- **Object Entries.** These entries form the leaves of the underlying tree structure. Object entries can store global attributes and also attributes that users associate with named objects. For example, one of the attributes stored for an object entry is typically the DNA$Towers attribute representing the address of the object in the network. (The DNA$Towers attribute is described in Chapter 11.)

- **Child Pointer Entries.** These entries name the arcs of the underlying tree structure. One of the global attributes stored for a child pointer entry consists of a pointer to a child directory in the namespace tree.

- **Soft Link Entries.** These entries name the arcs that augment the underlying tree structure to form a directed graph. One of the global attributes stored for a soft link entry is a pointer used to implement alias names.

Global Attributes

As introduced earlier, the meanings of global attributes are defined by the architecture and are the same for all entries stored by the naming service. Box 16.1 lists the global attributes assigned in the naming service architecture. Some of the global attributes are associated with directories and with all three types of directory entries; others apply only to directories, child pointer entries, soft link entries, or object entries. Most of them store values that the naming service uses to control its own operation. Therefore, the meanings of the global attributes give important insights into how the naming service performs its functions.

Directory Invariants

As discussed earlier, the child pointers in the directories making up the namespace always form a tree structure. A tree of directories makes up the entire namespace. The namespace enforces two *directory invariants*, conditions from which the directory structure is never permitted to deviate.

- **Directory Invariant 1.** Each directory has exactly one parent. This invariant guarantees that the namespace logical structure always forms a tree.

- **Directory Invariant 2.** No directory is a child of any of its descendants. This invariant ensures that the namespace logical structure does not contain any cycles.

Multiple Namespaces

In practice there is seldom a need for a given network to have more than one namespace. The implementation of a single logical namespace containing the names of all network resources allows everyone in the network to have access to any resource in the network. The naming service does, however, allow a network to implement multiple namespaces if an installation requires them. Multiple namespaces may be necessary in certain unusual cases for security purposes where an installation wishes to use the naming service in a compartmentalized environment that uses mandatory security controls. Support for multiple namespaces also helps when the namespaces for two isolated networks are about to be merged to form a single, integrated namespace.

Namespace Implementation

The function of mapping a name stored in a namespace into a set of attributes is relatively simple in concept. If the naming service were implemented in a centralized fashion, with the entire namespace contained in a single database stored on a single computing system, an existing file system could be used in a straightforward manner to implement the naming service. However, in a large network it is infeasible to store all the names in a single central location. One reason for this is that the naming service would then constitute a single point of failure in the network. Since the naming service is employed by all users to locate resources, failure of the naming service would mean failure of the entire computer network. Another reason to avoid a centralized naming service is that it would suffer from poor performance in a large network. The cost of accessing a centralized naming service from distant points in the network would be high, and the naming service would quickly become both a processing and a bandwidth bottleneck.

A major challenge in designing the naming service was to make the service operate in a highly distributed fashion and to make it work efficiently in a large, possibly global network. To meet its design objectives, the naming service must be highly available, highly robust, and highly distributed. To achieve the required performance and availability, the namespace is stored in a database that is both partitioned and partially replicated. The term *partitioned* means pieces of the database are stored in different physical locations on separate computing systems. The term *partially replicated* means the same piece of the namespace can be stored on multiple computing systems.

We next describe the major components that make up the naming service and examine the protocols by which naming service components communicate in carrying out naming operations.

BOX 16.1

Naming Service
Global Attributes

Global Attributes Associated with Directories and All Directory Entries

- **Creation Timestamp(DNS$CTS).** A single-valued attribute present and non-null for every directory entry. It contains a value, unique in space and time, that is assigned when the entry is created and is never changed. It also serves as a timestamp marking the time the object was initially created.

- **Update Timestamp (DNS$UTS).** A single-valued attribute present for every directory entry and non-null for every object that is updated. For object entries, it provides a timestamp indicating the time at which the most recent update of an object's attribute values was made.

- **Access Control Set (DNS$ACS).** A set-valued attribute containing a value for each access control element in the object's access control set.

Global Attributes Associated with Directories

- **Replicas (DNS$Replicas).** A set-valued attribute identifying all the clearinghouses storing a replica of this directory.

- **Convergence (DNS$Convergence).** A single-valued attribute describing how persistent a directory should be in keeping its replicas up to date. It contains three possible values: LOW, MEDIUM, and HIGH. The value LOW indicates that the propagator function is not to be run when updates are made and that the skulker should be run at least once every 24 hours for a directory having pending updates. The value MEDIUM indicates that the propagator is to be run once for each update and that the skulker should be run at least once every 12 hours for a directory having pending updates. The value HIGH indicates that the propagator is to be run once for each update and that a skulk should be scheduled for no more than 1 hour in the future for a directory having pending updates.

- **All Up To (DNS$AllUpTo).** A single-valued attribute giving a maximum value for how out of date the replicas of the directory are. All replicas are guaranteed to have received all updates whose time stamps are earlier than this value.

- **Clearinghouse Name (DNS$CHName).** A single-valued attribute containing a boolean variable used to enforce the clearinghouse invariants.

BOX 16.1

continued

- **Parent Pointer (DNS$ParentPointer).** A set-valued attribute containing a set of pointers to each directory's parent in the namespace tree from the directory in question up to the root. This attribute is maintained by nameservers to keep the graph of the namespace properly connected.

- **Directory Version (DNS$DirectoryVersion).** A single-valued attribute giving the current version of a directory.

- **Up Grade To (DNS$UpGradeTo).** A single-valued attribute used to control the upgrading of a directory from one version of the naming service to another.

Global Attribute Associated with Child Pointer Entries

- **Child Creation Timestamp (DNS$ChildCTS).** A single-valued attribute containing the creation timestamp of the child directory pointed to by this child pointer entry.

Global Attribute Associated with Soft Link Entries

- **Link Target (DNS$LinkTarget).** A single-valued attribute containing the full name of the entry the soft link entry points to.

- **Link Time Out (DNS$LinkTimeOut).** A single-valued attribute indicating the time after which the soft link is to be either checked or deleted.

Global Attributes Associate with Object Entries

- **Class (DNS$Class).** A single-valued attribute used to classify objects according to the type of object being named.

- **Class Version (DNS$ClassVersion).** A single-valued attribute used to allow the definition of an object class to be evolved over time.

- **Object Unique Identifier (DNS$ObjectUID).** A single-valued attribute used to store a unique identifier for the object assigned according to the rules of the Unique Identifier (UID) architecture described in Chapter 15.

- **Node Address (DNS$Address).** A single-valued attribute used only for compatibility with DNA Phase IV to store the address of the node on which the object resides. In a DNA Phase V network, the DNA$Towers attribute is used to store node address information.

Naming Service Components

The namespace database is implemented in the form of repositories called clearinghouses. The two major functional components of the naming service are clerks and nameservers. Users request naming service operations through a clerk, which communicate with nameservers on behalf of users. Nameservers retrieve information from and update clearinghouses on behalf of the clerks. Clearinghouses, clerks, and nameservers are distributed among the nodes in the network.

A nameserver can control one or more clearinghouses, but each clearinghouse is controlled by one and only one nameserver. A clerk can communicate with any of the nameservers in the network. These relationships are illustrated in Figure 16.5, which shows how a clerk might access two nameservers and two clearinghouses in satisfying a request for a naming operation.

Clearinghouses

The unit of both partitioning and replication of the namespace is the individual directory. A collection of directories stored on a particular sys-

FIGURE 16.5   Each nameserver is responsible for one or more clearinghouses. A clerk accesses the nameserver responsible for the clearinghouse that the clerk determines is most likely to contain the directories required to satisfy its request. A clerk may access several nameservers in satisfying a request for a naming service.

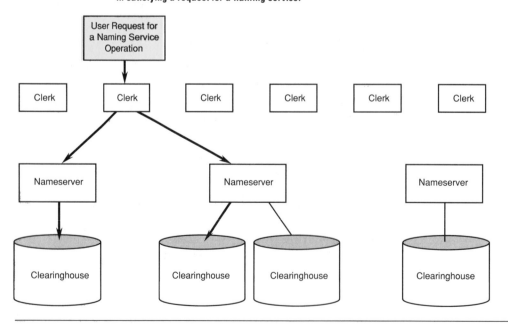

tem and accessible by a single nameserver is called a *clearinghouse*. Clearinghouses are either active or inactive. When at least one clearinghouse is active in a given system, the system is currently acting as a nameserver. Although a nameserver typically has access to a single clearinghouse, which contains all the directories the nameserver can directly access, it is possible for a nameserver to concurrently control and access multiple clearinghouses. This might happen when a nameserver fails and a clearinghouse has to be moved to a new nameserver.

Clerks

A *clerk* is the naming service component that implements the application programming interface to the naming service and that performs naming service operations on behalf of end users and application programs. All requests for naming operations that users make, either directly or indirectly, are made of a naming service clerk. Each node in the network contains an implementation of a clerk. Box 16.2 lists the functions a user of the naming service can ask a clerk to perform.

Nameservers

A *nameserver* is the naming service component that actually accesses the clearinghouses containing the directories making up the namespace. Not all nodes implement a nameserver component. A network should include enough nameservers to provide the performance, robustness, and availability required for a given size network. A nameserver can be implemented in a general-purpose computing system performing other tasks as well as naming. However, in large networks it is likely that the nameserver function will be performed by specialized processors, just as the routing function is generally performed by specialized routers.

A nameserver is composed of four major modules, as shown in Figure 16.6. The following are descriptions of the functions of the nameserver modules:

- **Control.** The *Control* module of a nameserver coordinates the overall operation of the nameserver, such as turning it on and off and bringing clearinghouses online. The Control module is also responsible for periodically advertising the availability of the nameserver.

- **Transaction Agent.** The *Transaction Agent* module performs the operations requested by clerks. The transaction agent is responsible for accessing one or more clearinghouses and for communicating with other transaction agents to coordinate the creation, deletion, and modification of directories.

BOX 16.2

**Naming Service
Clerk Functions**

- **EnumerateAttributes.** Enumerates the attributes of an object entry, directory entry, soft link, or clearinghouse.

- **ReadAttribute.** Returns the value(s) of the specified attribute.

- **ModifyAttribute.** Modifies (or deletes) an attribute or attribute value.

- **TestAttribute.** Tests for whether a value is a current attribute value.

- **CreateObject.** Adds an object entry to the namespace.

- **EnumerateObject.** Returns the names of object entries from the namespace.

- **DeleteObject.** Removes an object entry from the namespace.

- **CreateDirectory.** Creates a child directory under the specified parent directory.

- **AddReplica.** Adds a clearinghouse from the replica set of a directory.

- **RemoveReplica.** Removes a clearinghouse from the replica set of a directory.

- **DeleteDirectory.** Removes the specified directory from the namespace.

- **EnumerateChildren.** Returns information about child directories of the specified parent directory.

- **Skulk.** Skulks a directory to force convergence of its replicas.

- **CreateLink.** Creates a soft link entry.

- **DeleteLink.** Deletes a soft link entry.

- **EnumerateLinks.** Enumerates the soft link entries in a directory.

- **ResolveName.** Follows a chain of soft links and returns the full name of the entry pointed to. Cycles are detected.

- **TestGroup.** Tests for group membership, allowing for recursively defined groups and for detecting cycles.

- **Update Sender.** The *Update Sender* module is responsible for spreading changes made to directories in the local clearinghouse to all other clearinghouses that contain copies of that directory. This process is described later when we discuss directory updating.

- **Update Listener.** The *Update Listener* module receives directory updates from the update sender and records the changes in the appropriate clearinghouse. The update sender and the update listener are also responsible

FIGURE 16.6   **Nameserver modules.**

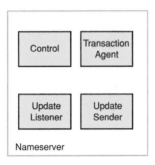

for ensuring that clearinghouses can find each other when a new clear-inghouse is created or when a clearinghouse is moved.

Naming Service Protocols

Four protocols are used in implementing the distributed algorithms that the naming service uses to perform its functions, as shown in Figure 16.7 and briefly described next:

- **Solicitation and Advertisement Protocol.** The *Solicitation and Advertise-ment* protocol (S.Protocol) is the means by which clerks learn about available nameservers. Nameservers periodically advertise their avail-ability by multicasting advertisement messages. Clerks can also solicit advertisements from nameservers.

FIGURE 16.7   **Naming service protocols.**

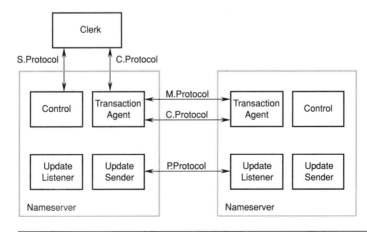

- **Clerk-Server Protocol.** The *Clerk-Server* protocol (C.Protocol) is the protocol a clerk uses to request naming information from a nameserver.

- **Directory Maintenance Protocol.** The *Directory Maintenance* protocol (M.Protocol) is used by Transaction Agent modules to coordinate their activities in creating, deleting, and modifying directory entries in clearinghouses.

- **Update Propagation Protocol.** The *Update Propagation* protocol (P.Protocol) is the protocol that Update Sender modules and Update Listener modules use to propagate directory updates from one clearinghouse to another.

We next describe methods used for partitioning and replicating the namespace. After that we will walk through a typical naming operation to see how a naming operation is performed.

Namespace Partitioning

Partitioning of the namespace is accomplished by deciding which clearinghouses will contain which directories. A particular clearinghouse need not contain all the directories that make up the underlying namespace tree structure. However, it must be possible for a naming service clerk to always be able to access any directory in the namespace.

As introduced earlier, a clerk must be able to find the root of the namespace by coming in from any clearinghouse, and the clerk must then be able to locate any directory once it has found the root. One way this could have been accomplished would be to require each clearinghouse to maintain a copy of the root directory. However, to enhance the scalability of the naming service, the architects of the naming service decided not to require this restriction. Instead, clearinghouses are assigned names so the naming service itself can be used to locate clearinghouses in the network. The architecture enforces certain invariants on the assignment of clearinghouse names to enable any clerk to locate any directory beginning in any clearinghouse.

Clearinghouse Invariants

Clearinghouse names are assigned according to a set of rules that ensure that a name lookup for a clearinghouse cannot fail because the clearinghouse in which a required directory is located cannot be found. These naming rules revolve around two clearinghouse invariants that are never violated during normal operation of the naming service:

- **Clearinghouse Invariant 1.** A clearinghouse must contain at least one directory whose name is closer to the root of the namespace than the name of the clearinghouse itself. This invariant guarantees that the root is always reachable by starting at any clearinghouse.

- **Clearinghouse Invariant 2.** Every directory must be replicated in at least one clearinghouse whose name is closer to the root than the name of the directory itself. This invariant guarantees that every directory is reachable from the root without having to look up a clearinghouse, which would in turn require looking up the subject directory.

Directory Replication

Namespace replication is accomplished by storing a given directory in more than one clearinghouse. A copy of a directory stored in a particular clearinghouse is called a *replica*. There are three kinds of replicas:

- **Master Replicas.** One and only one replica of a directory is designated the *master replica*. To simplify maintenance, certain types of update operations are performed only on master replicas. For example, the master replica is the only replica in which a new directory can be created by adding a child pointer to a higher-level directory.

- **Secondary Replicas.** Another type of replica is a *secondary replica*. New soft link or object entries can be added either to a master or a secondary replica, and existing directory entries can be updated in either master or secondary replicas.

- **Read-Only Replicas.** A third kind of replica is a *read-only replica*. It can handle requests for name lookups but cannot service user requests for adding or updating directory entries. Read-only replicas are updated only by the naming service itself.

We next walk through a typical naming service operation. We will see how the components of the naming service work together to access the partitioned and replicated namespace database in performing naming operations.

Naming Operation

A naming service user requests a naming operation by communicating with a clerk via the clerk-client interface. A typical naming operation might be to issue the ReadAttribute function to retrieve a particular attribute in a directory entry.

To satisfy a retrieval request for a directory entry, a clerk begins by choosing a clearinghouse likely to have the requested directory entry and establishing communication with the nameserver responsible for that clearinghouse. In most cases, the clerk will do this using information from a parent directory it already has stored in a cache.

Assuming the clerk can locate the appropriate clearinghouse from information available to it, the clerk communicates with the nameserver responsible for that clearinghouse using the C.Protocol and requests the desired directory entry. It then passes the attributes associated with the directory entry to the user.

Walking the Namespace Tree

In some cases, the clerk will not know which clearinghouse contains the required directory, and it must *walk the namespace tree* to locate the clearinghouse containing the directory entry it is looking for. Even though a clerk may not have information about the clearinghouse that contains the information the clerk is searching for, it must have some information to get started. This may be a directory entry for some ancestor directory above the desired entry's parent. In the worst case, the clerk may have to begin in any clearinghouse whose address is available to it. In the absence of any cached directory entries, the clerk uses the address of a nameserver that has advertised its availability or an address in a statically configured list of nameservers available to the clerk.

Depending on where it starts, the clerk may have to follow a number of pointers to reach the clearinghouse that contains the entry it is searching for. If the clerk has already found a clearinghouse containing the root of the namespace, it can start at the root and follow pointers found in child directory entries until it reaches the desired directory entry.

It is possible—especially when a clerk first becomes operational and has no cached directory entries—for the clerk to not yet have access to a clearinghouse that contains the root of the namespace. In such a case, one of the clearinghouse invariants described earlier guarantees that a clearinghouse not containing a replica of the root directory must contain a pointer to another clearinghouse closer to the root. The clerk can follow these pointers from clearinghouse to clearinghouse, moving up at least one level each time, until it eventually reaches a clearinghouse that has a root directory replica. It can then follow child pointers until it finds the entry it is looking for.

We next examine the way in which the naming service handles update operations and how directory replicas are brought into convergence.

Namespace Updating

The updating algorithms defined by the naming service architecture are designed to operate efficiently and correctly in a highly distributed environment. The updating algorithms operate so all updates are *total*, *idempotent*, and *commutative*:[*]

- **Total.** *Total* means that an update can always be applied without regard to any of the updates made in the past.
- **Idempotent.** *Idempotent* means that multiple applications of the same update to the database has the same effect as a single application of the update.
- **Commutative.** *Commutative* means that a series of updates can be applied in any order with identical results.

The total and idempotent aspects of attribute updating are facilitated through the limited types of allowed update operations. For example, attribute values can only be completely replaced and cannot be incremented or decremented. The commutative aspect of updating is handled via update timestamps. All updates made to the database implementing the namespace are time stamped and are always applied so the update entering the network most recently always wins.

Loose Consistency Guarantees

A first look at the features provided by the naming service can give the impression that it has many of the features associated with a general-purpose distributed database facility. However, the architectural specifications for the naming service specifically warn against using it for such general-purpose applications.

NETWORK ARCHITECT

Although the database used to maintain a namespace can be used to perform many of the functions a user might want in a distributed database system, the naming service has many characteristics making it ill suited for such uses. The naming service is intended to be used to store a small amount of information for a very large number of things, rather than a lot of information about a few things. Also, the level of replication the naming service supports is far beyond the level of replication typically associated with distributed databases. A typical

---

[*] The operation to create a new attribute does not satisfy these properties.

distributed database might implement two, three, or four replicas, but beyond that the overhead ordinarily gets too great. The naming service is designed to support possibly 100 replicas of the same directory scattered around a world-wide network.

The naming service provides very loose consistency guarantees to allow the namespace to be partitioned and replicated to provide for high levels of availability and performance. Immediately after a change is made to one replica of a directory, a temporary situation may exist in which different users may get different answers when querying the naming service.

Suppose I move from Boston to San Francisco. Before moving I update the address attribute associated with the ENG.NAC.JamesMartin user name in the Boston clearinghouse. In a large organization, it is likely that the directory storing the object entry for ENG.NAC.JamesMartin is replicated in a great many clearinghouses maintained by different nameservers. Immediately after I update the address attribute of my user name, those users that happen to be using the nameserver controlling the Boston clearinghouse will have immediate access to my new e-mail address. However, if someone in London attempts to send me an e-mail message immediately after I change my address, it is possible that the clearinghouse used in London may not yet have been informed of the change, and the message may go to Boston instead of San Francisco.

It is also possible for two users employing different clearinghouses to each attempt to register the same name in the naming service and both be allowed to do so. After the directories converge, only one of the names registered will be valid. To handle this type of situation, the naming service uses the notion of *safe* and *unsafe* names.

NETWORK ARCHITECT

One of the most unusual features of the naming service is this notion of loose consistency guarantees. If two people go to the naming service and both register the name Dave Oran, and they happen to go to two different nameservers, those two nameservers will both accept the name. Such a situation would be totally unacceptable in most distributed database applications. Instead of trying to do distributed synchronization with two-phase commits or trying to implement a quorum consensus algorithm, we implemented the notion of safe *names and* unsafe *names. When you first register your name, it's unsafe. At any time you can go in and ask the naming service: "Is my name safe yet? Is my name safe yet? Is my name safe yet?" And eventually either you will be told your name is safe, or you will be told someone else claimed that name before you did. In a well-managed, well-designed network, a name will become safe within minutes and often within seconds. And also, if the installation's naming conventions are well designed, name conflicts will occur very seldom, so the problems associated with unsafe names will be rare. But the architecture takes great pains to ensure that no matter what, at some point either a name becomes safe or you are notified that someone else claimed it first. The alternative was that we would have had to require a quorum of the nodes to be operational in order to be able to do an update. Many more people would be upset if they tried to give a name to something and they were told they couldn't do it than by allowing an operation to occasionally fail because the directories didn't converge immediately.*

Directory Update Convergence

When an update is made to a replica of a directory, the nameserver controlling that replica typically makes a one-time attempt to spread that change to all other clearinghouses containing replicas of that directory. This updating attempt is performed by a naming service function called the *propagator*. In most cases, the propagator causes convergence to take place relatively quickly. The function of the propagator as described in the naming service architecture is relatively simple and defines the function as being performed at the time each update is made. However, the architectural description of the propagator suggests a series of optimizations of this function that actual implementations might employ, including:

- running the propagator as a background thread, thus allowing responses to be returned to naming service clerks more rapidly than if propagation occurred synchronously
- waiting for a short time before running the propagator function to allow updates to be batched, thus potentially reducing the number of required connections to the same clearinghouse
- sequencing the transmission of updates by clearinghouse rather than by entry to make better use of network resources
- caching connections to clearinghouses to potentially reduce the overhead associated with connection establishment and authentication operations
- omiting the propagation function if an execution of the convergence algorithm (described next) is scheduled soon

The Skulker

A network manager can specify that the propagator should not be run for certain directories. Even if the propagator was executed, there may be situations where one or more clearinghouses were not available at the time the propagator function was run. There is another convergence algorithm, called the *skulker*, that operates periodically for each directory in the namespace. It forces convergence for those updates the propagator was not able to fully propagate.

NETWORK ARCHITECT

During the design of the naming service architecture we gave the convergence algorithm the nickname "the midnight skulker," and it sort of stuck. You're letting the system go on during the day, and then at night the skulker will skulk around through all the clearinghouses and fix everything up for you. The skulker is the background algorithm that runs around through the replicated directories, figures out what's different about them, and makes them all the same.

Skulk Operation   Execution of the convergence algorithm is called a *skulk*. Skulks operate independently on each directory in a namespace and can be done at intervals set individually by network managers for each directory. For each directory, the master replica is linked to the secondary replicas in a virtual ring structure. (A master replica that is not replicated simply points to itself.) The virtual ring keeps multiple skulks of a single directory from getting in each other's way. For a skulk operation to complete successfully, it is necessary for all clearinghouses containing replicas of the directory being skulked to be online during the time the skulk is executed.

The following is a simplified description of what the skulker does in bringing replicas of a directory into convergence:

1. The skulker gathers up all updates made to the master replica and all updates made to secondary replicas and applies them to the clearinghouse in which the skulker is running.

2. The skulker then spreads all the gathered updates to all other replicas of the directory so the master replica and all secondary replicas are brought into synchronization.

3. Finally, the skulker informs all the replicas of the timestamp of the latest update that all of them are guaranteed to have seen. This timestamp is maintained for each directory replica in the DNS$AllUpTo attribute.

The skulker is a distributed algorithm that can be started by any nameserver, and it is possible for skulks to be running concurrently in more than one replica of a given directory. The algorithm is designed so when this happens, resources may be wasted but the directory will not be corrupted and all replicas will still converge. To increase efficiency, a function of the skulker detects the operation of other skulkers in the same directory and terminates all the skulks except for the one most recently started. Once the skulk process has completed successfully for a given directory, all replicas are guaranteed to be in convergence as of the time contained in the DNS$AllUpTo attribute.

The more frequently skulks are run, the more up to date all the replicas of a directory will be. In a large network, skulks can be expensive to execute, so network managers must make tradeoffs between the cost of the computing resources required to maintain convergence and the cost of being somewhat out of synchronization for a period of time. (What is the cost of not being able to locate ENG.NAC.JamesMartin for a while?) Network managers can control the frequency of skulks either by adjusting one of the global attributes associated with each directory or by manually initiating skulks.

Skulk Operation Failure   In a large, global network, it is possible for a skulk operation to fail. If the skulker repeatedly fails to complete successfully, it is due to one of the following reasons:

- One or more replicas of a directory are not available because one or more clearinghouses are currently offline.
- The network has become partitioned, so communication with one or more clearinghouses is not possible.
- A clearinghouse has been destroyed due to a hardware failure or a serious operator error.
- The clocks in the network have gone out of synchronization to such an extent that updates to directories are being rejected.
- The structure of the namespace has been corrupted.
- A nameserver has a programming error causing it to operate incorrectly.
- There is an error in the naming service architecture itself.

If either of the first two situations occurs, the skulk operation will eventually complete successfully once the offline clearinghouses are placed online or after the required resources are made available to recover from the network partitioning. The next four situations require more elaborate recovery procedures typically requiring network management intervention. The naming service architecture describes these recovery procedures in detail. As for the last reason:

NETWORK ARCHITECT

We feel confident that we have addressed all seven reasons for a skulk operation failing. But the seventh type of failure would be rather serious and the prospect of that happening sometimes keeps us up at night.

X.500 and the OSI Directory

As introduced earlier, CCITT Recommendation X.500 and ISO 9594, the OSI Directory, describe an international standard for a naming service. The DNA Phase V naming service has some similarity to the OSI Directory. Both the naming service and an implementation of the OSI Directory allow a user to specify a name and get back either an indication that the name does not exist or the set of attributes associated with that name. There are, however, also a great many differences between the naming service and the OSI Directory. Perhaps the biggest difference is that the naming service operates only on primitive names, whereas the OSI Directory works with limited forms of descriptive names.

Distinguished Attributes

The OSI Directory stores sets of attribute names and attribute values. One type of attribute the OSI Directory stores is called a *distinguished attribute*, which functions as a name. Distinguished attributes can be used to provide a function similar to returning the set of attributes associated with a name. (For example, what attributes are associated with ENG.NAC.JamesMartin?)

Descriptive Searches

Another major function provided by the OSI Directory, not provided by the naming service, is the search function. The *search* function allows a user to request a search based on an arbitrary set of attribute name/attribute value pairs. These are called *attribute value assertions* (AVAs) in the terminology unique to X.500 and the OSI Directory. An example of an informally stated set of AVAs might be: "Give me information about all the users whose Group attribute has the value 'Network and Commu-

nications' and whose Division attribute has the value 'Engineering'."
The naming service does not provide such descriptive search capabilities.

Differences Between the Naming Service and the OSI Directory

The following is a list of the major differences between the naming service and the OSI Directory:

- The naming service maintains primitive names and allows only name-to-attribute mapping; the OSI Directory maintains descriptive names and allows limited descriptive searches in addition to name-to-attribute mapping.

- In the naming service graph structure, the arcs of the graph do not have types associated with them; in the OSI Directory, all the arcs of the graph are typed.

- In the naming service, there is no formal schema or enforced formal structure associated with a namespace. Users are able to structure a namespace in any desired manner. An OSI Directory namespace has a formal schema defining allowable data types and places constraints on the shape of the namespace graph structure.

- The naming service defines detailed methods for allowing portions of the namespace to be replicated. The OSI Directory currently provides no information on how replication should be handled. The OSI Directory standard currently includes a general discussion of replication but leaves the details of how it is to be accomplished to individual implementors.

- The naming service provides access control facilities for implementing security functions. The OSI Directory currently provides no access control facilities.

NETWORK ARCHITECT

To build an implementation of the OSI Directory today, you have to add a lot of things not discussed in the standard. This is a problem for interoperability. The things addressed in the standard will interoperate, but things that go beyond the standard may not. So if somebody implements replication, you can only replicate among nameservers of a given vendor. It is the intention of Digital to eventually merge the naming service with the OSI Directory. And when that is done, the user will get the best of both worlds. The real problem today is that the OSI Directory is not yet complete and won't be until about 1992.

Conclusion

The DNA Phase V naming service is a ubiquitous service, available on all network nodes, that users can employ to locate network resources. Another ubiquitous set of services pervading the entire DNA Phase V architecture concerns monitoring and controlling the vast array of resources that make up a computer network. The network management aspects of the DNA Phase V architecture are described in Chapter 17.

CHAPTER 17

Network Management

DNA network management allows network managers to control and monitor the operation of a DECnet Phase V communication network. It allows parameter values to be specified that describe how various aspects of the network are to operate and allows parameter values automatically set by DNA Phase V protocols to be fine-tuned as necessary. DNA network management allows network managers to start and stop network components as needed, to monitor the operation of the network, and to extract and analyze information relating to network traffic and network performance. Network management data is collected in real time and can be used to generate statistical and auditing information.

Digital's philosophy is that network management should be limited to the setting of options related to matters of policy rather than those related to the normal operation of the network. For example, all network protocols—such as the protocol controlling the distributed routing algorithm—have mechanisms built into them to control normal network operation. These mechanisms are outside the scope of network management. They automatically set parameters to the proper values as link failures occur and as nodes come up and down. No network management intervention is required to control the day-to-day operation of the network.

International Standards

DNA Phase V network management is based on the emerging international standards for network management. The draft international standards for network management that ISO is developing divide management functions into five specific management functional areas (SMFAs):

- configuration management
- fault management

- performance management
- security management
- accounting management

The current ISO draft international standards do not cover all aspects of managing communication networks. In cases where standards are not currently being developed, DNA Phase V uses proprietary solutions. Digital's intention is to migrate toward international standards when they become available.

Network Management Evolution

Network management has been a part of DNA since about 1978, when DNA Phase II was introduced. Until the development of the network management architecture included in DNA Phase V, DNA network management was defined in a single architectural specification defining the network management aspects of all components of DNA. Such a monolithic approach to network management led to a number of problems, including a large and unwieldy network management document and difficulties in keeping the network management architectural specification synchronized with the architectural specifications for other components.

In DNA Phase V, there is still a network management architectural specification. However, it describes only the general approach to network management. The details concerning the management aspects of each individual architectural module are contained in the architectural specification for the module itself. Such an approach moves the responsibility for the management aspects of an architectural module to the architectural group responsible for that part of the architecture. For such an approach to work, provision must be made for guaranteeing consistency in the management approach from one architectural module to another, both within and outside the DNA Phase V architecture. This led to a requirement for an overall management architecture within which the DNA Phase V network management architecture would fit.

Enterprise Management Architecture

While DNA Phase V was being developed, it became clear that with the advent of truly distributed systems, the distinction between the management of a local computing system and the management of the network was beginning to break down. What was needed was a much more general approach to management. This resulted in the development of the Enterprise Management Architecture (EMA), which defines a distributed system as a collection of individual computing systems tied together by a communication network for the purposes of sharing resources. EMA is a *meta-architecture* that ensures consistency among a family of management architectures in the same way an individual architecture ensures consistency among a family of implementations. EMA is based on object-oriented design principles. Object-oriented design views data values as being embedded within an object. Data values are accessed through the object itself rather than directly from the outside. The DNA Phase V network management architecture is only one of a series of management architectures that will eventually fall under the EMA umbrella. The DNA Phase V network management architecture describes how the components making up a DNA Phase V communication network are managed. Other management architectures describe how various other components in the total distributed system are managed.

The Entity Model

At the heart of the enterprise management architecture is the *entity model*. The entity model uses the term *entity* to refer to any type of object in a distributed system that must be managed. The concept of an entity closely corresponds to the concept of an *object* in object-oriented design. Management can be described as a feedback loop between a person (a manager) and a set of entities (the things that are managed) (see Figure 17.1). The entity model defines two major classes of software components:

- **Directors.** A *director* is a software system that managers use to manage the various components of a distributed system.

- **Agents.** An *agent* consists of a software component associated with the entity being managed.

FIGURE 17.1   **Monitor/control feedback loop.**

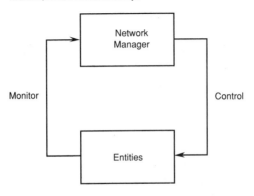

FIGURE 17.2   **Director, agent, and management protocol.**

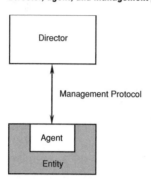

Directors communicate with agents by means of a *management protocol* that handles the flow of information between the two. The relationship between directors, agents, and a management protocol is shown in Figure 17.2.

The management information and operations that pass between directors and entities are described below:

- **Directives.** *Directives* flow from a director to an agent, and responses to directives flow back from an agent to a director. Directives consist of commands a director issues to an entity, possibly as a result of a manager issuing a command to the director. Most management needs are satisfied by two directives: *Show* to read a value of interest to management and *Set* to change a value. The directives *Add* and *Remove* are also defined for management information consisting of a set of values. Directives for certain types of entities also include *actions*. Examples of actions applying to many types of entities are *Enable* and *Disable*, which allow an entity to be turned on and off. Many other actions are specific to a particular type of entity. The detailed definitions of actions are entity specific.

- **Events.** *Events* flow from an agent to a director. An event is generated when some specific normal or abnormal condition occurs that is of interest to management.

Entity Hierarchy   A distributed system is constructed from manageable components, and the more computing systems there are in the distributed system, the more manageable components there are. To allow effective management of distributed systems using very large networks, the components must be organized into a logical structure, and they must be named so managers can deal with the complexity. EMA uses a hierarchical system for naming entities in which parent entities can have child entities subordinate to them.

Entity Classes

While all entities, from a management perspective, share a common architecture, they are far from similar in function. For example, a Transport layer entity performs functions very different from those performed by a Network layer entity. However, entities can be grouped into *classes*; all entity instances that are members of the same class are similar. In general, the architectural specification for a particular component—such as OSI transport—defines a specific entity class.

Within a particular class of entity, there may be a number of child entities. For example, within the OSI transport entity class, there is a child entity class called OSI Transport Port. A *port* defines an end point of an OSI transport connection. There is an instance of the Port entity class within the OSI Transport entity instance for every OSI Transport connection currently in operation. (See Figure 17.3.)

FIGURE 17.3　　**Entity hierarchical structure.**

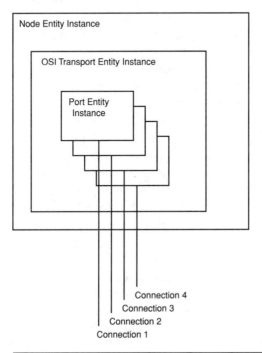

Instances of a class can vary slightly. For example, an OSI Transport Port entity instance requesting the establishment of a Transport connection is slightly different from an OSI Transport Port entity instance accepting a connection request. However, the differences are minor and both types of OSI Transport Port entity instances are members of the same entity class.

Entity Attributes

An entity has a set of internal variables defined for it. The variables that can be inspected or set by a management action are called *attributes*. The values of an entity's attributes represent all the information about the entity that are of concern to management. Box 17.1 describes the four types of attributes that can be associated with an entity instance.

Network Management Entities	With respect to DNA Phase V network management, systems making up the network are defined as the highest-level components in the naming hierarchy. Each system (end node, router, name server, etc.) in the network is represented to network management by an instance of the Node entity class. Each Node entity instance is assigned a globally unique name. The name of the Node entity instance is used as the highest-level identifier in the name assigned to each manageable entity within that node. Node entity instance names are registered with the naming service along with the attributes associated with that node, including the node's network-service-access-point (NSAP) address.

Below the Node entity instance in the entity hierarchy are class names of Module entities. A *module* consists of a group of networking functions that together provide a particular service. For example, there is a Module entity class associated with each different type of entity that can run in each of the architectural layers. The Transport layer includes an NSP Transport Module entity class and an OSI Transport Module entity class. At the next level down in the hierarchy are entity classes subordinate to the Module entity class. These are defined to allow individual management of some part of a module's functions. For example, the High-level Data Link Control (HDLC) module includes a child entity class named *Link*. Since there can be many links attached to the node over which the HDLC protocol can operate, there must be a separate Link entity instance for each HDLC link attached to the node. The network management architecture allows any number of levels of child entity classes to be specified. In the HDLC example, the hierarchy has three levels:

BOX 17.1

Entity Attribute
Types

- **Identification.** An *identification* attribute uniquely identifies an entity instance to management.
- **Characteristic.** A *characteristic* attribute allows a manager to control the operating parameters of an entity. For example, the parameters that determine the DDCMP polling rate or the cost of a routing circuit are characteristic attributes. In general, characteristic attributes take default values when the entity is created, and their values can be changed only through a network management action. The values of characteristic attributes are not changed during normal distributed system operation.
- **Status.** *Status* attributes allow a manager to inspect the current state of an entity. Unlike characteristic attributes, status attributes can change without management intervention. For example, the values of status attributes can change as a result of normal distributed system operation.
- **Counter.** A *counter* attribute indicates the number of times an operation has been performed by an entity or the number of times a particular condition has been detected. As with status attributes, counter attributes change in value as a result of normal distributed system operation.

1. an instance of the Node entity class
2. an instance of the HDLC Module entity class
3. an instance of the Link entity class

Entity Instance Names

The full name of an entity instance is made up by concatenating all the individual entity class and instance names in the hierarchy. Each entity name is made up of a global part and a local part. The *global* part consists of the name of the Node entity class and instance; the *local* part is made up of all the child entity classes and instances, up to the level of the Node entity instance. For example, the name "Node NAC.Dept57 HDLC Link DSV-0" might refer to HDLC link "DSV-0" attached to the computing system whose node name is NAC.Dept57.

The global part of the name is used to establish a connection between the node in which the access module resides and the node containing the required agent. An agent in the node entity then uses the local part of the entity name to identify the next level of child entity to which the directive is addressed. If there are multiple levels of child entities, the process is repeated by each child entity in the hierarchy until the destination agent is reached.

Entity Architectural Model

Although a distributed system employs many different types of entities that have very different characteristics, from a management perspective all entities have a common architecture. As we have seen, one or more Module entities are associated with each of the layers of the DNA Phase V architecture. The architectural model of the OSI Transport layer entity, from a management perspective, is shown in Figure 17.4. All entities are made up of the following:

- **Name.** Each entity has a *name* associated with it that uniquely identifies it in the distributed system. Global entity names—such as the names of instances of the Node entity class in DNA Phase V—are registered with the DNA Phase V naming service.

- **State Machine Definition.** An entity's *state machine definition* defines a set of state variables whose values define the entity's state at any given instant. For DNA Phase V entities, an entity's state machine definition is ordinarily a part of the entity's protocol specification and is not specifically related to network management.

FIGURE 17.4   OSI Transport entity architectural model.

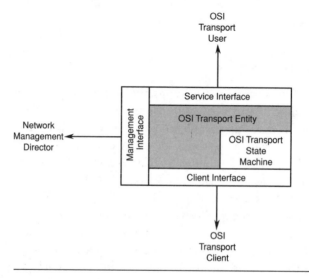

- **Interfaces.** *Interfaces* to the entity define the operations that provide input to and output from the state machine.

Interfaces

A typical entity, such as the Transport layer entity shown in Figure 17.4, has three types of interfaces, only the first of which is directly associated with management:

- **Management Interface.** The *management interface* defines the way in which a director access module issues directives to the agent and the way in which the agent sends information about events to the director access module.

- **Service Interface.** The *service interface* defines how the entity provides services to other entities. For example, the OSI Transport layer entity service interface defines the operations a user of the OSI Transport entity (such as the DNA Session Control layer) can request of the Transport layer entity.

- **Client Interface.** The *client interface* defines the operations the entity can request of other entities. For example, the OSI Transport layer entity client interface defines the operations the OSI Transport layer entity can request of a Network layer entity.

Director Architectural Model

Managers use the software that makes up a director to control and monitor a collection of entities. For example, to control and manage a communication network, a network manager might use director software specifically designed to manage a DECnet Phase V communication network. To control the operation of a distributed system, a distributed system manager might use director software designed to handle all aspects of the distributed system, with management of the communication network being only part of the management function. The director architecture has been specifically designed to be extensible to allow for the management function to be expanded in a consistent manner over time.

The director provides an interface between a manager and a collection of manageable objects, each represented by an entity. Directors are themselves manageable objects conforming to the entity model. Figure 17.5 shows the architecture of the director. It consists of the following components:

- **Kernel.** The *kernel* provides a set of services that support and integrate the other functions of the director.

FIGURE 17.5   **Management Director architectural model.**

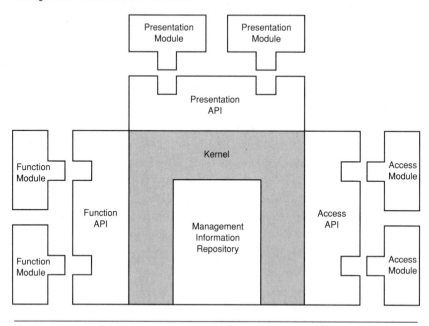

- **Management Information Repository.** The *management information repository* is a database of management information about the entities being managed.

- **Application Programming Interfaces.** A set of *application programming interfaces* (APIs) define how the other three types of director components can be plugged into the director. The director APIs allow the other three components to be implemented in a manner independent of the particular hardware or operating system on which the kernel and the management information repository are run.

- **Presentation Modules.** A *presentation module* consists of software that handles a particular style of user interface between a manager and a director. Any number of presentation modules can be plugged into the director to handle different user interface styles. Presentation modules are independent of the entities being managed and of the functions that can be applied to them.

- **Function Modules.** A *function module* consists of software that handles a set of specific management applications. It implements a set of specific management actions that can be applied to a collection of entities. Function modules are independent of the entities being managed and of the user interface style a manager employs.

- **Access Modules.** An *access module* consists of software that handles communication with one or more of the entities being managed. Access modules are independent of the functions that can be applied to the entities and of the user interface style a manager employs. An access module operates as a *sink* that receives information about events the managed entities generate.

Network Management Operation

The DNA Phase V network management architecture is designed to use many of the distributed computing services described in Chapters 15 and 16. For example, network management uses the naming service to manage names and the time service to obtain date and time-of-day values. Network management also uses the services of the DNA Session Control layer to provide communication capabilities for management components. The services of the Data Link layer are also sometimes used directly to handle some basic management operations, such as loading and dumping when not all Network protocols are operating, for example, during node initialization or after certain types of failures.

DNA Phase V Management Architectures

A number of architectures support DNA Phase V network management and the entity model. The following sections provide overviews of these architectures.

Common Management Information Protocol

In most cases, the network management director software will reside in one or more nodes remote from the node in which the managed entity and its agent reside. Communication between the director and the agent is controlled by an Application layer protocol called the *common management information protocol* (CMIP). DNA Phase V CMIP is based on the emerging ISO standards for CMIP. The DNA Phase V version of CMIP is a combination of two protocols:

- **Management Information Control and Exchange.** The *management information control and exchange* (MICE) protocol is used to send directives from a director to a node agent.

- **Management Event Notification.** The *management event notification* (MEN) protocol is used to send event reports from a node agent to a director.

DNA CMIP is a simple request-response protocol operating over a DNA Session Control connection. It provides operations to show and set management attribute values, to request the execution of management actions, and to report on events that occur.

Network Control Language

The *network control language* (NCL) defines a command line interface that network managers can use to communicate with a director. NCL is new to DNA Phase V and replaces the command interface to the network control program (NCP) used to manage DNA Phase IV networks. NCL provides network managers with access to the directives defined for all DNA Phase V entities. NCL specifies general syntax rules defining how network management commands must be entered and how responses are displayed. An implementation of NCL accepts input from a terminal and issues directives to entities using MICE protocol messages.

The NCL command syntax consists of a verb, an entity name, and a sequence of argument identifiers or identifier/value pairs. The following are examples of NCL commands:

- `Set node NAC.Littleton Routing Circuit 73 Cost 10`
- `Show Node NAC.Littleton DDCMP Link 67 All Counters`

NCL allows wildcards to be specified at various points in an NCL command to allow a network manager to specify a management operation for a group of entity instances. The following is an example of an NCL command with a wildcard:

- `Show Node NAC.Littleton DDCMP Link * All Counters`

This command would cause all the DDCMP link entities in the NAC.Littleton node to return all their counter values. NCL also provides commands that request naming service operations, for example, to register the name of a new node in the naming service. Additionally, NCL supports DNA Phase IV network management commands and allows a network manager to manage a DNA Phase IV node from a DNA Phase V node.

Event Logging

DNA provides mechanisms that enable the information generated as a result of events that occur to be distributed to points in the network where the event information can be stored and analyzed. DNA Phase V *event logging* consists of the following components:

- **Event Sources.** An *event source* detects events and initiates the generation of event reports.

- **Event Sinks.** An *event sink* accepts event reports from an event source and processes, stores, or displays them. Phase V event logging allows for an arbitrary number of event sinks, possibly with each providing different features.

- **Event dispatchers.** An *event dispatcher* serves as an intermediary between event sources and event sinks.

    Each entity in the network that reports events has an event dispatcher. Entities in a node post event reports to the local event dispatcher, which is responsible for buffering event reports and distributing them to event sinks using the management event notification protocol.

    Network management can be used to control the operation of event dispatchers. Event streams can be created defining the sinks for event information and event filters defining the types of event reports each event sink is to receive. An event sink can also perform further event filtering. Event filtering permits certain event sinks to process only certain types of events. For example, event filtering can be based on the types of events the event sink will accept or on the particular types of entities from which event reports will be accepted.

Maintenance Operations Protocol

Maintenance operations consist of simple functions that must be available in a node even when the services of the higher layers of the architecture are not available. For example, certain functions must be available even when a node is in the process of initializing itself and is not yet fully operational. DNA Phase V defines a simple management protocol called the *Maintenance Operations Protocol* (MOP). MOP requires the "managing" node to be on the same data link as the "managed" node. MOP uses the services of the Data Link layer directly and requires only minimal Data Link layer protocol support. The MOP modules handle all message acknowledgment and retransmission functions and do not require the services of any of the layers above the Data Link layer. MOP defines the following maintenance functions:

- **Downline Load.** The *downline load* function allows a node to request a memory image from an adjacent node on the data link. If the image is that of a program, the downline load function allows program execution to be started at a specified memory address following the load. On a broadcast data link, a node can multicast its downline load request and obtain the memory image from the first node responding to the request.

- **Upline Dump.** The *upline dump* function allows a node to send the contents of its own memory to an adjacent node over a single data link. On a broadcast data link, a node can multicast its dump request and then send its memory dump to the first node that responds.

- **Link Loopback Test.** The *loopback test* function can be issued to test a communication link by looping a test message at various points along the physical connection. By moving the loopback point and isolating components, a network manager can use this function to diagnose link problems and locate component failures.

- **System Console Control.** The *system console control* function can be used to control remote, possibly unattended, nodes through emulation of a console terminal. This function also allows the remote node to be restarted.

Conclusion

The network management provisions built into the DNA Phase V architecture provide an orderly means for the setting of network management policy and for monitoring and controlling the network. The final chapter in this part on related architectures and mechanisms concerns the role of packet-switched data networks (PSDNs) and CCITT Recommendation X.25 in a DNA Phase V network.

CHAPTER 18

X.25 Access

Many of today's public data networks use packet-switching techniques and conform to CCITT Recommendation X.25. Recommendation X.25 defines how a computer is attached to a *packet-switched data network* (PSDN). We begin by describing the characteristics of X.25. We then describe the DNA Phase V X.25 Access architecture and examine the various roles X.25 can play in a DECnet Phase V network.

A computer that uses a PSDN conforming to X.25 for communication must implement a *data terminal equipment* (DTE) function; the network device to which the DTE is connected implements a complementary *data circuit-terminating equipment* (DCE) function. Recommendation X.25 defines the interface between an X.25 DTE and an X.25 DCE. It is important to note that X.25 defines only this interface—the way a computer plugs into the network and exchanges packets with it—and does not specify how the network is implemented internally. Recommendation X.25 contains specifications for the interface between a DTE and a DCE at three levels (see Figure 18.1):

- **X.25 Level 1.** This interface defines the characteristics of the physical link between a DTE and a DCE. This part of Recommendation X.25 corresponds to the Physical layer of the OSI model. X.25 defines level 1 through reference to other standards, such as X.21, X.21bis, and the V series of modem standards.

- **X.25 Level 2.** This interface defines the protocol used to reliably pass frames of data between a DTE and a DCE. It corresponds to the Data Link layer of the OSI model and is defined by the Link Access Procedures—Balanced (LAPB) data link protocol. LAPB is a functional subset of the HDLC data link protocol described in Chapter 19.

FIGURE 18.1   **Comparison of Recommendation X.25 with DNA and the OSI model.**

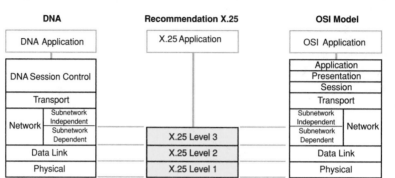

- **X.25 Level 3.** This interface defines the format and meaning of the data portion of the frames defined in level 2 and is often called the *X.25 packet level*. It corresponds to part of the Network layer of the OSI model and specifies the procedures by which X.25 packets are passed between a DTE and a DCE. This same interface is defined in ISO 8208, *Packet-Level Protocol for Data Terminal Equipment*. X.25 level 3 and ISO 8208 are essentially identical.

A PSDN might be constructed using a great many DCEs and a number of intermediate routing nodes, called *switches*, to construct networks having a complex topology, as shown in Figure 18.2. However, an X.25 DTE connected to an X.25 DCE perceives any other DTE on the network as being only one hop away. In this respect, a PSDN can be viewed as a subnetwork in the same manner as an HDLC point-to-point data link. A PSDN providing the X.25 interface is often represented in diagrams as a cloud. The complexities of the PSDN implementation are hidden from the user, and an X.25 DTE at one end of the network perceives only a point-to-point virtual circuit between itself and an X.25 DTE at the other end. (See Figure 18.3.)

X.25 Packets   The X.25 DTE/DCE packet-level interface consists of definitions of the formats of packets passed between a DTE and a DCE. Packets contain both user data and commands used to control the operation of the X.25 protocol. Box 18.1 contains brief descriptions of some of the X.25 command packets. The control information in each packet is used by devices in the PSDN to determine how to relay the packet through the network.

FIGURE 18.2   A possible X.25 network implementation.

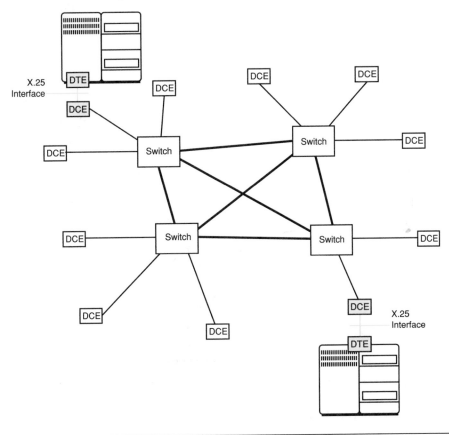

Routing functions in a PSDN are implementation dependent, and the algorithms used for routing are not defined by Recommendation X.25.

X.25 Features

A PSDN conforming to X.25 typically offers to its users two major types of facilities: *permanent virtual circuits* (PVCs) and *switched virtual circuits* (SVCs).[*] These facilities are described in the following sections. Other features of X.25 are briefly described in Box 18.2.

---

[*] The DNA architectural specifications use the term *switched virtual circuit* (SVC) for this type of facility, whereas CCITT Recommendation X.25 uses the term *virtual call* (VC). We will adopt the DNA Phase V terminology in this chapter and use the term *switched virtual circuit*.

FIGURE 18.3   **X.25 virtual circuit.**

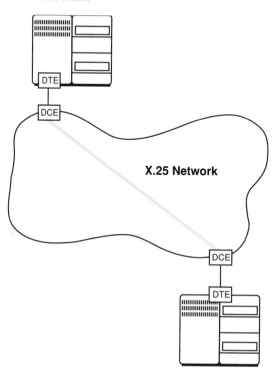

Permanent Virtual Circuits

A user of a PSDN may wish to be permanently connected with another network user in much the same way as two users are connected using a leased telephone connection. A permanent virtual circuit provides this facility. The users are permanently connected to their respective X.25 DCEs. They use the communication facilities of the network and consume network resources only when they are actually transmitting data; however, they remain logically connected permanently as though an actual physical circuit exists between them. Typically the users of a permanent virtual circuit pay a monthly connect charge plus a charge based on total data transmitted over the virtual circuit.

Switched Virtual Circuits

When an X.25 DTE requests the establishment of a switched virtual circuit, the network establishes a virtual circuit with another user, the two

BOX 18.1

X.25 Control
Packets

- **Call Request.** A DTE sends a Call Request packet to request the establishment of a switched virtual circuit.

- **Incoming Call.** A DCE accepts the Call Request packet and generates an Incoming Call packet, which it sends to the destination DTE. This asks the destination DTE if it can accept the request for the establishment of a switched virtual circuit.

- **Call Accepted.** The destination DTE transmits a Call Accepted packet as a positive response to an Incoming Call packet.

- **Call Connected.** The originating DTE accepts the Call Accepted packet and transmits a Call Connected packet as the final step in establishing a switched virtual circuit.

- **Clear Indication.** A Clear Indication packet is transmitted when a destination DTE is not able to accept an Incoming Call packet. It gives the reason for refusing to accept the call.

- **Clear Request.** A Clear Request packet is transmitted when a DTE wants to request the release of a switched virtual circuit.

- **Clear Confirmation.** A DTE transmits a Clear Confirmation packet as a positive acknowledgment to a Clear Request packet as the final step in releasing a switched virtual circuit.

DTEs exchange messages for a time over the virtual circuit, and then one of the two DTEs requests disconnection of the virtual circuit. A DTE requests an SVC by sending a Call Request packet to the DCE. When the DCE receives the Call Request packet from a DTE, it sends an Incoming Call packet across the network to the destination DTE. If the destination DTE accepts the call, the two DTEs can then begin exchanging Data packets with each other over the switched virtual circuit.

Users employing SVCs are generally charged based on connect time, quantity of data transmitted, or both. In requesting an SVC, the user perceives little difference between using a PSDN and using ordinary dial-up telephone facilities. All the complexities of routing through a packet-switched data network are hidden from the two communicating DTEs.

X.25 Access Architectural Model

Support for X.25 in DNA Phase V is defined in the X.25 access specification. This specification defines an architectural model consisting of modules and interfaces. These modules and interfaces, and some ways in

BOX 18.2

X.25 Features

- **Logical Channels.** A given DTE is allowed to concurrently establish up to 4095 different *logical channels* to other DTEs attached to the network by assigning a different 12-bit *virtual circuit number* to each (specific implementations may limit a DTE to fewer than 4095 logical channels). For example, a DTE might be implemented in a computing system supporting many users (people or application programs), many of whom may need to use the PSDN for communication at any given time. Virtual circuit numbers are assigned to both permanent virtual circuits and switched virtual circuits. Each SVC and PVC is assigned a separate logical channel with its own virtual circuit number. Each message a DTE transmits on behalf of a user contains the virtual circuit number to which the message is associated to distinguish it from message traffic generated by other users.

- **Flow Control.** An X.25 PSDN implements flow control mechanisms to control the rate at which it accepts packets from each DTE. Flow control is implemented independently in each direction on a logical channel through the use of a windowing mechanism. The window size represents the maximum number of sequentially numbered Data packets that may be outstanding at any given time.

- **Interrupt Packets.** A DTE can use Interrupt packets to send data that bypasses the normal packet sequence. Interrupt packets can be delivered even when the destination DTE is not accepting normal Data packets. A DTE sending Interrupt packets receives an Interrupt Confirmation packet for every Interrupt packet it sends. A DTE must wait until it receives a confirmation before sending the next Interrupt packet.

- **Reset Packets.** A DTE or the PSDN itself can send a Reset packet across the DTE/DCE interface to reinitialize a virtual circuit. A reset causes all Data and Interrupt packets in transit to be discarded.

- **Call Clearing.** A DTE receives an Incoming Call packet from its DCE when some other DTE is requesting that a switched virtual circuit be established with it. When a DTE receives an Incoming Call packet, it has the option of accepting or rejecting the request. A DTE rejects a request for a virtual circuit by sending a Clear Request packet. Either of the DTEs connected by an SVC can release the SVC by issuing a Clear Request packet. The DCE responds by sending a Clear Indication packet to the opposite DTE. That DTE then responds by sending a Clear Confirmation to its DCE. That DCE then sends a Clear Confirmation packet to the DTE originally requesting release of the SVC.

BOX 18.2

continued

- **Restart Facility.** Either a DTE or a DCE can issue a Restart Indication packet to clear all virtual circuits at the DTE/DCE interface. A DTE sends a Restart Indication packet to the DCE as part of its initialization procedure.

- **Closed User Groups.** This optional facility of X.25 allows network managers to form logical groups of X.25 DTEs. If a user requests the use of a closed user group and the destination DTE is in it, the destination DTE is informed that the user requested the closed user group. This provides a method for determining that the caller is a "friend" without the destination DTE needing to manage a list of DTE addresses.

- **Call Redirection.** This optional facility of X.25 allows an incoming request for a virtual circuit to be redirected to some other DTE. Capabilities of this facility include specifying a list of alternative DTEs to try to specify a logical chain of DTEs for continued redirection.

- **Network User Identification.** This optional facility of X.25 allows a DTE to provide information to the PSDN, on a per-call basis, for such purposes as security, network management, or billing.

- **Call Charging.** This optional facility of X.25 includes mechanisms for determining who is charged for a virtual circuit and for providing information for calculating charges.

which they are related, are illustrated in Figure 18.4. Keep in mind that the modules defined in the X.25 access specification are *architectural modules* and not actual modules of executable code. However, in the following discussion we will refer to the architectural modules as if they were physical modules, in order to conceptually describe how implementations might combine the architectural modules to provide X.25 access facilities.

X.25 Access Module

The X.25 access module is the module that allows a user to request the services provided by the X.25 interface. This is the only module that has to be implemented because it is the only module that provides an application programming interface to X.25 services. As we will show later, a user of the X.25 access module can be a DNA Network layer entity, a

FIGURE 18.4   **X.25 access modules and interfaces.**

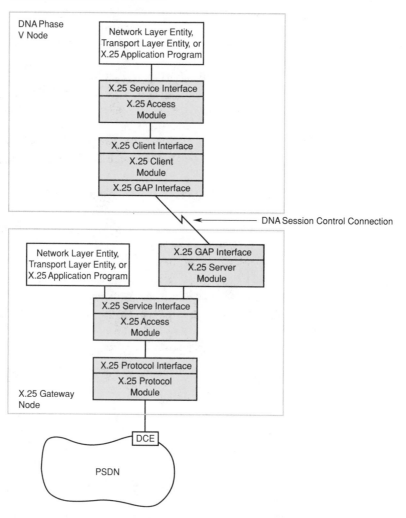

DNA Transport layer entity, an application program issuing requests for X.25 services, or an X.25 server module. The X.25 access module provides an X.25 service interface that allows its users to request its services via ports into the X.25 access module. *Ports* are data structures used to represent X.25 virtual circuits. The procedure declarations documenting the functions of the X.25 service interface are listed in Box 18.3. Note that this is an abstract interface; an implementation of the X.25 access

BOX 18.3

X.25 Service
Interface

The following function and procedure declarations define the abstract interface between the X.25 access module and a user of the X.25 access module in terms of the services the X.25 access module provides to a user.

- **OpenPort.** Opens a port into the X.25 access module. A port is a data structure that can be used for subsequent binding to an incoming or outgoing switched virtual circuit via a TakeCall or MakeCall function.

- **ShowPortStatus.** Reads the status of an X.25 access module port, which reflects the status of the virtual circuit with which it is bound.

- **ClosePort.** Releases a port and any of the resources associated with it.

- **OpenPvc.** Allocates a permanent virtual circuit for subsequent use and implicitly opens the port bound to the permanent virtual circuit.

- **AcknowledgeComsFailure.** Acknowledges that a failure of the PSDN has been detected for a port bound to a permanent virtual circuit.

- **MakeCall.** Establishes a switched virtual circuit and binds it to a specified port.

- **Read Accept.** Reads the data provided by some PSDNs when the PSDN accepts an outgoing call.

- **ListenForCall.** Adds a filter to the list of existing filters in the X.25 access module. Each filter defines the criteria for matching an incoming call to the listener defined when the function is invoked.

- **StopListeningFor.** Deletes a filter from the list of existing filters in the X.25 access module.

- **Listen.** Polls for an incoming call that satisfies any filter defined by a listener defined previously by an invocation of the ListenForCall function.

- **TakeCall.** Binds an incoming call that matches a listener's filter to a specified X.25 access port.

- **CannotTakeCall.** Indicates that the incoming call cannot be bound to the listener, even though it has matched one of the listener's filters.

- **AcceptCall.** Accepts an incoming call already bound to a port as a result of a TakeCall function.

- **ClearCall.** Clears an incoming or outgoing switched virtual circuit.

- **ReadClear.** Reads the data generated when the PSDN clears a virtual circuit.

BOX 18.3

continued

- **Reset.** Resets a virtual circuit bound to a port or acknowledges that the PSDN has reset a virtual circuit.

- **ReadReset.** Reads the data generated when the PSDN resets a virtual circuit.

- **TransmitData.** Queues a transmit buffer containing a Data packet to be sent over a virtual circuit.

- **TransmitPoll.** Polls a transmit buffer previously queued by a TransmitData function to determine if it has been transmitted.

- **ReceiveData.** Queues a receive buffer that can be used to receive a Data packet over a virtual circuit.

- **ReceivePoll.** Polls a receive buffer previously queued by a ReceiveData function to determine if it contains a Data packet.

- **InterruptTransmit.** Sends interrupt data over a virtual circuit.

- **InterruptPoll.** Polls for an Interrupt Acknowledgment received as a result of a previously issued InterruptTransmit function.

- **InterruptReceive.** Reads received interrupt data over a virtual circuit.

- **InterruptConfirm.** Acknowledges interrupt data previously received using the InterruptReceive function.

module must specify the actual application programming interface a program would use to request X.25 services.

The functions provided in the X.25 service interface are employed by users to request X.25 services, such as establishing SVCs and transmitting data over them. A user makes an outgoing request for the establishment of an SVC by issuing an OpenPort function followed by a MakeCall function. Once the SVC has been established, the user sends and receives data over the SVC by issuing TransmitData, TransmitPoll, ReceiveData, and ReceivePoll functions.

A user, called the *listener*, sets up a list of filters that indicates which incoming calls the local X.25 access module should inform the listener about. The listener maintains the filter list by issuing ListenForCall and StopListeningFor functions. When an incoming call matches the call criteria specified in a filter, the X.25 access module notifies the listener. The listener then has the option of accepting the call or explicitly refusing to accept it. If one listener rejects a call, the X.25 access module restarts its matching procedure and attempts to find a listener who will accept the call.

The X.25 Protocol Module

The X.25 protocol module performs the functions of the X.25 packet-level protocol to gain access to a PSDN. The X.25 protocol module provides an X.25 protocol interface. This interface is accessed only by the X.25 access module and is substantially similar to the X.25 service interface. An implementation of the X.25 protocol module performs the function of an X.25 DTE for the node in which it is implemented and communicates directly with an X.25 DCE in the PSDN.

X.25 Client and Server Modules

The X.25 client and X.25 server modules are necessary when the X.25 access module and the X.25 protocol module are in different nodes. The X.25 access module uses the services of an X.25 client module, which in turn communicates with an X.25 server module in another node. The X.25 server module can then use the services of the X.25 protocol module in that node to access the PSDN. The X.25 client module provides an X.25 client interface allowing the X.25 access module to request its services. Like the X.25 level 3 protocol interface, this interface is similar to the X.25 service interface.

The X.25 client and server modules communicate with one another using the gateway access protocol (GAP). The client and server modules each provide an X.25 gateway access interface allowing them to communicate using the GAP. The DNA Phase V X.25 access specification defines the GAP messages that the X.25 gateway server and client must be able to accept. These are listed in Box 18.4.

Although not shown in Figure 18.4, the X.25 client and server modules also implement an interface to the DNA Session Control layer allowing the GAP to operate over a DNA Phase V Session Control layer connection. This is the same interface described in Chapter 11.

Module Combinations

The architectural modules that make up X.25 access can be combined in various ways to allow the X.25 interface to be used for three purposes:

- Two Network layer entities in a pair of DECnet Phase V routers can use a virtual circuit as a point-to-point subnetwork to connect them.
- A Transport layer entity in a DECnet Phase V node can access a local X.25 access module to exchange data with another Transport layer entity using the ISO CONS, described in Chapter 8.

BOX 18.4

X.25 Gateway
Access Protocol
Messages

Messages Received by X.25 Gateway Server

- **Open.** Requests the establishment of a permanent virtual circuit.
- **Outgoing Call.** Requests an outgoing request for the establishment of a switched virtual circuit to the destination specified in the message.
- **Outgoing Accept.** Accepts a previously received incoming request for the establishment of a switched virtual circuit.
- **Clear Request.** Indicates that a user has issued a ClearCall function to the X.25 access module requesting that a virtual circuit be cleared.
- **Reset Request.** Indicates that a user has issued a Reset function to the X.25 access module requesting that a virtual circuit be reset.
- **No Comm Seen.** Indicates that a user has issued a AcknowledgeComs-Failure function to the X.25 access module indicating it has detected a failure of the PSDN for a port bound to a permanent virtual circuit.

Messages Received by X.25 Gateway Client

- **Open Accept.** Accepts an incoming request for the establishment of a permanent virtual circuit.
- **Open Reject.** Rejects an incoming request for the establishment of a permanent virtual circuit. The message indicates the reason for the rejection.
- **Incoming Accept.** Indicates to the Gateway Client acceptance of an outgoing request for the establishment of a switched virtual circuit.
- **Incoming Call.** Indicates to the Gateway Client that there is an incoming request for the establishment of a switched virtual circuit.
- **Clear Indication.** Indicates that the PSDN has issued a request to clear a switched virtual circuit.
- **Clear Confirm.** Indicates that the PSDN has confirmed a request to clear a switched virtual circuit.
- **Reset Indication.** Indicates that the PSDN has issued a request to reset a switched virtual circuit.

- An application designed to communicate using X.25 protocols can communicate, through a local X.25 Access module, with another X.25 application using the X.25 protocol.

Each of these uses of X.25 is described next with examples of the X.25 architectural modules that are used in each case.

BOX 18.4

continued

- **No Com.** Indicates that communication is currently impossible on the permanent virtual circuit.

Messages Received by Both Client and Server

- **Connect.** Establishes an association between an X.25 client module and an X.25 server module.
- **Accept.** Sent in response to the receipt of a Connect message to accept the establishment of an association between a client and a server.
- **Reject.** Sent in response to the receipt of a Connect message to reject the establishment of an association between a client and a server.
- **Call Reject.** Rejects a previously received Outgoing Call or Incoming Call message.
- **Clear Expected.** Indicates that a Clear Request or Clear Indication message is expected and that data should be discarded in order for the message to be read.
- **Reset Confirmation.** Confirms a previous request for reset of a switched virtual circuit.
- **Reset Confirmation Marker.** Indicates the point in the data at which a request for the reset of a switched virtual circuit occurred.
- **Data.** Contains outbound or inbound data.
- **Interrupt Complete.** Contains interrupt data completing an Interrupt message.
- **Interrupt Incomplete.** Contains incomplete interrupt data that are part of an Interrupt message.
- **Interrupt Confirmation.** Used for flow control to confirm receipt of an Interrupt message.

Using an X.25 Network as a Subnetwork

In this use of X.25, two routers can be connected using an X.25 virtual circuit as a data link. The virtual circuit is then used for the purpose of sending DNA network traffic between the two routers. When an X.25 virtual circuit is used to interconnect routers, the virtual circuit is used to implement what appears to the routers to be a simple point-to-point link. The X.25 access module and X.25 protocol module are used to implement such a use of an X.25 virtual circuit, as shown in Figure 18.5.

The DNA Network layer in this case is the user of the X.25 access module, and the X.25 protocol module is used to perform the function of an X.25 DTE in sending and receiving X.25 data packets and commands. In this use of X.25, the application programs using the network for communication are not aware of the fact that X.25 virtual circuits are being used. When a PSDN is employed in this manner, the PSDN can be viewed as a subnetwork in which any DECnet router attached to the PSDN is a single hop away from any other router attached to that PSDN.

FIGURE 18.5   Use of an X.25 virtual circuit as a subnetwork in a DECnet Phase V network.

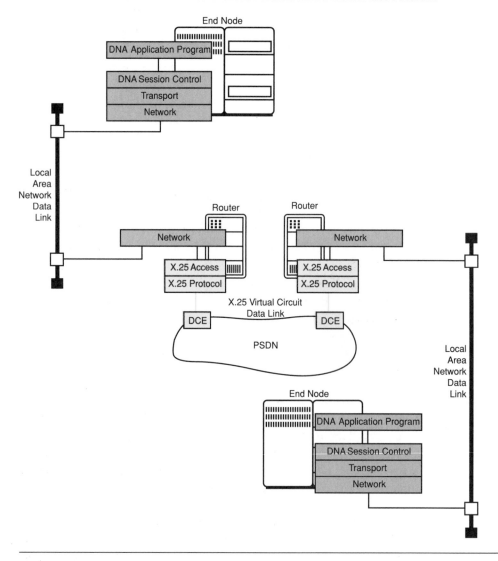

There are two ways routers can use an X.25 virtual circuit for carrying network traffic:

- **Data Link Mapping.** With data link mapping (DLM), an X.25 virtual circuit is set up by a network manager between two routers and remains available for use by those routers until a network manager releases it. Such a virtual circuit can be used without restriction—in the same manner as any other point-to-point connection—to exchange data traffic and routing control packets between the two routers.

- **Dynamic Assignment.** With dynamic assignment (DA), an X.25 SVC is set up when there is traffic requiring it. Dynamic assignment SVCs are used only to carry user data; they are not used to carry routing control information. Routing over DA SVCs is done using the static routing mechanisms for interdomain routing discussed in Chapter 9.

Using X.25 to Supply the CONS

As discussed in Chapters 7 and 8, the DNA Phase V Network layer also provides support for the connection mode Network service (CONS) for users who require the use of the CONS. This use of X.25 is illustrated in Figure 18.6. As with the previous use of X.25, only the X.25 access module and the X.25 protocol module are required to provide the CONS. In this case, the user of the X.25 access module is the DNA Transport layer.

FIGURE 18.6   Use of an X.25 virtual circuit to supply the CONS.

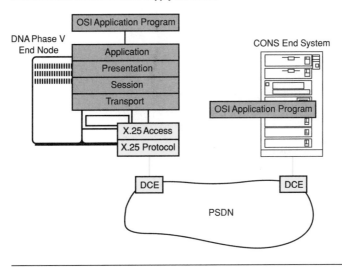

An implementation of the X.25 protocol module in a DECnet node attached to the PSDN provides the function of an X.25 DTE.

When X.25 is used to supply the CONS, one additional protocol is used: ISO 8878, *Use of X.25 to Provide the OSI Connection-Mode Network Service*. X.25 level 3 and ISO 8208 define a protocol that is sufficiently powerful to provide all the services needed to supply the CONS. However, because Recommendation X.25 predates the OSI model, it does not specifically provide information about *how* the X.25 protocol should be used to provide all the services specified in the CONS. ISO 8878 can be viewed as operating in a sublayer on top of ISO 8208 (X.25 level 3) defining how X.25 packets and procedures are used to supply all the services defined by the CONS.

X.25 Gateway Access

With this use of X.25, the X.25 access module can be used to allow an X.25 application running in a DECnet node to use the services of an X.25 protocol module in the same node or in some other node. A node implementing the X.25 access module to support either local or remote access by X.25 applications is called an *X.25 gateway node*. The services that X.25 applications request can be handled in various ways.

Figure 18.7 shows the simplest possibility in which an X.25 application, running in a DECnet node, is communicating with an X.25 application in a system (which may or may not be a DECnet node) attached to a PSDN. In this case the X.25 Access module allows the X.25 application

FIGURE 18.7   Use of an X.25 gateway node.

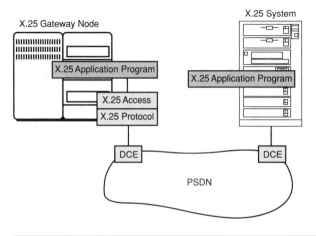

in the DECnet node to request X.25 services. The X.25 protocol module performs the function of the X.25 DTE and sends and receives X.25 control and data packets to communicate with the other X.25 application. In this example, implementations of the X.25 access module and the X.25 protocol module both reside in the same node and so no protocol is required for them to communicate with one another.

It is not necessary, however, for an X.25 application to reside in the X.25 gateway node. The use of the X.25 client module and the X.25 server module to support remote access to an X.25 gateway node is shown in Figure 18.8. Here, the X.25 application running in node A is the user of the X.25 access module in node A. It in turn uses the services of the X.25 client module to communicate with the X.25 server module

FIGURE 18.8   Remote access to an X.25 gateway node using the X.25 client and X.25 server modules.

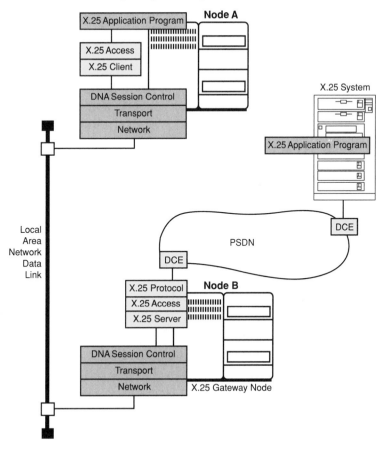

in node B. Implementations of the client and server modules use the gateway access protocol (GAP), running over a DNA Session Control connection, to handle communication between them. The X.25 server module in node B then uses another implementation of the X.25 access module in node B to request X.25 services. It in turn uses the X.25 protocol module, which performs the functions of an X.25 DTE to access the PSDN.

Internetworking between DECnet Phase V nodes and DECnet Phase IV nodes is fully supported. A node implementing a Phase IV X.25 access module can request the services of a Phase V X.25 gateway node and vice versa.

Multiple Uses of X.25

Implementations of the four X.25 architectural modules can be combined to allow X.25 to be used in a variety of ways in the same network. A DECnet network can be constructed using X.25 virtual circuits to implement some of the point-to-point connections between routers. At the same time X.25 Gateway nodes can operate as DTEs connected to one or more X.25 PSDNs. X.25 applications in DECnet nodes that do not implement X.25 DTEs can access the gateway nodes to request X.25 services. In the same network, any DECnet node can use a PSDN to provide the ISO CONS. The CONS users can then exchange data over the CONS connection.

Conclusion

This chapter, which concludes Part IV on related architectures and mechanisms, showed a variety of ways in which the virtual circuits provided by packet-switched data networks can be used in constructing a DECnet Phase V network. The final part of this book—Part V—examines the Data Link layer of the architecture in detail and discusses the various types of subnetworks the Network layer can use. Part V begins with Chapter 19 introducing High-level Data Link Control (HDLC), the main data link protocol used for point-to-point data links in the wide area networking environment.

PART V

Data Link Layer Protocols

CHAPTER 19

HDLC, SDLC, and LAPB Data Links

The types of data links described in this chapter and Chapter 20 are designed to implement wide area networking data links using conventional telecommunications facilities. As mentioned in the chapters in Parts II and III, it is a goal of ISO to define a single service definition and one or more protocol specifications for each layer of the OSI model. Currently, a single ISO standard defines a Data Link layer protocol specification for the wide area networking environment. This is *High-Level Data Link Control* (HDLC), documented in the standards documents listed in Box 19.1. Chapter 20 describes the *Digital Data Communication Message Protocol* (DDCMP), another protocol for wide area networking, provided in DNA Phase V mainly for compatibility with DNA Phase IV.

The original specification of ISO HDLC permits operation only over a physical circuit that supports synchronous transmission. However, an amendment to ISO 3309 defines the changes that are required to HDLC to allow the protocol to be used over an asynchronous (start-stop) line. DNA Phase V HDLC supports both synchronous and asynchronous transmission. (See Chapter 5 for a discussion of the differences between synchronous and asynchronous transmission.)

HDLC Service Definition and Protocol Specification

The HDLC protocol predates the OSI model, and the standards for HDLC do not separate the service definition from the protocol specification. The DNA Phase V documentation for HDLC, however, does specify a service definition in terms of procedure declarations the same as it does for the other layers of the architecture. We will examine these later when we look at the DNA Phase V architectural model for HDLC.

An HDLC entity operates in the Data Link layer of the architecture. It provides a set of services to a user of the HDLC entity and requests the ser-

BOX 19.1

ISO Standards That
Define HDLC

- ISO 3309, *HDLC Procedures—Frame Structure*
- ISO 4335, *HDLC Elements of Procedures*
- ISO 7776, *HDLC Procedures—X.25 LAPB-compatible DTE Data Link Procedures*
- ISO 7809, *HDLC Procedures—Consolidation of Classes of Procedures*
- ISO 8471, *HDLC Data Link Address Resolution*
- ISO 8885, *HDLC Procedures—General Purpose XID Frame Information Field Content and Format*

vices of a modem connect entity operating below it in the Physical layer. The HDLC protocol specification precisely defines the formats of the frames exchanged during protocol operation and describes, in detail, the procedures controlling the exchange of frames. We continue this discussion of the HDLC protocol by introducing some important terminology.

Stations and Data Links

Each device attached to a data link that handles data link protocol functions is called a *data station*, or a *station*. Data links connecting stations can be either *unbalanced* or *balanced*. An unbalanced link connects two or more stations, with one of the stations designated as the *primary station* and all the others designated as *secondary stations*. Such a communication facility is sometimes used to connect a computer to one or more terminals. With computer networks, balanced facilities more often are used. A balanced data link connects two stations only, with each station called a *combined station*, either of which can originate message transmission.

Commands and Responses

On an unbalanced data link, messages that the primary station sends are called *commands*; messages that the secondary station sends in reply to commands are called *responses*. With a balanced facility, either station can originate a transmission by sending a command; the other station then replies with a response.

HDLC Operating Modes

The HDLC protocol specification defines three operational modes to support three types of protocol operations. Only two of these are included in DNA Phase V HDLC. All three HDLC operational modes are described next.

Balanced Mode

Balanced mode, referred to as *asynchronous balanced mode* (ABM) in the ISO HDLC standard, supports a balanced data link that connects two combined stations using a full-duplex physical circuit. Either station can initiate frame transmission, and frame transmission can take place in both directions at the same time. DNA Phase V HDLC supports balanced mode, and this is the preferred operating mode of an HDLC data link in a DECnet Phase V network.

Normal Mode

Normal mode, referred to as *normal response mode* (NRM) in the ISO HDLC standard, is used to support unbalanced data links that connect two or more stations using a half-duplex physical circuit. One of the stations on the link is the primary station and the others are secondary stations. A secondary station cannot initiate transmission without first receiving permission from the primary station. DNA Phase V HDLC supports normal mode as an alternative to balanced mode.

Asynchronous Response Mode

The ISO HDLC standard also defines an *asynchronous response mode* (ARM), in which each station performs the function of both a primary and a secondary station. With ARM, the data link consists logically of two primary/secondary station pairs. In this mode either station can initiate transmission, but one of the stations typically retains responsibility for the data link. In practice, asynchronous response mode was found to have a number of limitations and is today considered obsolete by most authorities. It has been superseded in most cases by balanced mode. The DNA Phase V architecture does not support asynchronous response mode.

Nonoperational Modes

In addition to the three operational modes, there are three nonoperational modes:

- **Asynchronous Disconnected Mode.** The *asynchronous disconnected mode* (ADM) applies to a station on a balanced data link that is logically and/or physically disconnected from the link.

- **Normal Disconnected Mode.** The *normal disconnected mode* (NDM) applies to a station on an unbalanced link that is logically and/or physically disconnected from the link.

- **Initialization Mode.** The *initialization mode* (IM) is intended to be the mode a station is in before it actually becomes operational. One station can put another station into initialization mode when it is necessary to perform some hardware-specific initialization procedure. DNA Phase V HDLC does not employ initialization mode for station initialization or other types of maintenance procedures. Such functions are the responsibility of the DNA *Maintenance Operation Protocol* (MOP). The use of MOP is discussed later when we examine HDLC protocol operation.

Support for SDLC

The HDLC protocol has its roots in the *Synchronous Data Link Control* (SDLC) protocol developed by IBM in the early 1970s for use in SNA. At the time IBM developed SDLC, the predominant data link configuration consisted of a single primary station (typically a host computer or communications controller) connected to multiple secondary stations (typically terminals), using a multipoint, half-duplex physical circuit. IBM's SDLC is a functional subset of HDLC and is compatible with the normal mode of HDLC; a DNA Phase V station operating in normal mode can successfully communicate with a station conforming to IBM's SDLC specification. Normal mode requires one station to take the role of the primary station and the others to take the role of secondary stations. A management parameter must be set to designate one of the stations as the primary station for a link operating in normal mode.

Support for X.25 and LAPB

CCITT Recommendation X.25 (discussed in detail in Chapter 18) defines how a computer is attached to a packet-switched data network (PSDN). A portion of Recommendation X.25 defines the procedures that determine how frames of data are passed between the computer and the PSDN. This procedure is called *Link Access Procedures—Balanced* (LAPB) and is similar to the balanced mode of HDLC. An appendix on LAPB is included in the architectural specification for DNA Phase V HDLC.

Frame Format

As discussed in Chapter 6, the data unit transmitted over a data link is a *data-link-protocol-data-unit* (DLPDU), more typically called a *frame*. Some frames are originated by mechanisms operating in the Data Link layer itself and are used to control the operation of the data link. Other frames are used to carry the data-link-service-data-unit (DLSDU) passed down from an HDLC user for transmission over the data link. As shown in Figure 19.1, each frame is divided into three major parts: a header, a variable-length information field, and a trailer. Protocol-control-information (PCI) is carried in the header and the trailer. Frames originated in the Data Link layer sometimes use the information field to carry control information. The following sections describe the fields in an HDLC frame.

Beginning Flag Field

Each frame begins with a *flag field*, which consists of a single octet containing the unique bit configuration 0111 1110. A *bit stuffing* technique (described later) guarantees that only a flag field will contain six consecutive 1-bits.

Address Field

The field following the flag field is a single octet in length and is interpreted as the station address. The position of this field within the frame (the octet immediately following the beginning flag) defines this field as the address field. When a station originates a command, the command includes an address that identifies the station to which the frame is being sent. The address field value distinguishes whether a frame is a command or a response. A command always contains the station address of the receiving station; a response always contains the address of the sending station. The HDLC addressing scheme is an artifact of the multipoint data link orientation of the original SDLC specification, and, on a balanced data link that connects only two stations, the station address serves no real purpose. However, the address field is present in all HDLC frames for consistency of format.

FIGURE 19.1   **HDLC transmission frame.**

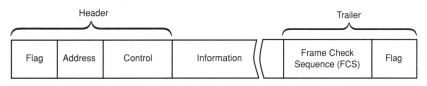

Control Field

The control field is 1 or 2 octets in length. The control field determines the type of frame being transmitted, conveys information necessary for the proper sequencing of frames, and carries control information. The position of the control field within the frame (the field immediately after the address field) defines this field as the control field.

Information Field

A variable-length information field is used to carry the data portion of the frame. It consists of either control information or data passed down from a user of the HDLC entity. Some frames originating in the Data Link layer do not use an information field. The HDLC specification allows the information field to be any number of bits in length. However, most implementations of HDLC require the information field to be some multiple of eight bits, as is the case with DNA Phase V HDLC. The size can be zero octets for some commands and responses. Although HDLC does not specifically define a maximum length for the information field, a particular HDLC implementation may set limits on the size of a frame based on the size of the available buffer. The receiving station knows where the first octet of the information field begins because it always immediately follows the control field.

Frame Check Sequence Field

The frame check sequence (FCS) field contains either a 16-bit or a 32-bit cyclic redundancy check (CRC) value used for error detection. The procedures used to generate and process the CRC are described in Chapter 6. Digital implementations of HDLC use a 32-bit CRC value but support a 16-bit CRC for communication with stations supporting only a 16-bit CRC.

NETWORK ARCHITECT

There is always a chance, no matter how small, that a frame will be damaged in such a way that the CRC value remains correct. We decided that, especially for high-speed links, 16-bit CRC values are inadequate for really good protection from errors. On a line operating at 10 megabits per second, a 16-bit CRC might allow an undetected error to get through about once per month. With a 32-bit CRC, there will be an undetected error about every 10 years.

The way in which stations determine whether to use a 16-bit or 32-bit CRC is discussed later in this chapter.

Ending Flag Field

The end of a frame is marked by another flag field containing the same bit configuration as the beginning flag field (0111 1110).

Frame and Control Field Formats	The three types of HDLC frames all share the same general format described previously. The following are brief descriptions of each frame type:

- **Information Frames.** The primary function of Information frames (I-frames) is to carry user data, although they sometimes also implicitly perform control functions, such as serving as positive acknowledgments to frames sent.

- **Supervisory Frames.** Supervisory frames (S-frames) are used to control the transmission of I-frames and are exchanged only when the link is in a state where it is possible to transmit and receive I-frames. They carry information necessary for supervisory control functions, which include requesting transmission, requesting a temporary suspension of transmission, acknowledging the receipt of I-frames, and reporting on status. Normal, routine transmission over a data link involves only I-frames and S-frames.

- **Unnumbered Frames.** Unnumbered frames (U-frames) are used to carry data and to perform control functions, such as performing initialization procedures, controlling the data link, and invoking diagnostic sequences.

1-Octet and 2-Octet Control Fields

I-frames and S-frames transmitted during HDLC operation can contain either 1-octet or 2-octet control fields; U-frames always contain 1-octet control fields. With DNA Phase V HDLC, a data link normally uses 2-octet control fields in I-frames and S-frames and runs using *modulo-128* operation. This is the preferred operating mode because it increases link throughput, especially on circuits having long propagation delays, such as satellite circuits. If one or both of the stations support only 1-octet control fields, then *modulo-8* operation is used with 1-octet control fields in I-frames and S-frames.

• **Modulo-8 Operation.** When stations operate in single-octet control field mode, 3 bits are used for frame sequence numbers. Three-bit sequence number values allow frame sequence numbers to range from 0 through 7. Modulo-8 operation allows a sending station to transmit up to seven frames in sequence before it must request an acknowledgment.

• **Modulo-128 Operation.** When stations operate in 2-octet control field mode, frame sequence numbers consist of 7-bit values, allowing values from 0 through 127. Modulo-128 operation allows a sending station to transmit up to 127 frames in sequence before an acknowledgment is required.

The following sections describe the formats of I-frames, S-frames, and U-frames.

I-Frame Format   Figure 19.2 illustrates the format of I-frames and shows how the control field bits are interpreted for 2-octet control fields. A 0 in bit position 1 in the first control field octet identifies the frame as an I-frame. The remainder of the bits in the 2-octet I-frame control field are used to contain a send count [N(S)], a receive count [N(R)], and a poll/final (P/F) bit. The count fields are used to control frame sequencing. The poll/final bit is used to request acknowledgments. For an unbalanced data link, the poll/final bit is also used by the primary station to poll the secondary stations.

FIGURE 19.2   **I-frame format.**

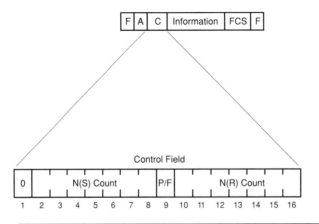

S-Frame Format   Figure 19.3 illustrates the frame format for S-frames, showing the control field layout for a 2-octet control field. The 2 bits provided for the function code allow up to four different S-frame commands and four different S-frame responses. S-frames do not carry information fields. When bit position 1 of the first control field octet is 1, bit position 2 further identifies the frame as being either an S-frame or a U-frame. A 10 in bit positions 1 and 2 identifies the frame as an S-frame. The remainder of the bits in the S-frame control octet are interpreted as containing a 2-bit function code, a receive count [N(R)], and a poll/final (P/F) bit. The function code bits identify the type of command or response the frame represents. Box 19.2 describes the three most commonly used S-frame commands and responses.

FIGURE 19.3   **S-frame format.**

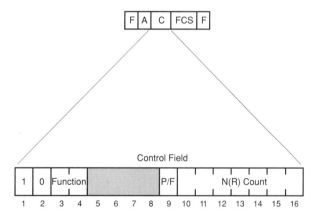

U-Frame Format   Figure 19.4 illustrates the format of U-frames, showing details for the control field. U-frames always have 1-octet control fields. Some U-frame commands and responses have information fields; others do not. An 11-bit configuration in bit positions 1 and 2 of the first control field octet identifies the frame as a U-frame. The remainder of the bits are interpreted as a poll/final bit and function code bits. The function code bits in a U-frame identify the type of command the frame represents. The five function code bits allow for up to 32 different commands and 32 different responses, only some of which are actually used in an implementa-

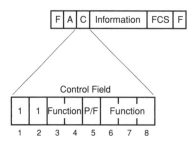

tion of HDLC. Box 19.3 (page 422) provides brief descriptions of the most commonly used U-frames.

DNA Phase V HDLC uses Exchange Station Identification (XID) and Unnumbered Information (UI) frames to support a *link initialization* procedure and defines how the information fields of UI-frames are used to support a *protocol multiplexing* function. These aspects of DNA Phase V HDLC are described later in this chapter.

HDLC Architectural Model

Figure 19.5 illustrates the DNA Phase V HDLC architectural model and shows how the HDLC entity relates to its users and to the Physical layer. Other higher-level protocols, such as the DNA *Maintenance Operations Protocol* (MOP), can also concurrently use the services of an HDLC entity over the same data link through the protocol multiplexing feature. A

FIGURE 19.5   HDLC architectural model.

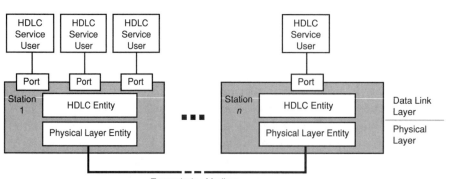

BOX 19.2

S-Frame
Commands and
Responses

- **Receiver Ready (RR).** Command or response sent to indicate that the station is ready to receive another I-frame or to acknowledge previously received I-frames.

- **Receiver Not Ready (RNR).** Command or response sent to indicate that the station is temporarily unable to accept additional I-frames.

- **Reject (REJ).** Command or response sent to request the retransmission of one or more I-frames.

user of the HDLC entity accesses its services through a port. A *port* is the point in the HDLC entity at which the HDLC service interface is located. Any number of users in a node can open a port into an HDLC entity.

HDLC Service Interface Procedure Declarations

The DNA Phase V architectural specification for HDLC defines the abstract interface between an HDLC entity and a user of its services. The function and procedure declarations that define this abstract interface are listed in Box 19.4 (page 423).

HDLC Protocol Operation

The ISO and DNA Phase V documentation for HDLC describe, in detail, the procedures controlling protocol operation. DNA Phase V HDLC supports all procedures required by a data link operating in either balanced mode or normal mode. DNA Phase V also defines a number of procedures that go beyond the ISO HDLC standard while remaining in conformance with it. We first describe a number of procedures defined by ISO HDLC.

Bit Stuffing and Synchronous Framing

When HDLC operates over a circuit using synchronous transmission, the data stream consists of a series of frames, each of which consists of a continuous stream of bits. HDLC always operates in *transparent mode*, meaning that any desired bit configurations can be carried in the data in the frame's information field. A requirement for achieving transparency is to ensure that flag octets, which contain six consecutive 1-bits, are not transmitted in any part of the frame other than in the beginning and ending flag field positions. If a flag field appeared anywhere else in the frame,

BOX 19.3

U-Frame
Commands and
Responses

- **Set Asynchronous Balanced Mode (SABM).** Command issued to place the data link into balanced mode.

- **Set Asynchronous Balanced Mode Extended (SABME).** Command issued to place the data link into balanced mode using 2-octet control fields. This is the normal operating mode of HDLC data links in a DECnet Phase V network.

- **Set Normal Response Mode (SNRM).** Command issued to place the data link into normal mode.

- **Set Normal Response Mode Extended (SNRME).** Command issued to place the data link into normal mode using 2-octet control fields.

- **Unnumbered Information (UI).** Used for transmitting unnumbered information frames between stations. DNA Phase V does not discriminate between the command and response forms of the UI-frame. In DNA Phase V HDLC, UI-frames are used to implement a protocol multiplexing facility allowing a data link to be used concurrently by more than one user.

- **Disconnect (DISC).** Command issued to terminate a previously set operational mode. On a dial-up line, the station receiving the DISC command also physically disconnects itself from the line.

- **Exchange Station Identification (XID).** Commands or responses issued to exchange and negotiate configuration information. The DNA Phase V HDLC specification uses XID commands and responses to implement a station identification procedure used to negotiate operational parameters, such as the use of either a 16-bit or a 32-bit FCS field.

- **Unnumbered Acknowledgment (UA).** Response issued to acknowledge receipt and acceptance of SABM, SABME, SNRM, SNRME, and DISC commands.

- **Frame Reject (FRMR).** Response issued to indicate abnormal conditions. The command contains bits indicating the reason for the rejection, such as an invalid or unimplemented command function code, a frame with an information field that should not have one, or a frame with an information field too big for the station's buffer.

- **Disconnect Mode (DM).** Response issued as a positive acknowledgment to a DISC command to indicate that the receiving station is now in disconnect mode.

BOX 19.4

HDLC Service
Interface
Procedure
Declarations

The following function and procedure declarations define the
abstract interface between a DNA Phase V HDLC entity and a user
of its services.

Port Control Functions

- **OpenPort.** Opens a port into an HDLC entity that can be used to
  request its services. A user can open only one port for exchanging
  I-frames and multiple ports for exchanging UI-frames.
- **ClosePort.** Closes a port into an HDLC entity.

Data Transfer Functions

- **Transmit.** Transmits sequenced data using I-frames.
- **TransmitPoll.** Polls for return of transmit buffers used to send
  I-frames.
- **TransmitUnsequenced.** Transmits data using UI-frames.
- **TransmitPollUnsequenced.** Polls for return of transmit buffers used
  to send UI-frames.
- **Receive.** Queues an empty buffer to receive I-frame or UI-frame data.
- **ReceivePoll.** Polls for received data and the status of the data.

Control Functions

- **AttachToCall.** Associates a call with a port.
- **InitializeLink.** Starts operation of the I-frame service of the HDLC
  protocol on a link.
- **StopLink.** Stops operation of the I-frame service on a link.
- **ShowLinkStatus.** Shows the status of the HDLC protocol on the link.

stations would have no way of knowing where a frame begins and ends.
If the protocol is to be transparent, however, frames must be capable of
containing bit sequences of any desired bit configuration, including
octets containing the flag configuration (0111 1110). When HDLC operates over a circuit that supports synchronous transmission, a technique
called *bit stuffing* handles this apparent contradiction.

In transmitting the data between a beginning and an ending flag, the
transmitting station inserts an extra 0-bit into the data stream each time

it detects a sequence of five 1-bits. The transmitter turns off the bit-stuffing mechanism when it transmits an actual beginning or ending flag. In this way, no consecutive sequence of six 1-bits is ever transmitted except when an actual flag is sent over the link. A complementary technique is used by the receiver in removing the extra 0-bits. Whenever the receiver detects five 1-bits followed by a 0-bit, it discards the 0-bit, thus restoring the bit stream to its original value. The bit stuffing technique ensures that six 1-bits in a row will never occur except in a flag field. When the receiver detects six consecutive 1-bits, it knows it has received a genuine flag.

At high bit rates, the time it takes to process each frame received may be greater than the minimum time between frames, which is defined by ISO HDLC as the time it takes to transmit a single flag sequence. To prevent a case where every other frame is lost on a high-speed link, DNA Phase V HDLC defines a procedure for informing the transmitter of the minimum acceptable time between frames. The transmitter uses this value to send additional flags between frames to provide the required delay.

Octet Stuffing and Asynchronous Framing

When HDLC operates over a circuit using asynchronous (start-stop) transmission, the data stream consists of a stream of octets. Octets are grouped into frames using a different procedure than that defined for synchronous HDLC. The ISO standard for asynchronous HDLC defines two octet values that are used to control the operation of the protocol: the *flag* octet value and the *control escape* octet value. The actual values to be used for the flag and control escape octets must be agreed upon in advance between the two communicating stations.

The transmitter begins a frame by sending a flag octet and ends a frame by sending another flag octet. The transmitter uses an *octet stuffing* procedure to ensure that no flag octets appear between the beginning and ending flags. Between the transmission of the beginning and ending flags, the transmitter checks each octet's value to see if it is equal to either the flag or control escape value. If the transmitter detects either a flag or control escape octet, it complements the octet's sixth bit. It then transmits a control escape octet followed by the modified flag or control escape octet. When a receiver receives a flag octet, it knows that it has received a genuine beginning or ending flag. When a receiver receives a control escape octet, it discards it and complements the sixth bit in the octet that follows, thus restoring the byte stream to its original value.

Pipelining and Acknowledgment

One of the primary responsibilities of HDLC is to detect corrupted and lost frames and, when they are detected, to cause required frames to be retransmitted. To achieve this, transmitted frames require acknowledgments from the receiving station indicating whether frames were received correctly. With HDLC, a technique called *pipelining* is used in which multiple I-frames can be sent before the sending station requires an acknowledgment. As discussed earlier, with 2-octet control fields, up to 127 I-frames can be transmitted between acknowledgments.

To ensure that no frames are lost and that all frames are properly acknowledged, the sequence numbers contained in I-frames and S-frames are employed to control I-frame transmission. All stations maintain counters that keep track of a *send count* value and a *receive count* value. These two counters are used to set the count fields in the control octets of the I-frames and S-frames the station transmits. The transmitter always keeps track of how many I-frames it has sent, and the receiver keeps track of how many I-frames it has received. When a station receives an acknowledgment, that acknowledgment contains the sequence number of the next I-frame the other station expects to receive. This implicitly acknowledges all I-frames up to, but not including, the frame having the specified sequence number. In this way a frame can acknowledge several previously transmitted I-frames. To ensure that acknowledgments are received in a timely manner, the HDLC specification allows a limit to be set on the number of frames the Physical layer can queue up for transmission at any time. This allows the Physical layer to maintain continuous transmission while ensuring that an up-to-date acknowledgment can be sent with minimum delay.

Flow Control

HDLC defines a simple flow control procedure that a station can use when it is temporarily unable to receive additional I-frames, possibly due to lack of buffers. A station indicates that the other station is to stop sending I-frames by transmitting a Receiver Not Ready (RNR) S-frame. This causes the opposite station to stop sending I-frames until it receives a Receiver Ready (RR) frame.

DNA Phase V Extensions to ISO HDLC

In addition to the HDLC procedures to support balanced mode and normal mode, DNA Phase V HDLC defines additional procedures that go beyond the ISO standard. These are described in the following sections.

Link Initialization

The DNA Phase V HDLC link initialization procedure ensures that two stations are able to establish, in an unambiguous manner, the initial state of the link or to restart a link after link failure. Information is exchanged during the link initialization procedure using the information fields of XID frames. The link initialization procedure has three phases:

1. **Station Identification.** In this phase, the stations exchange information about their capabilities to determine the operational parameters that will be used to govern link operation.

2. **Disconnection.** In this phase, each of the stations forces the link into one of the two disconnected modes by transmitting DISC U-frames.

3. **Link Establishment.** In this phase, one of the stations transmits a U-frame command to initialize the link. The U-frame command generally used is the Set Asynchronous Balanced Mode Extended (SABME) command. This places the link into balanced mode using 7-bit sequence numbers. The Set Asynchronous Balanced Mode (SABM) command is used if one or both of the stations supports only 3-bit sequence numbers. The Set Normal Response Mode (SNRM) command is used if the stations need to use normal mode, possibly for compatibility with IBM's SDLC.

CRC Negotiation

An important operational parameter negotiated during execution of the DNA Phase V link initialization procedure is whether 16-bit or 32-bit CRCs will be used. To determine this, an XID frame is sent during link initialization that carries a special 48-bit CRC sequence. This CRC sequence is produced using a polynomial designed so the last 16 bits of the 48-bit CRC will pass the 16-bit CRC algorithm and the last 32 bits will pass the 32-bit CRC algorithm. In this manner, the frame is received correctly by a station supporting only a 16-bit CRC, only a 32-bit CRC, or either. The stations then negotiate whether a 16-bit or 32-bit CRC will be used during link operation. A 32-bit CRC is used if both stations support it; otherwise, a 16-bit CRC is used.

Protocol Multiplexing

The ISO HDLC specification does not specify procedures allowing more than one higher-level protocol to concurrently use the same data link. The DNA Phase V architecture defines a protocol multiplexing facility in the Data Link layer, which, like the station identification procedure, goes beyond the ISO standard while remaining completely in conformance with it. DNA Phase V HDLC defines the way in which such multiplexing is handled through *protocol identifiers* that are assigned and registered by Digital. The DNA Phase V architecture assigns a protocol identifier to each protocol that can use the services of the Data Link layer. With HDLC, user data can be carried in I-frames by only one protocol at a time; thus, a user can open only one port into an HDLC data link for exchanging I-frames. The identifier of the protocol to be carried by I-frames is determined during the station initialization procedure. Data for any number of other protocols can be carried using UI-frames. A user can, therefore, open any number of ports into an HDLC data link for exchanging UI-frames. The DNA Phase V architecture defines a protocol identifier to be carried in the information field of UI-frames. The protocol identifier is specified when a port is allocated, and DNA Phase V implementations of HDLC ensure that a port receives only the UI-frames having the appropriate protocol identifiers.

Maintenance Functions

The protocol multiplexing facility allows the DNA Phase V Network layer protocol and the Maintenance Operations Protocol to run concurrently over the same data link. The DNA Phase V HDLC architectural specification documents how stations can use the HDLC protocol to support the maintenance functions defined by MOP. MOP is a Data Link layer user and can use an HDLC data link to perform such functions as message loopback testing of the link, upline dumping of memory contents, downline loading of initialization code, and console operations. MOP messages are carried in UI-frames. The protocol multiplexing facility allows these maintenance operations to be performed any time the link is operational without interfering with normal data transfer of I-frames over the link.

Protocol Error Detection

Each station must be able to detect errors in the operation of the protocol. Errors that can occur during data link operation include receipt of invalid frames, including frames containing invalid sequence numbers, frames having invalid frame type identifiers, and frames that are too long. When a station detects a protocol error, it generates a network management event and transmits a Frame Reject (FRMR) U-frame command. When a station receives a FRMR command, it also generates a network management event and begins the link initialization procedure.

Conclusion

This chapter introduced HDLC, the main data link protocol used to implement point-to-point links in the wide area networking environment. DNA Phase V HDLC supports all procedures required by a data link operating in either balanced mode or normal mode over both synchronous and asynchronous circuits and defines a number of procedures that go beyond the ISO standard. Chapter 20 examines DDCMP, a Digital proprietary protocol that can be used as an alternative to HDLC for wide area networking data links.

CHAPTER 20

DDCMP Data Links

The *Digital Data Communication Message Protocol* (DDCMP) was designed a number of years ago by Digital and is the primary wide area networking data link protocol in networks that conform to Phase IV and previous phases of DNA. It is an octet-oriented protocol but has many of the characteristics of bit-oriented protocols, such as HDLC, especially the characteristic of code transparency. DDCMP is concerned with the logical transmission of data grouped into physical blocks called *messages*. Even though we have been using the term *frame* to refer to the data unit exchanged in the Data Link layer, we will use the term *message* in this chapter to be consistent with the DDCMP documentation. Both the DDCMP service definition and protocol specification are described in the DDCMP architectural specification. The architectural specification for DDCMP has not changed from DNA Phase IV and has not been rewritten. The structure of the DDCMP architectural specification is, therefore, somewhat different from the structure of the Phase V architectural specifications. This chapter discusses some of the features of DDCMP, describes the DDCMP service interface, and examines the DDCMP protocol specification.

DDCMP Features   DDCMP is a versatile data link protocol that supports both point-to-point links connecting a pair of communicating stations and multipoint links in which a single control station communicates with two or more tributary stations over the same data link. Like HDLC, DDCMP can be used over both synchronous and asynchronous (start-stop) links. The following are some of the features of DDCMP:

- error detection using the 16-bit cyclic redundancy check (CRC) error detection polynomial

- error correction by means of retransmitting lost and corrupted messages
- message sequencing allowing up to 255 messages to be outstanding before an acknowledgment is required
- operation with a wide variety of communication hardware
- positive startup procedure that synchronizes both ends of the link
- simplicity of operation using a small number of message formats
- a maintenance mode for diagnostic testing and bootstrapping functions
- data transparency of any bit sequence using a length-field framing technique
- operation over full-duplex, half-duplex, point-to-point, and multipoint circuits

DDCMP Service Definition

Like the HDLC protocol described in Chapter 19, a DDCMP entity operates in the Data Link layer of the architecture. It provides a set of services to a user of a DDCMP entity and requests the services of a modem connect entity operating below it in the Physical layer.

DDCMP Service Interface Commands and Responses

The DDCMP architectural specification describes the interface between a DDCMP entity and a user of its services in terms of a set of abstract *commands* a user can issue to a DDCMP entity and a set of *responses* the DDCMP entity can send back to the user. These commands and responses are listed in Box 20.1.

DDCMP Protocol Specification

The DDCMP documentation contains a protocol specification that precisely defines the formats of the messages exchanged during protocol operation and describes in detail the procedures controlling the exchange of messages. The remainder of this chapter describes the DDCMP protocol specification. We begin with a look at the message formats defined in the protocol specification.

DDCMP Message Formats

The DNA Phase V architectural specification for DDCMP refers to data-link-protocol-data-units (DLPDUs) as *messages*. Two types of messages can be transmitted over the data link when DDCMP is in operation:

BOX 20.1

DDCMP Service Interface Commands and Responses

Commands to DDCMP

The following are commands a Data Link service user can issue to a DDCMP Data Link layer entity.

- **Initialize Link.** Starts DDCMP operation over the data link.

- **Stop Link.** Stops DDCMP operation over the data link. May disconnect the modem from the line by placing it "on hook" when the protocol is used with a dial-up link.

- **Transmit Message.** Passes a Data message to DDCMP for transmission over the data link.

- **Receive Message.** Provides one or more empty buffers to DDCMP for the receipt of Data messages.

- **Return Transmit Buffers.** Optional command issued after halting DDCMP operation to return outstanding transmit buffers to the user.

- **Enter Maintenance Mode.** Changes DDCMP operation to maintenance mode.

Responses from DDCMP

The following are the responses a DDCMP entity issues to a user of the DDCMP service in response to the above commands.

- **Initialize on Other End.** Issued when the station on the other end of the link has restarted or initialized. Protocol operation stops and must be restarted by issuing another Initialize Link command.

- **Initialization Complete.** Optionally issued in response to an Initialize Link command.

- **Message Transmitted.** Issued in response to a Transmit Message command after the message has been acknowledged by the other station.

- **Message Received.** Issued in response to a Receive Message command after a message has been successfully received.

- **Transient Error.** Issued after an error threshold counter has overflowed.

- **Persistent Error.** Issued in response to an error condition from which recovery might not be possible.

Data messages and *Control* messages. There are one Data message, five Control messages, and one Maintenance data message:

- Data messages
- Acknowledge (ACK) messages
- Negative Acknowledge (NAK) messages
- Reply to Message Number (REP) messages
- Start Message (STRT) messages
- Start Acknowledge (STACK) messages
- Maintenance data messages

The following sections describe the formats of the seven types of DDCMP messages.

Data Messages

Data messages contain sequence numbers and are employed to carry user data over a DDCMP link. Figure 20.1 shows the format of a Data message. A Data message contains the following fields:

- **Start of Header.** A Start-of-Header (SOH) code (hex '81') indicating a Data message.
- **Byte Count.** A 14-bit field containing a count of the number of octets in the Data field.
- **Flags.** A 2-bit field containing two flags. The first bit is a Quick Sync flag, indicating that resynchronization should follow this message; the second bit is a Select flag, used to give the receiver permission to transmit over a half-duplex or multipoint link.
- **Response Number.** Contains a number used to acknowledge correctly received messages from the other station.
- **Transmit Number.** Contains a number identifying this message.
- **Station Address.** Contains the address of the station on a multipoint link to which the message is being sent or the address of the originating station. Stations on point-to-point links use the address value hex '01'.

FIGURE 20.1   **DDCMP data message format.**

SOH X'81'	Byte Count	Flags	Response Number	Transmit Number	Station Address	Block Check 1	Data	Block Check 2

- **Block Check 1.** Contains a 16-bit Cyclic Redundancy Check (CRC) value calculated on the contents of the header fields from the SOH octet through the Station Address octet.
- **Data.** Contains the data transmitted in this message. It must contain the number of octets specified in the Byte Count field.
- **Block Check 2.** Contains a 16-bit CRC value calculated on the contents of the Data field.

Control Messages

A Control message is an unnumbered message that carries channel, transmission status, and initialization information over a DDCMP link. Figure 20.2 shows the format of a Control message. A Control message contains the following fields:

- **ENQ.** An ENQ code (hex '05') indicating a Control message.
- **Type.** An 8-bit code indicating the type of Control message.
- **Subtype or Reason.** A 6-bit code containing either a Subtype or Reason code for some types of Control messages. The Subtype field typically is not used and normally contains six 0-bits.
- **Flags.** Same as the Flags field for Data messages.
- **Receiver Field.** Used to pass control information from the Data message receiver to the Data message sender.
- **Sender Field.** Used to pass control information from the Data message sender to the Data message receiver.
- **Station Address.** Same as the station address field for Data messages.
- **Block Check.** Contains a 16-bit CRC value calculated on the contents of the fields from the ENQ octet through the Station Address octet.

   ACK and NAK Messages   The Acknowledge (ACK) and Negative Acknowledge (NAK) messages are used to provide positive and negative acknowledgments to Data messages. Their formats are similar and are shown in Figure 20.3.

FIGURE 20.2   **DDCMP control message format.**

ENQ X'05'	Type	Subtype or Reason	Flags	Receiver Field	Sender Field	Station Address	Block Check

FIGURE 20.3   Acknowledge (ACK) and negative acknowledge (NAK) message formats.

Acknowledge (ACK)

ENQ X'05'	ACK X'01'	Subtype 000000	F l g s	Response Number	Fill X'00'	Station Address	Block Check

Negative Acknowledge (NAK)

ENQ X'05'	NAK X'02'	Reason	F l g s	Response Number	Fill X'00'	Station Address	Block Check

- **ENQ.** An ENQ code (hex '05') indicating that this is a form of Control message.

- **ACK Type or NAK Type.** Contains the value hex '01' for an ACK and hex '02' for a NAK.

- **Subtype or Reason.** In an ACK this is a Subtype field containing six 0-bits; in a NAK this is a Reason field indicating the reason for the negative acknowledgment.

- **Flags.** Same as the Flags field for Data messages.

- **Response Number.** Contains a number used to acknowledge correctly received messages from the other station.

- **Fill.** Contains the value hex '00'.

- **Station Address.** Same as the station address field for Data messages.

- **Block Check.** Contains a 16-bit CRC value calculated on the contents of the fields from the ENQ octet through the Station Address octet.

REP, STRT, and STACK Messages   The Reply to Message Number (REP), Start (STRT), and Start Acknowledge (STACK) messages all have similar formats and are illustrated in Figure 20.4. The Reply to Message Number (REP) message is used to request status information from the data receiver. It is generally sent when the message sender has sent a message and has not heard back from the message receiver before a time-out occurs. The Start (STRT) message is used to establish initial contact and to perform synchronization on the link. The Start Acknowledge (STACK) message is used to respond to a STRT message after the station has completed its initialization. The fields contained in these messages are as follows:

- **ENQ.** An ENQ code (hex '05') indicating that this is a form of Control message.

FIGURE 20.4   **Reply to message number (REP), start (STRT), and start acknowledge (STACK) message formats.**

Reply to Message Number (REP)

ENQ X'05'	REP '03'	Subtype 000000	F l a g s	Fill X'00'	Message Number	Station Address	Block Check

Start (STRT)

ENQ X'05'	STRT X'06'	Subtype 000000	F l a g s	Fill X'00'	Fill X'00'	Station Address	Block Check

Start Acknowledge (STACK)

ENQ X'05'	STACK X'07'	Subtype 000000	F l a g s	Fill X'00'	Fill X'00'	Station Address	Block Check

- **REP Type, STRT Type, or STACK Type.** Contains the value hex '03' for REP, hex '06' for STRT, or hex '07' for STACK.
- **Subtype.** Contains six 0-bits.
- **Flags.** Same as the Flags field for Data messages.
- **Fill.** Contains the value hex '00'.
- **Message Number or Fill.** For REP, contains the number of the last sequential Data message (not including retransmissions) sent by the message sender. For STRT and STACK, contains the value hex '00'.
- **Station Address.** Same as the station address field for Data messages.
- **Block Check.** Contains a 16-bit CRC value calculated on the contents of the fields from the ENQ octet through the Station Address octet.

    Maintenance Data Messages   DDCMP operates in either *online* mode, which is the normal operating mode, or in *maintenance* mode. The Maintenance data message format is used when the link is operating in maintenance mode. Maintenance data messages are used for such functions as downline loading of program code and upline dumping operations. As shown in Figure 20.5, the Maintenance data message is similar in format to the Data message. Its fields are as follows:

- **Data Link Escape.** A Data Link Escape (DLE) code (hex '90') indicates that this is a Maintenance data message.

FIGURE 20.5   **Maintenance data message format.**

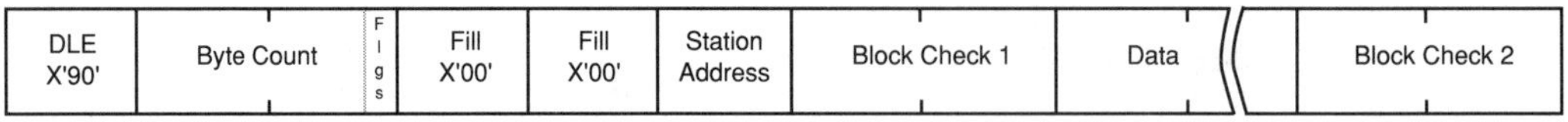

DLE X'90'	Byte Count	F l a g s	Fill X'00'	Fill X'00'	Station Address	Block Check 1	Data	Block Check 2

Byte Count. A 14-bit field containing a count of the number of octets in the Data field of the message.

Flags. Contains the value binary '11' for Maintenance data messages.

Fill. Contains the value hex '00'.

Fill. Contains the value hex '00'.

Station Address. Same as the station address field for Data messages.

Block Check 1. Contains a 16-bit CRC value calculated on the contents of the header fields from the DLE octet through the Station Address octet.

Data. Contains the data transmitted in this message. It must contain the number of octets specified in the Byte Count field.

Block Check 2. Contains a 16-bit CRC value calculated on the contents of the Data field.

Protocol Operation

The procedures used during protocol operation that govern the exchange of messages over a DDCMP data link can be divided into three major categories:

- framing procedures
- link management procedures
- message exchange procedures

Framing Procedures

Framing procedures concern both *byte framing* and *message framing*. The process of byte framing properly groups bits in the incoming bit stream into 8-bit octets. The protocol defines different byte framing procedures that can be used over asynchronous (start-stop) links and synchronous links. When the protocol operates over an asynchronous link, byte framing is inherent in the operation of the physical link. With a synchronous link, the sender begins transmission by sending four or more SYN patterns (binary 1001 0110). The receiver searches the incoming bit stream for two consecutive SYN patterns. Once it has located them, the receiver knows each successive group of 8 bits makes up an octet in the incoming bit stream. The receiver then ignores any subsequent SYN patterns and searches for the first octet containing a non-SYN pattern.

After it has achieved octet synchronization by using the appropriate byte framing procedure, the protocol achieves message framing by searching for one of the three starting message octets—SOH, ENQ, or DLE—in the incoming bit stream. One of these octets must appear immediately after the byte framing sequence or immediately after the final octet of the previous message. If one of these octets is not found in the proper location, the receiver assumes byte framing has been lost. The message framing procedures provide for a totally transparent data field; once a starting octet has been found, no more searching for a particular bit configuration is performed. The length field contained in each Data or Maintenance data message is used to tell the receiver where it will find the last octet of the message. Since Control messages have a fixed length, the receiver implicitly knows the location of the last octet of a Control message.

Link Management Procedures

Link management procedures coordinate the sending and receiving of data over half-duplex links in which data can be transmitted in only one direction at a time. They also coordinate transmission on a multipoint link, which contains one *control* station and two or more *tributary* stations. Transmission over a half-duplex circuit and over a multipoint link is controlled through the use of the *Select* flag in the header of each message. The transmitting station indicates that it is finished transmitting by setting the Select flag to 1 in its last message. Receipt of a message in which the Select flag is set to 1 gives the receiving station permission to begin transmitting. On a multipoint link, the control station identifies the tributary station to which a message is destined by including a station address in the header of each message. A tributary station receives all transmissions from the control station but ignores all messages except those whose station address values match its own station address. Messages from a tributary station are ignored by all the other tributaries and are processed only by the control station.

Message Exchange Procedures

The procedures governing the way in which messages are exchanged over the link ensure that messages are received in the order sent, that no duplicate messages are received, and that messages containing transmission errors are detected and eventually retransmitted. Transmission errors are detected using a CRC procedure in which the transmitter calculates 16-bit CRC values and includes them in the frames it transmits. The receiver calculates CRC values and compares them with the CRC values contained in the frames it receives. If a calculated CRC value does not match the corresponding received CRC value, the receiver discards the frame containing the erroneous CRC value.

Each frame contains an 8-bit message sequence number used by a receiving station to detect discarded frames and to request their retransmission. A receiver sends positive acknowledgments to indicate that it has received frames correctly. The 8-bit message sequence numbers are used by a *pipelining* procedure in which up to 255 frames can be sent before a positive acknowledgment is required. A time-out procedure detects errors signalled by the absence of a required positive acknowledgment. If messages are transmitted in both directions, a Data message can serve as a positive acknowledgment, thus eliminating the need for the transmission of a separate Control message. Since time-out values often are relatively long, provision is made for the immediate transmission of explicit negative acknowledgements to indicate certain types of error situations, such as CRC value mismatches.

Conclusion

This chapter and the previous one introduced the two data link protocols used to implement data links in the wide area networking environment. Both HDLC and DDCMP support both synchronous and asynchronous transmission over a wide variety of telecommunications circuits. HDLC is the preferred data link protocol in a DECnet Phase V network, with DDCMP provided primarily for compatibility with Phase IV of DNA. The remaining chapters in this book examine protocols that operate over local area network data links.

CHAPTER 21

Local Area Network
Data Links

The HDLC and DDCMP protocols discussed in Chapters 19 and 20 are designed to support the form of data link technology used with conventional, long-distance telecommunication facilities. This chapter and the next two examine a different class of protocol used to implement *local area networks* (LANs). The characteristics of the form of data link provided in the wide area networking (WAN) environment are very different from the characteristics of a LAN data link. Box 21.1 (page 441) summarizes some of the differences between the technology used to construct conventional telecommunications data links and the technology used to construct LAN data links.

Classifying Local Area Networks

A great many hardware and software systems are available for implementing local area networks. All share the general characteristics described in Box 21.1, but all are implemented in different ways. The following is a discussion of four ways in which local area networks are commonly classified:

- **Network Topology.** The network topology relates to the logical way in which devices attached to LAN are interconnected. The three major topologies are the *bus*, the *star*, and the *ring*, as illustrated in Figure 21.1. In many cases, a specific LAN implementation might use combinations of the three basic topologies to create hybrid configurations. We examine bus and ring topologies further in Chapters 22 and 23.

- **Transmission Medium.** The second criterion by which LANs can be classified is by the type of transmission medium used to interconnect processors. Most LANs use twisted-wire pairs, coaxial cable, or fiber-optic cable, although some LANs use radio transmission or infrared signaling.

FIGURE 21.1   Three LAN topologies.

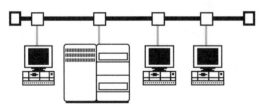

Bus Topology

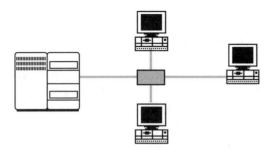

Star Topology

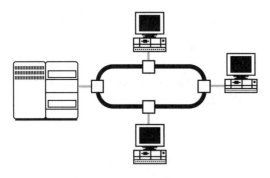

Ring Topology

- **Transmission Technique.** The third criterion for classifying LANs is according to the method used for transmitting signals over the transmission medium. There are basically two methods: *baseband* and *broadband*. With baseband signaling, information is carried over the transmission

Characteristics of Conventional Data Link Technology

- **Performance.** Transmission speeds are generally low, typically 9600
  bits per second or lower, with moderately high error rates. Some
  telecommunication links operate at higher speeds, such as 56,000 or
  1.544 million bits per second (T1 carrier), with relatively low error
  rates.

- **Distance.** Data communication can take place over any desired distance given the availability of the appropriate communication
  facilities.

- **Transmission Medium.** Public communication facilities, such as telephone circuits, are typically used for data communication.

- **Cost.** Cost for data transmission is relatively high due to common
  carrier tariffs.

- **Connectivity.** Conventional data link technology is most often used
  to connect pairs of communicating devices.

Characteristics of LAN Data Link Technology

- **Performance.** Transmission speeds are very high, typically in the millions of bits per second, with typically very low error rates.

- **Distance.** A LAN is designed primarily to support communication
  over a limited geographical area, for example, within a building or a
  group of related buildings (although extended LANs can span great
  distances).

- **Transmission Medium.** A LAN typically uses private, user-installed
  wiring as the communication medium.

- **Cost.** The cost for data transmission is relatively low because data
  are carried over privately owned transmission media having only a
  one-time installation cost.

- **Connectivity.** A LAN connects large numbers of devices, each of
  which can communicate with any other device attached to the LAN.
  The broadcast nature of a LAN also allows a station to multicast
  messages to groups of other stations.

medium in digital form; with broadband signaling, a data signal is super-
imposed on a carrier signal using some type of modulation technique.

- **Access Protocol.** A fourth way in which LANs can be classified is according to the rules governing the way individual LAN devices gain access to

the transmission medium. Any number of access protocols can be devised, but two major forms of access protocol dominate the LAN marketplace. With the *Carrier Sense Multi-Access with Collision Detection* (CSMA/CD) form of access protocol (described in detail in Chapter 22), a device first listens to the medium and then transmits if the medium is quiet. Procedures are provided to recover when the transmissions of two or more devices collide. With a *token passing* form of access protocol (described in detail in Chapter 23), access to the transmission medium is controlled through a special frame called the *token* that is passed from device to device.

International Standards for LANS

An important set of standards for local area networks has been published by the Institute of Electrical and Electronics Engineers (IEEE) (see Chapter 2) describing several ways for implementing LANs. These same standards have now also been accepted by ISO as international standards and are published by ISO as well. The DNA Phase V LAN data links include support for applicable IEEE/ISO LAN standards. In addition, the specifications for the DNA Phase V LAN data links define compatible extensions to the IEEE/ISO LAN standards to provide enhanced local area network services.

IEEE/ISO LAN Architecture

The IEEE/ISO LAN standards address the Physical and Data Link layers of the OSI model. As shown in Figure 21.2, the Data Link layer is divided into two sublayers to allow different forms of medium access control to be accommodated in the architecture. The following are descriptions of the layers and sublayers addressed by the IEEE/ISO LAN standards:

- **Physical Layer.** The *Physical* layer—the lowest layer in the IEEE/ISO LAN model—is concerned with the physical transmission of signals across a transmission medium. This layer defines procedures for establishing physical connections to the transmission medium and for transmitting and receiving signals over it. It includes specifications for the types of cabling to be used, plugs and connectors, and the characteristics of the signals that are exchanged. The Physical layer provides services to the Medium Access Control sublayer.

FIGURE 21.2   **Comparison of the layers of the OSI model with those of the IEEE/ISO LAN architecture.**

| Application |
| Presentation |
| Session |
| Transport |
| Network |
| Data Link |
| Physical |

OSI Model

| Logical Link Control |
| Medium Access Control |
| Physical |

IEEE/ISO LAN Architecture

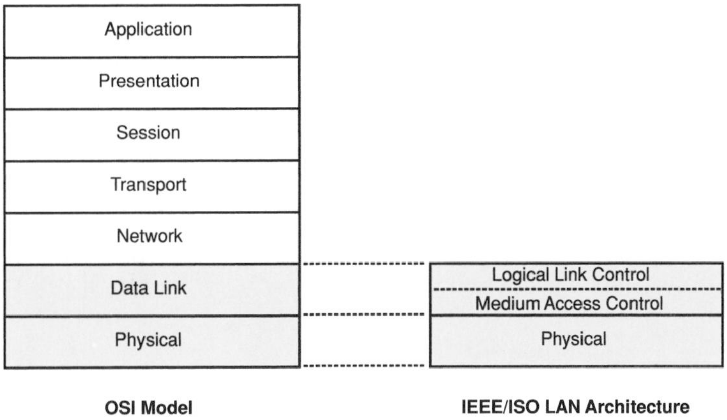

- **Medium Access Control Sublayer.** The *Medium Access Control* (MAC) sublayer of the Data Link layer is concerned with the medium access control method. It defines procedures for managing access to the transmission medium, describes addressing techniques, and specifies error detection and recovery procedures. The MAC sublayer provides services to the Logical Link Control sublayer.

- **Logical Link Control Sublayer.** The *Logical Link Control* (LLC) sublayer of the Data Link layer is responsible for medium-independent data link functions. It allows a user of the LLC sublayer to access the services of the LAN without regard to what form of medium access control is used. The LLC sublayer provides services to a user of the OSI Data Link layer, such as a Network layer entity.

IEEE/ISO LAN Standards

The IEEE/ISO LAN standards describe various ways in which local area networks can be implemented. These standards include:

- **IEEE 802.1d/ISO 10039.** IEEE 802.1 is a multipart standard that covers a wide range of topics. Of special interest in the DNA Phase V environment is the 802.1d standard that addresses *bridges* used to interconnect individual LANs to create extended LANS. ISO 10039 describes the ISO version of the standard for bridges. The DNA Phase V bridge and extended LAN architecture is described in Chapter 24.

- **IEEE 802.2/ISO 8802-2 Logical Link Control.** This standard describes the functions of the LLC sublayer of the IEEE LAN architectures. It describes the function of the LLC sublayer for all three forms of medium access control defined by the IEEE/ISO LAN architecture and can be used with Fiber Distributed Data Interface (FDDI) as well. The IEEE/ISO LLC standard is described in this chapter.

- **IEEE 802.3/ISO 8802-3 CSMA/CD.** This standard and a group of supplements to it describe the MAC sublayer and Physical layer functions for a bus- or tree-structured network using CSMA/CD as an access protocol. This standard has its roots in the Ethernet form of LAN, jointly developed by Digital, Xerox, and Intel, and used for many years in DECnet networks. Both IEEE/ISO CSMA/CD and Ethernet are supported by DNA Phase V. The DNA Phase V CSMA/CD LAN data link is described in Chapter 22.

- **IEEE 802.3/ISO 8802-3 CSMA/CD.** This standard and a group of IEEE 802.4/ISO 8802-4 Token Bus. This standard describes the MAC sublayer and Physical layer functions for a bus-structured LAN using token passing as an access protocol. This form of LAN was designed to meet the needs of factory automation applications.

- **IEEE 802.3/ISO 8802-3 CSMA/CD.** This standard and a group of IEEE 802.5/ISO 8802-5 Token Ring. This standard describes the MAC sublayer and Physical layer functions for a ring-structured network using a token passing access protocol. This standard is an outgrowth of the token ring form of LAN developed by IBM.

- **ISO 9314 Fiber Distributed Data Interface (FDDI).** This standard defines a very high speed form of LAN that was developed by a subcommittee of the American National Standards Institute (ANSI) and that has been accepted as an international standard by ISO. FDDI uses a logical ring-structured topology using a timed token-passing access protocol that is quite different from the token-passing protocol defined in the IEEE/ISO token ring standard. The DNA Phase V FDDI LAN data link is the subject of Chapter 23.

The standard for the LLC sublayer (IEEE 802.2/ISO 8802-2) is the basis for all the various LAN standards that are part of the IEEE/ISO LAN architecture and can be used in conjunction with FDDI as well. It allows all the various forms of LANs to present a common interface to a user of the local area network, such as the DNA Phase V Network layer.

At the time of this writing, DNA Phase V includes support for the

CSMA/CD and Ethernet forms of LAN and for FDDI. Because of the support for the IEEE/ISO LLC standard, it would be relatively easy to also accommodate products conforming to the IEEE/ISO token bus and token ring standards within the architecture.

We next describe the service definition and protocol specification for the IEEE/ISO LLC sublayer. After that, we will examine the features of the DNA Phase V LLC sublayer that go beyond the international standard while remaining in conformance with it.

The Logical Link Control Sublayer	Local area network data links implement a broadcast form of subnetwork in which each device attached to the data link receives all frames transmitted by all other devices. The broadcast data link can be implemented using either a multiaccess bus-structured circuit or a collection of point-to-point circuits forming a ring configuration. With a broadcast data link, a device can send each frame to multiple devices on the link. A broadcast form of data link can provide a broad range of services that allow different types of users to simultaneously employ the services of the link.

The IEEE/ISO standard for the LLC sublayer defines both a service definition for the LLC sublayer and a protocol specification. Although they are described in the same document, the service definition and the protocol specification are independent of each other, in keeping with other ISO standards for the OSI model. The service definition for the IEEE/ISO LLC sublayer describes the services an LLC sublayer entity provides to its users. These services are defined in the IEEE/ISO documentation in terms of service primitives and service primitive parameters. The relationship between the services the LLC layer provides to an LLC sublayer user and the protocol that governs its operation are shown in Figure 21.3. As shown there, the LLC sublayer protocol uses the services of the MAC sublayer to provide a defined set of services to a user of an LLC sublayer entity.

Figure 21.4 summarizes how a user of the LLC sublayer service (the Network layer in the diagram) transmits data from one node to another. An LLC sublayer user requests a data transfer service of the LLC sublayer and passes a *logical-link-control-service-data-unit* (LLC-SDU) to the LLC sublayer entity. The LLC sublayer entity adds PCI to the LLC-SDU in the form of a header to create a logical-link-control-protocol-data-unit (LLC-PDU). The LLC sublayer uses the services of the MAC sublayer to transmit the LLC-PDU over the transmission medium to its destination. The LLC sublayer entity in the destination device removes

FIGURE 21.3   Relationship between the LLC sublayer service definition and the LLC sublayer protocol specification.

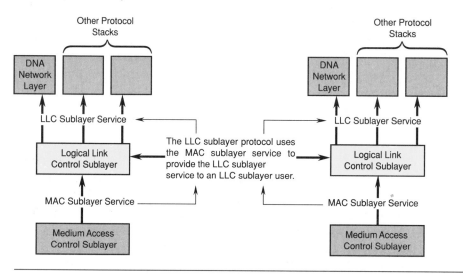

FIGURE 21.4   Providing the Logical Link Control sublayer service.

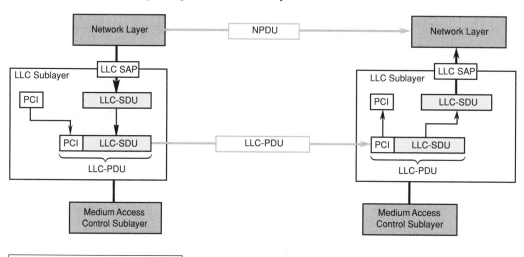

the PCI and delivers the enclosed LLC-SDU to the LLC sublayer user there.

To transmit an LLC-PDU over the network, an LLC sublayer entity passes the LLC-PDU down to a MAC sublayer entity in the form of a *medium-access-control-service-data-unit* (MAC-SDU). The MAC sublayer entity encapsulates the MAC-SDU with additional PCI, which takes the form of a header and a trailer, to create a *medium-access-control-protocol-data-unit* (MAC-PDU), or *MAC frame*. This procedure is shown in Figure 21.5. The format of the MAC frame varies, depending on the form of LAN used. MAC frame formats are examined in Chapters 22 and 23 for the CSMA/CD, Ethernet, and FDDI forms of LAN.

Local Area Networking Addressing

The IEEE/ISO LAN architecture provides for two levels of addressing: *station* addressing and *service-access-point* (SAP) addressing. A station address uniquely identifies each individual device attached to the LAN, and a SAP address identifies a particular type of LAN user. (The term *sta-*

FIGURE 21.5   **Providing the Medium Access Control sublayer service.**

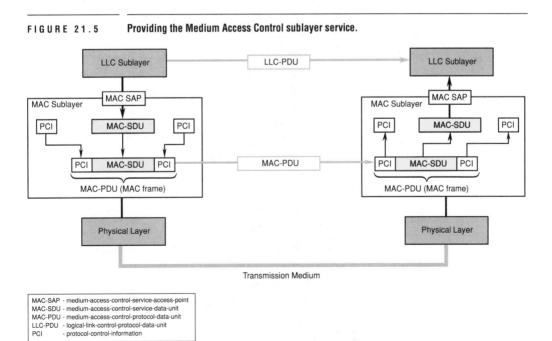

MAC-SAP - medium-access-control-service-access-point
MAC-SDU - medium-access-control-service-data-unit
MAC-PDU - medium-access-control-protocol-data-unit
LLC-PDU   - logical-link-control-protocol-data-unit
PCI   - protocol-control-information

tion is defined more precisely for each individual type of LAN in Chapters 22 and 23.) The definition of service-access-points allows many different types of users to share the same LAN.

The LLC sublayer is concerned only with the SAP address and not with the station address; the station address is the concern of the MAC sublayer. Even though the LLC sublayer does not examine or manipulate the station address, we describe it here to introduce the addressing scheme defined by the IEEE/ISO LAN architecture.

Station Addresses

A MAC-PDU contains destination and source station address fields. The destination address indicates the intended recipient (or recipients) of the frame. The destination address can refer to an individual station or to a group of stations. The source address refers to the station that transmitted the frame and always refers to an individual station. According to the IEEE/ISO LAN standards, station addresses can be either 16 bits or 48 bits in length. However, the DNA Phase V architecture mandates the use of 48-bit station addresses. The first bit of a source station address is always 0. If the first bit of a destination station address is 0, the address identifies an individual station. If the first bit is 1, the address refers to a group of stations. An address of all 1-bits is the broadcast address and refers to all the stations on the LAN.

The IEEE/ISO LAN standards define two forms of addressing that can be used for LAN implementations: *locally administered* and *globally administered*. All 16-bit addresses are locally administered. For 48-bit addressing, if the second bit is 0, addressing is globally administered; if the second bit is 1, addressing is locally administered.

- **Locally Administered Addressing.** When locally administered addressing is used, it is the responsibility of the organization installing the network to assign addresses to network devices.

- **Globally Administered Addressing.** With globally administered addressing, addresses must be 48 bits in length, giving 46 bits for individual MAC addresses. Each LAN manufacturer assigns a unique address to each LAN adapter it builds, thus guaranteeing that no two LAN adapters in the world have the same address. Digital strongly encourages the use of globally administered addresses in a DECnet Phase V network, and all current Digital LAN products are given a globally unique address during manufacture.

NETWORK ARCHITECT

A 46-bit address space gives over 70,368 billion unique addresses—so many that every device manufactured anywhere in the world can be assigned a unique address by its manufacturer. This guarantees that there will be no duplication of addresses when devices are added to a network or when networks are interlinked. Before Ethernet, users basically set network addresses with DIP switches. With Ethernet, we wanted to avoid addressing problems by providing a unique address for every device. The address is permanently set in the device at the factory. When we were developing the Ethernet specification, we originally thought a 32-bit address would be adequate (4 billion addresses), but we decided that administering so small an address space would prove impractical in practice, so we expanded the address to 48 bits. One proposal for generating an Ethernet address was to toss a coin 48 times, one toss for each bit. This actually would be adequate for up to 2^{24} different devices. But for more than 2^{24} you would tend to generate too many duplicates. Another proposal was to read the serial number from a dollar bill and to then tear up the dollar bill. That turned out to be illegal. The end result was to partition the 48-bit address space into blocks of 2^{24} different addresses that could be assigned to individual manufacturers. For a modest fee, you get a block of 2^{24} addresses. If you need more, you pay a fee for another block. The administration process of assigning Ethernet addresses has now been turned over to the IEEE. The idea behind a unique address for each individual device is that you can just plug any number of these devices together and not have to worry about address conflicts.

The IEEE assigns a value for the high-order 24 bits of the station address to any organization requesting one. The organization is then responsible for guaranteeing that a different address value is placed in the low-order 24 bits of the address for each device it manufactures. For example, one of the address block values assigned to Digital for station addresses is hexadecimal '08-00-2B'. When assigning a station address to a device, Digital places the value hex '08-00-2B' in the high-order three octets of the address and then assigns a value to the remaining 24 bits of the address so no two devices it manufactures have the same value in the last 24 bits.

SAP Addresses and User Multiplexing

A local area network can be used by an organization for many purposes. One collection of users might all be communicating using the ISO 8473

Internet protocol in the Network layer. Other users might be DNA Phase IV users employing Ethernet frames. Still other users might be employing some other architecture entirely, such as AppleTalk or Novell NetWare. These different types of users can all operate concurrently and can all use the LLC services on a station. They can all coexist on the same local area network without interfering with one another. The LLC SAP addresses, SNAP protocol identifiers, and Ethernet protocol types provide user-type multiplexing to achieve this concurrency. The SNAP protocol identifier and Ethernet protocol type multiplexing are described later in this chapter.

There are two types of SAP addresses. An *individual address* identifies a single type of LLC sublayer user, and a *group address* identifies groups of LLC sublayer user types. If the first bit of a SAP address contains a 0, the address is an individual address; if the first bit contains a 1, the SAP address is a group address.

LLC Sublayer Service Definition

The current version of the LLC sublayer standard defines two types of LLC sublayer services:

- connectionless-mode service
- connection-mode service

Conformance to the IEEE/ISO LLC standard requires the provision of only the connectionless-mode service, but a particular LAN implementation of the IEEE/ISO LLC standard might provide the connection-mode service as well. The DNA Phase V architecture uses only the connectionless-mode service for LANs, so we describe only the service primitives for the connectionless-mode service here. DNA implementations of the LLC sublayer also provide a *user-supplied LLC service* that can be used to implement a protocol to provide any desired LLC sublayer service, including the connection-mode LLC service, for those users requiring something other than the connectionless-mode service.

The Connectionless-Mode LLC Service

With the connectionless-mode LLC sublayer service, there is no need to establish a logical connection between the sending and the receiving LLC sublayer entities, and each LLC-PDU is sent and processed independently of any other LLC-PDUs. No sequence checking is done to ensure that data units are received in the same sequence in which they were sent, and the receiving LLC sublayer entity sends no acknowledgment that it has received an LLC-PDU. No flow control or error recovery procedures are provided as part of the connectionless service. With the connectionless service, data units can be sent to individual stations, to defined groups of stations, or to all stations on the LAN. Connectionless service is sometimes referred to as a *datagram* service. When the connectionless-mode service is used, all necessary flow control and error recovery services must be provided in the layers above the LLC sublayer, often in the Transport layer.

The DL_UNITDATA Data Transfer Service

A single DL_UNITDATA data transfer service is defined for the connectionless-mode service. Box 21.2 describes the service primitives for the DL_UNITDATA service. Figure 21.6 is a time-sequence diagram showing the sequence in which the two service primitives are issued in providing the DL_UNITDATA data transfer service. The DL_UNITDATA service is a nonconfirmed service in which the user of the LLC sublayer service is not informed of the success or failure of the data transfer operation.

LLC Sublayer Protocol Specification

The IEEE/ISO documentation of the LLC sublayer and the DNA Phase V documentation together provide a protocol specification for the LLC sublayer. The LLC sublayer protocol specification precisely defines the formats of the LLC-PDUs exchanged during protocol operation and de-

FIGURE 21.6   Time-sequence diagram for the DL_UNITDATA service.

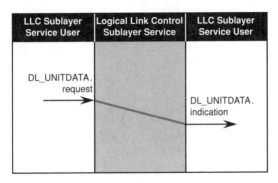

BOX 21.2

Service Primitives
for LLC
Connectionless-
Mode Service

```
    DL_UNITDATA.request    (
                            source_address
                            destination_address
                            data
                            priority
                            )


    DL_UNITDATA.indication  (
                            source_address
                            destination_address
                            data
                            priority
                            )
```

scribes in detail the procedures controlling the exchange of LLC-PDUs. We begin the discussion of the LLC sublayer protocol specification by examining the format of LLC-PDUs.

LLC-PDU Formats

An LLC-PDU conforms to the format shown in Figure 21.7. LLC-PDUs use a header format similar to that defined for the transmission frames in the HDLC standard (see Chapter 19). The following are descriptions of the fields in the LLC-PDU:

- **Source and Destination Service-Access-Point Addresses.** Each LLC-PDU begins with a 1-octet destination-service-access-point (DSAP) address and a 1-octet source-service-access point (SSAP) address. These fields identify the source and destination users of the LLC sublayer service. The uses of the SSAP and DSAP address fields are described later in this chapter.

- **Control Field.** Following the DSAP and SSAP address fields is a 1-octet or 2-octet control field that describes the PDU's type and contains control information.

- **Information Field.** After the control field is a variable-length information field.

FIGURE 21.7   **Logical-link-control-protocol-data-unit (LLC-PDU) format.**

Commands and Responses

An LLC-PDU can take the form of either a *command* or a *response*. A command is sent by an LLC sublayer entity initiating a data transfer operation; a response is sent by the opposite LLC sublayer entity in reply to a command. The low-order bit of the SSAP address indicates whether the PDU is a command or a response: 0 indicates a command and 1 indicates a response.

LLC-PDU Types

There are three types of LLC-PDUs, only one of which is used by the protocol supplying the connectionless-mode LLC sublayer service. All three are described here for completeness:

- **Unnumbered PDUs.** Unnumbered PDUs (U-PDUs) are used by the protocol supplying the connectionless-mode LLC sublayer service to carry user data. They are also used to perform initialization procedures and to invoke diagnostic sequences.
- **Information PDUs.** Information PDUs (I-PDUs) are used by the protocol supplying the connection-mode LLC sublayer service to carry user data.
- **Supervisory PDUs.** Supervisory PDUs (S-PDUs) are used by the protocol supplying the connection-mode LLC sublayer service to carry information necessary to control the operation of the protocol.

    U-PDUs carry 1-octet control fields; I-PDUs and S-PDUs carry 2-octet control fields. Since only U-PDUs are used in supplying the connectionless-mode LLC sublayer service, we examine only that format.

U-PDU Format

Figure 21.8 illustrates the format of U-PDUs, showing details for the control field. Some U-PDU commands and responses have information fields; others do not. An 11-bit configuration in bit positions 1 and 2 of the first control field octet identifies the PDU as a U-PDU and indicates

FIGURE 21.8   U-format LLC-PDU.

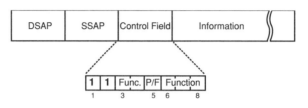

that the control field is only 1 octet in length. The remainder of the bits are interpreted as a poll/final bit and function code bits. The function code bits in a U-PDU identify the type of command or response the PDU represents.

Three U-format PDUs are used to support Type 1 operation. Each LLC-PDU has a full name and a mnemonic. The following descriptions of the three LLC-PDUs used for Type 1 operation give the full name of each LLC-PDU followed by the mnemonic in parentheses:

- **Unnumbered Information (UI).** Used to convey user data between a pair of LLC entities.
- **Exchange Identification (XID).** Used to exchange information about the types of service the LLC entities support.
- **Test (TEST).** Used to conduct a loopback test of the transmission path between two LLC entities.

LLC Operational Modes

The two operational modes that the IEEE/ISO LLC sublayer standard defines correspond to the two forms of service described earlier.

- **Type 1 Operation.** Supports the connectionless-mode service.
- **Type 2 Operation.** Supports the connection-mode service.

The IEEE/ISO LLC standard defines two classes of LLC protocol support:

- **Class I LLC.** Supports Type 1 operation only.
- **Class II LLC.** Supports both Type 1 and Type 2 operations.

The DNA Phase V architecture requires the use of only Class I LLC. As described earlier, the user-supplied LLC service can be used to build an implementation of Class II LLC if a user requires it.

LLC Sublayer Protocol Mechanisms

The protocol mechanisms operating in the LLC sublayer to support Type 1 operation are simple. No sequence checking, retransmission, or flow control procedures are defined. Error detection is, however, implemented by the MAC sublayer. If a MAC sublayer entity detects a corrupted frame, it discards the frame. Since this error detection mechanism is operating at the level of the MAC sublayer, the LLC sublayer never receives frames affected by transmission errors.

Data Transfer

The LLC sublayer carries out a request for a data transfer operation by encapsulating each received LLC-SDU in an Unnumbered Information (UI) PDU and then uses the MAC sublayer service to transmit it over the transmission medium. An LLC sublayer entity receiving a UI PDU does not acknowledge its receipt. In addition to handling the receipt of user data in UI PDUs, all implementations of the LLC sublayer standard must also be capable of correctly responding to Exchange Identification (XID) PDUs and Test (TEST) PDUs.

Exchanging XID LLC-PDUs

When an LLC sublayer entity receives an XID LLC-PDU command, it generates an XID LLC-PDU response specifying the class of service it can support. The response XID PDU indicates that it can support either Class LLC I (connectionless-mode service only) or Class II LLC (connectionless-mode and connection-mode service). Possible other uses for the XID LLC-PDU include determining if a particular station is available on the network, determining the stations assigned to a particular group address, checking for duplicate addresses, and announcing the presence of a station on the network.

Exchanging TEST LLC-PDUs

When an LLC sublayer entity receives a TEST LLC-PDU command, it generates a TEST LLC-PDU response. An exchange of TEST PDUs is used to perform a basic test of the presence of a transmission path between LLC sublayer entities. The source LLC sublayer entity sends a TEST command to a destination LLC sublayer entity, and the destination LLC sublayer entity replies by sending a TEST response back to the source LLC sublayer entity. An optional information field can be included in the TEST command. If one is included, the TEST response must echo it back.

We have now examined the service definition and the protocol specification for the IEEE/ISO LLC sublayer standard. The remainder of this chapter discusses the DNA Phase V LLC sublayer, concentrating on those LLC sublayer features that go beyond the international standards.

DNA Phase V LLC Architectural Model

Each of the two major forms of local area network supported in the DNA Phase V environment defines its own architectural model. The architectural models for the CSMA/CD and FDDI forms of LAN are described in Chapters 22 and 23. Although these two architectural models are different in the MAC sublayer and the Physical layer, both models include an LLC sublayer and define the same method for allowing a user to access LLC sublayer services. This is shown in Figure 21.9.

With both the CSMA/CD and FDDI forms of LAN, a LLC sublayer entity resides in a station. A *station* represents a physical point of attachment to the LAN transmission medium. A user requests the services of the LLC sublayer through a port. An LLC sublayer *port* is a data structure representing a particular user of an LLC sublayer entity. Each user of the LLC sublayer has its own port that it uses to request LLC sublayer services. A particular station can implement any number of ports, and a user can employ more than one port simultaneously. However, a port can service only a single user at a time.

FIGURE 21.9   **Local area network architectural model.**

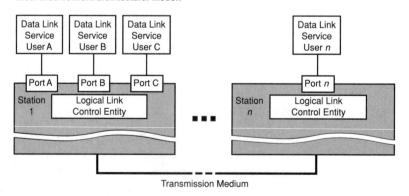

Transmission Medium

DNA Phase V LLC Sublayer Services

The LLC sublayer in the DNA Phase V architecture provides a number of services, many of which go beyond the IEEE/ISO specification for the LLC sublayer. The services provided by the DNA Phase V LLC sublayer include the following:

- **Class 1 Service.** With this service, the LLC sublayer handles all aspects of the LLC sublayer protocol to provide the service specified in the IEEE/ISO standard for the Type 1 connectionless-mode operation, including responses to XID and TEST frames.

- **Multiplexing.** This service makes it possible for more than one type of user to simultaneously use the Data Link layer service. Different types of users of the Data Link service might include DNA Phase V Network layer entities, Local Area Transport (LAT) users, and Maintenance Operations Protocol (MOP) users.

- **Address Filtering.** Each station on a broadcast data link receives the frames transmitted by all other stations on the data link. Each frame contains both a source and a destination station address. The address filtering function allows a station to specify the destination address value or values it will accept as being addressed to it.

- **Multicasting.** This service allows a station to send a frame to multiple destination stations on the data link.

- **User-Supplied Service.** With this service, the LLC sublayer provides all the preceding services except for processing of the LLC-PDU control field and the aspects of the LLC protocol associated with the control field. A user can employ the user-supplied service to implement any desired LLC sublayer protocol, including one to supply the LLC Type 2 connection-mode service.

LLC Sublayer Service Interface Procedure Declarations

The DNA Phase V architectural specification for the LLC sublayer defines the abstract interface between an LLC sublayer entity and its users. The function and procedure declarations defining this abstract interface are listed in Box 21.3. Services are provided that match the service primitives for the IEEE/ISO Type 1 operation and also provide the additional facilities that the DNA Phase V LLC sublayer provides over and above IEEE/ISO Type 1 operation.

BOX 21.3

LLC Service
Interface
Procedure
Declarations

The following function and procedure declarations define the abstract interface between the LLC sublayer and its users in terms of the services an LLC sublayer entity provides to a user.

Port Control Functions

- **OpenPort.** Opens a port into an LLC entity allowing an LLC user to transmit and receive LLC-SDUs. A port is a data structure that represents a particular LLC user's service-access-point and contains information needed by the LLC entity to service that user's requests.
- **Close.** Deallocates a port that was allocated with the OpenPort function.

Data Transfer Functions

- **Transmit.** Passes an LLC-SDU to the LLC sublayer for transmission.
- **TransmitPoll.** Checks for completion of a Transmit request.
- **TransmitAbort.** Aborts all outstanding Transmit requests for a port.
- **Receive.** Provides a receive buffer for use by an LLC sublayer entity.
- **ReceivePoll.** Checks for the completion of a Receive request.
- **ReceiveAbort.** Aborts all incomplete receive requests for a port.

Control Functions

- **EnablePromiscuous.** Indicates that a port is to receive LLC-PDUs having any destination station address value.
- **DisablePromiscuous.** Indicates that a port is no longer to receive LLC-PDUs having any destination station address value.
- **EnableProtocolType.** Adds an Ethernet frame protocol type value to the list of Ethernet frame protocol types a port maintains and begins receiving Ethernet frames having that protocol type value.
- **DisableProtocolType.** Removes an Ethernet frame protocol type value from the list of Ethernet frame protocol types a port maintains and stops receiving Ethernet frames having that protocol type value.
- **EnableProtocolIdentifier.** Adds a SNAP frame protocol identifier value to the list of SNAP frame protocol identifiers a port maintains and begins receiving SNAP frames having that protocol identifier value.
- **DisableProtocolIdentifier.** Removes a SNAP frame protocol identifier value from the list of SNAP frame protocol identifiers a port maintains and stops receiving SNAP frames having that protocol identifier value.

BOX 21.3

continued

- **EnableLLCSap.** Adds a group or individual SAP address value to the list of SAP address values a port maintains and begins receiving frames having that DSAP address value.

- **DisableLLCSap.** Removes a group or individual SAP address value from the list of SAP address values a port maintains and indicates that the port can no longer send or receive frames having that SAP address value.

- **EnableMACAddress.** Adds a group or individual MAC station address value to the list of MAC address values a port maintains and begins receiving frames having that destination MAC station address value.

- **DisableMACAddress.** Removes a group or individual MAC station address value from the list of MAC address values a port maintains and stops receiving frames having that destination MAC station address value.

- **GetLinkAttributes.** Reads the attributes of the data link

LLC Sublayer User Multiplexing and Filtering

All DNA Phase V LAN implementations are designed to accept frames and PDUs of different formats. Figure 21.10 shows the various formats of LLC-PDU that DNA Phase V nodes can accept. As described earlier, the DNA Phase V LLC sublayer provides services that each LLC sublayer user can request to specify the LLC-PDUs it would like to accept. The DNA Phase V LLC sublayer service then filters out all the other PDUs, so each LLC sublayer user receives only those it requested. The following are descriptions of the types of LLC-PDU the DNA Phase V LLC sublayer can process.

Network Layer LLC-PDUs

When the LLC sublayer user is a Network layer entity conforming to an ISO standard, the SSAP address identifies the protocol run by the Network layer entity that generated the frame, and the DSAP address identifies the protocol of the Network layer entity that is to receive the frame. For example, among the SAP address values defined by the IEEE is the value hex 'FE', which indicates the use of the ISO 8473 Internet protocol. A Network layer entity running the ISO 8473 Internet protocol to support the connectionless-mode Network service (CLNS) employs an SSAP value and DSAP value of hex 'FE' in the PDUs it sends.

FIGURE 21.10   **DNA Phase V LLC-PDU formats.**

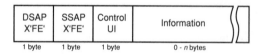

Network Layer ISO 8073 Internet Protocol LLC-PDU

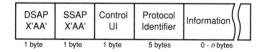

SNAP LLC-PDU

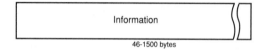

Ethernet LLC-PDU

SNAP PDUs

LLC sublayer users employing a protocol other than one defined by an international standard use *Subnetwork Access Protocol* (SNAP) LLC-PDUs. SNAP LLC-PDUs carry SSAP and DSAP values of hex 'AA'. Like SAP addressing, the SNAP protocol provides multiplexing of different user types. The SNAP protocol is an additional layer of multiplexing above that provided by SAP addressing. Data units generated by Digital proprietary protocols, such as those used to implement the naming service, are carried in SNAP LLC-PDUs. Data units generated by non-Digital protocols can also be carried in SNAP LLC-PDUs. SNAP LLC-PDUs are always U-format LLC-PDUs. The first 5 octets of the LLC-PDU's information field define the protocol that generated the SNAP PDU. The first 3 octets of the protocol identifier contain a value assigned to a vendor for station address values to distinguish each vendor's protocols. (As described earlier, hex '08-00-2B' is one such value assigned to Digital.) The remaining 2 octets identify the specific vendor protocol. For example, Digital's naming service uses the protocol ID value hex '08-00-2B-80-3C' in a SNAP LLC-PDU to advertise the availability of a name server on the LAN.

Ethernet LLC-PDUs

The *Ethernet Specification* does not make a clear distinction between the LLC sublayer and the MAC sublayer. Therefore, there is no notion of the LLC-PDU defined for Ethernet frames. As we will discuss in Chapter 22, the first 2 octets of the data portion of an Ethernet frame contain a *protocol type* field identifying the LLC-PDU as originating from Ethernet equipment. The way in which Digital LAN equipment identifies an Ethernet frame is discussed in Chapter 22. The Ethernet protocol type identifies the type of the user entity of the LLC service for Ethernet just as the SNAP protocol identifier does for the SNAP protocol.

Conclusion

This chapter examined the Logical Link Control sublayer of the Data Link layer—the sublayer shared by all the various forms of local area networks that can be used to construct a DECnet Phase V network. The next two chapters introduce the two major forms of LAN technology supported by DNA Phase V. Chapter 22 introduces the bus-structured Carrier Sense Multiple Access with Collision Detection (CSMA/CD) and Ethernet forms of LAN data link. Chapter 23 examines the ring-structured fiber distributed data interface (FDDI) LAN data link.

CHAPTER 22

IEEE CSMA/CD and Ethernet

Beginning in about 1972, the Palo Alto Research Center (PARC) of Xerox Corporation began developing a local area network (LAN) system that ran at 3 megabits per second (Mbps), which became known as *Research Ethernet*. Later, Digital, Intel, and Xerox jointly developed a substantially new design for a 10 Mbps Ethernet network that was documented in Version 1 of the *Ethernet Specification*. This design was later revised and is now documented in Version 2 of the *Ethernet Specification*. Digital has been one of the largest supporters of the Ethernet form of LAN, and LANs conforming to Version 2 of the *Ethernet Specification* are an integral part of DECnet Phase IV networks. DNA Phase V continues to support Version 2 of the *Ethernet Specification*.

The work done by Digital, Intel, and Xerox on Ethernet contributed substantially to the IEEE 802.3, *Carrier Sense Multiple Access with Collision Detection* (CSMA/CD), standard. The IEEE 802.3 standard is similar to Version 2 of the *Ethernet Specification*. IEEE 802.3 has been accepted by ISO as an international standard and is also published as ISO 8802-3. The IEEE/ISO CSMA/CD standard has been incorporated into the DNA Phase V architecture, and all DECnet Phase V LAN products support both the IEEE/ISO CSMA/CD standard and the *Ethernet Specification*. This chapter describes the DNA Phase V CSMA/CD specification, which goes beyond the IEEE/ISO CSMA/CD standard but is in complete conformance with it.

A CSMA/CD LAN uses building blocks of individual cable segments to which stations are attached in a bus-structured topology. A cable segment has a limited length, and devices called *repeaters* can be used to create a branching, nonrooted tree topology, as shown in Figure 22.1. A CSMA/CD LAN implements a multiaccess form of data link in which all stations in the network receive the transmissions of all other stations.

FIGURE 22.1   Simple CSMA/CD network using repeaters.

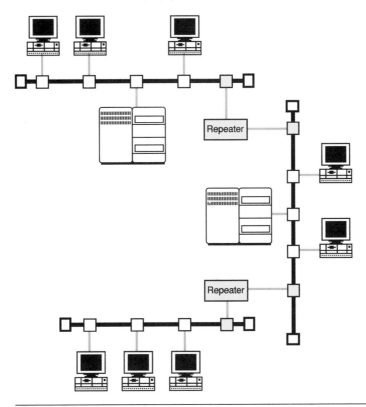

The CSMA/CD Architectural Model

The DNA Phase V specifications for the CSMA/CD form of data link defines an architectural model describing the organization of the Data Link layer and the Physical layer. This architectural model defines the components shown in Figure 22.2.

Data Link Layer Components

As described in Chapter 21, with a local area network data link, the Data Link layer is divided into a Logical Link Control (LLC) sublayer and a Medium Access Control (MAC) sublayer.

Logical Link Control Sublayer

The *Logical Link Control* (LLC) sublayer of the Data Link layer is responsible for medium-independent Data Link layer functions. It allows a

---

FIGURE 22.2

DNA Phase V CSMA/CD architectural model.

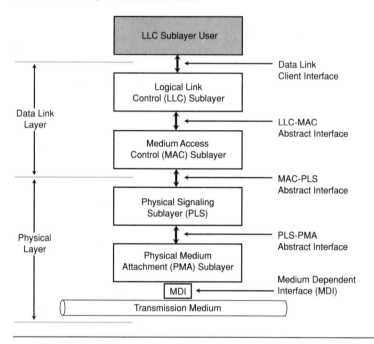

user of the LLC sublayer to access the services of the LAN without re-gard to what form of transmission medium is used and what method is used to control access to it. The LLC sublayer provides services to a user of the OSI Data Link layer, such as a Network layer entity. The functions of the LLC sublayer are described in detail in Chapter 21.

Medium Access Control Sublayer

The *Medium Access Control* (MAC) sublayer of the Data Link layer is concerned with the method used to control access to the transmission medium. The medium access control method defines procedures for managing access to the transmission medium, describes addressing tech-niques, and specifies error detection procedures. The MAC sublayer pro-vides services to the LLC sublayer.

   The interface between the LLC sublayer and the MAC sublayer (the LLC-MAC interface) is an abstract interface defining the set of services that a MAC sublayer entity supplies to an LLC sublayer entity above it. The relationship between the services the MAC sublayer provides to the

FIGURE 22.3   **The relationship between the MAC sublayer service and the MAC sublayer protocol.**

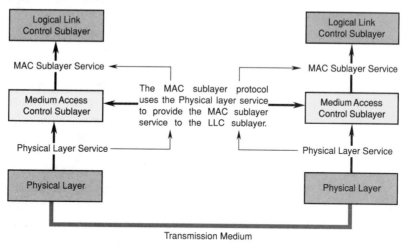

LLC sublayer and the protocol governing its operation are shown in Figure 22.3. As shown there, the MAC sublayer protocol uses the services of the Physical layer to provide a defined set of services to an LLC sublayer entity above it.

Physical Layer Components

The architectural components for the Physical layer address issues such as the physical characteristics of the transmission medium and the mechanical connection of devices to the transmission medium. The CSMA/CD Physical layer is divided into a Physical Signaling (PLS) sublayer and a Physical Medium Attachment (PMA) sublayer.

The Physical Signaling Sublayer

The *Physical Signaling* (PLS) sublayer provides a well-defined set of services to the MAC sublayer and enables the local MAC sublayer entity to exchange MAC frames with MAC sublayer entities in other stations. The interface between the MAC sublayer and the PLS sublayer (the MAC-PLS interface) is an abstract interface defining the services that a PLS sublayer entity supplies to a MAC sublayer entity.

The PLS sublayer is responsible for encoding the data passed down from the MAC sublayer in a transmitting station. The data encoding function is responsible for translating the bits being transmitted into the proper electrical signals that are then broadcast over the transmission medium. The PLS sublayer is also responsible for decoding the signal it receives. The decoding function translates received signals into the bit stream those signals represent and passes the resulting data up to the MAC sublayer.

With CSMA/CD, *Manchester encoding* is used to encode the bit stream into electrical signals. Manchester encoding has the desirable property that signal transitions occur on the transmission medium with predictable regularity. The Manchester encoding scheme used with an implementation of CSMA/CD is illustrated in Figure 22.4. With Manchester encoding, the signal state always changes at the midpoint of each bit time. For a 1 bit, the signal changes from low to high; for a 0 bit, it changes from high to low. This type of signaling allows data and clocking signals to be combined into a single transmission, since the receiving station can use the state change that occurs during each bit time for synchronization purposes.

The PLS sublayer is also responsible for listening to the transmission medium and for notifying medium access management whether the carrier is free or busy and whether a *collision* has been detected. Collisions, which occur when two or more stations attempt to transmit at the same time, are discussed later when we describe the operation of the CSMA/CD protocol.

Physical Medium Attachment Sublayer

The *Physical Medium Attachment* (PMA) sublayer provides services to the PLS sublayer. It performs a translation function between the PLS sublayer and the transmission medium itself and defines the characteristics of a particular type of transmission medium. The interface between the

FIGURE 22.4   **Manchester encoding for CSMA/CD.**

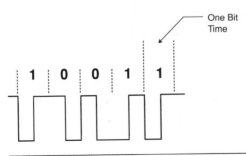

MAC sublayer and the PLS sublayer (the PLS-PMA interface) defines the services that a PMA sublayer entity supplies to a PLS sublayer entity.

The CSMA/CD standard allows the PLS and PMA sublayers to be implemented in the same device or in separate devices, as shown in Figure 22.5. A device implementing both the PLS and PMA sublayers is attached directly to the transmission medium. In such a device, the PLS-PMA interface is an abstract interface that defines services only. A device implementing only the PLS sublayer must use a separate device, called a Medium Attachment Unit (MAU), to implement the PMA sublayer. The function of the MAU is described later when we examine the devices that can implement the various architectural components.

Attachment Unit Interface

When a separate MAU is used to implement the PMA sublayer, the PLS-PMA interface consists of a concrete interface called the *Attachment Unit Interface* (AUI). The AUI defines the cable and the connectors used to connect the MAU to the device implementing the PLS sublayer. The AUI also specifies the characteristics of the signals exchanged across the interface.

FIGURE 22.5   **The PLS and PMA sublayers can be implemented in the same device or in different devices.**

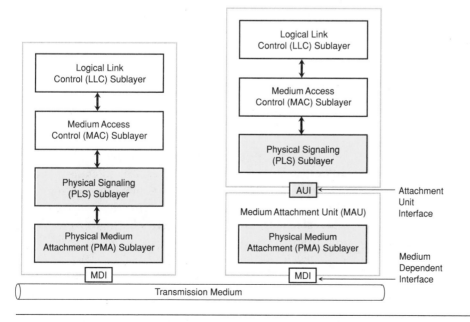

Transmission Medium

The transmission medium consists of the portion of the physical communication channel to which two or more PMA sublayer entities are connected. The interface between the PMA sublayer and the transmission medium (the PMA-Medium interface) is a concrete interface called the *Medium Dependent Interface* (MDI). The MDI for a particular form of transmission medium defines the characteristics of cable segments (sometimes called the *trunk cable*), connectors for joining cable segments, and terminators used at the ends of cable segments. Although the transmission medium ordinarily consists of a physical cable, such as coaxial cable, twisted-pair cable, or fiber-optic cable, it can also consist of a microwave link in some implementations.

CSMA/CD Medium Notation

A shorthand notation is used to describe a particular form of CSMA/CD transmission medium in which the data rate, signaling type, maximum cable segment length, and medium type are combined. An example of this notation is 10BASE5coax. The *10* refers to 10 Mbps (all current DECnet Phase V CSMA/CD implementations use a data rate of 10 Mbps), *BASE* refers to baseband signaling, *5* refers to a maximum of 500 meters, and *coax* indicates coaxial cable. If the medium type is omitted, coaxial cable is assumed, so 10BASE5 is equivalent to 10BASE5coax.

Digital CSMA/CD Transmission Media

The following forms of transmission media are supported by Digital implementations of CSMA/CD:

1. **10BASE5.** The 10BASE5 form of transmission medium is based on the original *Ethernet Specification* and uses baseband transmission over the original, thick (10 mm) form of 50-ohm Ethernet coaxial cable. This type of cable is often referred to as *thick Ethernet cable*. A 10BASE5 cable segment can be up to 500 meters in length.

2. **10BASE2.** The 10BASE2 form of transmission medium uses baseband signaling over 50-ohm coaxial cable, approximately 5 mm thick. This form of transmission medium is often called *ThinWire* cable or *Thinnet* cable. A 10BASE2 cable segment can be up to 185 meters in length.

3. **10BASE-T.** The 10BASE-T form of transmission medium uses baseband signaling over unshielded twisted-pair telephone wiring. The specification is designed for a typical distance of up to about 100 meters of 24 AWG twisted-pair cable.

4. **10BROAD36.** The 10BROAD36 form of transmission medium uses broadband signaling over the type of coaxial cable typically used in cable television. 10BROAD36 cable segments can be up to 1800 meters in length for a round trip distance of up to 3600 meters using a dual cable configuration.

5. **FOIRL.** The FOIRL form of transmission medium uses baseband signaling over a fiber-optic cable to implement a point-to-point connection between repeaters. Fiber-optic inter-repeater link cable segments can be up to 1000 meters in length. Repeaters and inter-repeater links are described later in this chapter.

Network Components

The components defined in the CSMA/CD architectural model can be combined to form three different types of devices: stations, medium attachment units (MAUs), and repeaters. Collections of those three types of devices can be combined in various ways to construct CSMA/CD LANs.

Stations

A *station* is a collection of hardware and software that appears to other stations as a single functional and addressable unit on the LAN. A station is a device that uses a CSMA/CD LAN for communication with other stations. A station is identified by a *station address*, which must be unique among all the stations attached to the LAN. Station addresses are described in Chapter 21.

Two types of stations can be attached to a CSMA/CD LAN, as shown in Figure 22.6. The first type of station—shown on the left in Figure 22.6—is one attached directly to the transmission medium. It implements the LLC, MAC, PLS, and PMA components and also the MDI concrete interface for attaching the station to a cable segment. The second type of station—shown on the right—is one that uses a separate medium attachment unit to implement the PMA sublayer functions. Hybrid stations are also possible that implement an internal MAU and also provide the MDI concrete interface for connecting to an external MAU to provide for alternative methods of connection to a cable segment. For

FIGURE 22.6   A station can implement an internal MAU or connect to an external MAU.

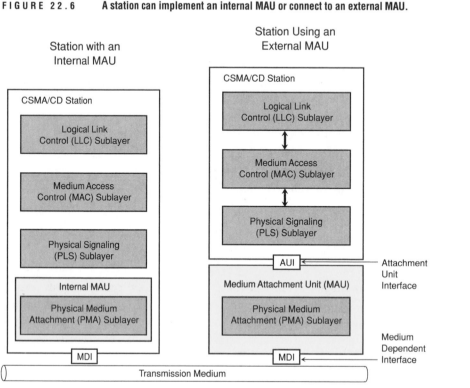

example, a station might implement the AUI for connecting the station to an external MAU for attachment to a 10BASE5 cable segment and an internal MAU for direct connection to a 10BASE2 or 10BASET cable segment.

Medium Attachment Units

The CSMA/CD standard anticipates that in many implementations the station will be located a short distance away from the transmission medium, which must often be installed behind a wall or in a ceiling. So, as described earlier, the CSMA/CD standard allows the physical medium attachment (PMA) component to be implemented in a separate device called a *Medium Attachment Unit* (MAU), also sometimes called a *transceiver*. An *attachment unit interface* (AUI) defines the interface between a station and the MAU. The AUI is a concrete interface that defines specifications for the cable and the connectors used to attach the station to the transceiver. The AUI also defines the characteristics of the electrical signals exchanged across the interface. An MAU provides the physical and electrical interface between a cable segment and a CSMA/CD station. The cable that connects the device implementing the PLS sublayer to the MAU is called the *AUI cable*.

The MAU handles all functions that depend on the specific transmission medium being used. By having an MAU separate from the station itself, the same station can be used with different transmission media simply by changing the MAU. The most common form of station that attaches to a 10BASE5 cable segment uses a separate MAU for attaching to the cable segment. The MAU typically has a contact that pierces the thick Ethernet coaxial cable shielding and makes appropriate contact with both the shielding and the central conductor. This is shown in Figure 22.7.

In most implementations of the 10BASE2 medium specification, the transmission medium is brought directly to the LAN adapter, and the PMA sublayer is implemented by the LAN adapter itself. A standard T-type BNC connector is used to attach the cable segment directly to the LAN adapter, and stations are connected together in a daisy-chain fashion, as shown in Figure 22.8. The 10BASE2 medium specification, however, does not preclude the use of a separate MAU.

A station that does not use a separate MAU and implements the PMA sublayer within the station is said to implement an *internal MAU*.

FIGURE 22.7   **Typical 10BASE5 implementation.**

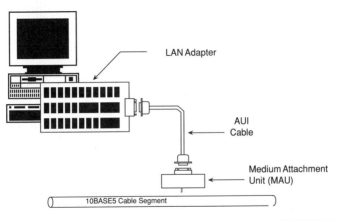

FIGURE 22.8   **Typical 10BASE2 implementation.**

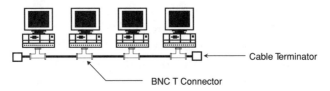

Therefore, the term *Medium Attachment Unit* can be used to refer to any point of physical attachment to a cable segment, whether or not a separate MAU is used to attach a station to the LAN.

Repeaters

As described earlier, a CSMA/CD cable segment is of limited length. A *repeater* can be used to relay signals from one cable segment to another, thus extending the reach of a LAN beyond that allowed by a single cable segment. Repeaters can be used to construct a network having a branching, nonrooted tree topology. A repeater's primary function is to relay all data units it receives from one cable segment to all other cable segments to which it is attached. The architectural model for a repeater is shown in Figure 22.9. It consists of a single repeater function and two or more *ports*. Each port consists of a PLS sublayer entity or the combination of a PLS sublayer entity and a PMA sublayer entity.

Like a station, a repeater port can have the PMA sublayer integrated into it, in which case the port is attached directly to the transmission medium. Alternatively, a repeater port can implement the AUI, which is a concrete interface, and can use a separate MAU for attachment to a cable segment. Both types of ports can be implemented in the same repeater.

FIGURE 22.9   **Repeater architectural model.**

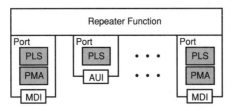

A repeater can implement ports that allow attachment to different types of transmission medias or different types of MAUs, as long as all support the same data rate. For example, the same repeater might allow data units to be relayed between 10BASE5 cable segments, 10BASE2 cable segments, and 10BASE-T cable segments.

CSMA/CD Network   Stations, MAUs, repeaters, and cable segments can be combined in a variety of ways to create networks that have a variety of topologies. Figure 22.10 shows a typical CSMA/CD network that suggests various ways in

FIGURE 22.10   **Typical CSMA/CD network.**

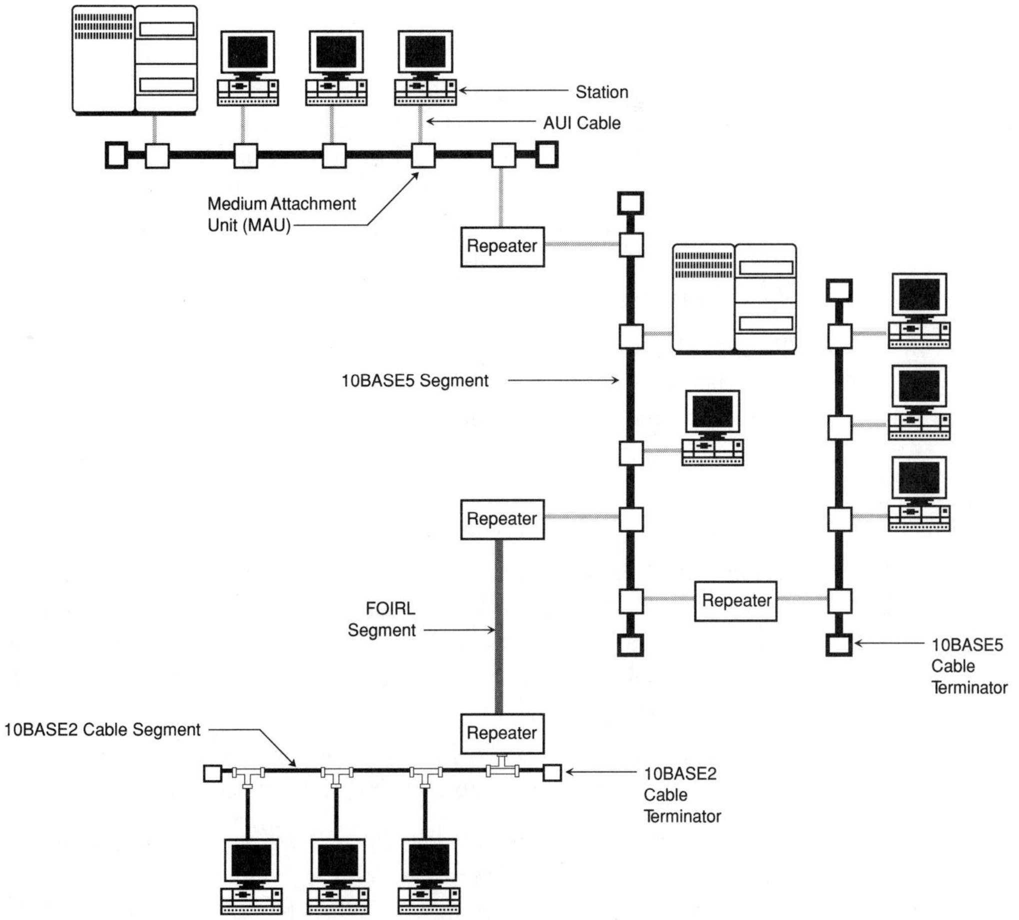

which components can be combined. The topology of a CSMA/CD network must always form a nonrooted, branching tree in which there is only one physical path between any two stations and in which the network can be extended or connected at any point.

Cable Segments

Two types of cable segments are defined in the DNA Phase V CSMA/CD specification: point-to-point and multiaccess. A *point-to-point* cable segment allows only two connections and is used to connect the MAUs of a pair of repeaters. A point-to-point cable segment is called an *inter-repeater link* (IRL). A *multiaccess* cable segment allows more than two connections and can be used to attach the MAUs of stations and repeaters to the LAN.

Station and Cable Segment Limits

An individual CSMA/CD network can contain up to 1024 stations. Certain additional limits must be placed on the network configurations that can be built based on signal propagation times. The following four types of transmission media are used most often today for constructing CSMA/CD LANs:

- **10BASE5 Multiaccess Cable Segments.** A 10BASE5 cable segment normally functions as a multiaccess cable segment. It can be up to 500 meters in length and can have a maximum of 100 MAUs attached to it.

- **10BASE2 Multiaccess Cable Segments.** A 10BASE2 cable segment can also function as a multiaccess cable segment. It can be up to 185 meters in length and can have a maximum of 30 MAUs attached to it.

- **10BASE-T Multiaccess Cable Segments.** A 10BASE-T cable segment can also be used as a multiaccess cable segment. The length of a 10BASE-T cable segment and the number of stations that can be attached to a single twisted-pair cable segment is implementation dependent. A maximum length of 100 meters is typical.

- **FOIRL Inter-Repeater Links.** A FOIRL cable segment can be used as an inter-repeater link and can be up to 1000 meters in length.

Between any two stations on the LAN, there can be a maximum of five cable segments, up to three of which can be multiaccess cable segments. There can be a maximum of 1000 meters of inter-repeater link cable segments between any two stations. Figure 22.11 shows a network

FIGURE 22.11   **Maximum span between two CSMA/CD stations with 10BASE5 multiaccess cable segments and FOIRL inter-repeater links.**

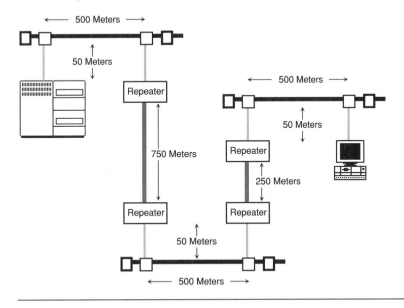

with the maximum span between station A and station B. This network uses three 500-meter multiaccess cable segments and two inter-repeater link cable segments totaling 1000 meters. Repeaters implementing inter-repeater links normally use internal MAUs for connection to a fiber-optic inter-repeater link (although the DNA Phase V CSMA/CD specification does not require this). Therefore, the total distance between any two stations is limited to 2800 meters. This includes 1500 meters of multiaccess cable segment, 1000 meters of inter-repeater link, and 300 meters for 6 AUI cables to external MAUs.

Interconnecting 10BASE2, 10BASE5, and 10BASE-T Segments

It is common to construct networks that use combinations of 10BASE2, 10BASE5, and 10BASE-T multiaccess cable segments. A possible combination is shown in Figure 22.12, in which a 10BASE5 network is used as a backbone for a number of smaller 10BASE2 and 10BASE-T cable segments. It is generally recommended that a 10BASE2 or 10BASE-T cable segment not be used between two 10BASE5 cable segments. This is because 10BASE2 and 10BASE-T cable segments are not as resistant to

FIGURE 22.12   Interconnecting 10BASE2 and 10BASE-T cable segments using a 10BASE5 backbone.

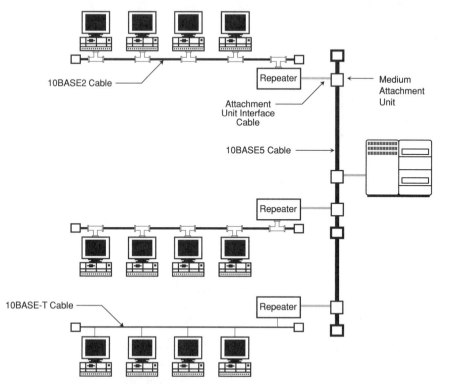

noise as a 10BASE5 cable segment, and a segment used as a backbone should be at least as resistant to noise as the segments it connects.

Star-Structured Networks

In the past, the CSMA/CD and Ethernet forms of local area networking have sometimes been criticized because of the difficulty of prewiring a building using a bus-structured network topology. This criticism is no longer valid because repeaters implementing multiple ports, sometimes called *multiport repeaters,* can be used to create star-structured networks that are often better suited to building wiring schemes than bus-structured networks. In many cases, the best solution to local area network wiring is to use a system of *satellite equipment rooms.* All the satellite equipment rooms in a building might be interconnected, and each network station then directly connected to the nearest satellite equipment room. Digital has long advocated the use of satellite equipment rooms to create a star-structured wiring scheme, as shown in Figure 22.13. The bus, in effect, operates as a high-quality backbone to which all the network stations can be connected. Multiport repeaters installed in the satellite equipment rooms allow a separate cable to connect each network station to the satellite equipment room.

Extended LANs

Devices called *bridges* can be used to interconnect individual CSMA/CD networks to create an *extended LAN*. Bridges can also be used to interconnect CSMA/CD networks with networks conforming to other stan-

FIGURE 22.13   **Star-wired topology using satellite equipment rooms.**

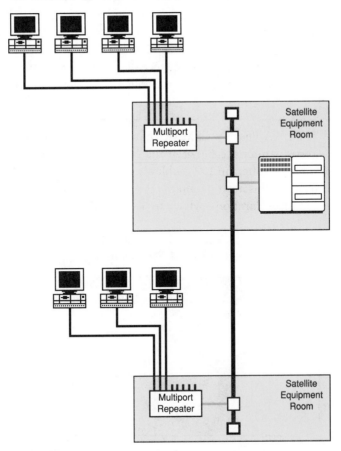

dards, such as FDDI. Bridges perform a Data Link layer relay function and are used to extend the LAN without affecting the basic services it provides. Bridges can be used to increase the maximum number of stations allowed, the maximum distance between pairs of stations, and the total available bandwidth. Bridges and extended LANs are discussed in Chapter 24.

The remainder of this chapter describes the CSMA/CD service definition and protocol specification and examines the format of the data units exchanged by CSMA/CD MAC sublayer entities during local area network operation.

CSMA/CD MAC Sublayer Service Definition

As with other ISO standards, the IEEE/ISO CSMA/CD documentation includes a service definition that defines the services the MAC sublayer provides to the LLC sublayer. The service definition is specified in terms of service primitives and service primitive parameters. The service definition describes a single, unconfirmed data transfer service. The service primitives that define the MAC sublayer service are shown in Box 22.1. Figure 22.14 is a time-sequence diagram showing the sequence in which the two service primitives are issued during normal frame transmission.

MAC Sublayer Service Interface Procedure Declarations

The DNA Phase V CSMA/CD architectural specification also defines the abstract interface between the MAC sublayer and a user of the MAC sublayer (often an LLC sublayer entity). As with other DNA Phase V interfaces, this abstract interface is defined using a set of function and procedure declarations, which are listed in Box 22.2.

FIGURE 22.14   Time-sequence diagram for the MA_UNITDATA service.

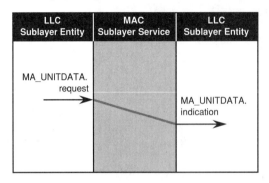

BOX 22.1

**MAC Sublayer
Service Primitives**

```
        MA_UNITDATA.request    (
                                destination_address,
                                user_data,
                                service_class
                               )


        MA_UNITDATA.indication    (
                                   destination_address,
                                   source_address,
                                   user_data,
                                   reception_status
                                  )
```

**CSMA/CD MAC
Sublayer Protocol
Specification**

The MAC sublayer Carrier Sense Multiple Access with Collision Detection (CSMA/CD) protocol uses a distributed contention resolution technique to decide which station transmits next. The remainder of this chapter describes, in a nontechnical fashion, how the distributed contention resolution technique evolved and how the CSMA/CD protocol operates.

The ALOHA Protocol

The CSMA/CD protocol had its roots in an early multiaccess protocol used in an experimental packet radio system called ALOHA, developed at the University of Hawaii in the early 1970s. The protocol developed for the ALOHA system uses a *free-for-all* technique, in which any station having a frame to send simply transmits it. The station then waits for a period of time equal to twice the round-trip *propagation delay*—the length of time it takes a signal to reach the far end of the network. Twice the round-trip propagation delay is called the *slot time* of the network. Since signals are propagated at the speed of light, the slot time is typically very short.

If the sending station hears an acknowledgment to its frame within the slot time, the sending station knows the frame was received correctly. If the sending station times out, it retransmits the frame. After repeated retransmissions, the sending station gives up (perhaps the receiving station is turned off).

If a second station attempts to transmit a frame while the first station is already transmitting, the two transmissions interfere, thus creat-

BOX 22.2

MAC Sublayer
Service Interface
Functions and
Procedures

The following function and procedure declarations define the abstract
interface between the MAC sublayer and a user of the MAC sublayer
in terms of the services a MAC sublayer entity provides to a user.

Control Functions

- **Enable.** Starts the operation of the services provided by the MAC
  sublayer and the Physical layer.
- **Disable.** Stops operation of the MAC sublayer entity and the Physical layer entity.
- **EnableReceiveAddress.** Adds a MAC station address value to the list
  of addresses of those frames the station wishes to receive. Only
  frames having the MAC station addresses in the current list are
  passed up to the LLC sublayer entity.
- **DisableReceiveAddress.** Removes a MAC station address value from
  the list of addresses of those frames the station wishes to receive.
- **ReadAttributes.** Allows the LLC sublayer entity to determine the
  values of the MAC sublayer entity parameters and state variables.

Data Transfer Functions

- **TransmitFrame.** Transmits a frame over the physical transmission
  medium. Control is not returned until either the frame has been successfully transmitted or the function fails.
- **ReceiveFrame.** Accepts an incoming frame. Control is not returned
  until either the frame has been received or the function fails.

ing a condition called a *collision*. When collisions occur, frames are damaged, the errors are detected through an error detection mechanism, and
receiving stations ignore the corrupted frames. Both stations then later
attempt to retransmit. The protocol is simple but inefficient with high
utilization of the channel capacity. It can be shown mathematically that
the maximum utilization of the available bandwidth with the pure
ALOHA protocol is less than 18 percent.

The CSMA Protocol

A problem with the ALOHA protocol is that collisions often occur when
a station begins transmitting a frame after some other station has already

begun transmitting. If each station would simply listen to the transmission medium before sending its own frame and then send only if the medium were quiet, many collisions could be avoided. This is the technique of *Carrier Sense Multiple Access* (CSMA). Each station senses the condition of the transmission medium and transmits only when no signal is being transmitted.

However, even with the CSMA technique, it can happen that two or more stations all listen at exactly the same time and then transmit simultaneously. Therefore, collisions can still occur. With the CSMA scheme, when frame transmission times are long compared to the propagation delay, a significant portion of channel capacity can be lost due to collisions because each station transmits its entire frame before discovering that a collision has occurred.

The CSMA/CD Protocol

The final refinement to the CSMA technique is to add the *Collision Detection* (CD) function, resulting in *CSMA/CD*. In addition to listening to the transmission system before transmitting, a sending station continues to listen as the frame is propagated throughout the network. If two or more stations have begun transmitting within a sufficiently short time interval, a collision occurs. When this happens, the transmitting stations immediately detect the collision, cease transmitting data, and all send out a short *jamming signal*. The jamming signal ensures that all stations on the network detect the collision. All stations that have been transmitting then stop transmitting, wait for a random period of time, and if the carrier is free, transmit their frames again. A station must listen while it is transmitting to ensure that a collision has not taken place.

Deference Process

The process of monitoring the state of the transmission medium and determining when to begin transmission is called the *deference process*. The deference process determines when the station can begin transmitting after it has detected that a transition between medium busy and medium idle has occurred. For example, when a collision occurs, all stations that have been transmitting stop, wait a period of time, and then if the carrier is free, start transmitting again. If all stations waited the same length of time before checking the carrier and starting transmission, then another collision would occur. The deference process avoids this. In executing the deference process, each station generates a random number that determines the length of time it must wait before testing the carrier. This time period is known as the station's *backoff delay*. Backoff delay is calculated in multiples of slot time, which is 51.2 microseconds on a CSMA/CD network.

Each station generates a random number that falls within a specified range of values. It then waits that number of slot times before attempting retransmission. The smaller the range of values from which the random number is selected, the greater the likelihood that two stations will select the same number and have another collision. However, if the range of numbers is large, all the stations may wait for several slot times before any station transmits, causing transmission time to be wasted.

Truncated Binary Exponential Backoff

To achieve a balance between these two considerations, the CSMA/CD protocol uses an approach called *truncated binary exponential backoff*. The range of numbers (r) is defined as $0 \leq r < 2^k$, where k reflects the number of transmission attempts the station has made. For the first attempt the range is 0 to 1; for the second attempt, 0 to 3; for the third, 0 to 7 and so on. If repeated collisions occur, the range continues to expand until k reaches 10 (with r ranging from 0 to 1023), after which the value for k stays at 10. If a station is unsuccessful in transmitting after 16 attempts, the MAC sublayer entity reports an *excessive collisions* error condition.

Binary exponential backoff results in minimum delays before retransmission when traffic on the network is light. When traffic is high, repeated collisions cause the range of numbers to increase, thus lessening the chance of further collisions. Of course, when the traffic is extremely high, repeated collisions can still begin to cause excessive collisions error conditions to be generated. However, this technique results in network utilizations that are extremely high, generally better than 90 percent.

Collision Detection

A station knows that a collision has occurred when the signal level on the cable equals or exceeds a predefined threshold. As a signal travels along the cable, it gradually attenuates, or weakens. If the signal is allowed to attenuate too much, a station's signal might not be recognized as a collision when it combines with the signal from another transmitter. This is one of the reasons that repeaters must be used at least every 500 meters to regenerate the signal to its optimal level (1000 meters over an inter-repeater link).

Figure 22.15 illustrates, in a simplified manner, worst-case collision detection for a network of maximum size. Stations 1 and 2 are the maximum distance apart. Station 1 begins transmitting, and just before its signal reaches station 2, station 2 also begins transmitting. The collision occurs near station 2, causing a signal that must travel back the full length of the network to reach station 1. The frame station 1 is transmitting must be large enough to ensure that station 1 is still transmitting when it detects the collision with station 2's transmission. Otherwise, it will assume its frame got through without a collision.

The maximum time it takes to detect a collision is equal to the slot time, twice the propagation time for the maximum cable length. This represents the time it takes station 1's signal to reach the far end plus the time it takes the collision signal to travel back the length of the network to reach station 1. The worst-case collision detection time on a valid CSMA/CD network of maximum size is less than 51.2 microseconds.

CSMA/CD Protocol Design Decisions It is interesting to note that many of the design decisions made during the development of the *Ethernet Specification* (which led to the CSMA/CD standard) were based on real-world engineering considerations and represented difficult tradeoffs between cost and performance. Box 22.3 gives a list of the design decisions that were made. Keep in mind that these decisions were made in 1980. We list the decisions in the order the

FIGURE 22.15   Worst-case collision detection.

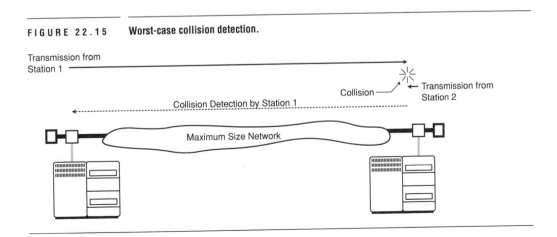

BOX 22.3

**Ethernet Design
Decisions**

1. The 10 megabits per second (Mbps) data rate was the first design decision. Given the scaling of semiconductor technology, the design team felt it would be feasible to put the logic to implement CSMA/CD at 10 Mbps on a single chip by about 1985, which would lead to LAN adapters that could be marketed at a reasonable cost.

2. The next design decision was that the total span of a CSMA/CD LAN needed to be at least a couple of kilometers in extent. This figure was based on the need to wire buildings from floor to floor and the requirement for wiring a campus of buildings.

3. The maximum length of 500 meters for a single multiaccess cable segment was decided next. This figure was based on a tradeoff between jitter increasing as the cable gets longer and the cost associated with building a transceiver increasing as the jitter increases.

4. The next design parameter was to allow a maximum of 50 meters for the AUI cable from the transceiver attached to the cable segment to the station itself. This figure was kept relatively small so the AUI cable could be implemented cheaply.

5. The next decision was to specify a maximum of two repeaters between any two stations and a maximum of 1000 meters of point-to-point link between any two stations. In the *Ethernet Specification,* a repeater could consist of two half-repeaters connected by a point-to-point link. This is the same as the present DNA Phase V CSMA/CD specification, which allows five cable segments, two of which must be inter-repeater links. These parameters were chosen to permit a maximum distance between any two stations of 2800 meters (three 500 meter multiaccess cable segments, 1000 meters of point-to-point link, and six 50-meter AUI cables to MAUs).

6. The above five design decisions led directly to the CSMA/CD slot time of 51.2 microseconds.

7. The slot time dictates the minimum frame size requiring at least 46 octets in the data field of a frame.

8. The maximum packet size of 1500 octets in the data field of a frame was then chosen based on a tradeoff between reducing latency and maximizing transmission efficiency. As the frame size gets longer, the probability increases that two or more other stations will have frames to send when the first station finishes sending its frame and that a collision will occur. Keeping the maximum

BOX 22.3

continued

frame size relatively small lowers this probability and increases channel efficiency.

9. The decision to use Manchester encoding was based on the fact that it is relatively simple and inexpensive to implement and that it has frequent, predictable transitions making synchronization easy to achieve.

10. The final design decision was to allow for a minimum of 9.6 microseconds between transmitted frames (interpacket gap). This decision was based on an analysis of the processing that had to be performed after each packet was received and on an estimate of the amount of time it would require to perform that processing based on the technology of the time.

Ethernet design team made them and give the key considerations that led to each decision.

MAC Frame and Packet Format

In using the data transfer service provided by the MAC sublayer, an LLC entity in the source station passes a *medium-access-control-service-data-unit* (MAC-SDU) to the MAC sublayer entity in that station. The MAC sublayer entity adds PCI to the MAC-SDU in the form of a header and a trailer to create a *medium-access-control-protocol-data-unit* (MAC-PDU)—also called a MAC frame—and passes it to the Physical layer. The Physical layer attaches additional PCI to the MAC frame to create a physical-protocol-data-unit (PPDU). The DNA Phase V CSMA/CD specification calls a PPDU a *packet.** The Physical layer then transmits the packet over the transmission medium. When a station receives a packet, the Physical layer entity in the receiving station extracts the MAC frame from the packet and passes it up to the MAC sublayer entity. The MAC sublayer then extracts the LLC-PDU from the MAC frame and passes it up to the LLC sublayer. This process is summarized in Figure 22.16.

---

* This is an unfortunate choice of terminology, since the term *packet* is also frequently used in networking literature to refer to the NPDUs that are exchanged by Network layer entities. The Physical layer packet is *not* the same as the Network layer packet.

FIGURE 22.16   Providing the Medium Access Control sublayer data transfer service.

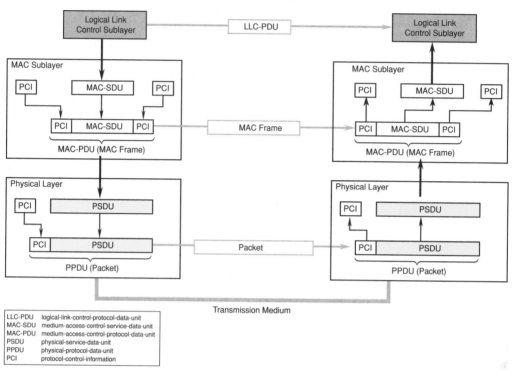

The general formats of a packet and a MAC frame are shown in Figure 22.17. The MAC frame is contained within a Physical layer packet and consists of destination and source address fields, a length/type field, a data field, and a frame check sequence field. The Physical layer creates a packet by adding a preamble, start frame delimiter, and end frame delimiter to the MAC frame. The following are descriptions of the fields that make up a MAC frame and a Physical layer packet:

- **Preamble.** A sequence of 56 bits having alternating 1- and 0-values that the Physical layer transmits prior to the beginning of a MAC frame to synchronize the transmitter and the receivers.

- **Start Frame Delimiter.** A sequence of 8 bits having the bit configuration 10101011 that the Physical layer transmits to indicate the beginning of a MAC frame.

- **Station Addresses.** Station addresses, described in Chapter 21, are often called *MAC addresses*. Address fields are 48 bits in length. The *source*

FIGURE 22.17   **DNA Phase V MAC frame and packet formats.**

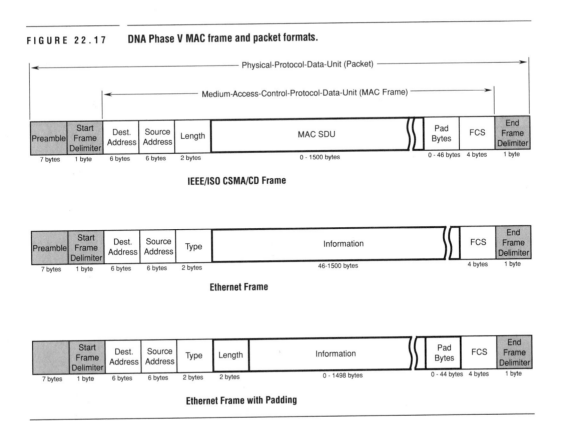

- *address field* always refers to an individual station, the station that transmitted the frame. The *destination address field* identifies the station or stations to receive the frame. The destination address can be either an individual address or a group address. An address referring to a group of stations is called a *multicast address*. The address referring to all stations on the network is called the *broadcast address*.

- **Length/Type Field.** The value contained in this field indicates whether the frame conforms to the IEEE/ISO CSMA/CD format or to the format defined by the *Ethernet Specification*. For an IEEE/ISO CSMA/CD frame, this field contains a count of the number of octets contained in the data field. For an Ethernet frame, this field contains a value used to identify the protocol employed by the Data Link layer user. Later in this chapter we discuss how the length/type field is used to distinguish between IEEE/ISO CSMA/CD and Ethernet frames.

- **Data Field.** Contains the MAC-SDU passed to the MAC sublayer by a user of the MAC sublayer. The data field can contain from 0 to 1500 octets.

- **Pad Field.** To properly detect collisions, there must be at least 46 octets of data between the length/type field and the frame check sequence field. If the data field is not at least 46 octets in length, Pad octets are added to bring the size of the data field plus the Pad field up to 46 octets.
- **Frame Check Sequence (FCS).** When the sending station assembles a frame, it performs a cyclical redundancy check (CRC) calculation on the bits in the frame. The specific algorithm used is documented in the IEEE/ISO CSMA/CD standard and is also described in the DNA Phase V CSMA/CD specification. The algorithm always results in a 32-bit value. The sending station stores this value in the frame check sequence (FCS) field and then transmits the frame. When the receiving station receives the frame, it performs an identical CRC calculation and compares the results with the value in the FCS field of the received frame. If the two values do not match, the receiving station assumes that a transmission error has occurred and discards the frame; thus, the user of the MAC sublayer service does not receive corrupted frames. It is the responsibility of higher layers to detect lost frames and to request their retransmission.

Ethernet Frames

A DECnet Phase V CSMA/CD LAN device distinguishes between an Ethernet frame and an IEEE/ISO CSMA/CD frame by examining the 2-octet length/type field. The maximum frame size restriction specifies that the length of the data field must be within the range of 0 to 1500 octets; therefore, the length field value in an IEEE/ISO CSMA/CD frame must be less than 1500. Since no Ethernet protocol identifier values are less than 1500, the LLC layer knows that if the length field value is 1500 or less, the frame is an IEEE/ISO CSMA/CD frame. If the length field value is larger than 1500, it is an Ethernet frame.

Digital's DECnet Phase V LAN devices are designed to normally transmit IEEE/ISO CSMA/CD frames but to accept incoming frames in either the IEEE/ISO CSMA/CD or the Ethernet format. When a Phase V CSMA/CD device receives an Ethernet frame from a station, it replies to that station with Ethernet frames.

Ethernet Frames with Padding

Although not defined by either the ISO/IEEE CSMA/CD standard or the *Ethernet Specification*, the DNA Phase V architecture defines a special Ethernet frame format that makes it possible to avoid the requirement for a data field to be at least 46 octets in length. It carries a 2-octet length field after the protocol identifier field. The remainder of the user data portion of the frame is then padded. The header portion of the frame does not distinguish between the padded and nonpadded variants. It is up to the two LAN users to agree on which format to use.

Conclusion

The CSMA/CD form of local area network data link and its Ethernet predecessor will be widely used in DECnet Phase V networks as easy-to-use methods for interconnecting host computers, workstations, personal computers, and terminals within a relatively small geographic area. Chapter 23 describes the *Fiber Distributed Data Interface* (FDDI) standard that defines a higher-speed LAN than CSMA/CD that will be important in the 1990s for high-performance networking applications.

CHAPTER 23

Fiber Distributed
Data Interface

Like a CSMA/CD local area network, a Fiber Distributed Data Interface (FDDI) local area network implements a broadcast form of data link in which all stations in the LAN receive the transmissions of all other stations. However, instead of using a multiaccess circuit to implement the LAN, FDDI uses full-duplex, point-to-point fiber-optic physical links between stations to form a logical ring-structured network. A special data unit called the *token* circulates around the ring. A station can transmit frames only when it is in possession of the token. An FDDI LAN operates at a data rate of 100 Mbps, 10 times that of a CSMA/CD network.

The FDDI standard is designed to meet requirements for both high-performance individual networks and high-speed connections between networks. The FDDI standard was developed by the Accredited Standards Committee (ASC) X3T9.5 of the American National Standards Institute (ANSI). It has also been accepted by ISO as an international standard and is published in ISO 9314. The DNA Phase V FDDI specification defines an implementation model that can be used to build FDDI LAN equipment that will successfully interoperate with any implementation of the ANSI FDDI specification. Like the CSMA/CD specification, the DNA Phase V FDDI specification defines many services that go beyond those described in the ANSI standard while remaining fully conformant with it.

The FDDI standard addresses the requirements associated with three types of networks: backend local networks, high-speed office networks, and backbone local networks.

- **Backend Local Networks.** Backend local networks are used to interconnect mainframe computers and large data storage devices where there is a need for a high-volume data transfer rate. Typically, in a backend local network there will be a small number of devices to be connected, and they will be close together. This was the original use for which FDDI was intended, but FDDI LANs will probably be used much more extensively for the following two uses.

- **High-Speed Office Networks.** The need for high-speed office networks has arisen from the increased use of image and graphics processing devices in the office environment. The use of graphics and images can increase the amount of information that needs to be transmitted on a network by orders of magnitude. A typical data processing transaction may involve 500 bits, while a document page image may require the transmission of half a million bits or more.

- **Backbone Local Networks.** Backbone local networks are used to provide a high-capacity network that can be used to interconnect lower-capacity LANs.

In the DNA Phase V environment, an important use of an FDDI LAN will be to serve as a high-speed backbone for connecting lower-speed CSMA/CD and Ethernet LANs. To this end, the DNA Phase V FDDI specification includes a mapped Ethernet service for allowing Ethernet stations to communicate with FDDI stations and for allowing an FDDI LAN to transmit traffic between Ethernet LANs.

The FDDI Architectural Model

The DNA Phase V specification for the FDDI form of data link defines an architectural model describing the organization of the Data Link and Physical layers of the OSI architecture. This architectural model is illustrated in Figure 23.1. The components in the architectural model can be divided among those components associated with the Data Link layer, those associated with the Physical layer, and those associated with the station management (SMT) function. An FDDI *station* is defined as a device that implements a single instance of the SMT component and the components SMT controls. A station has exactly one SMT component; zero, one, or two link components; and one or more PHY port components.

Data Link Layer Components

As described in Chapter 21, with a LAN data link, the Data Link layer is divided into a Logical Link Control (LLC) sublayer and a Medium Access Control (MAC) sublayer. An instance of an LLC sublayer entity and a MAC sublayer entity in the FDDI model is called a *link*. A station can implement zero, one, or two links, depending on the use to which the

FIGURE 23.1   **DNA Phase V FDDI architectural model.**

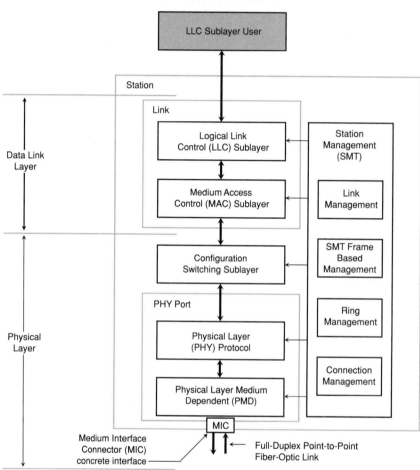

station is put. Different types of FDDI stations are described later in this chapter.

Logical Link Control Sublayer

The *Logical Link Control* (LLC) sublayer of the Data Link layer is responsible for medium-independent Data Link layer functions. It allows a user of the LLC sublayer to access the services of the local area network without regard to what form of transmission medium is used and what method is used to control access to it. The LLC sublayer provides services to a user of the OSI Data Link layer through an *LLC port*, as described in Chapter 21. The functions of the FDDI LLC sublayer are effectively the same as those described in Chapter 21. In addition to providing the IEEE/ISO Class I service, the DNA Phase V FDDI LLC sublayer provides the following services:

- multiplexing and demultiplexing for multiple users employing the service-access-point (SAP) address and subnetwork access protocol (SNAP) protocol identifiers
- address filtering
- XID and Test frame procedures
- a mapped Ethernet service to allow Ethernet and FDDI networks to interoperate in the same extended LAN

The DNA Phase V FDDI architectural specification defines the interface to the FDDI LLC sublayer in terms of function and procedure calls. These function and procedure calls are essentially the same as those specified in Chapter 21 (Box 21.3) and are not repeated here.

Medium Access Control Sublayer

The *Medium Access Control* (MAC) sublayer of the Data Link layer is concerned with the protocol used to handle the transmission of tokens and data frames around the logical ring. The interface between the LLC sublayer and the MAC sublayer is an abstract interface defining the set of services that a MAC sublayer entity supplies to an LLC sublayer entity above it. The relationship between the services the MAC sublayer provides to the LLC sublayer and the protocol governing its operation are shown in Figure 23.2. As shown there, the MAC sublayer protocol uses the services of the Physical layer to provide a defined set of services to an LLC sublayer entity above it.

The DNA Phase V FDDI MAC sublayer performs the following functions in supplying its services:

- ring initialization
- providing fair and deterministic access to the transmission medium
- address recognition and address filtering
- generation and verification of frame check sequence (FCS) fields
- frame transmission and reception
- frame repeating and frame stripping (removal of frames from the ring)

FIGURE 23.2   **The relationship between the MAC sublayer service and the MAC sublayer protocol.**

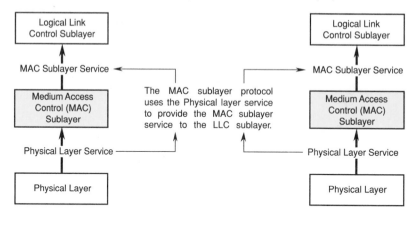

Transmission Medium

Physical Layer Components

The architectural components for the Physical layer address issues such as the physical characteristics of the transmission medium and the mechanical connection of stations to the transmission medium. The FDDI Physical layer is divided into a Configuration Switching sublayer, a Physical Layer Protocol (PHY) sublayer and a Physical Layer Medium Dependent (PMD) sublayer. A single instance of a PHY sublayer entity and a PMD sublayer entity within a station is called a *PHY port*. A station can implement one or more PHY ports.

Configuration Switching Sublayer

The *Configuration Switching* sublayer allows the PHY ports in a station to be interconnected in various ways. This allows the station configuration to be changed to determine the local topology of the network and any link or PHY port to be enabled or disabled as a result of a network management action. The Configuration Switching sublayer can determine the path that information takes through the station when new connections become available or when connections are removed.

The Physical Layer Protocol Sublayer

The *Physical Layer Protocol* (PHY) sublayer provides a well-defined set of services to a MAC sublayer entity and enables the local MAC entity to exchange MAC frames with MAC sublayer entities in other stations. The interface between the MAC sublayer and the PHY sublayer is an abstract interface defining the services that a PHY sublayer entity supplies to a MAC sublayer entity. The PHY sublayer performs the following functions:

- encoding and decoding data and control information
- transmitting data received from the MAC sublayer
- performing clock synchronization and recovering the data coming in from the PMD sublayer
- transmitting and receiving groups of code bits, called *line states*, that are used to initialize and condition the transmission medium

Symbol Coding

The encoding system used by FDDI is designed to provide ease of synchronization as well as data transmission. Data and control information is carried on the transmission medium in the form of code bits. A *code bit* is the smallest signalling entity and is represented using *Nonreturn to Zero Inverted* (NRZI) encoding. With NRZI, a 1 code bit is represented by a transition in the signal and a 0 code bit by no transition. A *code group* is a consecutive sequence of 5 code bits that is used to represent a *symbol* on the transmission medium. A 4b/5b code is used to assign interpretations to the various code groups, as shown in Figure 23.3. Each 5-bit data symbol corresponds to a 4-bit binary data value. The code groups used to represent data symbols were chosen so there are never more than three consecutive 0-bits and thus no more than three bit times without a transition. An additional 8 symbols are used for control purposes. Other possible 5-bit values are invalid.

Physical Layer Medium Dependent Sublayer

The *Physical Layer Medium Dependent* (PMD) sublayer provides services to the PHY sublayer. The interface between the PHY sublayer and the PMD sublayer is an abstract interface defining the services that a PMD sublayer entity supplies to a PHY sublayer entity. The functions performed by the PMD sublayer include:

- Providing the services required to transport an encoded digital bit stream from one station to the next over a point-to-point transmission medium.

FIGURE 23.3   FDDI symbol coding.

Code Group	Symbol	Interpretation
Data		
11110	0	hex 0
01001	1	hex 1
10100	2	hex 2
10101	3	hex 3
01010	4	hex 4
01011	5	hex 5
01110	6	hex 6
01111	7	hex 7
10010	8	hex 8
10011	9	hex 9
10110	A	hex A
10111	B	hex B
11010	C	hex C
11011	D	hex D
11100	E	hex E
11101	F	hex F
Control		
00000	Q	Quiet
11111	I	Idle
00100	H	Halt
11000	J	Starting Delimiter (1st symbol)
10001	K	Starting Delimiter (2nd symbol)
01101	T	Ending Delimiter
00111	R	Reset
11001	S	Set

- Defining the *Medium Interface Connector* (MIC) and the keying of various types of MIC receptacles for different types of MIC connections. The MIC is a fully specified concrete interface described in the FDDI standard. There are four types of MIC connectors defined: A, B, M, and S. The functions of the four types of connectors are discussed when we describe various types of FDDI stations.

- Specifying the characteristics of fiber-optic drivers and receivers, fiber-optic transmission media, connectors, power budgets, and other physical, hardware-related characteristics.

Another function performed by the PMD sublayer is the *Signal Detect* function, which determines when an actual signal is being received by a receiver. This function is particularly important in determining when there is an active PHY port at the other end of a transmission medium segment.

NETWORK ARCHITECT

With a metallic interface, the cable is either not connected or it's connected. With fiber, the unconnected fiber starts out dark. Then, as the fiber moves closer to the LED transmitter, the fiber gradually gets lighter. As the fiber approaches the transmitter, the signal starts to get through, but with a very high bit error rate at first. This process of connection could take maybe 100 milliseconds or so when a transmission medium segment is plugged into a station. That may seem fast, but 100 milliseconds at 100 megabits represents a lot of bits. Now given that stations are all in series, you don't want to put a physical link into the network that has an error rate of 10^{-3} or 10^{-2}, when everything else is running at an error rate of 10^{-10}. So because of that, FDDI uses a protocol to initialize a physical link. It runs a bit error rate test on a physical link before it is incorporated into the ring to make sure there are no bad physical links in the ring. A bad physical link in the ring, with a physical link that has a bit error rate of 10^{-5} or 10^{-6}, means you'll be losing a token every few seconds. This protocol is something that Digital was involved in developing.

FDDI Transmission Medium

The transmission medium consists of the portion of the physical communication channel to which two or more PMD sublayer entities are connected. Each transmission medium segment implements a full-duplex transmission path, typically using a fiber-optic medium. Each segment ordinarily implements two optical fibers, one for transmission in each direction. Although an implementation of FDDI typically uses a fiber-optic transmission medium, it is interesting to note that the DNA Phase V FDDI architectural specification does not require fiber optics to be used. Implementations of FDDI that interoperate with all layers above the PMD sublayer could be built using transmission media other than optical fibers.

Station Management

The station management (SMT) component is responsible for monitoring the operation of the station and for controlling the various management-oriented attributes of other station components. The ANSI FDDI standard contains detailed specifications for the SMT function, and the DNA Phase V FDDI specification is fully conformant with the ANSI FDDI specification. However, the DNA Phase V FDDI specification goes further than the ANSI SMT specification in many areas to provide enhanced network management functions. The SMT component implements the following functions:

- **Link Management.** Monitors and controls the link components in a station.

- **SMT Frame Based Management.** Monitors and controls functions associated with the transmission of SMT PDUs used by SMT components in communicating with each other over the network.

- **Ring Management.** Monitors and controls functions associated with ensuring the proper operation of the logical ring, such as identifying when a break in the logical ring has occurred.

- **SMT Connection Management.** Monitors and controls the operation of the various PHY Ports implemented in a station.

Station Types

As described earlier, a station is defined as a single instance of the SMT component and the components SMT controls. Different types of stations can be implemented that contain the other architectural components in various combinations. We will examine three types of stations that will be commonly implemented and show how these stations can be interconnected to create various types of network topologies. The three station types we describe here are the single-attachment station (SAS), the dual-attachment station (DAS), and the dual-attachment concentrator (DAC).

Single-Attachment Station

A *single-attachment station* (SAS) implements a single link component and a single PHY port. This type of station is attached to one end of a single full-duplex, point-to-point transmission medium segment. An architectural model of the single-attachment station is shown in Figure 23.4. A single-attachment station can be connected to another single-attachment station using a single transmission medium segment, thus forming a ring consisting of a single pair of stations. Such a configuration, shown in Figure 23.5, represents the simplest possible FDDI network. Such a configuration is not very useful since it does not allow for a third station to be connected.

A single-attachment station implements a single Medium Interface Connector (MIC) of type S (short for *slave*). As we will see after we examine the architectural model for a concentrator, a single-attachment station is typically connected, via a single transmission medium segment, to a concentrator implementing a MIC connector of type M (for *master*).

FIGURE 23.4   **FDDI single-attachment station (SAS).**

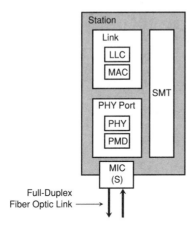

Dual-Attachment Station

A *dual-attachment station* (DAS) is designed to connect to two separate full-duplex transmission medium segments. A dual-attachment station can implement either one or two link components and contains exactly two PHY ports. An architectural model of the dual-attachment station is shown in Figure 23.6. A configuration switch component is used to form data paths between the two PHY ports and the links to control the flow of data through the station.

Dual Counter-Rotating Rings

Each of the PHY ports is associated with its own MIC. A dual-attach-ment station implements one MIC of type A and one MIC of type B. Figure 23.7 shows a simple FDDI network consisting of 4 dual attachment stations. The network is formed by connecting the A MIC of one station to the B MIC of the next station with a single transmission medium seg-

FIGURE 23.5   **Simplest FDDI network topology.**

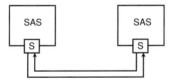

FIGURE 23.6 FDDI dual-attachment station (DAS).

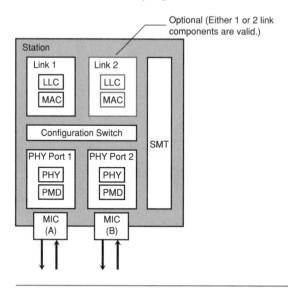

ment. When all the MICs are properly connected to the end of a transmission medium segment, a dual counter-rotating ring structure is formed. For a set of dual-attachment stations, each MIC type A must be connected to a MIC type B for a primary ring and a secondary ring to be formed. The type A and type B MICs are defined as follows:

- **MIC Type A.** A MIC of type A is defined to be the input of a physical link that forms part of the path for the primary ring.

- **MIC Type B.** A MIC of type B is defined to be the output for a physical link that forms part of the path for the primary ring.

FIGURE 23.7 Simple ring of dual-attachment stations.

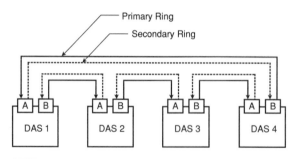

Dual-Attachment Concentrator

A *dual-attachment concentrator* (DAC) is a station that has three or more PHY ports, each associated with its own MIC. The concentrator implements one MIC of type A, one of type B, and at least one of type M. Typical concentrator implementations will contain from 4 to 16 MICs, although the ANSI standard and the DNA Phase V FDDI specification permit many more than that. An architectural model of the dual-attachment concentrator is shown in Figure 23.8. A dual-attachment concentrator can implement zero, one, or two link components. If a station performs a concentrator function only, it is likely to implement no link components, because the concentrator will not be the source or the final destination of any frames.

A dual-attachment concentrator is used to create a network topology called a *dual ring of trees*, in which tree structures branch off the dual counter-rotating ring. A simple concentrator network is shown in Figure 23.9. Notice that the type A and type B MICs are interconnected in exactly the same way as in the example in Figure 23.8, which consisted of four dual-attachment stations. Each of the type M MICs is connected via a single full-duplex, point-to-point physical link to a single attachment station implementing a type S MIC.

FIGURE 23.8   FDDI dual-attachment concentrator (DAC).

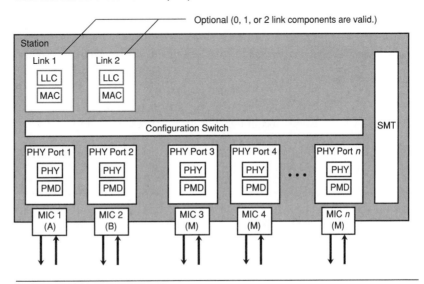

FIGURE 23.9   **A simple concentrator network showing token flow on the primary ring. Boldface numbers indicate when a MAC entity in each station receives the token. (This example assumes that each concentrator implements one link and, thus, one MAC entity.)**

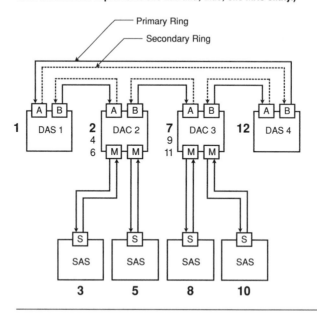

Token Path

Before any single-attachment stations are connected to the concentrators, the primary and secondary rings are identical to those shown in Figure 23.7. As each single-attachment station is attached to its concentrator, the SMT component in the concentrator sets the configuration switch appropriately to add that station to the logical ring. The numbers next to the stations in Figure 23.9 show the path the token takes as it travels from station to station around the primary ring. In this example, we are assuming that each concentrator implements a single link component and, thus, contains a single MAC entity.

Physical Link and Station Failures

The ANSI FDDI standard does not specify how the primary and secondary rings are to be used. This is left to the implementors. In the DNA Phase V FDDI implementation, the primary ring is used to carry data; the secondary ring may be idle and is used to recover from physical link and station failures.

Physical Link Failure

If a physical link failure occurs, stations perform procedures to detect the failure and set their configuration switches to use the secondary ring to bypass the failure. This is shown in Figure 23.10. The redundant physical links that implement the secondary ring are used to bypass the missing physical link, thus reconfiguring the primary ring. The numbers in the diagram show the sequence in which the token flows around the ring both before and after the failure.

Station Failure

The secondary ring can also be used to bypass a station that either fails or is disconnected from the ring. This is shown in Figure 23.11. Stations on either side of the physical link reconfigure using the secondary ring. Again, numbers show the sequence in which the token flows around the ring both before and after the failure.

Interconnecting FDDI and CSMA/CD LANs

Bridges can be used to interconnect individual FDDI networks with CSMA/CD networks to create an *extended LAN*. Bridges perform a

---

FIGURE 23.10   **Reconfiguration after physical link failure.**

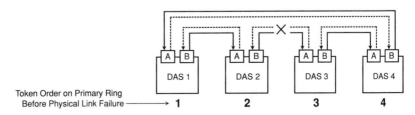

Token Order on Primary Ring
Before Physical Link Failure ⟶ 1   2   3   4

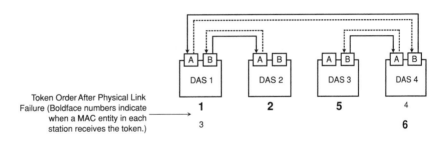

Token Order After Physical Link
Failure (Boldface numbers indicate
when a MAC entity in each
station receives the token.)

FIGURE 23.11   **Reconfiguration after station failure.**

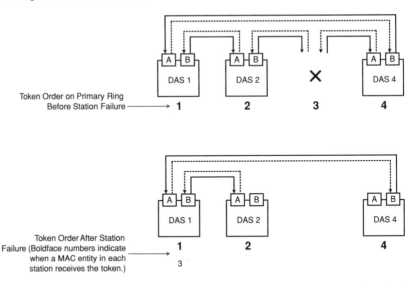

Data Link layer relay function and are used to extend the LAN without affecting the basic services it provides. Bridges and extended LANs are discussed in Chapter 24.

The remainder of this chapter describes the FDDI service definition and protocol specification and examines the format of the data units exchanged by FDDI MAC and PHY sublayer entities during local area network operation.

FDDI MAC Sublayer Service Definition

The ANSI FDDI specification for the MAC sublayer follows the ISO model and includes a service definition that describes the services the MAC sublayer provides to the LLC sublayer. The DNA Phase V FDDI architectural specification does not define this interface in terms of function and procedure calls as in the CSMA/CD architectural specification. It simply references the ANSI MAC standard.

The service definition is specified in terms of service primitives and service primitive parameters. The service definition describes an unconfirmed data transfer service and a token request service. The service primitives defining the MAC sublayer services are shown in Box 23.1. Figure 23.12 contains time-sequence diagrams showing the sequence in which the service primitives are issued.

FIGURE 23.12   Time-sequence diagrams for FDDI MAC sublayer service primitives.

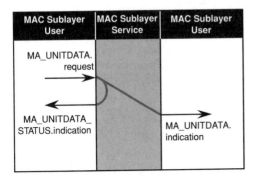

The MA_UNITDATA Data Transfer Service

The data transfer service uses three primitives. A single MA_UNIT-DATA.request primitive can include multiple sets of parameters, one for each MAC-SDU that is to be transmitted. Thus, a single service request can cause multiple MAC-SDUs to be sent. The MA_UNITDATA_STATUS.indication primitive is returned by the MAC sublayer to the LLC sublayer in the sending station to indicate the success or failure of an attempt to transmit a frame. It does not indicate whether the frame was successfully received by the destination station. As with the MAC sublayer service for the CSMA/CD type of LAN, the FDDI MAC sublayer data transfer service is an unconfirmed service in which data transfer is not guaranteed.

The MA_TOKEN Token Request Service

This is an optional service, not used in the DNA Phase V FDDI specification, that can be used by the LLC sublayer to request the capture of the next token. The ANSI FDDI standard states that it is to be used only in certain special cases when time-critical data must be transmitted. Its use can minimize the effects of ring latency and can reduce the waiting time for the next token but at the expense of reducing transmission capacity.

FDDI MAC Sublayer Protocol Specification

The FDDI MAC sublayer uses a timed-token ring access protocol that governs the way in which a MAC sublayer entity gains access to the ring to transmit data. The IEEE/ISO standards include the *token ring* form of local area network described by IEEE 802.5 and ISO 8802-5. However,

BOX 23.1

**MAC Sublayer
Service Primitives**

```
                    MA_UNITDATA.request    (
                                           FC_value(1),
                                           destination_address(1),
                                           M_SDU(1),
                                           requested_service_class(1),
                                           stream(1),

                                           FC_value(2),
                                           destination_address(2),
                                           M_SDU(2),
                                           requested_service_class(2),
                                           stream(2),
                                                   •
                                                   •
                                                   •
                                           FC_value(n),
                                           destination_address(n),
                                           M_SDU(n),
                                           requested_service_class(n),
                                           stream(n)
                                           (
                 MA_UNITDATA.indication    (
                                           FC_value,
                                           destination_address,
                                           source_address,
                                           M_SDU,
                                           reception_status,
                                           stream(n)
                                           (
        MA_UNITDATA_STATUS.indication    (
                                           number_of_SDUs,
                                           transmission_status,
                                           provided_service_class
                                           )
                      MA_TOKEN.request    (
                                           requested_Token_class
                                           )
```

the IEEE/ISO token ring access protocol is quite different from the timed-token ring access protocol used by FDDI.

NETWORK ARCHITECT

Some presentations that I have seen give the impression that FDDI is based on IEEE 802.5 Token Ring and has evolved from it. The fact that the word token *and the word* ring *appear in the description of FDDI is leading people to believe that FDDI has something to do with IBM. But this is not the case. The essence of this is that when the two competing LAN standards were Ethernet and 802.5 Token Ring, the world divided, and we had the Ethernet camp and the 802.5 Token Ring camp. What we have now is FDDI versus nothing. FDDI is the only 100-megabit-per-second LAN, and everybody wants to claim heritage. FDDI uses a dual timed-token ring access protocol that is not based on the IEEE 802.5 protocol. It is actually more closely related to the protocol defined in the IEEE 802.4 Token Bus standard than it is to the 802.5 protocol. FDDI uses a distributed algorithm instead of a centralized algorithm. FDDI's algorithm is more robust than the one used in 802.5. Another difference between FDDI and 802.5 Token Ring is that FDDI reclocks the signal on each physical link as opposed to having a single clock for the whole network. As a result it doesn't have problems with the accumulation of jitter in the clock that the 802.5 protocol has. This allows FDDI to scale up to a much larger number of nodes on the ring.*

The FDDI timed-token ring access control protocol passes a special data unit, called the *token*, around the logical ring from one link entity to the next. When the token arrives at a PHY port associated with a link component, the token is passed up to the MAC entity in that link component, and the MAC entity is allowed to transmit data frames. If the MAC entity has frames to send, it holds the token and uses its PHY port to transmit as many frames as desired onto the ring until a predefined time limit is reached. When the MAC entity either has no more frames to send or reaches the time limit, it transmits the token. When a frame circulates all the way around the ring and returns to the MAC entity originating it, that MAC entity is responsible for stripping the frame from the ring by not repeating it. As MAC entities repeat frames around the ring, they set status bits in the frames indicating whether errors have been detected, addresses recognized, or frames copied for processing.

Since the token is transmitted as soon as a MAC entity is finished transmitting frames, it is possible for a MAC entity to transmit new frames while frames transmitted by other MAC entities are still circulating around the ring. Thus, it is possible for there to be multiple frames, from multiple stations, on the network at any given time. The FDDI token passing procedure is illustrated in Figure 23.13.

FIGURE 23.13   **FDDI token-passing protocol.**

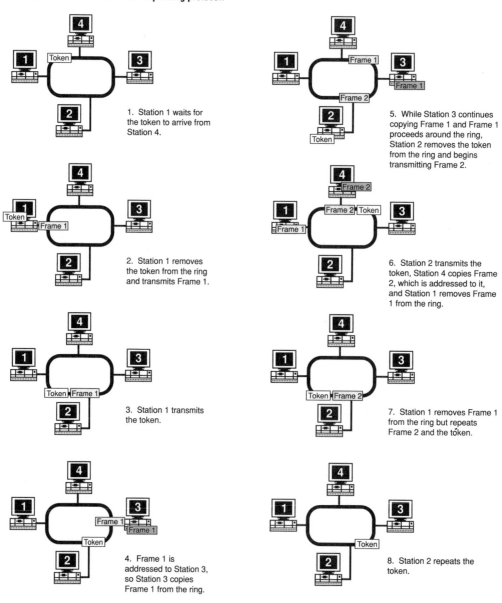

1. Station 1 waits for the token to arrive from Station 4.

2. Station 1 removes the token from the ring and transmits Frame 1.

3. Station 1 transmits the token.

4. Frame 1 is addressed to Station 3, so Station 3 copies Frame 1 from the ring.

5. While Station 3 continues copying Frame 1 and Frame 1 proceeds around the ring, Station 2 removes the token from the ring and begins transmitting Frame 2.

6. Station 2 transmits the token, Station 4 copies Frame 2, which is addressed to it, and Station 1 removes Frame 1 from the ring.

7. Station 1 removes Frame 1 from the ring but repeats Frame 2 and the token.

8. Station 2 repeats the token.

Ring Monitoring Functions

All stations on the ring participate in distributed algorithms that monitor the operation of the ring to check for invalid conditions that require the ring to be reinitialized. An example of an invalid condition is a ring that currently has no token circulating. To detect the absence of a circulating token, each station maintains a *token rotation timer* (TRT), which it resets each time it receives the token. If the timer expires twice before the station next receives the token, the station assumes the token has been lost and begins the ring initialization procedure. Other types of incorrect activities can also cause a station to begin the station initialization procedure. A station begins the ring-initialization process by performing a claim token procedure.

Claim Token Procedure

In performing the *claim token* procedure, a station bids for the right to initialize the ring. The station begins the claim token procedure by issuing a continuous stream of control frames called *Claim frames*. Each Claim frame contains a suggested *Target Token Rotation Time* (TTRT) value. If a station sending Claim frames receives a Claim frame from another station, it compares TTRT values. If its TTRT value is lower, it keeps transmitting Claim frames. If the TTRT value in a claim frame a station receives is lower than its own TTRT value, it passes on the received Claim frame instead of its own. If the values are the same, the MAC addresses are used to determine which station takes precedence. Eventually, the Claim frame with the lowest TTRT value will be passed on by other stations and will return to the station that sent it. At this point the sending station recognizes itself as the winner in the claim token procedure. That station has won the right to initialize the ring and continues by performing the ring initialization procedure. As a result of the claim token procedure, all stations now have the TTRT value to be used in subsequent ring operation because all stations have seen the TTRT value in the Claim frame sent by the winning station.

The claim token procedure sounds complex and time consuming, but it takes only a millisecond or two to complete, even on a large ring.

Ring Initialization

The station winning the claim token procedure sets its own token rotation timer (TRT) to the negotiated TTRT and transmits a token onto the ring. Each station that receives the token then sets its own TTRT to the negotiated value and transmits the token. No frames are transmitted until the token has passed once around the ring. The purpose of the initial token rotation is to align TTRT values and TRT times in all stations on the ring.

Beacon Process

When a serious failure occurs, such as a break in the ring, stations use a *beacon process* to locate the failure. The SMT component in a station can also cause the station to initiate the beacon process. When a station that has been sending Claim frames recognizes that a defined time period has elapsed without the claim token process being resolved, it begins the beacon process by transmitting a continuous stream of Beacon frames. If a station receives a Beacon frame from another station, it stops sending its Beacon frames and passes on the Beacon frames it has received. Eventually, Beacon frames from the station immediately following the break will be propagated through the network. Some process external to the MAC entity must then be invoked to diagnose the problem and to reconfigure the ring to bypass the failure. If during the beacon process a station receives its own Beacon frames, it assumes the ring has been restored and initiates the claim token procedure.

Optional FDDI MAC Protocol Features

The ANSI FDDI standard specifies optional mechanisms that implement a capacity allocation scheme. This scheme is designed to support a mixture of stream and burst transmissions and transmissions involving dialogs between pairs of stations. Two types of frames are defined by the ANSI FDDI standard: *asynchronous* frames and *synchronous* frames.[*] In normal FDDI protocol operation, only asynchronous frames are transmitted. The use of synchronous frames is optional, and an FDDI implementation need not support them. The DNA Phase V FDDI specification currently supports only asynchronous frames and does not include the optional synchronous frame service.

ANSI FDDI also provides an optional mechanism for implementing *multiframe dialogs* between pairs of stations. When a station needs to enter into a dialog with another station, it can do so using its asynchronous transmission capacity. After the station transmits the first frame in the dialog, it transmits a *restricted token*. Only the station re-

---

[*] Note that the terms *asynchronous* and *synchronous* have meanings here very different from those in Chapter 5.

ceiving the first frame is allowed to use the restricted token for transmitting asynchronous frames. The DNA Phase V implementation of FDDI does not include support for the restricted token for multiframe dialogs.

MAC Frame and Packet Format

In using the data transfer service provided by the MAC sublayer, an LLC entity in the source station passes a *medium-access-control-service-data-unit* (MAC-SDU) to the MAC sublayer entity in that station. The MAC sublayer entity adds PCI to the MAC-SDU in the form of a header and a trailer to create a *medium-access-control-protocol-data-unit* (MAC-PDU)—also called a MAC frame—and passes it to the Physical layer. The Physical layer attaches additional PCI to the MAC frame to create a physical-protocol-data-unit (PPDU). The DNA Phase V FDDI specification calls a PPDU a *packet*.* The Physical layer then transmits the packet over the transmission medium. When a station receives a packet, the Physical layer entity in the receiving station extracts the MAC frame from the packet and passes it up to the MAC sublayer entity. The MAC sublayer then extracts the LLC-PDU from the MAC frame and passes it up to the LLC sublayer. This process is summarized in Figure 23.14.

The general formats of a packet and a MAC frame are shown in Figure 23.15. The MAC frame is contained within a Physical layer packet and consists of a frame control field, destination and source address fields, a data field, and a frame check sequence field. The Physical layer creates a packet by adding a preamble, starting delimiter, ending delimiter, and frame status field to the MAC frame. The following are descriptions of the fields that make up a MAC frame and a Physical layer packet:

- **Preamble.** The *preamble* is used to synchronize each station's clock.

- **Starting Delimiter.** The *starting delimiter* is a unique signal pattern that identifies the beginning of a frame.

- **Frame Control.** The *frame control* field identifies the frame's type. It has the bit format CLFFZZZZ, where C identifies this as a synchronous or asynchronous frame, L specifies whether 16 or 48 bit addresses are used, FF indicates whether this is an LLC or a MAC frame, and ZZZZ provides control information for MAC frames. The DNA Phase V FDDI specification allows for only asynchronous frames and 48-bit addresses.

---

* As mentioned in Chapter 22, this is an unfortunate choice of terminology since the term *packet* is also often used in networking literature to refer to the NPDUs that are exchanged by Network layer entities. The Physical layer packet is not the same as the Network layer packet.

FIGURE 23.14   Providing the Medium Access Control (MAC) sublayer data transfer service.

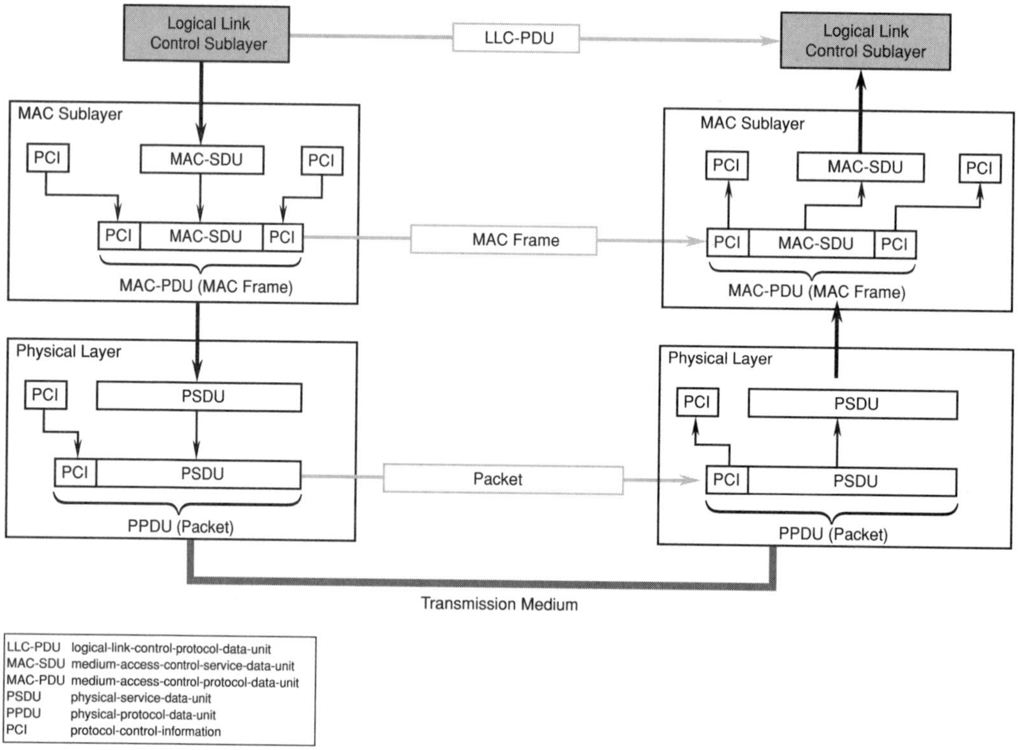

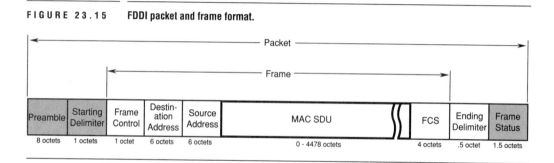

LLC-PDU	logical-link-control-protocol-data-unit
MAC-SDU	medium-access-control-service-data-unit
MAC-PDU	medium-access-control-protocol-data-unit
PSDU	physical-service-data-unit
PPDU	physical-protocol-data-unit
PCI	protocol-control-information

- **Destination and Source Addresses.** The DNA Phase V FDDI specification requires the use of 48-bit addresses. The *destination address* can be an individual address, a group address, or a broadcast address. The *source address* always identifies an individual station.

FIGURE 23.15   FDDI packet and frame format.

- **Data Field.** The *data field* can contain data passed from the LLC layer or control information supplied by the MAC layer. The maximum length of the data field is 4478 octets.

- **Frame Check Sequence.** The *frame check sequence* contains a 32-bit cyclic redundancy check value. The value is calculated based on the contents of the frame control field, destination address, source address, and information field. The receiving station performs the same calculation. If the received value does not match the calculated value, the frame is considered to be in error.

- **Ending Delimiter.** The *ending delimiter* identifies the end of the frame.

- **Frame Status Field.** The *frame status field* contains information about the status of a frame, including whether an error was detected, the address recognized, and the frame copied.

Frame Types

The frame control field contains bits that indicate a frame's type. The DNA Phase V FDDI specification defines seven types of frames:

- **Void Frame.** Used by DNA Phase V enhancements to the ANSI MAC protocol, such as the frame stripping algorithm and ring purging algorithm discussed later.

- **Token.** Indicates the data unit is a token and not a data frame.

- **SMT Frame.** Frames sent by station management components to control their operation.

- **MAC Frame.** Frames used to control the operation of the MAC protocol, including the Claim and Beacon frames.

- **LLC Frames.** Frames containing data passed down from the LLC sublayer.

- **Implementor Frame.** Frames reserved for the implementor. DNA Phase V FDDI does not define any Implementor frames.

- **Reserved.** Reserved frames are intended for use by future versions of the standard.

Token Frame Format

A special frame format, illustrated in Figure 23.16, is used for the token, consisting only of a preamble, starting delimiter, frame control field, and ending delimiter.

FIGURE 23.16   **FDDI token format.**

Mapped Ethernet Frames

As discussed in Chapter 22, on a CSMA/CD LAN, frames conforming to the IEEE/ISO CSMA/CD format and frames conforming to the Ethernet format can coexist on the same LAN. The LLC sublayer multiplexes and demultiplexes the two frame types by using the length/type field that is part of the CSMA/CD MAC frame header. The FDDI MAC frame does not contain a length/type field. To allow an extended LAN to be constructed of both CSMA/CD and FDDI local area networks, the DNA Phase V FDDI specification includes support for a mapped Ethernet frame type. On an FDDI LAN, an Ethernet frame is contained within an IEEE/ISO SNAP PDU, which is then encapsulated within an FDDI MAC frame. The DNA Phase V FDDI mapped Ethernet service allows an Ethernet application to use the services of an FDDI LAN in communicating with another Ethernet application across an extended LAN.

The following sections describe two enhancements to the FDDI standard that the DNA Phase V version of FDDI implements that deal with removing frames from the ring.

Frame Stripping   The ANSI FDDI standard specifies a single method for removing frames from the ring, a process called *frame stripping*. As described above, a MAC entity that transmits a frame onto the ring has the responsibility of removing it when the frame has circulated all the way around the ring and returns to the originating MAC entity. A MAC entity does this by recognizing the source address in a frame it receives as being equal to its own MAC address. This method for stripping frames from the ring is adequate when a transmitting MAC entity transmits only frames having its own MAC address as the source address. However, in an extended LAN that implements bridges, a MAC entity in a bridge may transmit frames onto a ring that have originated in a station on some other local area network. In such a case, a MAC entity in a bridge may transmit frames onto the ring with source addresses different from the bridge's own MAC address. A MAC entity in a bridge must implement an additional frame stripping algorithm, allowing it to strip frames from the ring that have a source address different from the MAC entity's own MAC address.

Frame Content Independent Stripping

The DNA Phase V FDDI specification defines a *Frame Content Independent Stripping* (FCIS) algorithm that FDDI MAC entities use to remove frames from the ring. To implement this algorithm, each MAC entity maintains a local count of the frames it has transmitted onto the ring but has not yet stripped since the last time it received the token. The station also transmits a special delimiter frame, called a *Void* frame, after it finishes transmitting a set of frames onto the ring. Stations that do not implement the FCIS algorithm do not copy Void frames but simply repeat them. The MAC entity transmitting the Void frame sets the Void frame's source address field equal to the MAC entity's own MAC address. The MAC entity then strips from the ring any frame it receives— even if the frame's source address field value is not equal to its own MAC address—and reduces its transmitted frame count by one for each error-free frame it strips. The MAC entity continues stripping the frames it receives until one of three termination conditions occurs:

- The station's transmitted frame count reaches 0.
- It receives a token.
- It receives its own error-free Void frame, a Claim frame, or a Beacon frame.

NETWORK ARCHITECT

The frame stripping algorithm we designed works because of an important invariant on a properly operating FDDI token ring: the frames a station receives first after it has transmitted the token will always be the frames that it transmitted. Frames generated by stations downstream on the ring must always follow the frames the station itself transmitted onto the ring. The three termination conditions ensure stable operation of the algorithm. They guarantee that there is a low probability of overstripping (stripping too many frames from the ring) and a very low probability of understripping (not stripping enough frames) even when one or more frames are affected by errors as they circulate around the ring.

Ring Purging

One of the properties of a local area network that uses a ring topology and a token passing access protocol is that it is possible for a frame to circulate indefinitely. A frame that is not removed after its first traversal of the ring is called a *no-owner frame*. The FDDI standard does not specify a guaranteed method of removing no-owner frames.

The DNA Phase V version of FDDI includes a simple, robust algorithm, called the *ring purger algorithm*, that reliably removes no-owner frames from the ring. The ring purger algorithms consist of two parts:

- **Election Algorithm.** An election algorithm is used to choose, in a distributed manner, one of the stations on the ring to be the *ring purger*. The primary purpose of the ring purger election algorithm is to ensure that there is one and only one ring purger operating in the ring. It recovers from ring initializations and from failure of the station acting as the ring purger.

- **Purging Algorithm.** The station designated as the ring purger runs the purging algorithm to remove no-owner frames and frame fragments from the ring.

Election Algorithm

Each time the ring is initialized, a station becomes the ring purger if it is the winner of the claim token procedure or if it was the ring purger prior to ring initialization. A ring purger periodically announces its presence on the ring by transmitting a Purger Hello frame.

If there is no ring purger after ring initialization or at any time during the operation of the ring, a new ring purger is elected using a broadcast election protocol. The election algorithm is designed to elect one and only one station to be the ring purger. The overhead of the purger election algorithm is negligible, with the ring purger periodically (approximately every 10 seconds) sending a short frame to the other stations on the ring.

Purging Algorithm

In running the purging algorithm, the station designated as the ring purger waits for a token. Once that station captures a token, if it has frames to transmit, it transmits them. After the ring purger's transmissions are completed, it transmits two Void frames. The Void frames mark the end of transmission of the ring purger's frames.

When the ring is operating normally, the ring purger should receive only the frames it sent, followed by its own Void frames. The ring purger strips from the ring all frames and frame fragments that it receives until it receives its Void frames. It then strips the two Void frames and ceases stripping frames from the ring. If there are no owner frames circulating on the ring, the ring purger will strip these from the ring while stripping the frames that precede its Void frames. The ring purger does not begin another purging operation until it receives the token. The ring purger also stops the purging algorithm if it receives a Beacon frame or a Claim frame.

With a ring purger active on the ring, no frame will circulate as a no-owner frame for more than one traversal around the ring. These frames will therefore be received at most only twice by any destination station.

Conclusion

The Fiber Distributed Data Interface standard defines a 100-Mbps local area network using a timed-token ring access control protocol. FDDI LANs will be extremely important in the 1990s to provide high-bandwidth connections between individual lower-performance local area networks and as a high-speed broadcast data link to serve the needs of host computers and high-performance workstations. The final chapter in this book describes bridges that can be used to interconnect LANs of various types to create extended LANs.

CHAPTER 24

Bridge and Extended
LAN Architecture

DNA Phase V provides facilities that allow collections of local area networks to be combined using devices called *bridges* to form an *extended LAN*. A bridge is a device whose main functions operate in the Logical Link Control (LLC) sublayer. Each bridge in an extended LAN is attached to two or more local area networks and acts as a link between them. The bridge architecture is defined in the DNA Phase V *Bridge and Extended LAN Architecture* specification. This architecture is based on the IEEE 802.1d, *MAC Bridges*, standard, which is also described in ISO 10038.

A bridge is only one type of device that can be used to interconnect network segments to form a complete DECnet Phase V network. Other types of devices, some of which have already been described in other chapters, are repeaters, routers, gateways, and portals. Box 24.1 describes the five types of devices that can be used to interconnect networks and network segments.

Extended LANs

A *bridge* is a device that is attached to two or more local area networks. The extended LAN created by interconnecting local area networks using bridges does not have to be made up of LANs of the same type. A bridge can be designed to connect LANs using different protocols in the Physical layer and in the Medium Access Control sublayer, as long as they use a common protocol in the Logical Link Control sublayer. For example, an extended LAN can be constructed of CSMA/CD LANs connected to an FDDI LAN. Figure 24.1 shows how an FDDI LAN can be used as a high-speed backbone to interconnect a number of CSMA/CD LANs using bridges.

A bridge can also be designed to connect a local area network to a wide area network data link instead of to another LAN. For example, two local area networks could be connected via bridges to a full-duplex,

FIGURE 24.1   Bridges connecting two CSMA/CD LANs and an FDDI LAN.

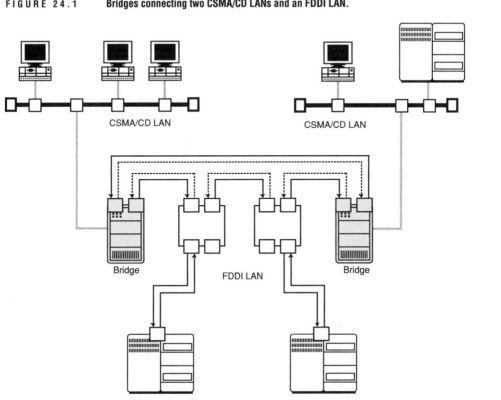

point-to-point telecommunications facility, as shown in Figure 24.2 (page 522). When two bridges are connected using such a telecommunications facility, the distance limitation inherent in the LAN architecture can be overcome, and the extended LAN can span any desired distance. A station in a network at one end of the full-duplex communication facility can communicate with a station at the other end of the link as if they were attached to the same local area network.

Bridge Operation   The DNA Phase V bridge and extended LAN architecture describes a form of bridge often called a *transparent* bridge, because ordinary stations on the LAN communicate with one another in an identical manner whether or not one or more bridges lie in the path between them. The fact that the local area network consists of an extended LAN having bridges is hidden from ordinary stations.

BOX 24.1

Network
Interconnection
Devices

- **Repeaters.** The simplest facility used for network interconnection is the repeater. Repeaters are used in bus-structured local area networks to connect individual cable segments to form a larger local area network. In ring-structured local area networks, every station performs the function of a repeater. In a local area network there is generally a limit on the length of any single cable segment. This limit is based on the physical medium and the transmission technique used. A repeater operates in the Physical layer and its use is hidden from any of the layers above. The function of a repeater is to receive a signal from one cable segment and to retransmit it over one or more other cable segments, thus regenerating the signal at its original strength. The number of repeaters that can be used in tandem on a bus-structured local area network is generally limited by the LAN architecture. Stations connected by repeaters can use different Physical layer procedures but must share a common protocol in the medium access control sublayer.

- **Bridges.** A bridge is used to join together two separate local area networks to create an extended LAN. It operates in the Logical Link Control sublayer. A bridge can be designed to join networks using different protocols in the Physical layer and in the Medium Access Control sublayer, as long as they use a common protocol in the Logical Link Control sublayer.

- **Routers.** Routers provide the ability to route packets from one end node to another where there may be multiple paths between them. The routers participate in a distributed algorithm to decide on the optimal path each packet should travel from the source end node to the destination end node. The router function operates in the Network layer. When routers are used to interconnect local area networks, all the stations on the LANs being interconnected must ordinarily use the same Network layer protocols. However, it is possible to construct multiple-protocol routers that can route traffic conforming to two different architectures, such as DNA Phase V and TCP/IP. Stations connected using routers can use different protocols operating in the Physical and Data Link layers but must share common protocols in the Network layer and above.

- **Gateways.** A gateway can be used when an application running on a node in a DECnet Phase V network must be able to communicate with an application running in a node conforming to a different network architecture. For example, the X.25 gateway facility allows a DECnet Phase V node to communicate over a PSDN with a node conforming to CCITT Recommendation X.25. (See Chapter 18.)

BOX 24.1

continued

Gateways can also be used to allow a DECnet Phase V node to communicate with nodes conforming to the TCP/IP architecture or to IBM's Systems Network Architecture (SNA). The function of a gateway is to convert the protocols of one network architecture to the protocols of the other network architecture. A gateway replaces the control information from one network with control information required to perform comparable functions in the other network. Stations connected using gateways can run different protocols in any of the layers in the protocol stack.

- **Portals.** A portal provides a method for allowing nodes conforming to some other network architecture to use a DECnet Phase V network for communication. Unlike a gateway, a portal does not perform protocol conversion. Instead, a portal *encapsulates* the foreign protocol messages within DNA Phase V protocol messages for transmission through the DECnet Phase V network. An example of such a device includes Digital's Internet Portal. The Internet protocol allows a node conforming to the TCP/IP architecture to use a DECnet Phase V network for communication with another node that also conforms to the TCP/IP architecture. The TCP/IP node at one end of the DECnet Phase V network generates protocol messages conforming to the TCP/IP architecture. The portal encapsulates these messages within DECnet Phase V packets and then forwards these packets through the network to the portal at the opposite end. The portal there removes the original TCP/IP messages from the DECnet Phase V packets and hands them to the destination TCP/IP node. A pair of portals is sometimes said to implement a facility called a *tunnel*, with each portal providing an opening into a tunnel through a network conforming to a foreign network architecture.

A bridge performs three basic functions:

- frame forwarding
- learning the addresses of stations on the LANs to which it is attached
- converting an arbitrary extended LAN physical topology to a spanning tree

Frame Forwarding

A bridge receives all frames on each LAN to which it is attached. Each bridge maintains a filtering database in which it maintains the MAC addresses of all the stations on those LANs and identifies which physical

Bridges connecting two LANs using a full-duplex, point-to-point data link.

port in the bridge can be used to communicate with each station. The bridge then takes one of the following actions for each frame it receives:

- When a station receives a frame having a multicast destination address, it forwards the frame over all its physical ports except the one from which it received the frame.

- When a bridge receives a frame having an individual MAC station address, it looks up the destination MAC address in its filtering database. If it finds the address and determines that it can reach the destination station using the same physical port as the one through which it received the frame, the bridge discards that frame.

- If the bridge determines the destination station is reached using a different physical port than the one through which it was received, it forwards the frame using the appropriate physical port.

- If the bridge does not find the address in its filtering database, it forwards the frame over all its physical ports except the one from which it received the frame.

In this manner, a bridge forwards traffic for unknown destinations and multicast traffic over the entire spanning tree. This guarantees that it will be seen by the destination station wherever that station may be, if the destination station is in the extended LAN. However, if the bridge knows the location of the destination station, it avoids unnecessarily forwarding traffic over those local area networks that do not contain the destination station.

Learning Addresses

When a bridge first comes up, its filtering database is empty. A bridge builds up its filtering database by examining the source MAC address fields in all the frames it receives. If a bridge receives a frame having a MAC address not currently in its filtering database, it adds the address to its filtering database along with an indication of which physical port was used to receive the frame. The bridge then knows which physical port to use to forward traffic when it next receives a frame having that destination MAC address. When traffic arrives from the same port as a known destination station, the bridge does not have to forward that traffic.

If the bridge receives a frame from a station already in the database, it updates the database entry for that station. This handles the situation where a station is moved from one local area network to another. Entries are maintained in the filtering database only for a predetermined period of time. If no new frames are received from a particular station, the entry for that station is eventually removed from the filtering database. This handles the situation where a station is powered down for a long period of time or is removed from the network.

Creating a Spanning Tree

Individual local area networks can be connected in any desired way using bridges. For example, networks can be physically interconnected, if desired, in an arbitrary mesh topology such that there is more than one path between any two stations. However, during the operation of the extended LAN, the bridges ensure that there is no more than one *active* path used to carry traffic between any two stations. The bridges convert the physical topology of the extended LAN into a *logical* topology that always consists of a *spanning tree*. A spanning tree is a graph structure that includes all the bridges and stations on the extended LAN but in which there is never more than one active path connecting any two stations.

To create the spanning tree, bridges run a distributed algorithm in which each bridge periodically multicasts Hello messages called *bridge-protocol-data-units* (BPDUs) to all other bridges on the extended LAN. The BPDUs each bridge receives are used by that bridge to calculate the spanning tree. Redundant links not part of the spanning tree are treated as spares and are used only if some other link fails. After a link failure, the BPDUs the bridges periodically transmit allow them to quickly calculate a new spanning tree, possibly using redundant links.

Source Routing

IEEE Project 802 is currently in the process of defining an optional enhancement to the 802.1d bridge specification called *source routing*. With source routing, each station on the extended LAN is expected to know the route over which to send each frame it transmits. If a station does not know the route, or if a previously known route is no longer active, the station sends out *route discovery* frames. Each bridge along the eventual path to the destination station adds routing information to the route discovery frame. The destination station then sends a response back to the source station indicating the route that should be used to reach that destination station. A source routing technique is often used with IEEE/ISO Token Ring LANs.

A major disadvantage of the source routing technique is that the operation of bridges is not hidden from ordinary stations on the LAN. Individual stations must participate in the routing of traffic through the extended LAN. The DNA Phase V bridge and extended LAN architecture does not currently specify the use of source routing.

Extended LANs versus Routers

At first glance, it appears that an extended LAN, using bridges and point-to-point telecommunications facilities to connect multiple LANs, provides a function similar to that of a system of interconnected routers. However, bridges and routers each have different roles to play in the design of a geographically dispersed network.

Bridges must be used, instead of routers, to interconnect LANs when traffic from protocols that expects to flow over a single local area network must flow between stations on two different LANs. An example of such a protocol is Digital's Local Area Transport (LAT) protocol. Routers, on the other hand, can make better use of the topology, since the logical topology of the network created using routers is not confined to a single spanning tree. Routers also separate the individual local area networks they connect in the sense that the multicast traffic that is sent over each LAN can be confined to those LANs. Multicast traffic is not relayed from one local area network to another by routers. Routers also provide enhanced network management capabilities. The most efficient design for any large DECnet Phase V network will usually involve a combination of strategically placed repeaters, bridges, routers, gateways, and portals.

Conclusion	This concludes this book on Phase V of the Digital Network Architecture. Following this chapter are two appendices. Appendix A lists the ISO standards that DNA incorporates, and Appendix B is a list of the architectural specifications that make up DNA Phase V.

APPENDIX A

ISO Standards for the OSI Model

Wide Area Networking Data Link Layer Standards

ISO 8886, *Data Link Service Definition*

ISO 3309, *HDLC Frame Structure*

ISO 4335, *HDLC Control Elements of Procedures*

ISO 7776, *HDLC Procedures—X.25 LAPB DTE*

ISO 7809, *HDLC Procedures—Consolidation of Classes of Procedures*

ISO 8885, *HDLC XID Frames*

Local Area Network Data Link Layer Standards

ISO 8802-2, *LAN Logical Link Control*

ISO 8802-3, *LAN CSMA/CD*

ISO 8802-4, *LAN Token Bus*

ISO 8802-5, *LAN Token Ring*

ISO 9314-1, *Fiber Distributed Data Interface (FDDI)—Part 1: Physical Layer Protocol (PHY)*

ISO 9314-2, *Fiber Distributed Data Interface (FDDI)—Part 2: Media Access Control (MAC)*

ISO 9314-3, *Fiber Distributed Data Interface (FDDI)—Part 3: Physical Layer Medium Dependent (PMD)*

ISO 10038, *LAN MAC Sublayer Interconnection (MAC bridging)*

Network Layer Standards

ISO 8208, *X.25 Packet Level Protocol*

ISO 8348, *Network Service Definition*

ISO 8473, *Protocol for Providing the Connectionless-Mode Network Service and Provision of the Underlying Service*

ISO 8648, *Internal Organization of the Network Layer*

ISO 8878, *Use of X.25 to Provide the OSI Connection-Mode Network Service*

ISO 8880-1, *Protocol Combinations to Provide and Support the OSI Network Service—General Principles*

ISO 8880-2, *Protocol Combinations to Provide and Support the OSI Network Service—Provision and Support of the Connection-Mode Network Service*

ISO 8880-3, *Protocol Combinations to Provide and Support the OSI Network Service—Provision and Support of the Connectionless-Mode Network Service*

ISO 8881, *Use of X.25 over Local Area Networks to Provide the OSI Connection-Mode Network Service*

ISO 9542,   *End System to Intermediate*
               System Routing Exchange
               Protocol for Use with the
               Protocol for Defining the
               Connectionless-Mode Network
               Service

ISO 10589,   *Intermediate System to*
               Intermediate System Intra-
               Domain Routing Exchange
               Protocol for Use in Conjunction
               with the Protocol for Providing
               the Connectionless-mode
               Network Service (ISO 8473)

TR 9575,   *OSI Routing Framework*

TR 9577,   *Protocol Identification in the*
               Network Layer

Transport Layer Standards

ISO 8072,   *Transport Service Definition*

ISO 8073,   *Connection Oriented Transport*
               Protocol Specification

ISO 8602,   *Protocol for Providing the*
               Connectionless-Mode Transport
               Service

Session Layer Standards

ISO 8326,   *Session Service Definition*

ISO 8327,   *Session Protocol Specification*

Presentation Layer Standards

ISO 8822,   *Presentation Service Definition*

ISO 8823,   *Presentation Protocol*
               Specification

ISO 8824,   *Specification of Abstract Syntax*
               Notation One (ASN.1)

ISO 8825,   *Specification of Basic Encoding*
               Rules for ASN.1

Application Layer Standards

ISO 8571,   *File Transfer, Access, and*
               Management (FTAM)

ISO 8649,   *Service Definition—Association*
               Control Service Element (ACSE)

ISO 8650,   *Protocol Specification—*
               Association Control Service
               Element (ACSE)

ISO 9040,   *Virtual Terminal Service: Basic*
               Class

ISO 9545,   *Application Layer Structure*

APPENDIX B

DNA *Phase V*
Architectural Specifications

Glossary

10BASE2 An IEEE/ISO CSMA/CD transmission medium specification that uses baseband signaling over 50-ohm coaxial cable, approximately 5 mm thick. This form of transmission medium is often called *ThinWire cable* or *thinnet cable*. A 10BASE2 cable segment can be up to 185 meters in length.

10BASE5 An IEEE/ISO CSMA/CD transmission medium specification based on the original *Ethernet Specification*. 10BASE5 specifies baseband transmission over the original, thick (10 mm) form of 50-ohm Ethernet coaxial cable. This type of cable is often referred to as thick Ethernet cable. A 10BASE5 cable segment can be up to 500 meters in length.

10BASE-T An IEEE/ISO CSMA/CD transmission medium specification that specifies baseband signaling over unshielded twisted-pair telephone wiring. The specification is designed for a typical distance of up to about 100 meters of 24 AWG twisted-pair cable.

10BROAD36 An IEEE/ISO CSMA/CD transmission medium specification that specifies broadband signaling over the type of coaxial cable used in cable television. 10BROAD36 cable segments can be up to 1800 meters in length for a round-trip distance of up to 3600 meters using a dual cable configuration.

abstract interface A description of the semantics of a set of services that an entity in a func-tional layer of the OSI model provides to a user of that layer's services. An abstract interface does not specify implementation details, nor does it describe the syntax that must be used to implement the interface.

abstract syntax Definition, using some form of formal notation, of the information content of a set of data types. An abstract syntax specifies nothing about how values of those data types are represented in a computer or encoded for transmission.

abstract syntax notation (ASN) A notation used to define abstract syntaxes. See *abstract syntax* and *Abstract Syntax Notation One*.

Abstract Syntax Notation One (ASN.1) International standard notation, defined in ISO 8824, widely used in the OSI environment to define abstract syntaxes. See *abstract syntax*.

Accredited Standards Committee (ASC) An organiza-tion, accredited by ANSI, that develops stan-dards in the United States.

address resolution component of DNA Session Control The component that accesses the naming service clerk to determine, given the name of an object (possibly residing in a remote node), all the various sets of communication protocols and associated addressing infor-mation that can be used to support commu-nication between the local object and the remote object.

address selection component of DNA Session Control
The component that takes the set of towers that could support communication—as computed by the address resolution component—orders them in some manner, and tries each in turn until either a connection is successfully established or it becomes clear that further attempts would be futile.

addressing authority An organization responsible for allocating the initial octets of NSAP addresses such that the network entity title an organization assigns to each end node and router in the administrative domains it creates is globally unique.

adjacency The combination of a circuit and a node attached to that circuit.

adjacent nodes Network nodes that are reachable by a single hop over a subnetwork to which a given node is attached.

adjacent systems See *adjacent nodes*.

administrative domain An individual DECnet Phase V network—consisting of a collection of end nodes, routers, and data links—operated by a single organization. An administrative domain is not an architecturally defined entity; thus, the boundaries of an administrative domain are determined by network management policy.

advertisement A protocol message that makes the presence of a service known to all the nodes on a broadcast form of data link.

AM Amendment.

Amendment (AM) A document, published by ISO, that makes an accepted modification to an international standard. A modification to an international standard begins as a *Committee Draft Amendment* (CDAM), progresses to a *Draft Amendment* (DAM), and finally becomes an *Amendment* when it is accepted by ISO as an official part of an international standard.

American National Standards Institute (ANSI) The standards organization in the United States that serves as the U.S. member organization in the International Organization for Standardization (ISO). ANSI is a nonprofit organization that writes the rules for standards bodies to follow and publishes standards produced under its rules of consensus. ANSI accredits standards committees to write standards in areas of their expertise.

ANSI American National Standards Institute.

APDU application-protocol-data-unit.

API Application programming interface and application-process-invocation.

application-association A logical binding between two application-entity-invocations, one of which is called the *initiator* and the other the *responder*.

application-context Definition of a common set of rules shared between a pair of communicating application-entity-invocations, each including a set of ASEs (possibly only ACSE) and an association between them. An application-context defines a particular set of communication capabilities for two communicating application-entity-invocations. Each application-association has only one application-context.

application-entity The part of an application-process that provides resources for OSI communication and describes a set of Application layer capabilities used for a specific purpose.

application-entity-invocation A particular use of the resources defined by an application-entity to perform a particular OSI communication activity.

application-entity-title A unique identifier, unambiguous in the OSI environment, that is assigned to an application-entity.

Application layer The functional layer that provides a means for application processes to access the system interconnection facilities in order to exchange information. The Application layer provides services used to establish and terminate associations between application processes and to monitor and manage the processes being interconnected and the various resources they employ.

application-process A set of resources, including processing resources, within an open system that can be used to perform information processing activities.

application-process-invocation A particular use of the resources defined by an application-process to perform a particular information processing activity.

application-process-title A unique identifier, unambiguous in the OSI environment, assigned to an application-process.

application programming interface (API) A form of concrete interface that defines how an application program invokes a set of services.

application-protocol-data-unit (APDU) The protocol-data-unit exchanged between peer Application layer entities.

application-service-element (ASE) An element within an application-entity that provides a set of OSI communication functions for a particular purpose.

architecture The term used in the information technology industry to refer to an overall scheme or plan that may be evolving together with the details needed to guide implementors in creating products that will interoperate with other implementations of the architecture.

area The largest subdivision of a network defined by the DNA Phase V architecture. Each node (end node or router) resides in exactly one area. Routing in a multiple-area routing domain is classified as either *level 1 routing* or *level 2 routing*.

ASC Accredited Standards Committee.

ASE application-service-element.

ASN abstract syntax notation.

ASN.1 Abstract Syntax Notation One.

Association Control Service Element (ACSE) The application-service-element, defined by international standards ISO 8649 and ISO 8650, responsible for establishing and releasing application-associations. An application-

association binds an application program executing in one open system with an application program executing in another open system for the purposes of exchanging information between them.

asymmetric cryptography algorithm A cryptography algorithm in which the key used to decipher a message is different from the key used to encipher it.

asynchronous transmission A form of data communication, sometimes called *start-stop* transmission, in which a small number of bits, such as the 8 bits representing a single character, is sent at a time. Two devices using asynchronous transmission must be in synchronization only for the time it takes to transmit and receive a single character.

authentication The process of verifying the identity of a person, program, or service. See also *authorization*.

authorization The process of determining whether a person, program, or service is allowed to perform a particular process. See also *authentication*.

balanced data link In HDLC, a data link connecting two stations only. Each station is called a combined station, and either station can initiate message transmission. See *High-level Data Link Control*.

Basic Encoding Rules (BER) The international standard, defined in ISO 8825, specifying a set of encoding rules that define how the information content of ASN.1 values are encoded for transmission over the network. BER is a commonly used method for producing transfer syntaxes in the OSI environment.

Bellman-Ford routing algorithm See *distance-vector routing algorithm*.

BER Basic Encoding Rules.

bridge A device operating in the Logical Link Control sublayer and used to join together two separate local area networks to create an *extended LAN*. A bridge is attached to two or more local area networks and selectively copies frames from one local area network to another. A bridge can be designed to join together stations using different protocols in the Physical layer and in the Medium Access Control sublayer, as long as they use a common protocol in the Logical Link Control sublayer.

broadcast data link A data link that can connect two or more stations and in which the data units a station sends are seen by all the other stations attached to the data link. On a broadcast data link, a station can send a data unit to an individual station or multicast a data unit to any number of other stations attached to the data link.

byte A collection of 8 bits in a storage system.

call sharing A feature of the DNA Phase V Modem Connect specification that allows calls on a switched line to be accessed concurrently by more than one user of the Physical layer.

Carrier Sense Multiple Access with Collision Detection (CSMA/CD) An IEEE/ISO local area network standard, defined in IEEE 802.3 and IEEE 8802-3, that describes the Medium Access Control sublayer and Physical layer functions for a bus-structured network using a distributed contention resolution mechanism. The CSMA/CD standard has its roots in version 2 of the *Ethernet Specification,* jointly developed by Digital, Xerox, and Intel.

CCITT International Telegraph and Telephone Consultative Committee.

CD Committee Draft.

CDAM Committee Draft Amendment.

centralized routing A routing technique in which end nodes and routers report information about their local environments to a centralized facility. The centralized facility accumulates routing information from all the nodes in the network, computes routes, and sends to each router the information it needs to handle routing decisions.

circuit A DNA Phase V generic term used in routing that includes any type of data link, including a local area network broadcast link, a point-to-point link, an attachment to a node on a DDCMP multipoint link, a dial-up link, or an X.25 virtual circuit. See *subnetwork.*

clearinghouse A naming service repository for a portion of the namespace.

CLNS connectionless-mode network service.

collision A condition that occurs on an IEEE/ISO CSMA/CD or Ethernet data link when two or more stations attempt to transmit at the same time.

Committee Draft (CD) A proposed international standard in an early stage of ISO's standardization process. An international standard begins as a working draft and is assigned an ISO number when it becomes a *Committee Draft.* It then progresses to a *Draft International Standard* (DIS) and finally to an accepted international standard. Formerly a *Draft Proposal* (DP).

Committee Draft Amendment (CDAM) A document constituting a preliminary modification to an international standard in the first stage prior to its formal acceptance by ISO. A modification to an international standard begins as a *Committee Draft Amendment,* progresses to a *Draft Amendment* (DAM), and finally becomes an *Amendment* (AM) when it is accepted by ISO as an official part of an international standard. Formerly *Proposed Draft Addendum* (PDAD).

concatenation A protocol function in which multiple protocol-data-units are combined into a single block for transmission through the network as a single unit.

concentrator In FDDI, a component that has one or more ports used to connect single-attached stations, dual-attached stations, and other concentrators in a physical tree configuration. See *Fiber Distributed Data Interface, dual-attachment station, dual-*

attachment concentrator, and *single-attachment station*.

concrete interface A point in an architecture at which a physical connector is used or at which an application programming interface is defined.

confirm A service primitive in an ISO service definition issued by a service provider to notify the service requester of the results of one or more request primitives that the service requester previously issued.

confirmed service A service in an ISO service definition in which the service requester is informed by the distant peer entity of the success or failure of the service request.

Connection Control component of DNA Session Control The component that accesses Transport layer communication services on behalf of an object residing on the local node, the address selection component of Session Control, or the naming service.

connection-mode Network service (CONS). A reliable Network layer service in which a Network service user requests that a connection be established, the Network service and the user at the other end both agree, and the Network service establishes the connection. Data units can then be reliably exchanged over the connection.

connection-mode service. A reliable, sequenced service performed by a layer entity consisting of three phases: connection establishment, data transfer, and connection release.

connectionless-mode Network service (CLNS) A best-efforts, datagram Network layer service in which routing decisions are made independently for each data unit. Delivery is not guaranteed, and error detection and recovery procedures, if they are required, must be implemented by higher layers or by the application itself.

connectionless-mode service An unreliable, best-efforts service in which the service accepts each data unit for transmission and attempts to deliver it to its intended recipient or recipients. A connectionless-mode service is sometimes called a *datagram* service.

CONS connection-mode network service.

CSMA/CD Carrier Sense Multiple Access with Collision Detection.

DAC dual attachment concentrator.

DAD Draft Addendum.

DAM Draft Amendment.

DAS dual attachment station.

data circuit-terminating equipment (DCE) Circuitry implemented in a signaling device, such as a modem or line driver, that allows a computing device, such as a computer or terminal, to be attached to it.

data link Combination of a physical circuit and a data link protocol that defines how data can be transmitted over the data link in an error-free fashion.

Data Link layer The functional layer responsible for providing data transmission from one system to another and for shielding higher layers from any concerns about the physical transmission medium.

data link protocol Procedures operating in the Data Link layer that define how two adjacent nodes transmit data over a physical circuit.

data-link-protocol-data-unit (DLPDU) The protocol-data-unit exchanged between peer Data Link layer entities. An informal name for the DLPDU is *frame*.

data-link-service-access-point (DLSAP) Service-access-point to the Data Link layer, the point at which a user accesses the services of a Data Link layer entity.

data-link-service-data-unit (DLSDU) The service-data-unit passed to a Data Link layer entity by a user of the Data Link layer service.

data terminal equipment (DTE) Circuitry implemented in a computing device, such as a computer or a terminal, that allows the computing device to be attached to a signaling device, such as a modem or line driver.

datagram service See *connectionless-mode service*.

DCE data circuit-terminating equipment.

DDCMP Digital Data Communication Message Protocol.

DECnet Term used in the names of Digital hardware and software products that conform to the Digital Network Architecture.

default context A presentation context known to two communicating Presentation layer entities that can be used when the defined context set is empty. See *presentation context* and *defined context set*.

deference process The process in an IEEE/ISO CSMA/CD or Ethernet data link of monitoring the state of the transmission medium and determining when to begin transmission.

defined context set A set of presentation contexts that are negotiated by two peer Presentation layer entities. See *presentation context*.

descriptive name A name that identifies an object by specifying information about the attributes of that object.

designated router A router attached to a broadcast data link that is selected using an election process and that periodically multicasts to other routers information about that data link.

Digital Data Communication Message Protocol (DDCMP) A Digital proprietary protocol for the Data Link layer, included in DNA Phase V mainly for compatibility with DNA Phase IV.

Digital Network Architecture (DNA) Digital proprietary network architecture, first defined in the mid-1970s, that has evolved through a series of phases. DNA Phase V, the current phase of the architecture, is based on international standards for the OSI model. DECnet hardware and software products are implementations of the Digital Network Architecture.

Digital time service architecture The architecture that defines services and algorithms for maintaining and providing in all network nodes a consistent, correct date and time of day.

distance-vector routing algorithm A routing algorithm in which each node in the network learns about the network topology by exchanging routing information packets with its neighbors. Each router learns from its neighbor routers the distances between those neighbors and the other nodes. From these measurements it computes the distance between itself and the other nodes. The process is repeated and eventually stabilizes when all the nodes learn they have the same description of the network topology. Also sometimes called a *Bellman-Ford algorithm*. The routing algorithm defined by DNA Phase IV is a distance-vector algorithm.

distributed adaptive routing A routing technique in which nodes dynamically sense their local environments and exchange this information with each other—and compute routes accordingly—in a distributed fashion.

Distributed Authentication Security Service (DASS) Architecture An architecture that defines a comprehensive set of security services that can be used in implementing distributed systems.

DLSAP data-link-service-access-point.

DLSDU data-link-service-data-unit.

DLPDU data-link-protocol-data-unit.

DNA Digital Network Architecture.

DP Draft Proposal.

Draft Addendum (DAD) Obsolete ISO term for *Draft Amendment* (DAM).

Draft Amendment (DAM) A document constituting a preliminary modification to an international standard in the final stage prior to its formal acceptance by ISO. A modification to an international standard begins as a *Committee Draft Amendment* (CDAM), progresses to a *Draft Amendment*, and finally becomes an *Amendment* (AM) when it is accepted by ISO as an official part of an international standard. Formerly *Draft Addendum* (DAD).

Draft International Standard (DIS) A proposed international standard in the final stage of ISO's standardization process. An international standard begins as a *Committee Draft* (CD), progresses to a *Draft International Standard*, and finally is accepted by ISO as an international standard.

Draft Proposal (DP) Obsolete ISO term for *Committee Draft* (CD).

DTE data terminal equipment.

dual-attachment concentrator (DAC) On an FDDI data link, a station having three or more PHY ports and 0, 1, or 2 link components. The concentrator implements one MIC of type A, one of type B, and one or more of type M. Used to connect single-attached stations, dual-attached stations, and other concentrators in a physical tree configuration. See *dual-attachment station* and *single-attachment station*.

dual-attachment station (DAS) On an FDDI data link, a station designed to connect to two separate full-duplex transmission medium segments. A dual-attachment station can implement either one or two link components and contains exactly two PHY ports.

duplex A form of communication in which information can be transmitted in both directions simultaneously. Also called *full-duplex*. Contrast with *half-duplex*.

EIA-232-D A commonly implemented Physical layer standard defining 25 interchange circuits, carrying positive and negative voltages in the range of from about 5 to 15 volts, used to connect a computing device (DTE) to a signaling device (DCE). EIA-232-D is the successor to the RS-232-C standard. See *data terminal equipment* and *data circuit-terminating equipment*.

element of procedure Description in an ISO protocol specification of a protocol mechanism.

EMA Enterprise Management Architecture.

end node A term used in the DNA Phase V architecture to refer to a node that can act only as the source or the final destination of user data and that does not perform the routing and relaying functions of routers. Contrast with *router*.

end system See *end node*.

Enterprise Management Architecture (EMA) A Digital architecture that defines a general approach to the management of distributed systems. EMA characterizes a distributed system as a collection of individual computing systems tied together by a communication network for the purposes of sharing resources.

entity model A model of distributed system management, used to organize objects in a distributed system that must be managed, their attributes, and management operations, into a consistent structure.

entity An OSI term that refers to an active element within a layer. Also a term used in conjunction with the entity model to refer to an object in a distributed system that must be managed.

Ethernet A network conforming to the *Ethernet Specification*. Also sometimes used generically to refer to a local area network conforming either to the *Ethernet Specification* or to the IEEE/ISO CSMA/CD standard.

Ethernet Specification A local area network standard, jointly developed by Digital, Intel, and Xerox, on which the current IEEE/ISO CSMA/CD standard is based. See *Carrier Sense Multiple Access with Collision Detection*.

FDDI Fiber Distributed Data Interface.

Fiber Distributed Data Interface (FDDI) A local area network standard, developed by the Accredited Standards Committee (ASC) X3T9.5 of ANSI and also published in ISO 9314, that uses a ring topology and supports a data rate of 100 megabits per second over a fiber-optic transmission medium.

File Transfer, Access, and Management (FTAM) An international standard, defined in ISO 8571, for an application-service-element that defines a standardized way for accessing and transferring data files between open systems in a heterogeneous network environment.

flooding Process in a link-state routing algorithm in which a router propagates routing control packets throughout the network.

FOIRL An IEEE/ISO CSMA/CD transmission medium specification that specifies baseband signaling over a fiber-optic cable to implement a point-to-point connection between repeaters. Fiber-optic inter-repeater link cable segments can be up to 1000 meters in length.

frame Informal name for the data-link-protocol-data-unit (DLPDU) that is exchanged by peer Data Link layer entities.

FTAM File Transfer, Access, and Management.

full name A complete name maintained by the naming service that consists of a concatenation of all the simple names assigned to a set of arcs that begins at the root of the tree and ends with the object in question.

full-duplex See *duplex.*

gateway A device used to connect networks that conform to different network architectures. The function of a gateway is to convert the protocols of one network architecture to the protocols of the other network architecture. A gateway replaces the control information from one network with control information required to perform comparable functions in the other network. Nodes connected using gateways can run different protocols in any of the layers in the protocol stack.

half-duplex A form of communication in which data units can be transmitted in both directions over a connection but in only one direction at a time. Contrast with *duplex.*

HDLC High-level Data Link Control.

High-level Data Link Control (HDLC) An international standard protocol of the Data Link layer,

included in DNA Phase V, used to implement telecommunications data links in the wide area networking environment.

hop Term used in routing to refer to a traversal from one node to an adjacent node across a single data link.

IEEE Institute of Electrical and Electronics Engineers.

indication A service primitive in an ISO service definition issued by the service provider to notify a service requester that a significant event has occurred.

Institute of Electrical and Electronic Engineers (IEEE) A professional society, whose members are individual engineers, that is engaged in information technology standardization. The IEEE became the focus for development of local area network standards under its Project 802.

Integrated Services Digital Network (ISDN) International standards that describe the provision of unified public voice and data communication services.

interface data The data portion of the data unit that is passed in a single interaction across the abstract interface between two layer entities at the service-access-point.

interface-control-information (ICI) The control information portion of the data unit that is passed in a single interaction across the abstract interface between two layer entities at the service-access-point.

interface-data-unit (IDU) The data unit, consisting of *interface data* and *interface-control-information* (ICI), that is passed in a single interaction across the abstract interface between two layer entities at the service-access-point.

intermediate node The term used in the DNA Phase V architecture to refer to a system that functions as a router in moving data units through the network from a source end node to a destination end node. See *end node.*

intermediate system See *intermediate node.*

International Electrotechnical Commission (IEC) A standards organization whose role in the field of information technology standards is generally limited to Physical layer considerations, such as electrical safety. ISO and IEC have merged their technical committees working on information technology into a single organization, called *ISO/IEC Joint Technical Committee 1* (JTC1).

International Organization for Standardization (ISO) The world's dominant standardization organization, which creates standards of all types and plays an important role in creating standards for the information technology industry. The members of ISO are individual national standards organizations that represent national positions. The ISO member organization from the United States is the American National Standards Institute (ANSI).

International Telegraph and Telephone Consultative Committee (CCITT) The world's leading organization involved in the development of standards relating to telephone and other telecommunications services. CCITT is a part of the International Telecommunications Union (ITU), a body of the United Nations.

ISDN Integrated Services Digital Network.

ISO International Organization for Standardization.

Joint Technical Committee 1 (JTC1) A combination of ISO and IEC technical committees working on information technology standardization.

JTC1 ISO/IEC Joint Technical Committee 1.

LAN local area network.

LAPB Link Access Procedures—Balanced.

level 1 router A router that performs the level 1 routing function.

level 1 routing Routing within an area. A level 1 router routes network traffic directly toward destination nodes within its own area and toward a level 2 router when it determines a packet's destination node is in a different area.

level 2 router A router that performs both the level 1 and level 2 routing functions.

level 2 routing Routing of network traffic between areas. Level 2 routing also includes interdomain routing for traffic destined to other routing domains and to other administrative domains. Such interdomain traffic is handled using static routing techniques.

Link Access Procedures—Balanced (LAPB) A subset of High-level Data Link Control used in conjunction with CCITT Recommendation X.25. (See *X.25* and *High-level Data Link Control*.)

link state routing algorithm A routing technique in which a router determines what its individual area of the network looks like and then broadcasts that information to all the other routers.

LLC Logical Link Control.

LLC-PDU logical-link-control-protocol-data-unit.

LLC-SDU logical-link-control-service-data-unit.

local area network (LAN) A form of subnetwork that meets the needs for high-speed, relatively short-distance communication among intelligent devices. Local area networks are normally constrained to being within a single building or within a "campus" of buildings. They do not ordinarily cross public thoroughfares and normally operate over private cabling.

local concrete syntax The definition of how the information content of presentation-data-values is represented in a computing system.

Logical Link Control (LLC) sublayer The upper sublayer of the Data Link layer in the IEEE/ISO LAN architecture. The LLC sublayer, described in IEEE 802.2 and ISO 8802-2, is responsible for medium-independent data link functions. It allows a user of the LLC sublayer service to access the local area network without regard to the form of medium access control used. The LLC sublayer requests services of the Medium Access Control sublayer. See *Medium Access Control sublayer*.

logical-link-control-protocol-data-unit (LLC-PDU) The protocol-data-unit exchanged by peer Logical Link Control sublayer entities.

logical-link-control-service-data-unit (LLC-SDU) The service-data-unit passed to a Logical Link Control sublayer entity by a user of the Logical Link Control sublayer service.

MAC Medium Access Control.

MAC-PDU medium-access-control-protocol-data-unit.

MAC-SDU medium-access-control-service-data-unit.

MACF multiple-association-control-function.

MAN metropolitan area network.

Manchester encoding Encoding scheme used with an IEEE/ISO CSMA/CD and Ethernet data link to encode the bit stream into electrical signals. Manchester encoding has the desirable property of signal transitions occurring on the transmission medium with predictable regularity.

Medium Access Control (MAC) sublayer The bottom sublayer of the Data Link layer in the IEEE/ISO LAN architecture. The MAC sublayer is responsible for performing the procedures that manage use of the physical transmission medium. The MAC sublayer provides services to the Logical Link Control sublayer. See *Logical Link Control sublayer*.

medium-access-control-protocol-data-unit (MAC-PDU) The protocol-data-unit exchanged by peer Medium Access Control sublayer entities.

medium-access-control-service-data-unit (MAC-SDU) The service-data-unit passed to a Medium Access Control sublayer entity by a user of the MAC sublayer service.

message interface to DNA Session Control An interface that allows end users of the Session Control layer service to send and receive individual messages of any desired size. Senders and receivers work with messages contained in buffers.

message transfer agent (MTA) In Recommendation X.400, the component that delivers messages that have been submitted from users to one or more recipients. See *X.400.*

metropolitan area network (MAN) A form of subnetwork that supports relatively high-speed communication over a geographic area roughly the size of a large city.

Modem Connect A DNA Phase V specification that defines how the DNA Phase V Physical layer operates over wide area network telecommunications links. Modem Connect supports any type of modem or service unit for communication over a conventional analog telecommunications link or over a digital data service.

MTA message transfer agent.

multicast facility Facility implemented by a broadcast form of data link in which a station can send a single transmission to a number of other stations on the data link.

multiple-association-control-function (MACF) An Application layer control function that is associated with an entire application-entity-invocation and that maps each service the application-entity-invocation provides to one of the associations and coordinates the interactions taking place on these associations.

nameserver A component of the naming service that, on behalf of naming service clerks, retrieves information from and updates clearinghouses containing the directories making up the namespace.

namespace A logical collection of the names of all the objects that can be referenced, anywhere in a possibly global network.

naming service A service that allows users to assign names to objects that mean the same thing anywhere in the network and to maintain a set of attribute values associated with each name, including the address of the node on which the object resides. The naming service accepts an object's name from a user and passes back the set of attributes associated with that name.

naming service clerk The component of the naming service that implements the application programming interface to the naming service and that performs naming service operations on behalf of end users and application programs. Clerks communicate with nameservers.

NET network entity title.

network architecture A comprehensive plan and set of rules that govern the design and operation of the hardware and software components used to create computer networks.

network entity title (NET) The entire NSAP address of a node, including a zero selector field value. A node's network entity title must be unambiguous within the OSI environment.

Network layer The functional layer concerned with routing data from one open system to another. The facilities provided by the Network layer supply a service employed by higher layers to move bits from a source end node to a destination end node, where the bits may flow through any number of routers. See *end node* and *router*.

network-protocol-data-unit (NPDU) The protocol-data-unit exchanged by peer Network layer entities. An informal name for the NPDU is *packet*.

network-service-access-point (NSAP) Service-access-point to the Network layer, the point at which a user accesses the services of a Network layer entity. The NSAP address forms the network address of an end node or router.

network-service-data-unit (NSDU) The service-data-unit passed to a Network layer entity by a user of the Network layer service.

Network Service Protocol (NSP) A Digital proprietary Transport layer protocol included in DNA Phase V mainly for compatibility with DNA Phase IV.

node A term used in DNA to refer to a device containing at least an instance of the Network layer and the Data Link and Physical layers below it. Synonymous with the OSI term *system* or *open system*.

nonbroadcast data link A data link implemented using a point-to-point connection between exactly two stations.

nonconfirmed service A service in an ISO service definition in which the service requester is not informed of the completion of the service request.

NPDU network-protocol-data-unit.

NSAP network-service-access-point.

NSDU network-service-data-unit.

NSP Network Service Protocol.

null modem An EIA-232-D cable or connector that crosses the appropriate conductors to allow two DTEs to be connected to simulate the presence of a pair of DCEs between the two communicating devices. See *EIA-232-D*, *DTE*, and *DCE*.

octet OSI term for a collection of 8 bits.

open system The representation within the OSI model of those aspects of a computing system that are pertinent to OSI communication. Systems are said to be open to each other because of their mutual adherence to a set of applicable standards.

OSI architecture The network architecture that the International Organization for Standardization (ISO) is developing based on international standards. Together, the standards developed around the OSI model framework make up the OSI architecture. See *Reference Model for Open Systems Interconnection*.

OSI Directory See *X.500 Directory*.

OSI Model See *Reference Model for Open Systems Interconnection*.

OSI Upper Layer (OSUL) architecture The DNA Phase V architecture that describes the Digital implementation of the OSI Session, Presentation, and Application layers.

packet An informal name for the network-protocol-data-unit (NPDU).

PCI protocol-control-information.

PDAD Proposed Draft Addendum.

PDU protocol-data-unit.

PDV presentation-data-value.

peer entities Two communicating entities, associated with the same layer but existing in different nodes, that communicate using the services of the layer below them.

permanent virtual circuit A facility provided by a packet-switched data network that provides the appearance of a permanent point-to-point connection between two DTEs. The two DTEs use the communication facilities of the network and consume network resources only when they are actually transmitting data; however, they remain logically connected permanently as though an actual physical circuit always exists between them.

Physical layer The functional layer responsible for the transmission of bit streams across a physical transmission medium. It involves a connection between two machines that allows electrical or other types of signals to be exchanged between them.

physical-protocol-data-unit (PPDU) The protocol-data-unit exchanged between peer Physical layer entities.

physical-service-access-point (PSAP) The service-access-point to the Physical layer, the point at which a user accesses the services of a Physical layer entity.

physical-service-data-unit (PSDU) The service-data-unit passed to a Physical layer entity by a user of the Physical layer service.

point-to-point data link A data link that implements a connection between exactly two nodes.

port A data structure, defined by the DNA Phase V architecture and implemented in a layer entity, providing access to the services of that entity. Typically, a port is assigned to a user upon request and remains associated with that user until it is explicitly released. Each user generally has its own port assigned; and many users may be able to access the services of a layer entity, each

through its own assigned port.

portal A facility for allowing nodes that conform to some other network architecture to use a network for communication. Unlike a gateway, a DNA Phase V portal does not perform protocol conversion. Instead, a portal encapsulates the foreign protocol messages within DNA Phase V protocol messages for transmission through the DECnet Phase V network. A pair of portals is sometimes said to implement a facility called a *tunnel*, with each portal providing an opening into a tunnel through a network conforming to a foreign network architecture.

PPDU Physical-protocol-data-unit or presentation-protocol-data-unit.

presentation context In the OSI Presentation layer, the association of the name of an abstract syntax with the name of a particular transfer syntax used to transfer the information content defined by that abstract syntax.

presentation-data-value (PDV) Definition of the information content of an application-protocol-data-unit (APDU) or a part of an APDU.

Presentation layer The functional layer concerned with preserving the information content of user data and with the way in which it is represented and encoded for transmission through the network.

presentation-protocol-data-unit (PPDU) The protocol-data-unit exchanged between peer Presentation layer entities.

presentation-service-access-point (PSAP) The service-access-point to the Presentation layer, the point at which a user accesses the services of a Presentation layer entity.

presentation-service-data-unit (PSDU) The service-data-unit passed to a Presentation layer entity by a user of the Presentation layer service.

primitive name A character string that uniquely identifies a resource.

propagator A function of the DNA Phase V naming service that attempts to propagate updates made to the namespace to all replicas of a directory at the time the update is made.

Proposed Draft Addendum (PDAD) Obsolete ISO term for *Committee Draft Amendment* (CDAM).

protocol A set of data units and the procedures that define how the data units are exchanged between peer entities. A layer entity in one node communicates with a complementary layer entity in another node using a protocol.

protocol-control-information (PCI) Information a layer adds to the data from one or more of its service-data-units to produce a protocol-data-unit.

protocol-data-unit (PDU) Data units that are sent from a layer entity in one node to a peer layer entity in another node.

protocol specification ISO standard defining the formats of the data units that are exchanged between two peer layer entities and the procedures by which those data units are exchanged.

proxy mapping A mechanism of the DNA Session Control layer through which a user on one node in the network can be given access to accounts on another node in the network without knowing the access control information associated with the target accounts.

pseudonode An imaginary node used with a link-state routing algorithm to model a broadcast data link as a logical star structure in which the pseudonode represents the transmission medium itself. All nodes are viewed as being connected to the pseudonode with a separate point-to-point logical link.

public key cryptography system See *asymmetric cryptography algorithm.*

quasi-static routing A routing technique similar to static routing except the routing information that is computed and provided to each node includes information about alternative paths that can be used when certain types of failures occur. See *static routing.*

Reference Model of Open Systems Interconnection (OSI model) An international standard, described in ISO 7498, that documents a generalized model of system interconnection. The primary purpose of the OSI model is to provide a basis for coordinating the development of international standards relating to the flexible interconnection of systems using data communication facilities.

referential transparency A property of a name maintained by the naming service that guarantees that a full name always refers to the same thing no matter which user provided the name, and that these names can be freely passed outside the naming service from one user to another without the possibility of confusion.

relaying The function of a router in moving a packet from one node to the next over the route it travels through the network.

remote procedure call (RPC) architecture The architecture that defines services by which a procedure executing in one computing system can pass control to a procedure residing in some other computing system attached to the network using a conventional procedure call mechanism.

repeater A device used to relay signals from one cable segment to another in a local area network. A repeater operates in the Physical layer, and its use is hidden from any of the layers above. The function of a repeater is to receive a signal from one cable segment and to retransmit it over one or more other cable segments, thus regenerating the signal at its original strength. Repeaters are used in bus-structured local area networks to connect individual cable segments to form a larger local area network. In ring-structured local area networks, every station performs the function of a repeater.

replica A copy of a naming service directory stored in a particular clearinghouse. See *clearinghouse.*

request A service primitive in an ISO service definition issued by a service requester to request that a particular service be performed by a service provider and to pass parameters needed to fully specify the requested service.

response A service primitive in an ISO service definition issued by the service requester to acknowledge or complete some procedure previously invoked by the service provider through an indication primitive.

router The informal name for intermediate system or intermediate node. A router provides the ability to route packets from one end node to another where there may be multiple paths between them. The routers participate in a distributed algorithm to decide on the optimal path each packet should travel from the source end node to the destination end node. The router function operates in the Network layer.

routing The function of the Network layer that determines the best path for moving each packet to its destination based on the current topology of the network.

routing domain A set of end nodes and routers that share routing information, operate according to the same routing protocol, and are contained within a single administrative domain. The definition of a routing domain is associated with a network policy, since a routing domain is not an architecturally defined entity. See *administrative domain*.

RPC remote procedure call.

RS-232-C See *EIA-232-D*.

SACF single-association-control-function.

SAP service-access-point.

SAS single-attachment station.

SDLC Synchronous Data Link Control.

SDU service-data-unit.

segment interface to DNA Session Control The interface that allows end users of the Session Control layer service to send messages limited in size to the maximum allowable trans-

port-protocol-data-unit (TPDU) size. Senders and receivers work with messages contained in buffers.

segmentation function A protocol function in which a service-data-unit is divided into segments, each of which is transmitted in a separate protocol-data-unit.

service-access-point (SAP) The point at which the services of a layer are provided. A service-access-point is identified by an SAP address.

service-data-unit (SDU) A data unit passed from a higher-layer entity that is requesting a service down to a lower-layer entity that is providing the service.

service definition An ISO standard that defines the services that one layer of the OSI model provides to a user of that layer's services without specifying how those services are to be provided.

service primitive A description of the semantics of a particular service that an entity in a functional layer of the OSI model provides to a user of that layer's services.

Session layer The functional layer that provides services used to organize and synchronize the dialog between application programs and to manage the data exchanges between them.

session-protocol-data-unit (SPDU) The protocol-data-unit exchanged between peer Session layer entities.

session-service-access-point (SSAP) The service-access-point to the Session layer, the point at which a user accesses the services of a Session layer entity.

session-service-data-unit (SSDU) The service-data-unit passed to a Session layer entity by a user of the Session layer service.

simple name In the naming service, a string of octets having no internal structure. Simple names are concatenated with periods to form full names. See *full name*.

simplex A form of communication in which information flows in only one direction.

single-association-control-function (SACF) An Application layer control function that is associated with a single association and thus a single application context.

single-attachment station (SAS) In FDDI, a station that implements a single link component and a single PHY Port. This type of station is attached to a concentrator using a single full-duplex, point-to-point transmission medium segment. See *concentrator* and *dual-attachment concentrator*.

skulk Execution of the skulker convergence algorithm. See *skulker*.

skulker The naming service convergence algorithm that forces convergence for those updates the propagator was not able to fully propagate.

slot time On an IEEE/ISO CSMA/CD or Ethernet data link, twice the maximum round-trip propagation delay.

SNA Systems Network Architecture.

SNAcP Subnetwork Access Protocol Role.

SNDCP Subnetwork Dependent Convergence Protocol Role.

SNICP Subnetwork Independent Convergence Protocol Role.

SPDU session-protocol-data-unit.

SSAP session-service-access-point.

SSDU session-service-data-unit.

static routing A routing technique in which all routing information for each node is pre-computed and is provided to each router through a management action.

station With most types of data links, a station corresponds to a particular instance of a Data Link layer and a Physical layer entity and corresponds to a single point of attachment to a transmission medium segment. A particular node must implement at least one station in order to attach that node to the network. With an FDDI data link, a station can contain zero, one, or two Data Link layer entities, and a station can attach to either one or two full-duplex optical-fiber cable segments.

stream interface to DNA Session Control An interface that allows end users to view data as a continuous stream of octets, in which an occasional "end-of-message" marker may be inserted. The stream interface is similar to the segment interface, but the buffer size is not restricted by the maximum allowable TPDU size. See *segment interface to DNA Session Control*.

subnetwork A collection of nodes that are attached to a single virtual transmission medium.

Subnetwork Access Protocol Role (SNAcP) The Network layer protocol role of directly accessing the services of the Data Link layer in helping to provide the requested Network service.

Subnetwork Dependent Convergence Protocol Role (SNDCP) The Network layer protocol role of augmenting the functions provided by a protocol operating in the SNAcP role to provide the services the subnetwork independent sublayer requires to provide the requested Network service. See *subnetwork access protocol role*.

subnetwork dependent layer The lower of the two sublayers of the Network layer whose major function is to access the underlying services of the Data Link layer upon request of the subnetwork independent sublayer. See *subnetwork independent layer*.

Subnetwork Independent Convergence Protocol Role (SNICP) The Network layer protocol role of providing the requested Network service to a user of the Network layer service using a well-defined set of underlying capabilities. It interfaces directly with the Network layer service user and is independent of the Data Link layer services used to provide the Network service.

subnetwork independent layer The upper of the two sublayers of the Network layer whose function is to provide either the connectionless-mode network service (CLNS) or the connection-mode network service (CONS) upon request of a user of the Network layer service. See *subnetwork independent layer, connectionless-mode network service,* and *connection-mode network service.*

SVC switched virtual circuit.

switched virtual circuit (SVC) A facility provided by a packet-switched data network that provides the appearance of a point-to-point connection between two DTEs. It is established upon request of either of the two DTEs and is released when the connection is no longer required. Sometimes called a *virtual call* (VC).

Synchronous Data Link Control (SDLC) A data link protocol, defined by IBM, that is a functional subset of the international standard High-Level Data Link Control (HDLC) data link protocol defined by ISO. SDLC includes only the normal response mode of HDLC, in which one station is designated the primary station and is in control of the data link while one or more other stations are designated secondary stations.

synchronous transmission A form of data communication in which bits are sent in a continuous stream and in which the receiving device must stay in synchronization with the transmitting device for the transmission of an entire block of information.

system A set of one or more computers, the associated software, peripherals, terminals, human operators, physical processes, transfer means, and so forth, that forms an autonomous whole capable of performing information processing and/or information transfer. Often referred to in DNA Phase V as a *node.*

Systems Network Architecture (SNA) IBM's network architecture, widely used in the IBM large-system environment.

TCP/IP Transmission Control Protocol/Internet Protocol.

Technical Report (TR) An ISO publication that covers subject matter for which support can-

not be obtained for the development of an international standard, when a subject is still under technical development, or when a technical committee has collected data different from data normally published as a standard.

time-sequence diagram A diagram in an ISO service definition in which service primitives are represented by arrows and in which time flows down. A time-sequence diagram shows the sequence in which service primitives are issued in performing a particular service.

token bus LAN A standard for local area networks, defined by IEEE 802.4 and ISO 8802-4, that describes the Medium Access Control sublayer and Physical layer functions for a bus-structured LAN using a token passing access protocol.

token passing access protocol A local area network procedure in which access to the physical transmission medium is controlled through possession of a special data unit called the token, which is passed from device to device.

token ring LAN A standard for local area networks, defined by IEEE 802.5 and ISO 8802-5, that describes the Medium Access Control sublayer and Physical layer functions for a ring-structured LAN using a token passing access protocol.

tower A data structure, maintained in the naming service, that contains protocol and addressing information for an object that can be located via the network.

TPDU transport-protocol-data-unit.

TR Technical Report.

transfer syntax A definition of how the information content of data is encoded for transmission over a network. See *local concrete syntax* and *abstract syntax.*

Transmission Control Protocol/Internet Protocol (TCP/IP) A network architecture and protocol suite, typically used in conjunction with the UNIX operating system, used for communication in an internet made up of interconnected subnetworks of various types.

Transport layer The functional layer responsible for providing an end-to-end data transfer service between any two end systems at an agreed-upon level of quality. The Transport layer builds on the services of the Network layer and the layers below it to form the uppermost layer of an end-to-end data transport service. The Transport layer shields higher layers from any concern with the actual moving of data from one computer to another and shields the users of the data transport service from the complexities of the layers below.

transport-protocol-data-unit (TPDU) The protocol-data-unit exchanged between peer Transport layer entities.

transport-service-access-point (TSAP) The service-access-point to the Transport layer, the point at which a user accesses the services of a Transport layer entity.

Transport-service-data-unit (TSDU) The service-data-unit passed to a Transport layer entity by a user of the Transport layer service.

TSAP transport-service-access-point.

TSDU transport-service-data-unit.

tunnel A facility, consisting of a pair of portals, that allows nodes conforming to some other network architecture to use a network for communication. See *portal.*

UA user agent.

UID unique identifier.

unbalanced data link A data link that connects two or more stations, with one of the stations designated the primary station and all the others designated as secondary stations.

unique identifier (UID) An identifier, globally unique over space and time, created through use of the DNA Phase V unique identifier architecture. See *unique identifier architecture.*

unique identifier architecture The architecture that defines a service that distributed systems and the DECnet software itself use to obtain an

identifier guaranteed to be globally unique over space and time.

user agent In X.400, the component that allows individual users of the system to submit messages to the system for delivery to one or more recipients and to receive and view messages that have been sent by other users.

VC virtual call.

virtual call (VC) See *switched virtual circuit.*

virtual circuit A facility, implemented via a packet-switched data network, that gives the appearance of a point-to-point connection between two nodes. See *switched virtual circuit* and *permanent virtual circuit.*

virtual filestore In FTAM, a conceptual model of a file service that can be implemented in any desired way in an open system. The virtual filestore is an abstraction that can be emulated by the file service existing in a real computing system.

WAN wide area network.

wide area network (WAN) A network constructed using public telecommunications facilities that extends over large geographic areas.

window mechanism A mechanism, often used in flow control procedures, to control the rate at which protocol-data-units are sent between the transmitter and the receiver. A window mechanism is used to limit the number of frames a transmitter can send before it must wait for an acknowledgement from the receiver.

X.25 Interface The recommendation of the CCITT that defines how a computer is attached to a packet-switched data network (PSDN).

X.400 Message Handling System The recommendation of the CCITT for a message handling system that defines standard methods for transferring electronic mail messages among users of heterogeneous computing systems.

X.500 Directory The international standard for a descriptive naming service in the OSI environment. Also called the *OSI Directory.*

INDEX